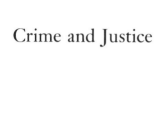

Crime and Justice

Crime and Justice
An Annual Review of Research

Edited by *Michael Tonry and Norval Morris*
with the Support of The National Institute of Justice

VOLUME 5

The University of Chicago Press, Chicago and London

The University of Chicago Press, Chicago 60637
The University of Chicago Press, Ltd., London

ISSN: 0192-3234
ISBN: 0-226-80799-1

LCN: 80-642217

This volume was prepared under Grant Number 80-IJ-CX-0022(S2)
awarded to the University of Maryland by the National Institute
of Justice, U.S. Department of Justice, under the Omnibus
Crime Control and Safe Streets Act of 1968 as amended. Points
of view or opinions expressed in this volume are those of the editors
or authors and do not necessarily represent the official position
or policies of the U.S. Department of Justice. Additional support was
provided by The German Marshall Fund of the United States under
Grant Number 1-31536.

Contents

Introduction

Volume 5 carries forward the ecumenical character of the earlier volumes, with essays on incapacitation research, prison labor, womens' prisons, and sexual offenses and offenders. Thus, like the earlier volumes, it speaks to current and important concerns in the better understanding and control of crime. But something new has been added. This volume also presents a collection of five shorter essays on a single theme—the organization of criminological research in several foreign countries and a consideration of the major directions of their research endeavors.

The essays by Cohen on incapacitation research, by Hawkins on prison labor, by Rafter on the history of womens' prisons, and by West on sexual offenses and offenders need no introduction by us—all are excellent state-of-the-art overviews of obviously important topics. But perhaps the collection of brief essays on comparative research organization and research directions permits us as editors of this series to offer a few comments on those questions in this country.

None of the comparative surveys demonstrates a bursting ebullience about the present state of criminological research; everywhere there is uncertainty about funds for research and where criminological research is and should be headed, and that is certainly true in this country at this time. We seem unsure not only of the broad direction and general structure of our research efforts but even of the wisdom of continuing existing initiatives.

The story of the last twenty years of research in criminal justice has been told in detail in several studies. Two important supporters of research appeared at about the same time: the Ford Foundation, to fund the establishment of several Centers for Studies in Criminal Justice at private and public universities, sometimes providing the bulk of the funding, sometimes in alliance with state and federal funds; and the federal government, to make a substantial investment in research through LEAA (though it had a variety of titles, LEAA was its longest lasting acronym), itself a product of President Johnson's Crime Commission, and its report, "The Challenge of Crime in a Free Society."

Federal funds flowed through state and local planning agencies, but they also combined with the Ford Foundation's resources to support the development of a nucleus of university-based research and evaluative projects in the prevention and treatment of crime and delinquency, as well as the development of several private enterprise research agencies and corporations supported on contract by federal funds. The federal initiative also developed larger sophistication and precision in the data bases of crimes, in particular by planning, launching, and supporting a series of victim surveys.

There were other structural and organizational developments worthy of note—an overview like this will be sure to alienate a few of our friends whom we have forgotten to mention—the Police Foundation, the Vera Institute in New York, the School of Criminal Justice at the State University of New York at Albany, and several others.

On these then-new foundations, twenty years ago a fresh start was made toward a better understanding of crime and its control, using greater resources than had ever before been so directed in this country. And yet, pervasively, there remains a sense of disappointment in the results, a sense of unmet objectives.

Why is this so? Part of the answer is obvious: economic recession has not spared the criminological researcher. The flow of research funds has been severely reduced, and many promising projects have been abandoned. It is a period of retrenchment when excellent scholars are inhibited from following promising avenues of research.

There is, however, more to the current depression about criminal justice research than its economic aspect. There is a sense of failure. And this, we think, is unjustified, a product of the same unrealistic expectations that bedevil the entire field of criminal justice.

Police are judged on whether their efforts prevent and inhibit crime. So are prosecutors, criminal courts, and correctional agencies. But it is surely clear that those modulations in the work of the police, the prosecutors, the judges, and the prison, probation, and parole officers that might be politically acceptable and achievable are unlikely to make any measurable impact on phenomena as deep-seated as crime and juvenile delinquency. All that can be expected realistically are incremental and marginal inhibitions and controls. We can, of course, without necessarily at all varying the incidence or prevalence of crime, make our governmental processes more efficient and more respectful of the proper interests of the victim and the criminal—and much along this line has been done in the twenty years of which we write. But the broad sweep of crime is unlikely to be measurably influenced in a democratic society by reforms within legislative or administrative competence.

All this will be seen as obvious enough when it is directed toward the police, the prosecutor, the judge, and the correctional official. Our point is that it is surely even more applicable to the work of the researcher of the criminal justice system. Of course there has been no dramatic breakthrough in understanding the etiology of crime—nor will there be. Glimpses of important relationships in the origins of some crimes by some criminals there have been, and that is no small contribution. And in crime control, it is likely that the criminologist will be better able to measure what can be done without making any differences to the frequency of criminality than in devising what might properly be done to reduce it. It is a barb, but it is also the truth: the criminologist gradually learns what is not so about crime and crime control, but not what to do about it.

And in this country, as in the others covered in our series of reports on criminological research, there has been one greatly encouraging development over the past twenty years: a number of well-trained, sophisticated researchers of the criminal justice system have emerged where previously there were very few. In the universities and a few of the service agencies one now finds skilled analysts of the criminal justice system where previously none were to be found. A research capacity has been developed. But there is a dark side even to this encouraging development. At present too many career lines in criminological research are being threatened for the serious younger scholar to turn his career in this direction without considerable anxiety. In the next few years ways must be found to encourage and support criminological research over the long haul of established career patterns, and not in the fits and starts of fashionable public and private research funding.

Is all this a counsel of despair? Not at all. It is merely an argument for the recognition of how knowledge grows in the social sciences and an insistence that we persevere along paths that have gradually been cleared over the past two decades. Many of those paths have been described in the first five volumes of this series, which report a history of achievement and not of failure in the study of crime and its control in this country.

Jacqueline Cohen

Incapacitation as a Strategy for Crime Control: Possibilities and Pitfalls

ABSTRACT

A number of estimates of incapacitative effects from incarceration of convicted offenders are available. While these estimates vary in absolute magnitude, the studies consistently find that crime reduction achieved by existing collective incapacitation policies is modest, at under 20 percent of crimes prevented. Further crime reduction from alternative policies that would impose fairly stringent mandatory five-year prison terms after convictions for serious offenses is similarly modest. Implementing these alternative policies, however, would result in dramatic increases in already record-size prison populations. In view of the limited crime reduction and enormous increases in prison population associated with collective incapacitation policies, recent research has explored the potential benefits of more selective or targeted incapacitation. If a small number of high-rate offenders commit a disproportionately large amount of crime, targeting limited prison resources on these offenders should achieve increased crime control without increasing prison populations unreasonably. Such a policy depends on identifying high-rate offenders prospectively, and early in their careers. Recent efforts to use predictions of individual crime rates as a basis for selective incapacitation are plagued by ethical and empirical problems. An alternative approach relies on observed differences in the criminal career patterns of offenders charged with different offenses to identify offenses committed by offenders who on the average commit crimes at higher rates and have longer careers. This approach may achieve differential incapacitation effects while avoiding many of the ethical and empirical problems posed by sentencing policies that employ individual-level predictions to distinguish among offenders.

Jacqueline Cohen is research associate and associate director, Urban Systems Institute, School of Urban and Public Affairs, Carnegie-Mellon University. The final formulation of this paper has benefited from many helpful suggestions by Alfred Blumstein, David Greenberg, Michael Tonry, James Q. Wilson, and Franklin Zimring.

Incapacitation involves denying an offender the opportunity or ability to commit future crimes. In recent years, there has been growing interest in incapacitation as a strategy for controlling crime. The logic is simple: an offender who is locked up cannot commit crimes in the community.

Interest in incapacitative strategies heightened in the early 1970s because of public concern about continuing increases in crime and widespread disillusionment with efforts to rehabilitate offenders or otherwise meaningfully affect their future criminal behavior. Martinson's widely influential article on the general failure of correctional evaluations to document the rehabilitative effects of treatment programs appeared in 1974 (Martinson 1974; see also Lipton, Martinson, and Wilks 1975). At about the same time, arguments for an incapacitative strategy appeared in the academic press (Avi-Itzhak and Shinnar 1973; Shinnar and Shinnar 1975), while James Q. Wilson argued for incapacitation to a broader public audience (Wilson 1975a, 1975b, 1977).

Support for incapacitation policies, especially for high-rate offenders, has gained momentum in the 1980s, partly as a result of the increasing strains on existing prison resources experienced throughout U.S. jurisdictions. State and federal prison populations have been growing steadily since 1974; by the end of 1982 there were 412,303 prisoners under state or federal jurisdiction. The national incarceration rate rose from 139 per 100,000 resident population in 1980 to 170 in 1982. In 1982, the annual growth rate in prison population set a new record of 12.2 percent (U.S. Department of Justice 1983). Prison capacity has not kept pace. In 1981, thirty-one states were under court orders to reduce prison overcrowding and thirty-seven states were involved in litigation about some aspect of prison conditions.

For both fiscal and policy reasons, prison capacity is not likely to increase rapidly. State governments face growing citizen resistance to taxes and increased demands for state support for other public services for which federal support has declined. These fiscal concerns have combined to limit support for increased prison expenditures out of states' annual operating budgets and contributed to the defeat by voters of proposed bond issues to cover the costs of new prison construction in New York and Rhode Island. (Recent approvals of bond issues in California and New Jersey are notable exceptions to this pattern.)

Demographic projections of prison populations provide another basis for limiting the growth of prison capacity. Projections in Pennsylvania suggest that when individuals born during the postwar baby boom, from 1947 to 1962, move out of the most crime-prone ages of the late teens by 1980, crime rates will begin to decline. The baby boom population, however, will reach the ages most vulnerable to imprisonment—the middle and late twenties—and so commitments to prison can be expected to increase through 1985, when they will level off and begin to decline. Because time served in prison averages several years, the daily prison population will continue to grow until 1990 (Blumstein, Cohen, and Miller 1980). These projections for Pennsylvania, where the population is stable but aging, are likely to be representative of many states in the United States, especially in the Northeast and Midwest. In states with growing young populations, particularly in the South and West, the growth in prison populations is likely to continue beyond 1990.

The most recent data on reported crimes for 1981 and 1982 are fully consistent with these projections. Between 1980 and 1981, there was essentially no change in the reported number of index crimes (excluding arson) in the United States.[1] Over this same period, index crimes decreased by about 1 percent in the northeast and north central regions of the country and increased slightly in the South and West (Federal Bureau of Investigation 1982, table 3). As expected from the demographic projections, index crimes then decreased a full 5 percent in the first six months of 1982 from the same period in 1981 (Federal Bureau of Investigation, press release, October 19, 1982). In the northeast and north central regions with their older populations, the decrease was larger at 9 percent; the decline was less at 2–3 percent in the South and West. This contrasts with national average annual increases of 4.4 percent between 1974 and 1980 (Federal Bureau of Investigation 1982, table 2). A continuation of the recent declines in reported crimes in coming years would provide additional support for the expected turnaround in prison populations to begin in the early 1990s.

Nevertheless, we will continue to confront a prospect of rapidly increasing prison populations in the 1980s, and there is a growing interest in finding ways to use the limited available prison space in the most effective manner for achieving crime control. The problem of *allocation*—deciding which offenders are to be incarcerated—has emerged as an important consideration in developing imprisonment policies.

[1]The index offenses include homicide (murder and nonnegligent manslaughter), rape, robbery, aggravated assault, burglary, larceny of more than $50, and auto theft. The index offenses were expanded in 1973 to include all larcenies regardless of value and were augmented in 1981 to include arson.

From an incapacitation perspective, incarceration should be used primarily for those offenders who are likeliest to continue to commit serious crimes at reasonably high rates. Conversely, offenders who do not present a significant social threat could be released from prison early or not imprisoned at all. Such a policy has the potential of directly preventing the most crimes for a given level of prison resources, but it requires reasonably accurate bases for distinguishing among offenders and faces a variety of challenges to the legitimacy of differential sanctions.

Two different types of incapacitation policy are often distinguished: *selective* incapacitation and *collective* incapacitation (Greenberg 1975). Selective incapacitation involves *individually based* sentences, in which sentencing decisions are tailored to the particular individual. Such sentences would be individualized to vary with differences in predictions of the individual's propensity to commit future crimes. Selective incapacitation permits quite different sentences for the same offense in order to accommodate the differences in crime control potential among offenders convicted of the same crime. The effectiveness of a selective incapacitation policy in preventing crime rests on the predictive capability to identify the worst offenders—those who commit crimes at high rates.

Collective incapacitation refers to *aggregate-offense-based* sentencing policies. Unlike a selective incapacitation policy, under an aggregate policy, individuals are sentenced solely on the basis of their present offense and perhaps their prior criminal record. Aggregate policies do not invoke any predictions about the expected future behavior of a particular individual. Within certain bounds (reflecting, e.g., a concern that sentences be commensurate with the seriousness of the offense), aggregate policies may vary in the types of offense that are subject to imprisonment and in the average length of prison terms applied to different offenses. But within an offense and prior record class, all convicted offenders would be sentenced uniformly. To the extent that individual offending patterns vary with the nature of the present offense and prior record, the choices among different aggregate policies have the potential for differential impact in preventing crimes. In estimating these effects the variations across particular individuals are ignored, and only the average consequences of a collective incapacitation policy are considered.

This essay reviews the findings of several bodies of incapacitation research that have developed in recent years. Section I is a general introduction to incapacitation research. It sets out and explains a model for criminal careers that is generally employed by researchers and discusses several assumptions on which incapacitation research is based. Sections II, III, and IV, respectively, consider collective incapacitation research, selective incapacitation research, and research on an alternate collective incarceration strategy that avoids many of the objections to selective incapacitation that have been raised.

Section II, on collective incapacitation strategies, reviews research findings on the crime reduction effects of existing incarceration practices and on the crime reduction and prison population effects of various hypothetical sentencing policies (e.g., five-year minimum sentences for all felony convictions). Generally the estimated crime reduction effects are small. Section II concludes by examining differences in the sizes of the various estimates and suggests some absolute limits on crime reduction effects that result from the nature of individual criminal careers and the response of criminal justice systems.

Section III, on selective incapacitation, examines the major research, reviews various ethical and policy problems posed by selective incapacitation strategies, and identifies a number of empirical and methodological problems that plague the existing research.

Section IV then describes a hybrid collective incapacitation strategy that uses criminal career information as the basis for sentencing. Such a policy is based on the emerging evidence that there are pronounced regularities in criminal career patterns that can be used to distinguish offenders. Such a strategy would be based only on conviction information and would thereby avoid both many of the ethical problems that beset selective incapacitation and the overaggregation problems that characterize collective incapacitation.

Finally, Section V, the conclusion, places the preceding sections in perspective and identifies promising strategies for future development of incapacitation research.

I. The Criminal Careers Framework

A key consideration in evaluating the merit of incapacitative strategies is the estimated crime control effects of those policies in the free community. When studying incapacitative effects, it is useful to characterize the nature of an individual's criminal activity as a "criminal career" (see Avi-Itzhak and Shinnar 1973; Shinnar and Shinnar 1975).

A. Criminal Careers

The period during an individual's lifetime when crimes are likely to be committed can be viewed as a criminal career.[2] As illustrated in figure 1, during a criminal career there is some chance that the individual will commit crimes; before and after a career the individual is crime free. The likelihood of committing crimes during a career is represented by the individual crime rate, r. An individual with a crime rate of ten crimes per year, for example, has a .027 likelihood (10/365) of committing a crime on any day in a year. Whether a crime is actually committed will depend on the circumstances of the offender and the opportunities for crime on that day.

It is unlikely that an individual will commit exactly r crimes each year. In the example above, the offender with a rate of ten crimes per year will actually commit less than ten crimes in some years and more than ten crimes in others; there may even be years when no crimes are committed, even though the rate remains at ten that year. If it were possible, however, to observe this same individual over many years during a career, or to observe the careers of many different individuals who each commit crimes at a rate of ten per year, we would expect that in the long run the average number of crimes per year per individual would be ten.

Careers begin when the chance of committing crimes becomes r. This may be at or before the first crime committed. Likewise, careers

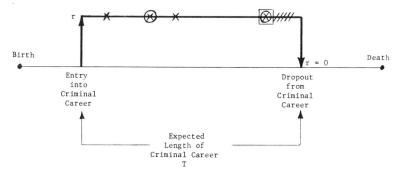

FIG. 1.   An individual criminal career. x: crimes (committed at rate r); circle: arrest for a crime (with probability q_A); box: conviction after arrest (with probability q_c); hatching: time served after conviction (with probability J and mean length S).

[2]This characterization of an individual's criminal activity as a "career" is not meant to imply that offenders derive their livelihood exclusively or even predominantly from crime. Here the concept of a "criminal career" is intended merely to structure the series of criminal events for an individual. Some criminal careers may consist only of one offense. Others may include many offenses over a lengthy period.

end when there is no longer any chance of committing crimes, which may occur at or after the last crime committed. The period during lifetimes when there is some chance of committing crimes is the observed length of an individual's career, t.

The actual beginning and end points of a career will vary with chance for an individual. If it were possible to let the same individual repeat his career over many different lifetimes, the observed length of the career would likely vary across these different lifetimes. In the long run, the expected length of an individual's career would be the mean length, T, found over all those hypothetical careers.

This mean T cannot be estimated by replicating lifetimes for any single individual. An alternative way to estimate T would be to find a population in which all individuals have the same chances of beginning and ending their careers at any point during their lifetimes. Because these careers begin and end by chance, it is unlikely that any two individuals will begin their careers at the same point or have the same career lengths, even though their chances are the same at each point in their lifetimes. The mean career length, T, observed across all those individuals, however, would give the long-run expected length of a career for any individual in the population.

During a career, not only the crimes committed by an individual but also the responses of the criminal justice system are the result of a chance process. Offenders commit crimes at rate r, with some crimes resulting in arrest with chance q_A. Arrested offenders are convicted with chance q_c and those who are convicted then have a chance, J, of being incarcerated. The average time served by those who are incarcerated is then given by S.

In this formulation of a criminal career, the criminal activities of an individual are not deterministic, fixed events. Instead, they are the result of a chance process. With such a chance process it is important to distinguish between the particular realization of a career that is actually observed and the underlying rates and chance processes that give rise to that realization. In the case of coin flipping, this distinction is between the outcome on any particular flip (say a head) and the underlying stable process for a fair coin where the chance of a head is one-half. With enough coin flips, we expect the underlying process to be revealed, with about one-half of the outcomes being heads.

A similar distinction applies to criminal careers. The number and timing of crimes committed and the responses of the criminal justice system (e.g., arrests) vary according to a chance process. It is this chance process that characterizes criminal careers. For each individual we can observe only one particular realization of that process. If it were possible to replicate an individual's lifetime repeatedly, or if we have many different individuals all subject to the same chance process, the particular course of the criminal career observed would undoubtedly be different each time. The long-run average pattern of career realizations, however, would accurately reflect the underlying chance process that characterizes criminal careers.

Having characterized the elements of an individual criminal career, we can now turn to developing estimates of the incapacitative effect of incarceration in reducing crimes during a career. The crime control effects of any incapacitation policy will vary with the magnitude of individual crime rates, r, and with the expected length of criminal careers, T. When a criminal career is not interrupted by incarceration, it can be expected to generate a total of rT crimes. Incarceration for a period of S years could potentially avert rS of those crimes. In general, the higher the individual crime rate and the longer the career, the more crimes can be averted through incapacitation. Larger individual crime rates mean more crimes averted for each unit of time incarcerated. Longer careers, on the other hand, decrease the likelihood of wasting incapacitation on offenders who end their careers while incarcerated and who would thus not be committing any further crimes whether incarcerated or not. The incapacitative effect actually achieved will depend on the effectiveness of the criminal justice system in identifying and ultimately incarcerating offenders. The less likely offenders are to be incarcerated, the smaller the incapacitative effect.

B. Critical Assumptions

All existing estimates of incapacitative effects share certain basic assumptions. To begin with, all offenders are assumed to be vulnerable to arrest and incarceration; there is no subpopulation of offenders who will—with certainty—never be caught and incarcerated and who are responsible for a substantial portion of unsolved crimes. If there were such an invulnerable group, incapacitative effects would be reduced and would only affect the smaller number of crimes committed by offenders who do have some chance of arrest and incarceration. The likelihood that such a group of invulnerable offenders exists is not great (Shinnar and Shinnar 1975). The more unsolved crimes are attributed to invulnerable offenders, the fewer unsolved crimes remain to be committed by the offenders who do get caught. This would greatly increase the chance of arrest after a crime for the offenders who do get caught. In the extreme case, all unsolved crimes would be committed by invulnerable offenders, and the vulnerable population would be arrested for every crime they commit—a very unlikely scenario.

It is also assumed that the crimes of offenders who are taken off the streets are not replaced by those of other offenders. This could happen if, for example, the offender were part of an organized illegal economic activity like drug sales or burglaries organized by a fence; in this event a replacement might simply be recruited from an available "labor market" to continue the crimes that would otherwise be committed by the incarcerated offender. Alternately, if the offender were part of a crime-committing group, the remaining members of the group might continue their criminal activity, with or without recruiting a replacement. The potential impact of replacement and group offending in reducing incapacitative effects is considered in greater detail in Reiss (1980). The social networks capable of sustaining the crimes of an incarcerated offender are more likely to be found among juveniles; they are less of a problem in estimates of incapacitative effects for adults.

A final assumption generally invoked in estimates of incapacitative effects is that periods of incarceration do not alter criminal careers by changing the expected length of criminal careers, T, or the individual crime rate, r. More specifically, it is assumed that there are no rehabilitative or criminogenic effects of prison terms on the careers of incarcerated offenders, and no general deterrent effects that curtail the criminal careers of nonincarcerated offenders. To the extent that these effects, when they exist, are not immediate, but rather affect the future course of careers after release, the short-run estimates of incapacitative effects would be unaffected.

Long-run outcomes, by contrast, would be more vulnerable to violations of this assumption. A criminogenic effect of incarceration that increases individual crime rates or lengthens careers after release would perversely lead to future *increases* in the incapacitative effect that could be achieved from continuing the same incarceration policies. As the mean individual crime rate or the expected career length increases, so also does the number of crimes that can be averted through incapacitation from each man-year incarcerated. Similarly, the long-run crime reduction directly associated with incapacitation would decrease if the mean individual crime rate or expected career length declined in the future as a result of rehabilitation or deterrence. Fewer crimes would be averted by the same incarceration level. In each case, the gains from one form of crime control are counteracted by losses from another form. With criminogenic effects, failure to account for changes in criminal careers would lead to long-run underestimates of the incapacitative effect; in the presence of rehabilitation or deterrence, the long-run incapacitative effect would be overestimated.

The weight of the evidence strongly suggests that there is no aggregate effect of imprisonment in altering the subsequent criminal activity of incarcerated offenders.[3] While some studies have found a difference in the recidivism rates of incarcerated and nonincarcerated offenders, these differences largely disappear when satisfactory controls for prior differences between the two populations are introduced (see Robison and Smith 1971; Lipton, Martinson, and Wilks 1975; Greenberg 1977; Sechrest, White, and Brown 1979). The assumption of no long-run criminogenic or rehabilitative effects on incarcerated offenders thus appears to be reasonable.

The evidence for a general deterrent effect is unconvincing. On the whole, studies of deterrence have consistently reported a negative association between crime rates and sanction levels, which has been interpreted as evidence of a deterrent effect. These studies, however, suffer from a variety of methodological problems that undermine the credibility of the results (Blumstein, Cohen, and Nagin 1978). At best, whatever deterrent effect has been estimated must be viewed as representing the combined effects of deterrence and other inadequately controlled factors, including incapacitation. Deterrence may play a role in overestimating incapacitative effects. The importance of this bias, however, will vary with the magnitude of the estimated incapacitative effect; the smaller the estimated incapacitative effect, the less serious are any errors that would have inflated that estimate.

At a minimum, the accuracy of estimates of incapacitative effects will depend on the accuracy of these assumptions. Failure of any of the assumptions will result in over- or underestimates of incapacitative effects. For the most part, the available estimates of incapacitative effects are similarly vulnerable to these various sources of error. So while the absolute magnitudes of the different estimates might be subject to errors, the relative magnitudes in comparisons across estimates are less likely to be affected.

[3]Particular individuals may experience either a criminogenic or rehabilitative effect, but in the aggregate these individual effects largely offset one another to yield no effect for the group as a whole.

These three assumptions appear, in general, to be well-founded. Except for offenses, like retail drug trafficking, in which imprisoned offenders are likely to be replaced by other offenders, weakness in these assumptions should not vitiate the general credibility of the findings of incapacitation research.

II. Collective Incapacitation

Several major studies of the effects of collective incapacitation strategies have been published. They can be divided into those that attempt to determine the crime reduction effects of existing sanctioning policies and those that examine both the crime reduction effects and the impact on prison population size of hypothetical sanctioning policies. The incapacitative effects of existing and of plausible hypothetical policies are only modest in size. A movement toward general increases in the use of incapacitation strategies is likely to exacerbate present levels of prison crowding. Analysis of existing offending patterns suggests that there are real limits on the maximum crime reduction obtainable under any incapacitation policy.

A. Estimates of the Incapacitative Effects of
Current Imprisonment Policies

Table 1 summarizes several estimates of the collective incapacitative effects of existing imprisonment policies. In each case, the estimate of the reduction in crime is derived using a constant average crime rate for all offenders and applying a uniform sentencing policy to these offenders.[4] The estimates in table 1 are vulnerable to a number of different problems that affect the credibility of the individual estimates. The first four studies are reviewed in considerable detail elsewhere (Cohen 1978), and their limitations are only briefly summarized here.

The studies in table 1 rely on estimates of the mean individual crime rate of active offenders. When estimating incapacitative effects it is important to distinguish between the individual crime rate during freedom, r, and the *effective* crime rate for individuals, r^*. To estimate the decrease in crime that would result from incapacitation during periods of incarceration, the desired quantity is the *free* crime rate, the rate at which crimes would be committed while the offender is free on the

---

[4]Clarke (1974) is a minor exception; that study allows for different age-specific arrest rates and incarceration rates. These rates, however, are assumed to apply uniformly within each age category.

TABLE 1
Alternative Estimates of the Collective Incapacitative Effect of Current Imprisonment Policies

Study	Data Base	Assumptions	Crime Reduction from Incapacitation	
			Percentage of Current Level of Crime with Incapacitation	Percentage of Potential Level of Crime without Incapacitation
Clarke (1974)	Juvenile index* arrests in Philadelphia (applied to 1972 reported offenses)	Age-specific arrest rates (.287 to .385 arrests per year); age-specific incarceration rates; constant probability of arrest for a crime	1%–4% of *all* (adult and juvenile) *reported* index crimes	1%–3.8% of all reported index crimes
Greenberg (1975)	Index offenses nationally in 1965	Individual crime rate constant at .5 to 3.33 crimes per year†	1.2%–8% of reported and unreported index crimes	1.2%–7.4% of reported and unreported index crimes
Ehrlich (1974)	Index offenses nationally in 1960	Individual crime rate constant at one reported crime per year	9.5% of reported index crimes	8.7% of reported index crimes
Shinnar and Shinnar (1975)	Safety crimes in New York State in 1970: homicide, rape, robbery, aggravated assault and burglary	Individual crime rate constant at ten reported crimes per year; Expected prison stay per crime = 0.024 years	25% of reported safety crimes	20% of reported safety crimes
Peterson and Braiker, with Polich (1980)	California prison inmates in 1976	Crime-specific individual crime rates constant at: .815 armed robberies per year; 3.89 burglaries per year; .82 auto thefts per year	22% of reported and unreported armed robberies; 6% of reported and unreported burglaries; 7% of reported and unreported auto thefts	18% of reported and unreported armed robberies; 5.7% of reported and unreported burglaries; 6.5% of reported and unreported auto thefts

* In all the analyses above, the index offenses used were defined by the FBI to include homicide, rape, robbery, aggravated assault, burglary, larceny and auto theft.

† The estimates of individual crime rates are those reported in the original study. These differ from the estimates attributed to Greenberg in Moore, Estrich, and McGillis (1982, table II-2); the latter reflect various corrective adjustments made to the original estimates by Moore et al.

streets. Any time that is spent incarcerated will reduce the annual free crime rate to yield the effective crime rate for offenders. For example, an offender may commit crimes at a rate of ten per year while free. If this offender is incarcerated for six months during a year, he can only commit crimes at rate ten for the six months he is free. His free rate is ten crimes per year, but his effective rate during the entire year is only five, since he is only free to commit crimes for one-half of the year. The crimes that are observed for a sample of offenders generally reflect their effective crime rates. Any time served by these offenders must be removed to estimate their free crime rates.

Two studies, Clarke (1974) and Greenberg (1975), rely on official data on arrests as a basis for estimating the individual arrest or crime rates of active offenders. Clarke (1974) uses data on individual records of "arrests" before age eighteen for a cohort of 9,945 Philadelphia boys.[5] This cohort included all boys who were born in 1945 and who resided in Philadelphia from ages ten to eighteen (Wolfgang, Figlio, and Sellin 1972). Using data on the arrests and incarcerations for the 381 boys from the cohort who were ever incarcerated by age eighteen, Clarke estimates the average annual arrest rate for juvenile offenders while free to be .287 for whites and .385 for nonwhites. Applying these rates to the periods of incarceration, Clarke estimates the number of arrests averted by incarceration of these juveniles. The resulting incapacitative effect of the then-prevailing use of incarceration for juveniles is estimated to be from 5–15 percent of reported index crimes by juveniles and from 1–4 percent of all (adult and juvenile) reported index crimes.

The resulting incapacitative effect is likely to be underestimated in Clarke (1974). In estimating individual arrest rates Clarke fails to consider variations in the ages of onset and dropout from criminal activity. Instead, all identified juvenile offenders are considered criminally active from ages seven to seventeen. Such a procedure will yield underestimates of individual arrest rates, especially at younger ages when many juveniles have not yet started their criminal careers and at older ages when some juveniles have already terminated their careers. The underestimates in individual arrest rates while free will yield underestimates of the incapacitative effect.

---

[5]Here "arrests" refer to the juvenile equivalent of offenses resulting in arrests for adults: they include all offenses attributed to the juvenile by the police without formal arrest charges against the juvenile.

Greenberg (1975) uses 1965 Federal Bureau of Investigation (FBI) data on criminal careers to estimate the annual index arrest rate of 0.5 for persons with at least one arrest. This arrest rate estimate is combined with an estimate of the probability of arrest for a crime, q_A, to yield an estimate of the individual crime rate. At one extreme, the upper bound on q_A is 1.0, where all crimes result in arrest. This results in a lower bound estimate of 0.5 for the individual crime rate. By means of an analysis set out in Appendix A, Greenberg calculates an upper bound of 3.3. Using the bounds $0.5 < r < 3.33$, Greenberg estimates that the incapacitative effect of the then-prevailing incarceration policies was from 1.2 to 8.0 percent of the estimated 8.34 million index crimes in 1965.

Greenberg's estimate rests on certain arbitrary assumptions about the rate at which offenses are reported to the police and about the proportion of virgin arrests among all arrests (V/A). The total number of index crimes, C, is estimated from the number of reported crimes and an assumed combined reporting rate of one-third for police agencies reporting to the FBI and citizens reporting to the police. As demonstrated in Cohen (1978), holding the values of all other variables constant, the upper bound on the individual crime rate, r, is found to be very sensitive to minor changes in the assumed reporting rate. Within the most probable range of citizen reporting rates to the police of 25 to 50 percent,[6] the combined reporting rate ranges from 17.5 to 35 percent,[7] and the upper bound on the crime rate varies between 6.4 and 3.1, respectively.

Similarly, the virgin arrest ratios, V/A and V_I/A, which play an important part in Greenberg's calculations (see App. A), are arbitrarily set at 0.25 and 0.20, respectively, by Greenberg (V = all first arrests and V_I = first arrests for index offenses). The only constraints on these values are that $V/A < 0.286$ and $V_I/A < V/A$. The choice of V/A is an important factor in the value of the upper bound for the individual

[6]Victimization surveys in eighteen U.S. cities (U.S. Department of Justice 1975, 1976a) indicate relatively little variation in reporting rates among cities, about 33 percent for all crimes in the personal sector, 45 percent for crimes of violence, and 25 percent for crimes of theft.

[7]The combined reporting rate is derived by multiplying the citizen reporting rate by the rate of police agencies reporting to the FBI. The latter rate is estimated as 70 percent using the ratio of the covered population to the total U.S. population in 1965 (135/194). This assumes that the rate of crimes for agencies that do not report to the FBI is like the rate found in reporting agencies.

crime rate; values of V/A marginally smaller than 0.25 lead to larger values for the crime rate.

Alternative and equally plausible values of the input variables lead to higher estimates of the individual crime rate than were used by Greenberg. The combination of a lower combined reporting rate and a lower proportion of virgin arrests significantly increases the upper bound on the crime rate. If the combined reporting rate is taken as 30 percent rather than one-third and V/A is set at 0.15 rather than 0.25 ($V_t/A = 0.10$), the upper bound for the individual crime rate is 6.25, and not 3.33. Because of the likely underestimated value of the individual crime rate, the incapacitative effect is underestimated as well. While Greenberg estimates the maximum crime reduction from adult incarceration in 1965 to be 8 percent of 1965 levels of index crimes, a different plausible set of assumptions (involving a 30 percent reporting rate and an individual crime rate of 6.25) yields a reduction that is 13.5 percent of 1965 levels of index crimes.

The estimates of individual crime rates used in Ehrlich (1974) and Shinnar and Shinnar (1975) are not empirically based. Ehrlich (1974) is principally concerned with estimating the deterrent effect of imprisonment policies. Since deterrence and incapacitation operate in the same direction in reducing crimes, at least some part of the estimated deterrent effect can be attributed to incapacitation. Ehrlich estimates that at prevailing levels of imprisonment in 1960 the incapacitative effect was no more than 10 percent of the total estimated effect of imprisonment in reducing crimes, or approximately a 0.1 percent reduction in crime from a 1 percent increase in imprisonment. Based on this estimate, the total crime reduction from 1960 levels of incarceration was estimated to be 9.5 percent of the 1960 levels of reported index crimes.

Ehrlich's estimate of the incapacitative effect is likely to be underestimated because of his use of an unusually low estimate of one index crime per year for the individual crime rate. This value of $r = 1$ is never reported directly; it is only uncovered by a careful reconstruction of his assumptions and estimates.

In Ehrlich (1974), the desired incapacitative effect is derived as a function of two imprisonment policy variables: $P =$ the probability that an offender at large is apprehended and imprisoned (e.g., the number of prison commitments per offender at large); and $S =$ the average time actually served in prison by an incarcerated offender. Both of these variables are offender based; they reflect the costs in prison time incurred by an offender and not the costs associated with any single offense. The problem arises in the empirical estimates of these variables used by Ehrlich.

Both P and S are estimated using 1960 data from the national prisoner statistics published annually by the U.S. Department of Justice. The estimate of S is straightforward using the time served for released inmates; P is estimated by the ratio of the number of prison commitments to the number of reported offenses, P^*. The number of prison commitments reflects the desired number of *offenders* committed to prison. The denominator of the ratio, by contrast, reflects *offenses* and not the total number of offenders who are at large. The required number of offenders can be estimated by dividing the number of offenses by an estimate of the individual crime rate, r, to yield the desired estimate $P = rP^*$.

By using P^* instead of P in his estimate of the incapacitative effect, Ehrlich has in effect assumed that active offenders commit on average only one reported index offense per year per offender ($r = 1$). To the extent that the individual crime rate for reported offenses is indeed larger than 1, the estimated crime reduction from incapacitation would also increase. An increase in r from one to five reported crimes per year per offender increases the estimated incapacitative effect in 1960 from 9.5 percent of the prevailing level of reported index crimes to 34.4 percent (see Cohen 1978).[8]

The Shinnar and Shinnar (1975) estimate of incapacitative effects is based on a model of individual criminal activity like that found in figure 1. The basic relationship derived from the model is the ratio of the expected volume of crime under some criminal justice policy to the expected volume of crime if there were no imprisonment. If a criminal is arrested, convicted, and imprisoned during a career, the total number of crimes committed in a career will be reduced by the same proportion that his time free during a career is reduced.[9] For comparatively long

---

[8]It is not clear whether the estimates of P^* in Ehrlich include federal prisoners in addition to state prisoners. In the event that federal prisoners were excluded, including them would increase the estimate of P^* and P by about 12 percent in 1960. The other estimates for the incapacitative effect reviewed in this section do include federal prisoners.

[9]In deriving this result, Shinnar and Shinnar (1975) explicitly invoke the assumption discussed earlier in which time spent incarcerated does not affect the progress of criminal careers. In particular, the expected career length and the individual crime rate are assumed to be unaltered by any time spent incarcerated.

careers, T large with respect to S, the reduction in time free, or the incapacitative effect, is approximately[10]

$$I = \frac{rqJS}{I + rqJS} \, . \tag{1}$$

The expression for the incapacitative effect in equation (1) is derived rigorously in Avi-Itzhak and Shinnar (1973) and only an intuitive justification is provided here. For long careers, in which T is much longer than S, the average time between prison commitments is just the reciprocal of the rate of prison commitments in a year, $1/rqJ$. With S the average prison stay, the fraction of a total career that a criminal is incapacitated is given by

Average prison stay/(Average time between commitments + Average prison stay) =

$$\frac{S}{(1/rqJ) + S} = \frac{rqJS}{1 + rqJS} \, .$$

The incapacitative effect in Shinnar and Shinnar (1975) is estimated by substituting values for the variables in equation (1). The criminal justice policy variable, qJS, is just the expected time spent in prison for a crime. Estimates of qJS are obtained by taking the ratio of the average daily prison population to the number of reported crimes in a year. For 1970, qJS was estimated at .024. The individual crime rate, r, is estimated from data on the average number of arrests per year observed during the past careers of offenders who were arrested on federal charges during 1970 combined with estimates of the criminal justice system variables. This estimate includes all past arrests for the offender sample and not just the federal charges. For safety crimes— defined to include murder, rape, robbery, aggravated assault, and burglary—the resulting individual free crime rate for *reported* crimes is estimated at between six and fourteen safety crimes per year, and the midpoint ten is used to estimate an incapacitative effect of a 20 percent reduction from the potential level of safety crimes in 1970.

The range of r provided by Shinnar and Shinnar for reported saftey crimes is likely to be overestimated. First, the estimated rate of *total*

[10]This expression for I represents an approximation of the reduction in time free when T is large with respect to S (i.e., $T/(T + S)$ is very close in value to 1). The exact expression for I for any values of S and T is

$$\frac{rqJS[T/(T + S)]}{1 + rqJS[T/(T + S)]} \, .$$

arrests per year is divided by the lower clearance rate of .15 to .20 that prevailed for all *index* offenses in cities. The clearance rate for safety crimes in cities is higher (at .25 or more) and would result in a *lower* estimate of the effective crime rate for individuals. The final estimate for the range of r while free is also circular, relying as it does on estimated values of the incapacitative effect that are themselves based on an *assumed* value of $r = 10$ for safety crimes. As we shall see later, this rate of 10 is likely to be an overestimate. Use of lower values for the crime rate, r, would result in lower estimates of the incapacitative effect. At the 1970 value of $qJS = .024$, the incapacitative effect is reduced from 20 percent of potential safety crimes to 11 percent by lowering the individual crime rate from ten to five reported safety crimes per year.

In the final estimate reported in table 1, Peterson and Braiker, with Polich (1980) use individually based empirical estimates of individual crime rates to estimate the incapacitative effect. Using data on self-reported crimes and prior incarcerations from a 1976 survey of California prison inmates, mean individual free crime rates are estimated for all inmates. These estimated rates of .815 armed robberies, 3.89 burglaries, and .82 auto thefts per inmate per year free are then multiplied by the total prison population in 1976 to estimate the total number of crimes that would have been committed in 1976 by all California prison inmates.[11] This is an estimate of the number of crimes prevented by incapacitation in prison. The total number of crimes (reported and unreported) actually experienced in California in 1976 is then estimated by dividing total crimes reported by police in the *Uniform Crime Reports* (Federal Bureau of Investigation 1976) by estimates of the rate at which victims report crimes to the police (available from annual victimization surveys). Comparing the number of crimes averted to the number actually experienced, the incapacitative effect in 1976 was estimated to be 22 percent for armed robbery, 6 percent for burglary, and 7 percent for auto theft.

The resulting estimate of the incapacitative effect is likely to be *overestimated* somewhat, because it is based on probable overestimates

---

[11]The individual crime rates used for each offense are averaged across all inmates including those who report that they never committed that offense. The mean individual crime rates while free for those inmates who admitted committing the offense are 5.61 armed robberies, 14.15 burglaries and 3.9 auto thefts per inmate per year free (Peterson and Braiker, with Polich [1980], table 10a; also available in Peterson and Braiker, with Polich [1981]).

of individual crime rates. Peterson and Braiker, with Polich (1980, p. 34) note that the sample of prison inmates used in the survey was not representative of all prison inmates in California; inmates with more serious prior records were more likely to be found in the sample. To the extent that inmates with more serious prior records are also more likely to have higher crime rates, the incapacitative effect for all inmates would be overestimated when the higher self-reported crime rates of the sample are used.

The Peterson and Braiker estimate is also not directly comparable to the other estimates of collective incapacitation in table 1. Prison inmates as a whole are likely to be more serious offenders than offenders in general, and so they would have higher crime rates than the average for all offenders. The incapacitative effect estimated by Peterson and Braiker based on the higher crime rates of prisoners is likely to be higher than the other estimates in table 1, which are based on lower estimates of individual crime rates for *all* offenders.

All the estimates in table 1 share a common reliance on some estimate of the average individual crime rate, r. Indeed, the differences in the magnitudes of the estimated incapacitative effect are due largely to differences in the estimates of the average crime rate for individual offenders while free. In general, the larger the average crime rate used, the greater the estimated incapacitative effect.

Although central to the above estimates of collective incapacitative effects, the individual crime rate is generally a poorly known quantity. More recent research has focused explicitly on providing estimates of individual crime rates for active offenders.

Peterson and Braiker, with Polich (1980) use self-reported crimes to estimate individual crime rates for California prison inmates. As already mentioned, because the estimates were based on the more serious of-fenders likely to be found in prison, the self-report estimates are likely to be biased toward higher individual crime rates than would be found in the total population of offenders both in and out of prison. To correct for this bias, Chaiken (1980) uses models of the crime-committing and imprisonment processes to estimate the probability that an active "street offender" will be in prison at some time t.[12] Using these probabilities, the individual crime rates estimated for prison inmates can be adjusted to obtain estimates of individual crime rates for all active "street of-

[12]The population of "street offenders" refers to the "offenders who commit serious crimes and have a nonzero probability of imprisonment" (Chaiken 1980, p. 226).

fenders." The resulting estimates of individual crime rates from these self-reports are presented in table 2.

Blumstein and Cohen (1979) analyze the officially recorded arrest histories of over 5,000 adults arrested for murder, rape, robbery, aggravated assault, burglary, or auto theft in Washington, D.C., during 1973. Using data on the number of past arrests and previous time served, mean individual arrest rates while free are estimated.

These individual arrest rates, u, result from individual crime rates, r, and the probability that an offender is arrested for a crime, q, with $u = rq$. Thus, going from the recorded arrests of an offender to his crimes requires some estimate of the probability that an offender is arrested for a crime. A crude measure of this probability is just the ratio of the number of arrests to the number of reported crimes. This ratio is then adjusted to account for unreported crimes by using esti-

TABLE 2

Individual Crime Rates while Free:
Alternative Estimates from Self-Reports and
from Arrest Histories

Estimate	Index Crimes*	Index Crimes without Larceny	Safety Crimes†
Self-Reports‡	Not available	6.5	5.6
Arrest Histories:ǁ			
Robbers	12.0	7.1	6.5
Assaulters	10.4	6.0	5.5
Burglars	15.8	9.0	8.2
Auto thieves	10.5	7.5	4.5

* The index crimes include murder, rape, robbery, aggravated assault, burglary, larceny, and auto theft.

† Safety crimes include murder, rape, robbery, aggravated assault, and burglary.

‡ The self-report estimates are derived from data in Peterson and Braiker, with Polich (1980). The aggregate rates for index crimes and safety crimes are just the sum of rates for each crime type weighted by the proportion of the population ever committing that crime type, from Peterson and Braiker, with Polich (1980: table II). Rates for larceny are unavailable. Also unarmed robberies are not included in the aggregate rates. Based on the *Uniform Crime Reports* for 1973, unarmed robberies are 34.1 percent of total robberies reported to the police that year. Using this proportion to increase the individual armed robbery rate would add only .33 to the aggregate rates from self-reports.

ǁ The arrest history estimates are calculated from data in Blumstein and Cohen (1979). The aggregate rates are just the sum of the individual crime rates for each type of crime found for offenders who are ever arrested for robbery (robbers), those ever arrested for aggravated assault (assaulters), those ever arrested for burglary (burglars), and those ever arrested for auto theft (auto thieves).

mates of the reporting rate to the police, R, available from victimization survey data on victim reporting. A further adjustment is required to account for the fact that the number of arrests often includes arrests for multiple offenders for the same crime incident. This correction uses an estimate of the rate of multiple offenders in crimes, M, available from victim accounts of the number of offenders per crime in the victimization surveys. The final estimate of the probability of arrest for a crime (whether reported or not) is given by

$$q = \frac{\text{number of arrests}}{(\text{number of reported offenses}) \, (M/R)}.$$

The resulting estimates of individual crime rates derived from arrest rates are presented in table 2.

The two estimates of individual crime rates for active offenders are vulnerable to different sorts of errors. Self-reports are subject to in-evitable response biases arising from simple memory-recall difficulties or from deliberate efforts to mislead. Analyses based on official arrest histories, by contrast, invoke various assumptions that may not be appropriate about the crime-committing and arrest processes in order to infer conclusions about unobserved crimes from observed arrests. Despite the potential sources of error, the two estimates of individual crime rates of table 2 are strikingly close at about twelve index crimes and six safety crimes per offender per year free. These estimates, based on data on individual criminal careers, are higher than the rates for index offenses that were used by the studies in table 1 and lower than the rate for safety crimes. Taken together, however, the five estimates in table 1 provide a reasonable range for the magnitude of the current collective incapacitative effect. That range is generally low; the esti-mated reduction from the potential level of crime for prevailing col-lective incapacitation policies never exceeded the 20 percent estimated for safety crimes in New York State.

B. Estimates of the Effects of Alternative
Collective Incapacitation Policies

The various estimates of prevailing incapacitative effects are couched in considerable uncertainty, largely because they rely on questionable estimates of individual crime rates. In addition to the estimate already discussed in table 1, Greenberg (1975, p. 573) also proposes an alternative procedure for estimating collective incapacitative effects that does not require explicit estimates of individual crime rates. This procedure, which measures the additional crime reduction effects of changes from current imprisonment policies, takes the arrestees in a year and examines their past criminal records for previous convictions. It is then determined whether the arrestees would have been incarcerated at the time of the current sampling arrest if they had been sentenced under alternative sentencing options at the time of previous convictions. This provides an estimate of the portion of currently sampled arrests that would have been averted by alternative incarceration policies.

The estimated incapacitative effect is most accurate for the portion of arrests that would be averted. To the extent that *all* offenders are vulnerable to arrest for their crimes, and the arrestees who have arrests averted are like the collection of other arrestees in arrest vulnerability, the proportion of arrests averted is also an estimate of the proportion of crimes that would be averted.[13] In this event, the portion of arrests averted would accurately reflect the incapacitative potential of alternative sentences on the level of crimes.

The estimate of the incapacitative effect also assumes that implementation of the alternative sentencing strategy would not have differentially altered offending patterns in the two groups of offenders. As long as any deterrent effect would similarly affect both offenders who have arrests averted and all other offenders, the estimated incapacitative effect would not be affected by deterrence.

Table 3 summarizes the estimated collective incapacitation effects on crime of alternative imprisonment policies in a number of jurisdictions. These estimates all use the general Greenberg procedure of retrospectively searching for prior convictions in the arrest histories of a sample of offenders. The estimates represent the incapacitative potential

---

[13]The proportion of arrests averted can be represented by $n_1 r_1 q_1 / (n_1 r_1 q_1 + n_2 r_2 q_2)$, where n_1 is the number of offenders with arrests averted, n_2 is the number of remaining offenders, r_i $(i = 1, 2)$ is the mean individual crime rate and q_i $(i = 1, 2)$ is the probability of arrests for a crime for the n_1 and n_2 offenders, respectively. For $q_1 = q_2 = q$, the proportion of arrests averted is equal to the proportion of crimes averted, $n_1 r_1 / (n_1 r_1 + n_2 r_2)$. If, however, the arrestees with *arrests averted* have a higher arrest probability than other arrestees, the reduction in arrests would overestimate the incapacitative effect on crimes. In this case the incarceration policies would be particularly effective in targeting offenders who are more vulnerable to arrest. The incapacitative effect on crimes would be underestimated if the arrestees with arrests averted have a lower probability of arrest than do other arrestees, as might occur if incarceration policies effectively target offenders who are more adept at avoiding detection and arrest.

TABLE 3
Estimates of the Collective Incapacitative Effect of Alternative Imprisonment Policies

Study	Data Base	Alternative Sentencing Policy	Target Offense	Estimated Incapacitative Effect: Reduction in Target Offense (%)
Greenberg (1975)	Arrestees in California during 1971	One year added to time served for those previously sentenced to prison	Index offenses (murder, rape, robbery, aggravated assault, burglary, larceny of more than $50, and auto theft)	3–4
Van Dine et al. (1977, 1979)	Arrestees in Franklin County, Ohio, during 1973	Five-year mandatory prison terms after any felony conviction as an adult	Violent index offenses (murder, rape, robbery, and aggravated assault)	17.4
		Five-year mandatory prison terms after repeat felony convictions as an adult	Same	6.0
Petersilia and Greenwood (1978)	Convictions in District Court in Denver, Colorado, between 1968 and 1970	Five-year mandatory prison terms after any felony convictions as an adult	Violent offenses (murder, kidnapping, rape, robbery, and aggravated assault)	
			Burglary	31
		Five-year mandatory prison terms after repeat felony convictions as an adult	Violent offenses	42
				16
			Burglary	15
Cohen (1982)	Arrestees in Washington, D.C., during 1973	Five-year mandatory prison terms after any conviction for a "criterion" offense as an adult	"Criterion" offenses (index offenses other than larceny)	13.7
		Five-year mandatory prison terms after repeat conviction for a "criterion" offense as an adult	Same	3.8

to be gained from alternative sentencing strategies measured as a fraction of prevailing levels of crime.

Greenberg (1975) uses data on arrestees for index offenses in California in 1971. The portion of arrestees who were on parole at the time of arrest is used to estimate the portion of arrestees who were released from prison within one year of their 1971 sampling arrest. Using this proportion, Greenberg estimates that the incapacitative effect of one additional year in prison for these releases would have been a 3–4 percent reduction in index offenses.

Van Dine, Conrad, and Dinitz (1979) examine the prior criminal records of all adults arrested for violent felonies (murder, rape, robbery, and aggravated assault) in Franklin County, Ohio (Columbus), whose cases were disposed in court during 1973. These 342 individuals accounted for 638 arrests for violent felonies in 1973. Searching the criminal histories of these individuals, it was found that 111 of the 638 arrests were preceded by a prior felony conviction as an adult within five years of the 1973 arrest (Van Dine et al. 1979, tables 3-25, 3-32). Thus, a five-year mandatory prison term imposed on any felony conviction would have prevented 17.4 percent of the 638 violent felony arrests in 1973. If the arrestees with arrests averted are just as likely to be arrested for their crimes as are other arrestees, the incapacitative effect of five-year mandatory prison sentences on violent felonies committed is also 17.4 percent. Focusing the five-year terms only on repeat felony convictions, the incapacitative effect is reduced to 6.0 percent (derived from Van Dine et al. [1979], tables 3-25, 3-33).

The estimates in Petersilia and Greenwood (1978) are based on prior criminal history data for a random sample of 625 persons convicted of serious offenses in District Court during a two-year period 1968–70 in Denver, Colorado. The criminal histories of these individuals were searched for prior convictions, which would allow mandatory prison terms under the alternative sentencing strategies considered. Based on their prior histories of convictions, 31 percent of the violent-crime convictions and 42 percent of burglary convictions in the sampling period would have been prevented by five-year mandatory sentences after any felony conviction. Restricting the five-year sentences to repeat felony convictions would have prevented 16 percent of violent convictions and 15 percent of burglary convictions. If offenders who have prior felony convictions have the same likelihood of conviction on serious charges for their subsequent crimes as do other offenders, the reduction in convictions provides a direct estimate of the reduction in crimes from incapacitation.

In the final estimate in table 3, Cohen (1982) uses data on the criminal histories of adults arrested for a "criterion" offense—murder, rape, robbery, aggravated assault, burglary, or auto theft—in Washington, D.C., during 1973. Based on the prior convictions for criterion offenses experienced by these offenders, five-year mandatory prison terms after any conviction for a criterion offense would have prevented 13.7 percent of the criterion arrests in 1973. Imposing the five-year terms only after repeat convictions would have prevented 3.8 percent of criterion arrests in 1973. Once again, if the arrestees whose arrests would be prevented because of prior convictions have the same chance of arrest for their crimes as do other arrestees, the reduction in arrests also measures the potential reduction in crimes from the alternative imprisonment strategies.

For a variety of reasons, the estimates in table 3 are not fully comparable. Unlike any of the other estimates, Greenberg's (1975) estimate is limited to a policy of increasing the time served by those previously sentenced to prison. All the other estimates also involve an increase in the likelihood of prison sentences, by imposing mandatory five-year prison terms after previous convictions. This difference combined with the shorter increment in time served of only one year accounts for the smaller incapacitative effect estimated in Greenberg (1975).

The estimate of crime reduction through collective incapacitation for Denver, Colorado, is substantially greater than any of the other estimates. Petersilia and Greenwood (1978) report that five-year prison terms imposed after any felony conviction as an adult could have prevented 31 percent of adult convictions following arrests for violent offenses and 42 percent of adult convictions following arrests for burglary. When the five-year terms are restricted to repeat felony convictions, the reductions decrease to 16 percent and 15 percent, respectively. These estimates, however, are based on a sample of convictions in the court of felony jurisdiction in Denver and they are likely to overstate the incapacitive potential more generally.

To the extent that case processing, particularly early dismissals and charge reductions by the prosecutor as well as the final charge at conviction, are influenced by a prior record of felony convictions, offenders convicted of serious offenses in the past would be more likely among current felony convictions than they would be among arrestees or offenders in general. This disproportionate overrepresentation in a sample of convicted offenders would inflate the estimated incapacitative effect of sentences applied to prior felony convictions. In this case, the differential process of charge transformation after arrest that is likely to apply to offenders with prior felony convictions makes the assumption of equal vulnerability less reasonable among a sample of convictions. While the resulting estimates reflect the potential reduction in convictions accurately, they will overestimate the potential incapacitative effect on crimes.

The Van Dine et al. (1979) estimate of a 17.4 percent reduction in violent felonies listed in table 3 is only one of several estimates provided by the authors. An alternative estimate of only a 4 percent incapacitative effect is obtained from applying the same stringent five-year mandatory prison terms after any felony conviction to the same data base (Van Dine et al. 1979); in Van Dine, Dinitz, and Conrad (1977), the 4 percent reduction is the primary estimate. The difference between the two estimates lies in how reported but uncleared offenses are treated.

In arriving at a 4 percent reduction, the crimes potentially averted by the five-year prison terms are limited to reported offenses that result in charges in 1973. The base figure of crimes, on the other hand, includes all reported offenses whether they result in charges or not. In this estimate, *none* of the uncleared crimes are attributed to the arrestees who are affected by the sentencing option. Since the 1973 arrestees are certainly responsible for at least some of the reported but uncleared offenses that year, 4 percent underestimates the incapacitative effect. This point was made in three separate rejoinders published one year after the original article (Boland 1978; Johnson 1978; Palmer and Salimbene 1978). In responding to these critiques, Van Dine, Dinitz, and Conrad (1978) acknowledge that there is surely some additional incapacitative effect to be derived from the uncleared offenses of incapacitated arrestees, and they emphasize that 4 percent represents the *minimum* incapacitative effect that would result from the stringent sentencing option considered. Unfortunately, these qualifications to the estimate are less well known and the admittedly low 4 percent estimate has been cited as a basis for rejecting the efficacy of incapacitation strategies (Currie 1982; Wicker 1982).

The 17.4 percent estimate of the incapacitative effect, which appears in their later work (Van Dine et al. 1979), reflects an alternative treatment of uncleared offenses. In this case, all offenders are assumed to have a nonzero probability of arrest for their crimes; that is, none of the reported offenses are committed by offenders who will never be arrested. In addition, arrestees with arrests averted are no more or less likely to be arrested for their crimes than are other arrestees. Under these minimal conditions, the proportion of arrests averted, 17.4 percent, is also the proportion of crimes averted.

The estimates in table 3 from Van Dine et al. (1979) and Cohen (1982) are directly comparable. Their similar magnitudes based on arrestees in two very different jurisdictions suggest a generalized expectation of a potential reduction in serious crimes of about 15 percent from mandatory five-year prison terms imposed after any felony conviction and about a 5 percent reduction from the same terms imposed only after repeat felony convictions. To the extent that offenders with prior felony convictions have a higher chance of arrest for their subsequent crimes than do other offenders (perhaps because they are known to the police and more likely to be considered as suspects), these estimates will overstate the potential incapacitative effect of these sentencing strategies on crimes. As such, they represent upper bounds on the crime reduction from incapacitation that can be expected from fairly stringent policies of mandatory five-year prison terms after conviction.

C. Limits to the Maximum Benefits to be
Derived from Incapacitation

The most striking feature of the estimated collective incapacitative effects in tables 1 and 3 is the generally limited size of the reductions in crimes achieved through incapacitation. Whether we consider prevailing imprisonment policies or the alternative of reasonably stringent five-year prison terms after any conviction for a serious offense, the incapacitative effect is generally modest at a 10–20 percent reduction in crimes. While a reduction in crime of this magnitude is certainly not trivial, representing from 131,000 to 262,000 reported violent index offenses in the United States during 1980, incapacitation does not make the dent in crime that might have been expected from a "lock-em-up" strategy.

Several recent estimates indicate that the *maximum* potential benefits from incapacitation are likely to be similarly modest. Based on the prior conviction histories of adult index arrestees in Washington, D.C., Cohen (1982) finds that imposing life terms in prison after *any* previous adult conviction for a "criterion" offense (homicide, rape, robbery, aggravated assault, burglary, or auto theft) would have prevented no more than 24 percent of the adult arrests—and by inference of the adult crimes—for these same offenses in Washington, D.C., during 1973. The reasons for this low incapacitative potential are found in the nature of the prior criminal records of adult arrestees. In particular, in the District sample, 21 percent of adult arrestees had no prior *arrests* as adults at all, and another 55 percent had prior arrests but no prior adult *convictions* for criterion offenses. Thus, 76 percent of 1973 adult index arrests in Washington, D.C., could not have been prevented by prior prison terms of any length imposed on convicted adult offenders.

In part, the limits on the maximum potential incapacitative effect result from the failure of prior arrests to result in conviction. Some portion of the 55 percent with prior arrests had prior arrests for criterion offenses but no conviction for a criterion offense. To the extent that the conviction rate could be increased, that would increase the potential incapacitative effect. Further increases in incapacitation would require increases in the chances of arrest for a crime. (The implications of arrest and conviction effectiveness for incapacitation are discussed more fully in Moore et al. [1982].)

The upper bound on incapacitation effects for crimes by adults was similar in Columbus, Ohio, where only 32.2 percent of adult arrestees for violent offenses had at least one prior felony conviction as adults (Van Dine et al. 1979). If the incapacitative strategy of life terms were imposed after *juvenile* felony convictions as well, the violent offenses of 47.1 percent of 1973 adult arrestees could have been prevented. Less severe, mandatory five-year terms after any felony conviction as an adult *or* juvenile would have prevented 27.4 percent of the violent offenses by adults.[14] A somewhat cruder estimate based on the portion of convicted offenders who have prior prison records in Michigan puts the maximum incapacitative effect at 30 percent for violent index offenses by adults (Johnson 1978).

These data indicate that the maximum incapacitative effect is inherently limited. The limits on the potential crime reduction from incapacitation arise principally from the large number of offenders who have no prior convictions. Their crimes could not have been prevented by any incapacitative strategy that required a conviction before imposing imprisonment terms. To the extent that arrestees are not grossly unrepresentative of offenders in their offending patterns, these results represent a sobering influence on expectations about the potential crime-reduction benefits of incapacitation strategies. The attractiveness of

---

[14] These potential incapacitative effects are derived from the numbers of actual and preventable arrests provided in tables 3-25, 3-46 of Van Dine et al. (1979).

incapacitation as a crime control strategy, which derives from the certainty that some crimes will indeed be prevented when offenders are locked up, pales with the recognition that the maximum crime reduction that can be expected if there are no improvements in achieving arrests and convictions is inherently limited.

D. Impact on Prison Populations

The analysis so far has indicated that the likely crime reduction effects from collective incapacitation are low for alternative sentencing strategies. By contrast, the effects of these same sentencing strategies on the size of prison populations are likely to be substantial. The alternatives considered in table 3 all involve committing additional offenders to prison or extending the lengths of prison terms served. To estimate the impact on prison population requires data on the number of convictions vulnerable to the new sentencing option and data on the size of the prison population under existing policies. The results in table 4 indicate that the expected increases in prison populations in the three jurisdictions studied would be substantial, representing threefold, fourfold, and fivefold increases from prevailing prison populations.

In each case, only the impact on the prison population for the target offenses is presented. The impact on the *total* prison population would be smaller, the smaller the proportion of target offenses in the total prison population. In Washington, D.C., for example, the target criterion offenses accounted for 74.5 percent of the total prison population in 1973 (U.S. Department of Justice 1976b), for a 231 percent (.745 × 310 percent) increase in the total prison population.

In the case of Denver (Petersilia and Greenwood 1978) and Franklin County (Van Dine et al. 1979), the estimates represent the impact on prison populations for only those jurisdictions. To the extent that prevailing imprisonment patterns (in terms of the expected man-years in prison after conviction)[15] are similar statewide for those jurisdictions, the proportional increases in table 4 would apply to the state as a whole.

E. Variations in the Size of Collective
Incapacitation Effects

The estimate of collective incapacitative effects reported in tables 1, 3, and 4 vary considerably in magnitude. This variation results from

[15] The expected sentence length after conviction is obtained by multiplying the proportion of convictions with prison sentences times the average sentence length.

TABLE 4
Impact on Prison Populations of Mandatory Five-Year Prison Terms after Conviction

Study	Jurisdiction	Target Offenses	Annual Number of Convictions for Target Offenses	Current Annual Prison Population for Target Offenses (Man-years)	Expected Increase in Prison Population for Target Offenses (%)
Petersilia and Greenwood 1978	Denver, Colorado, 1968–70	Any felony convictions	Not reported	Not reported	450
Van Dine et al. (1979)	Franklin County, Ohio, 1973	Any felony convictions	1,091	876*	523
Cohen (1982)	Washington, D.C., 1973	Convictions for any "criterion" offense (i.e., index offense other than larceny)	1,266†	1,573	310

*The number sentenced to prison for target offenses in Franklin County, Ohio, was 438. The resulting prison population is estimated using an assumed average time served of two years for all felonies. This average is consistent with data on time served in other jurisdictions. In Pennsylvania in 1980, e.g., average time served in prison was 2.18 years (Pennsylvania Bureau of Corrections 1981). Persons released to parole supervision from state and federal institutions in 1977 accounted for 67.8 percent of all releases. These parole releases had a median time served of 1.43 years and an average time served of 2.25 years (U.S. Department of Justice 1980). Since average time served for unconditional releases is generally shorter than that for parole releases, average time served for all prison releases in 1977 will be somewhat less than 2.25 years. An approximation of this average time served can be obtained by dividing the average daily population in state and federal prisons in 1977 by total admissions that year. In 1977, the resulting estimated average time served is 2.17 years (U.S. Department of Commerce 1979, table 332).

†Convictions in Washington, D.C., are approximated by applying crime-type-specific estimates of probability of conviction given arrest to available number of arrests for each crime type in that jurisdiction.

differences both in the magnitude of individual crime rates and in the current use of prison for the target offenses in the different jurisdictions. The simple model of incapacitation in equation (1) is used in Appendix B to illustrate the sensitivity of incapacitation effects to variations in these variables. That analysis indicates that variations in average individual crime rates and in existing sanctioning policies have implications for the size of the collective incapacitation effect in different jurisdictions and for different crime types. Crime reduction from collective incapacitation will be larger and prison population increases smaller where average individual crime rates or the expected prison terms for a crime are already large.

The differences in tables 3 and 4 between Franklin County, Ohio, and Washington, D.C., can be at least partially accounted for by the likely differences in average individual crime rates and in the expected prison term for a crime for the different target crime types considered in those jurisdictions. In table 3, the results for Franklin County are based on the narrower target crime group of violent felonies. While the individual crime rate for the subset of violent felonies is likely to be somewhat lower than for the broader class of index offenses other than larceny used in the Washington, D.C., analysis, the expected prison stay per crime is likely to be much higher for the violent felonies, resulting in the potential for slightly greater crime reduction in Franklin County. In table 4, on the other hand, the target crime group of index offenses other than larceny in Washington, D.C., is narrower than the class of *all* felonies considered for five-year prison terms in Franklin County. This use of a broader target crime group for imprisonment would result in higher increases in prison population in Franklin County if the target crime group of all felonies includes many offenses that rarely go to prison under current policies.

III. Selective Incapacitation

Based on the estimates considered so far, the potential reductions in crime from incapacitation are modest, even with fairly stringent sentencing policies involving mandatory five-year prison terms after conviction. All these estimates refer to the collective incapacitative effect achieved from sentencing policies applied uniformly to all offenders convicted of the target offenses. Marsh and Singer (1972) and Cohen (1978), however, have demonstrated that when offenders vary in their offending rates and high-crime-rate offenders are more likely to be incapacitated, substantially higher incapacitative effects are possible.

The frequent observation that a small number of offenders account for a disproportionately large share of offenses is often cited as evidence of high variability in individual offending rates. These two factors combined have contributed to a growing interest in pursuing policies of selective, or targeted, incapacitation.

To the extent that limited prison resources can be effectively targeted on these high-rate offenders, the potential exists to achieve the same, or improved, rates of crime control (through incapacitation) with reduced numbers in prison. The key to implementing such a selective, or targeted, incapacitation policy rests on our ability to identify these high-rate offenders prospectively, at relatively early stages in their careers.

Several ongoing projects have been examining this possibility since the mid-seventies. Two major efforts, conducted at the Rand Corporation and at Carnegie-Mellon University, are reviewed below. Section III A begins by suggesting that the findings of "disproportionate crime by high-rate offenders" remain hypotheses and that the findings may be at least in part statistical artifacts. A number of ethical and empirical problems associated with predicting high-rate offenders for selective incapacitation strategies are then discussed. Section III concludes by examining the Rand Corporation research. Section IV then discusses the Carnegie-Mellon work.

A. Findings of a Small Number of High-Rate Offenders

Several studies report that a small number of offenders account for a disproportionately large share of the offending found in the full study sample. This result, as summarized in table 5, is found for both adults and juveniles, among arrestees and prison inmates, and for arrests and self-reported crimes.

This disproportionality in observed offending has been taken as evidence of the existence of a small number of high-rate offenders (e.g., Wolfgang 1978; Williams 1980). There is, however, a strong possibility that the disproportionality in observed offending is at least partially a reflection of a simple distributional artifact: any statistical distribution will have a right-hand tail and the individuals found in that tail will of necessity account for a large portion of offending. The question is the extent to which these individuals "in the tail" are characteristically different in their offending behavior from other offenders as opposed to merely manifesting extreme realizations of a common underlying statistical process.

TABLE 5
Summary of Findings on
Small Number of High-Rate Offenders

Study	Sample Characteristics	Measure of Disproportionality	Ratio of Disproportionality
Wolfgang, Figlio, and Sellin (1972)	Any police contacts as juveniles for 1945 Philadelphia birth cohort	18% of delinquents account for: 71% of homicides; 73% of rapes; 70% of robberies; 69% of aggravated assaults; 52% of all arrests	3.94:1 4.06:1 3.89:1 3.83:1 2.89:1
Williams (1979)	Adult arrests brought to Superior Court in Washington, D.C., between January 1, 1971 and August 31, 1975	7% of arrestees with > 4 arrests during 56 month period account for 24% of all arrests in that period	3.43:1
		14% with ≥ 3 arrests account for 36% of all arrests	2.57:1
Peterson and Braiker, with Polich (1980)	Self-reported crimes by adult inmates in California prisons	10% among most criminally active offenders identified by model* accounted for: 46% of auto thefts; 23% of armed robberies; 25% of burglaries; 19% of assaults; 13% of rapes; 4% of homicides	4.60:1 2.30:1 2.50:1 1.90:1 1.30:1 .40:1

* Similar data are not provided for the 10 percent of inmates with the highest self-reported crime rates.

Consider a hypothetical sample of one hundred "identified" offenders (e.g., individuals arrested in a year or inmates in prison), all of whom commit serious crimes (e.g., index offenses) at the same rate of, say, five crimes per year per offender while they are free. In other words, the chance of committing a crime at any time while free is the same for all offenders in the sample. In this example, there are no characteristically different high-rate offenders. Nevertheless, because of the chance process involved in committing crimes, different offenders will commit different numbers of crimes in the same time free with some committing only one crime and others committing many.

The expected distribution of crimes for these one hundred offenders during an observation period of one year free is presented in table 6. Despite the fact that all offenders have the same individual crime rate, under 4 percent of the sample can be expected to appear as high-rate offenders with ten or more crimes in a year. These individuals would account for over 8 percent of the total crimes accumulated by the sample in a year for a disproportionality ratio of 2.24 to 1. If all the offenders in the sample also have the same chance of arrest for each crime, similar disproportionality would be observed among their arrests. In fact, the results in table 6 would apply exactly to arrests observed in a five-year period for offenders who all have the same crime rate of five crimes per year *and* the same one-in-five chance of arrest for each crime.

TABLE 6
Expected Distribution of Crimes in One Year for
One Hundred Offenders Who Have the Same Individual
Crime Rate of Five Crimes per Year Free*

$$P(X = k) = e^{-rt}(rt)^k/k!$$

One-Year Total Crimes per Individual (k)†	Expected Number of Offenders with k Crimes	Total Number of Crimes for Individuals with k Crimes	Percentage of Total Crimes for Offenders with $k +$ Crimes	Percentage of Offenders with $k +$ Crimes
10+	1.94	24.60	4.83	1.94
10	1.81	18.10	**8.39**	**3.75**
9	3.63	32.67	14.80	7.38
8	6.53	52.24	25.06	13.91
7	10.46	73.22	39.44	24.37
6	14.64	87.84	56.69	39.01
5	17.57	87.85	73.95	56.58
4	17.57	70.28	87.75	74.15
3	14.05	42.15	96.03	88.20
2	8.43	16.86	99.34	96.63
1	3.37	3.37	100.00	100.00
Total	100.00	509.18	100.00	100.00

*Expected distribution is estimated from statistical distribution that characterizes a Poisson process. In such a process (1) all offenders are assumed to commit crimes at the same rate, r; (2) this rate is constant over time; and (3) the chance of a crime at any time is independent of whether any previous crimes have already been committed.

†All offenders have at least one crime as the basis for their entering the sample.

The disproportionality ratio varies with the magnitude of the common individual crime rate. Interpolating from the results in table 6, the top 5 percent of offenders are responsible for about 10.6 percent of all crimes for a disproportionality ratio of 2.12. If the common crime rate were higher at ten crimes per year, the top 5 percent of offenders would be responsible for only 7.93 percent of all crimes by the sample and the disproportionality ratio would drop to 1.59. Correspondingly, if the common individual crime rate were lower at 2.5 crimes per year, the top 5 percent of offenders would be responsible for 11.65 percent of crimes and disproportionality ratio of 2.33. Thus, as the crime rate decreases, the extent of disproportionality in a sample of offenders increases.

The empirical findings in table 5 are generally consistent with this expectation. In Wolfgang et al. (1972), for example, as the crime type is focused more narrowly on low-rate offenses like murder and rape, the disproportionality ratio is larger. For more aggregate crime types which are likely to be committed at higher aggregate rates (i.e., the category of "all arrests"), the disproportionality ratio is smaller.[16] Also, the disproportionality ratio is generally higher for arrests (Wolfgang et al. 1972; Williams 1979) which are likely to occur at a lower individual rate per year than are crimes (Peterson and Braiker 1980).

Blumstein and Moitra (1980) extend the same general concept to consider an underlying population of offenders all of whom have the same chance of recidivism. In their model, offenders cannot be distinguished by their prior records; those with three or more arrests are all assumed to have the same chance of recidivating with another arrest. Under that assumption, Blumstein and Moitra use the empirical estimates of recidivism provided for juvenile offenders in Wolfgang et al. (1972) to calculate the expected distribution of arrests for these juvenile offenders. As seen in table 7, the expected distribution fits the observed distribution of arrests in Wolfgang et al. (1972) quite closely and results in the same disproportionality of arrests as observed in the Philadelphia cohort data. This means that the observed disproportionality in arrests

---

[16]The results on self-reported crimes in Peterson and Braiker, with Polich (1980) are not in the form necessary to compare the disproportionality ratios across individual offenses. The 10 percent high-rate offenders are identified by a regression model; the only supporting evidence provided on the accuracy of the model indicates that the model is not very accurate at all in identifying high-rate homicide offenders (Peterson and Braiker, with Polich 1980, p. 187). Also the criterion for the 10 percent most criminally active offenders is an *average* of the respondent's reported crime rates in eleven different offenses, rather than an aggregate rate as used in Wolfgang et al. (1972).

TABLE 7

Distribution of Arrests Observed in Data and
Expected from Model with a Constant Chance of Recidivism
after Third Arrest

Arrests per Individual	Observed Arrest Distribution (Wolfgang et al. 1972)	Expected Arrest Distribution with Constant Chance of Recidivism
0	.65	.65*
1	.16	.16*
2	.065	.065*
3	.034	.032
4	.024	.023
5	.016	.017
6	.010	.012
7	.009	.009
8	.006	.006
9	.004	.004
10	.004	.003

SOURCE.—Blumstein and Moitra (1980, table 1).
*These values are constrained to fit exactly by the parameter values.

found among juveniles in Philadelphia could have been produced by a population of offenders who all have the same chance of recidivism.

Thus, while observed disproportionality like that found in table 5 is no doubt an indicator of some variability in true underlying rates of offending in the offender population, substantial disproportionality can occur when there is *no* variability in offending rates, and any variability that does exist need not be extreme to explain the observed disproportionalities. As illustrated in tables 6 and 7, the same offending rate for all offenders will result in considerable disproportionality in the observed distribution of offenses. The possibility of distributional artifacts of this sort makes identification of high-rate offenders based on retrospective examination of past offending patterns particularly vulnerable to misperception regarding high variability in individual offending. The identified "high-rate" offenders may have the same (or nearly the same) crime rates as other offenders, but because crimes are committed according to a chance process they appear in the right-hand tail of the observed distribution of crimes. In this event, the retrospectively identified high-rate offenders are likely to be indistinguishable from other offenders in their *future* offending behavior and a selective incapacitation policy based on identification of artifactually high-rate offenders will involve an unacceptable level of errors.

B. Predicting High-Rate Offenders

The effectiveness of any selective imprisonment policy depends critically on the ability to identify high-rate persisters prospectively, before they have been arrested sufficiently often that they can be identified retrospectively. Use of these prospective predictions for purposes of differential sentencing introduces a number of difficult ethical and empirical problems.

1. *Ethical Concerns.* Whatever other social purposes—such as crime control—may be served, punishment for past wrongdoings is a fundamental feature of criminal sentences. The ethical considerations derive in large part from the nature and role of sentences as punishments for past criminal behavior. Whether defining the limits on who is liable for sanctioning or by how much, incarceration sanctions are in large part constrained by the nature of the offense being punished.

A selective imprisonment policy introduces the concern that particular individuals would be imprisoned for long terms based on predictions of the crimes they would commit if they were not incapacitated. Such a policy selectively applied would result in the imposition of very different sentences on individuals convicted of the same current offense. Such a selective policy distinguishes between offenders who will go to prison or not and determines differential lengths of terms for those selected for prison; both liability to imprisonment and the amount of imprisonment are determined by predicted offenses.

Some would argue that justice requires that punishment be based on convicted crimes, and that punishment for predicted crimes would be unjust. A potentially more acceptable selective policy might base liability to imprisonment on the past convicted offense and invoke predicted offenses as a basis for determining the amount of imprisonment. It could be argued further, however, that this selective policy would violate the principle that punishment should be commensurate with the seriousness of the current offense (Von Hirsch 1976).

There are contrary considerations that might legitimate differential sentencing for the same convicted offense. Some would argue (Morris 1974) that, for obvious epistemological reasons, there can be no commonly agreed single appropriate sentence for any individual offense. At best we can identify only a range of acceptable penalties for an offense. Within that range, the argument continues, it is permissible and may be desirable to sentence defendants differently for crime control purposes. To the extent that the range of acceptable penalties is constrained by the convicted offense, differential sentences within those bounds would both be just and further crime control objectives.

There are other important ethical problems. The predictor variables used to distinguish high- from low-rate offenders should be statistically valid, reliable predictors of high-rate offending. Some of these variables, however, may be objectionable to many as criteria for sentencing on ethical grounds. Age, race, and sex are variables often found to be associated with offending. There are, however, powerful ethical and political objections to transforming these variables from possible predictors of high-rate offending to explicit criteria for differential sentencing.

Race is universally considered an illegitimate criterion for differential sentencing. From a legal perspective, race is a "suspect classification," and it is widely viewed as an inappropriate criterion on moral grounds.

Age and sex are more ambiguous. These variables can be objected to on grounds akin to those that make race an unacceptable criterion. Age, sex, and race are ascribed characteristics; an individual cannot control them through intent or actions. Used as criteria for sentencing, they can be said to involve punishing the offender for what he is, rather than for what he intentionally did. This contravenes the principle that punishment be based on the blameworthiness of the offender. Various status variables, such as education, income, unemployment, and occupational prestige, might be similarly viewed as ascribed characteristics to the extent that individuals are seen as having limited opportunities to affect their status outcomes.

It can also be argued that many status variables are highly associated with race, and to the extent that race is an illegitimate criterion for sentencing, these status variables would be similarly suspect. The argument is that a sentencing system that is intended to punish minorities more severely ("an extra year for all blacks") would be unacceptable and that a system that is not intended to discriminate, but that is known to punish minorities more severely after controlling for variables like offense type and prior record, would be equally objectionable. Indeed, when various status variables have been explicitly considered as potential criteria for sentencing, as by the Minnesota and Pennsylvania sentencing guideline commissions, the problems associated with these variables have led to their rejection as valid considerations in sentencing decisions.

Arguments can, however, be offered that variables like age and un-employment are legitimate criteria for sentencing. Age has long been the basis of special sentencing provisions for juvenile and youthful offenders. Youthfulness is often regarded as a mitigating factor based on a presumption of diminished culpability for young offenders. Un-employment, as another example, is often regarded as a legitimate sentencing consideration because it is a reliable indicator of greater risk of further crime for offenders placed under supervision in the com-munity. The arguable status of many predictor variables is likely to provoke significant controversy, and represents a potential basis for undermining the legitimacy and feasibility of prediction efforts.

Underlying many of the ethical controversies raised by selective incapacitation policies is a fundamental question about the philosophical premises of punishment. For those who regard retribution, or just deserts, as a *limiting* principle of punishment that establishes a range of just punishments (as sketched above), selective incapacitation poses no inherent ethical problem as long as the selective policy is consistent with the range of acceptable options for the offense.

For those who regard retribution, or just deserts, as a *defining* principle of punishment, selective incapacitation based on predicted crimes is inconsistent with the principle that punishment should be limited by the blameworthiness of the offender. Traditionally, this has been in-terpreted to mean that particular individuals are deserving of punish-ment because of their intentional, overt actions, and not because of any properties or propensities that inhere in the person. To make selective incapacitation consistent with the principle of blameworthiness would require a radical transformation in this fundamental principle through a shift away from actions and to the person as the basis for blame. In particular, if blameworthiness were to rest in the individual—in who or what they are rather than what they do—many of the ethical ar-guments against selective incapacitation would no longer apply. The latter perspective is implicit in the rhetoric of selective incapacitation where the target is variously described as "dangerous offenders," "vi-olent offenders," "career criminals," "habitual offenders," or "high-crime-rate offenders." In each of these instances, the basis for selective in-capacitation is fundamentally an attribute of the *offender* that is pre-sumed to reflect a disposition or propensity toward a certain kind of behavior.

In large measure, whether any individual approves or disapproves of selective incapacitation policies rests on which of these conflicting principles he or she accepts. The key point here is not to take a position in these debates, but to acknowledge that there is substantial controversy about the appropriateness of selective incapacitation crime control strategies.

2. *Empirical Problems in Prediction.* There are also important underlying empirical problems in using predictions in sentencing. These problems, which relate primarily to the limited accuracy of predictions, must be resolved before any such instruments can be used.

Until very recently, prediction research has been largely limited to attempts to predict future violence, especially among released mental patients. The various efforts at predicting future crimes have not been very successful. (Many of these prediction efforts are reviewed in Von Hirsch [1974], Greenberg [1975], and Monahan [1976, 1978, 1981].) These predictions involve two different types of errors: (1) incorrectly identifying individuals as violent recidivists (false positives), and (2) failing to identify recidivists (false negatives). Monahan (1981, p. 79) reports false-positive rates in which 60 percent or more of the individuals predicted to be violent in the future were *not* observed to be violent during follow-up periods in several studies involving clinical predictions of violent behavior. Various statistically based prediction devices intended to assess the risk of recidivism for use in parole-release decisions also report 50–60 percent favorable (i.e., false-positive) outcomes (typically measured by no new arrests, parole violations, or revocations during the follow-up period) in their predicted worst risk groups.[17] Other statistical efforts to identify the worst recidivists among arrestees have comparably high false-positive rates. In Williams (1979), for example, a model to predict the worst recidivist third of the sample correctly identified two-thirds of the actual worst 10 percent and 58 percent of the actual worst 25 percent. The predicted worst recidivist third, however, included 56 percent false positives who were *not* among the actual worst 25 percent and 79 percent false positives who were *not*

[17]In a 1976 validation of the Federal Parole Commission's Salient Factor Score, only 44 percent of the poor risks (20.3 percent of the sample) were rearrested or had a parole violation warrant issued in a one-year follow-up after release on parole (Hoffman and Beck 1980). Monahan (1981, p. 103) reports that a similar risk-assessment device developed by the Michigan Department of Corrections found only a 40 percent recidivism rate (i.e., arrest for a new violent crime while on parole) in their "very high risk" group (4.7 percent of the sample). Gottfredson, Mitchell-Herzfeld, and Flanagan (1982) report only a 49.6 percent readmission rate to state correctional institutions in a five-year follow-up for the "high-risk" group, 16.3 percent of their sample of 1972 releases from correctional institutions in a Northeastern state.

among the actual worst 10 percent (derived from Williams [1979], p. 27).

Such high false-positive rates are characteristic of attempts to predict relatively rare events. In the studies examined here, the recidivism variables being predicted were relatively rare; they occurred in from 10 to 35 percent of each sample. If a small number of offenders does account for a large portion of offending (see table 5), these high-rate offenders are likely to be comparably rare in offending samples, and thus difficult to identify without also incorrectly "identifying" many who are not high-rate offenders.

The degree to which a democratic society is willing to tolerate very high false-positive rates may depend on the consequences that result from these predictions (Monahan 1981). High rates of false positives in predicting high-rate offenders are particularly troubling when there are large differences in the consequences that result from this prediction. This would occur, for example, if predicted high-rate offenders received long prison terms while predicted low-rate offenders received probation or only very short prison or jail terms. The problem would be exacerbated even further if the resulting prison terms for predicted high-rate offenders were excessive in relation to the acceptable range of sentences for the convicted offense.[18] To the extent that an imprisonment policy attempts to maximize crime control benefits by selectively incarcerating some offenders for long terms, it is likely to involve sharp differences in sentence outcomes between the predicted high-rate offenders and other offenders. Such a policy would be difficult to justify without considerable improvements over the levels of predictive accuracy that have characterized past research.

Some argue that to demand such a high standard for accuracy in predictions is excessive (Greenwood, with Abrahamse 1982; Moore et al. 1982). In fact, that criminal justice system already makes extensive use of predictions in virtually all aspects of decision making from bail release to release on parole. These predictions about the likely future behavior of the offender, however, are often informally applied and based on subjective judgments by the decision maker. In this context, the test of acceptability for explicit, statistical predictions should be

---

[18]Similar problems would accompany excessively lenient sentences for false negatives (i.e., those incorrectly predicted to be low-rate offenders). This downside problem, however, is likely to be far less frequent because of the wide range of offenses for which probation terms are viewed as acceptable sentence outcomes.

whether they perform more accurately than current practices within the criminal justice system.

This is a fair point. For purposes of evaluating selective incapacitation policies, however, use of a standard that is based on current practices would require empirical estimates of the accuracy of current imprisonment practices in distinguishing between high- and low-rate offenders. Such estimates are generally not available. One indicator of the relative accuracy of subjective predictions is the accuracy of various clinical predictions about future violence. As indicated by the false-positive rates reported above, available statistical predictions have not been found to do markedly better than subjective predictions. This suggests no relative advantage over current practices for the evaluated efforts at statistical prediction.

3. *The Rand Corporation Research.*   Recent research at the Rand Corporation (Greenwood, with Abrahamse 1982) has renewed interest in predicting high-rate offenders as a basis for a selective incapacitation policy. The research is based on a survey of a sample of 2,190 inmates in prisons and jails in three states: California, Michigan, and Texas. In addition to self-reports of crimes committed while free, the survey also elicited self-reported information on prior arrests, convictions, and incarcerations as well as previous offending as a juvenile and various indicators of prior social adjustment (e.g., employment and drug use). For purposes of assuring the accuracy of the self-reports, the surveys were not anonymous and official criminal records were coded for prison inmates. Also, redundant questions were asked throughout the survey, and the survey was repeated one week later for 250 respondents. Analysis of detected response errors indicated that these errors were not systematically related to various attributes of the respondents, including age, race, main convicted offense on the current sentence, and self-reported crime rates.

The analysis of selective incapacitation focused on the inmates currently convicted for robbery or burglary. Based on their self-reported armed robberies and burglaries during the time they were free in the two years preceding the current incarceration, the inmates were divided into low-, medium-, and high-rate offenders for robbery and burglary.[19] Using one variable at a time, a variety of other characteristics were

[19]Low-rate offenders had individual crime rates "below the median for their offense type and state"; the individual crime rates of high-rate offenders were "above the 75th percentile for their offense type and state"; medium-rate offenders fell between these two (Greenwood, with Abrahamse 1982, p. 49).

then examined for their association with individual crime rates. Based on the strength of their relationships with individual crime rates and their appropriateness in sentencing, seven variables were selected to form a simple additive scale for characterizing offenders (see table 8).

The score on this scale was used to repartition inmates into low-, medium-, and high-rate offenders. The mean and median crime rates (crimes per offender per year free) for these scale-identified groups were then calculated from the self-reported crime rates of group members. As indicated in table 9, the mean crime rate varies sharply for the different scale groups identified for robbery and burglary; the mean for predicted high-rate offenders is twelve to fifteen times that found for predicted low-rate offenders.

The basic model of incapacitation in equation (1) was used to assess the potential effects of alternative selective incapacitation policies applied to California inmates. The effects of alternative strategies on adult crimes and on the size of the incarcerated population (prison and jail) for robbery and burglary were measured in relation to the levels of these variables found under current sentencing practices. The analysis used the mean crime rates (r) from table 9 combined with estimates of the size of the adult offender population (N) and of sentencing practices (qJS) in equations (B2) and (B3) (App. B) to estimate the number of

TABLE 8

Variables Used in Scale to Distinguish Inmates
by Individual Crime Rates

Variable*	Source
1. Prior conviction for same charge	Official criminal record (prison inmates only)
2. Incarcerated more than 50 percent of preceding two years	Self-Report
3. Convicted before age sixteen	Self-Report
4. Served time in state juvenile facility	Self-Report
5. Drug use in preceding two years	Self-Report
6. Drug use as a juvenile	Self-Report
7. Employed less than 50 percent of preceding two years	Self-Report

SOURCE.—Greenwood, with Abrahamse (1982, p. 50)

*All variables are scored as one or zero depending on the presence or absence of the attribute.

TABLE 9
Mean Individual Crime Rates
from Self-reported Crimes for Groups Identified by Scale

Convicted Offense	Scale Predicted Crime Rate for Convicted Offense		
	Low	Medium	High
Robbery	2.0	10.1	30.8
Burglary	12.6	87.6	156.3

Note.—Rate = mean offenses per offender per year free.

Values reported here are truncated means. All individuals reporting individual crime rates above the ninetieth percentile for an offense were assigned the ninetieth percentile rate. This was intended to reduce the extreme sensitivity of the mean to very large self-reported crime rates (Greenwood, with Abrahamse 1982, pp. 55–58).

crimes and the size of the incarcerated population in each offender group. The results were summed over low-, medium-, and high-rate offenders to yield total adult crimes and total incarcerated population for robbery and for burglary under various sentencing strategies. The results for an alternative strategy were then compared with the results from current sentencing practices.

The analysis assumes that the mean crime rates found in a sample of incoming prisoners apply to all offenders and that the chance of arrest and conviction for a crime (q) and the chance of being incarcerated after conviction (J) are the same for all three offender groups. These three variables (r, q, and J) are all assumed to remain the same under alternative selective incapacitation strategies. Only the distribution of inmates between jail and prison and the length of prison terms are varied in the alternatives. In the most selective policy considered, all incarcerated low- and medium-rate offenders are sent to jail for the current average jail term and all incarcerated high-rate offenders are sent to prison for increasingly longer terms.

Based on the analysis of expected crimes and expected incarcerated populations, it is reported that this highly selective policy of imposing long prison terms on predicted high-rate offenders and current average jail terms on all other incarcerated offenders could reduce armed robberies by adults by 20 percent without any increase in the incarcerated population for armed robbery. Smaller increases in the length of prison terms under this highly selective policy may result in smaller reductions in robberies, while also reducing the incarcerated population for robbery. This occurs because reductions in the numbers of low- and medium-rate offenders who are incarcerated are not offset by corresponding increases in incarcerated high-rate offenders. Using a less selective policy of leaving the incarceration sentences for low- and medium-rate offenders unchanged but increasing the length of prison terms for high-rate offenders, it is reported possible to reduce armed robberies by 20 percent with only a 10 percent increase in incarceration for robbery (Greenwood, with Abrahamse 1982, p. 79).

These results on selective incapacitation have received considerable attention in the media (Anderson 1982; "Cutting Crimes Tied to Jailing of Busiest Criminals" 1982; Lewin 1982; "Lock Them Up" 1982). They are attractive both because of the apparent simplicity and potentially easy application of the prediction scale and because they seem to offer ready solutions to crime control and prison overcrowding. There is no question that the results will be provocative to legislators and other policymakers. Because of this potential for widespread use—and the associated danger of misuse—considerably more caution and critical attention to the strength of the results are needed.

While this research has advanced efforts to evaluate the feasibility of selective incapacitation crime control strategies, it is subject to a number of important shortcomings that limit its usefulness as the basis for current sentencing policies. Particularly, there are a number of important validation problems that must be addressed. First, the analysis is entirely retrospective, relating past attributes of the offenders to their past offending. There is no basis for judging the potential utility of the scale in prospectively identifying high-rate offenders.

The success of the scale as a prospective prediction tool depends on the extent to which offenders observed to have high rates of offending in the past will continue as high-rate offenders into the future. Such prospective accuracy of predictions is, of course, crucial to the effectiveness of selective imprisonment policies that are based on those predictions. In part, prospective accuracy will be influenced by the degree to which observed high-rate offenders in the past are indeed offenders with stable underlying high rates of offending as opposed to extreme realizations of the same offending rates (see Sec. III *A* above). Even if the prediction instrument can successfully distinguish truly high-rate offenders retrospectively, the prospective accuracy of the instrument requires that the past behavior continue for some time into the future. Prospective accuracy becomes particularly important when the selective policy involves long prison terms. While retrospectively estimated crime rates may be reasonably accurate for short-term prospective predictions, they are likely to be increasingly in error when predicting crime rates to continue prospectively for longer terms.

Second, the scale lacks internal validation. Typically, when only a single sample is available for analysis, internal validation is achieved with a split-sample design in which part of the sample is used for constructing the prediction scale and the remainder of the sample is used to validate that scale. Such a design was not feasible within individual samples because of the limited number of inmates who qualified as convicted robbers or burglars in each state sample. Robbers numbered 178, 150, and 117 in California, Michigan, and Texas, respectively; there were 160, 124, and 203 burglars, respectively. If, as appears to have happened, the separate samples were aggregated across states and robbers and burglars were combined to develop a single scale for use in all these settings, the 781 individuals without missing data could have reasonably been split to form a construction and validation sample. Without some such internal validation, the scale will overfit the data used in construction, and its predictive accuracy on a split sample (with identical population characteristics), if one were available, would decline by some amount.

Third, there is no external validation of the scale. When considering external validation, it is important to distinguish two different components of selective incapacitation strategies, decisions whether to incarcerate and decisions on the lengths of terms for those incarcerated. As currently formulated in Greenwood (1982), both the prediction scale and the selective incapacitation strategies considered focus narrowly on inmates; the decision whether to incarcerate or not is left unchanged. Without external validation on other independently drawn inmate samples, there is cause for concern that the predictive accuracy of the scale may be peculiar to the construction samples. Large declines in that accuracy in other samples would seriously limit application of the scale elsewhere.

There is also the risk that the scale may be inappropriately used as the basis for the full sentencing decision, including the decision to incarcerate. Using the scale in this way would require external validation of the scale with respect to *non-inmate* samples of convicted robbers or burglars. The scale may be very useful among inmates who already represent a highly selected sample of offenders, but may be of more limited value when applied to convicted offenders more generally. In particular, because of the narrowness of the construction sample, it may be that there are other offenders who are convicted and who have the same predictor attributes as found among high-rate offenders in prison, but who are *not* high-rate offenders. Or it may be that the high-rate offenders among the non-inmate population display very different attributes from those offenders who do end up in prison. Before applying the scale at sentencing, its usefulness and validity in distinguishing among convicted offenders must be established.

The absence of any internal or external validation highlights the problem of shrinkage for the present prediction model. No matter how well a prediction device performs on the construction sample, there will be some shrinkage in predictive accuracy when that scale is applied to new independent samples. The greater the differences between the construction and validation samples, the greater the shrinkage. Shrinkage is thus likely to be especially severe in going from inmates to a sample composed of convicted offenders.

A fourth problem with the current scale is its heavy reliance on self-reported items as independent scale variables (see table 8). Variables relating to past incarceration experiences, drug-use, employment, and age at first conviction are all based on self-reports by inmates; the only scale variable reflecting official record information is past convictions for the same charge. The self-reported items are vulnerable to exclusion on legal grounds if the scale were used for sentencing decisions. A companion report analyzing the same data (Chaiken and Chaiken 1982) concludes that the predictive quality of any scale applied to these data deteriorates if it is limited to officially recorded legal variables such as convictions and arrests. Among inmates currently convicted of robbery, for example, official record items alone explain one-third less of the variance in individual robbery crime rates. Obviously, if such a scale were to be implemented as a basis for sentencing, one could not rely on access to reliable data on many of the variables, especially if they depend on reporting by the offender.

Past convictions for the same charge is the only variable in the scale that is based on official records, and even that variable is problematic. Official records were available only for prison inmates; all jail inmates were simply assigned a value of zero for the prior convictions variable. To the extent that some jail inmates do have prior convictions for the same charge, prior convictions as measured would be less an indicator of prior convictions and more a proxy measure distinguishing between jail and prison inmates in the sample. Use of the current jail or prison outcome in predicting high-rate offenders reflects the accuracy of current sentencing decisions in choosing between jail and prison for high-

and low-rate offenders. In effect, the outcome of current subjective sentencing decisions is being used to distinguish high- and low-rate offenders. When using a prediction scale that is intended to inform sentencing decisions, we would not have access to the sentence outcome to enter it into the prediction.

Another fundamental problem relates to the degree of predictive accuracy of the scale, even in the construction sample. The mean and median crime rates do differ sharply for the predicted offender groups (see table 9). There are, nonetheless, serious problems in the accuracy of scale predictions for individuals. Two different aspects of accuracy are important:

1. predictive accuracy: the degree to which the predictive offending rates are correct (based on self-reported crime rates); and

2. identification accuracy: the degree to which actual offending rates (based on self-reported crime rates) are correctly identified.

The data on predicted versus actual crime rates provided in Greenwood, with Abrahamse (1982, table 4.5) were used to calculate the accuracy of the scale's predictions (table 10) and its ability to identify high- and low-rate offenders correctly (table 11). Only the accuracy rate among predicted low-rate offenders is reasonably high, with 76 percent correct predictions among predicted low-rate offenders (table 10). The scale does not perform nearly as well in correctly identifying self-reported low-rate offenders; only 41 percent of self-reported low-rate offenders are correctly predicted to be low-rate offenders (table 11).

The scale's performance is more uniformly poor for high-rate offenders. Among those predicted to be high-rate offenders, only 45

TABLE 10
Predictive Accuracy of the Greenwood Scale

Scale Score	Predicted Offense Rate (%)	Self-reported Offense Rate (%)			Distribution of Offenders across Predicted Offense Rate	
		Low	Medium	High	Total N	Percentage of Total
0–1	Low (100)	**76**	16	8	209	27
2–3	Medium (100)	52	**27**	22	336	43
≥4	High (100)	25	30	**45**	236	30

Note.—Percentage correct among predictions shown in bold type.

TABLE 11

Accuracy of Identification by the Greenwood Scale:
Percentage Correct among Self-reported Offense Rates

Self-reported Offense Rate	Predicted Offense Rate (%)			Distribution of Offenders across Actual Offense Rate	
	Low (0–1)	Medium (2–3)	High (≥4)	Total N	Percentage of Total
Low	**41**	44	15	390	50
Medium	17	**46**	37	196	26
High	9	37	**54**	195	24

NOTE.—The percentage of correctly identified offenders is shown in bold type.

TABLE 12

Distribution of Offenders by Predicted and Actual
Offense Categories (%)

Predicted Offense Rate	Self-reported Offense Rate			Total
	Low	Medium	High	
Low	20	5	2	27
Medium	22	12	9	43
High	8	9	13	30
Total	50	26	24	100

percent actually were high-rate offenders. This involves a false-positive rate of 55 percent. For purposes of selective incapacitation, where predicted high-rate offenders will be subject to longer prison terms than all other offenders, much better discrimination of the high-rate offenders would seem to be required.

Table 12 provides an overall picture of the predictive accuracy of the scale. A total of 45 percent of the respondent inmates (the sum of the diagonal entries) were correctly labeled by the scale. Among the errors, 8 percent of all respondents were predicted to be high-rate offenders when they were actually low-rate offenders (false-positives), while 2 percent were predicted to be low-rate offenders when they were actually high-rate offenders (false-negatives). To assess the comparative accuracy of the scale over current sentencing decisions, Greenwood categorized offenders as low-, medium-, or high-rate offenders based on their sentence lengths. The accuracy of sentence lengths in distinguishing individual crime rates was then determined by comparing these predictions with the self-reported crime rates. Table 13 compares the predictive accuracy of current sentences (as implied by sentence lengths) with the Greenwood scale. The seven-point scale does only marginally better overall and results in slightly more false-positives than existing subjective judgments in distinguishing offenders by their crime commission rates.[20]

On the general question of scale validation, it is important to distinguish between the success of a scale in producing differential crime control effects, and its success in identifying individual high-rate offenders. From the perspective of impact analyses, the scale may be

TABLE 13

Relative Predictive Accuracy of the Greenwood Scale:
Comparison with Current Sentence Lengths

Accuracy in Distinguishing Offenders by Crime Rates	Greenwood's Seven-Factor Scale	Current Sentence Lengths
Predicted correctly (%)	45	42
Predicted to be high rate, actually low rate (False-positives) (%)	8	7
Predicted to be low rate, actually high rate (False-negatives) (%)	2	5

[20]The predictive accuracy of the scale reported in tables 12 and 13 differs from the numbers reported in Greenwood, with Abrahamse (1982, table 4.8). The numbers reported here are based on analysis of the entries in Greenwood's table 4.5. The differences between the two tables result from a change in the criteria used to partition self-reported crime rates into low-, medium-, and high-rate offenders. The break points between categories changed as in the table below.

Self-reported Offense Rate	Percentiles	
	Table 4.5	Table 4.8
Low	Lower fiftieth	Lower thirtieth
Medium	Fiftieth to seventy-fifth	Thirtieth to seventy-second
High	Upper twenty-fifth	Upper twenty-eighth

Table 4.5 uses the original criteria as reported in Greenwood, with Abrahamse (1982, p. 49). Without offering any reasons, the high- and esp. the medium-rate categories have been expanded in table 4.8. The greater scale accuracy reported in table 4.8 results primarily from redefining many originally low-rate offenders as medium-rate offenders and some originally medium-rate offenders as high-rate offenders.

quite useful in making aggregate-level distinctions among groups of offenders with different *average* crime rates, as was evident in table 9. Considerations of justice, equity, and due process, however, seem to require that if it is to be the basis for differential sentencing of individuals, the scale must be a reasonably accurate predictor for *individuals*. The present scale is inadequate on the level of individual predictions.

Aside from the questions surrounding the predictive validity of the Greenwood scale, there are also problems with the estimates of the potential incapacitative effects under alternative strategies. These estimates rest on the model of incapacitation developed in equations (1), (B2), and (B3), combined with estimates of average individual crime rates (r), the size of the offender population (N), and the sanction levels (qJS). Using the reported values of all the variables and the description of the alternative sentencing policies (Greenwood, with Abrahamse 1982, table 5.1, p. 49), I have been unable to replicate the results on incapacitation effects reported in Greenwood, with Abrahamse (1982, fig. 5.1, p. 79). The differences between the original results and the replication for the most highly selective policy (policy 6) are presented in figure 2. The required incarcerated population in the replication (the dashed line in fig. 2) is always smaller than the original Greenwood results.

One factor contributing to this poor match is a serious error in the size of the low-rate offender population reported in Greenwood, with Abrahamse (1982, table 5.1, app.). The proportion of offenders who are incarcerated at any time is given by I in equation (1), and the size of the incarcerated population (R) is just $R = I \cdot N$, where N is the total offender population. With estimates of R and I for each offender category, the total number of offenders (N) in a category can be estimated. Greenwood's estimates of R and I for each offender group are given in table 14 along with the associated size of the offender population. The correct estimate for the number of low-rate offenders is 49,714; the number reported in Greenwood is 20,471. Using the corrected size estimate results in a much closer match to the original Greenwood results (the dotted line in fig. 2).

The Greenwood analysis reports the potential for achieving reasonable levels of crime reduction without any increases in the incarcerated population, through use of selective policies that increase prison use for high-rate offenders and lengthen their prison terms. Selective policies like this take advantage of the differences in individual crime rates to achieve greater crime reduction for high-rate offenders. The potential

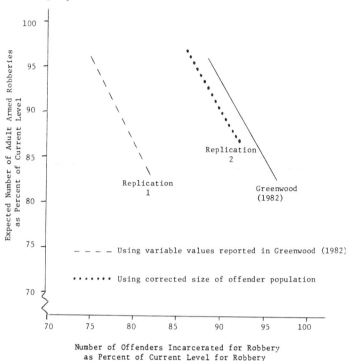

Fig. 2. Attempt to replicate estimates of incapacitative effects for highly selective policy (all incarcerated low- and medium-rate offenders to jail for average term and all incarcerated high-rate offenders to prison for increasing terms).

for larger incapacitative effects when crime rates vary in the population of offenders was originally demonstrated in Marsh and Singer (1972) using hypothetical data. The Greenwood results augment this earlier analysis with empirical estimates of individual crime rates and of existing sentencing practices.

While empirically based, the estimates are only preliminary and there is room for some variation in the magnitudes of the input variables. Given the tentative nature of many of the basic variable values, it is important to explore the sensitivity of the results to use of different variable values. In particular, we would want to know whether the potential incapacitative effects are relatively insensitive to the input variables, or whether they depend critically on the particular values used for these variables. No such sensitivity analyses are reported in Greenwood.

Three assumptions in the model particularly merit consideration. First, it is assumed that the chance of arrest and conviction for a crime

TABLE 14
Estimating the Size of the Offender Population in
Each Offender Category in California

Offender Category	Proportion of Population Incarcerated (I)	Size of Incarcerated Population (R)	Size of Total Offender Population ($N = R/I$)
Robbery:			
Low rate	.07	3,480	49,714*
Medium rate	.37	4,401	11,895
High rate	.67	6,049	9,028
Burglary:			
Low rate	.18	4,159	23,106
Medium rate	.56	6,812	12,164
High rate	.77	3,540	4,597

* The number of low-rate robbers is incorrectly reported to be 20,471 in Greenwood, with Abrahamse (1982).

(q) and the chance of being incarcerated after conviction (J) are the same for low-, medium-, and high-rate offenders. This assumption is made largely because data limitations do not permit distinguishing these variables by offender group. While there is as yet no empirical basis for assessing the assumption of a homogeneous chance of arrest and conviction for a crime, the survey data for California inmates provide evidence that casts doubt on the assumed same chance of incarceration after conviction for different offender groups.

The chance of prison, given that an individual is incarcerated, is found to vary substantially with the predicted crime rate. Among the sample inmates convicted of robbery, for example, the chance of prison terms (as opposed to jail) was 40.9 percent, 74.8 percent, and 82.1 percent, for low-, medium-, and high-rate offenders, respectively (Greenwood 1982, table B.5). A similar pattern was observed for sample inmates convicted for burglary. This suggests that judges in California are more likely to send predicted high-rate offenders to prison, rather than jail, than low-rate offenders. The same selectivity by offense rate is likely to be found in the decision to incarcerate or not, thus violating the assumption that all offender groups have the same chance of incarceration after conviction.

As it turns out, the incarceration rates observed in California are very high, $J = .86$ for robbery convictions and .72 for burglary convictions. At these high aggregate rates for all offenders, there is little room to vary the incarceration rates for different offender groups while still maintaining the overall aggregate rate. The same argument applies to the assumed homogeneous chance of arrest and conviction for different offender groups. The aggregate rate is very low at $q = .03$ for both robbery and burglary. At this low aggregate rate there is once again little room for variation in different offender groups. The estimated incapacitative effects are thus not likely to be vulnerable to violations of the assumption of homogeneous q and J.

The second assumption of concern applies the mean crime rates in a sample of incoming prisoners to all offenders. As argued in Peterson and Braiker, with Polich (1980), and Chaiken (1980), offenders who are incarcerated are likely to be more serious offenders with higher crime rates than the general offending population. The incapacitative effect varies with the magnitude of the mean individual crime rate; the lower the crime rate, the lower the crime reduction achieved through incapacitation and the greater the size of the prison population (see Sec. IIE above). Similarly, use of lower mean individual crime rates would reduce the relative advantage over current sentencing practices found for selective incapacitation policies in Greenwood.

Figure 3 illustrates the effect on the Greenwood results of reducing the mean individual crime rate in each offender group by 25 percent. (These alternative values are presumably within the range of normal variation in the estimates of mean individual crime rates given the sensitivity of the mean to extreme outliers.) At these lower crime rates, the highly selective policy achieves slightly greater reductions in crime, but lower reductions in the incarcerated population. Estimates of incapacitative effects on the order of magnitude of 8 percent reductions in crime and 11 percent reductions in the incarcerated population are sensitive to the shifts of about three percentage points observed in figure 3.

The last assumption involves the distribution of inmates over the different offender groups. This is the most fundamental assumption in Greenwood's analysis; it is used to estimate the chance of prison for those incarcerated in each group and the size of the total offender population in each group. Figure 4 illustrates the sensitivity of the results to a minor shift in this distribution that increases the proportion of high-rate offenders among inmates from 45 to 50 percent. There is little effect on the reduction in crime, but once again the reduction in the incarcerated population shifts about three percentage points.

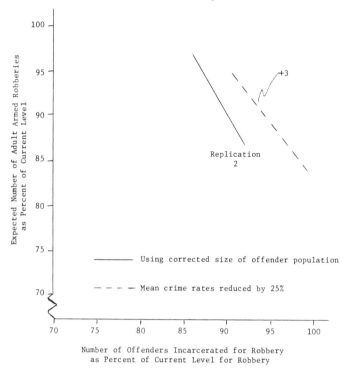

Fig. 3. Sensitivity of estimates of incapacitative effects for highly selective policy to variations in average crime rates (policy: all incarcerated low- and medium-rate offenders to jail for average terms and all incarcerated high-rate offenders to prison for terms of increasing lengths).

The analyses in figures 3 and 4 indicate that the results are somewhat sensitive to the values used for individual crime rates and to the distribution of inmates across different offender groups. The general conclusion, that it is possible to reduce crime while also reducing the incarcerated population through selective policies, is unaffected. However, the magnitudes of those effects, and thus their attractiveness for implementation, are affected.

Greenwood's results are an important illustration of the potential of selective incapacitation policies. Given the crucial issues of low predictive accuracy and the tentativeness of the estimated impacts, however, they do not yet provide a basis for implementing selective incapacitation policies. The problems found in the Rand research on selective incapacitation suggest that the results of that research must be approached cautiously and that alternative strategies for achieving increased incapacitation be considered.

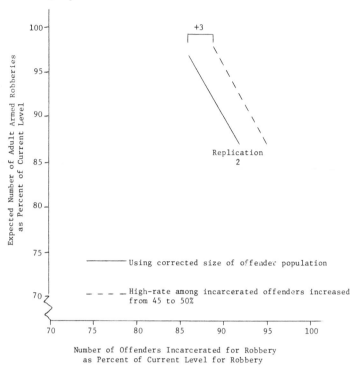

Fɪɢ. 4. Sensitivity of estimates of incapacitative effects for highly selective policy (see figs. 2, 3) to variations in distribution of offenders among crime-rate categories.

IV. An Alternative Strategy

Section III highlighted the difficult ethical and empirical problems involved in identifying high-rate offenders prospectively. In Section II, I suggested likely limits on the crime-reduction benefits to be derived from any incapacitation policies, selective or otherwise. This section explores the feasibility of an alternative approach to incapacitation, designed to avoid many of the ethical and empirical problems that characterize past research efforts.

The approach relies on empirical estimates of various aspects of criminal careers (e.g., individual arrest rates and crime rates and the length of criminal careers) derived directly from officially recorded arrest histories and variations in these careers associated with the type of crime of the current charge and with prior criminal record. To the extent that variations in the career patterns are observed, the convicted offense and prior record can then be used as bases for identifying classes of offenders who can be expected as a group to commit offenses at high rates and to have long careers. These differential offending patterns can then be exploited to develop sentencing policies that achieve differential incapacitation effects.

The incapacitation policy will target on increasing incarceration for selected offenses. When selecting sentences, the policy will rely exclusively on the type of crime charged and prior criminal record of the offender. This avoids reliance on potentially objectionable predictor variables like the personal attributes of the offender. Sentences that are commensurate with the seriousness of the offense will be applied uniformly to all offenders convicted of the same charge who have the same prior criminal record. Such sentences will meet the objections that sentences should be just and equitable.

The feasibility of the policy as a means of achieving increased crime reduction through incapacitation rests on finding target offenses that are both viewed as serious enough to deserve increased incarceration and characterized by active offenders who on the average have high crime rates and long careers. For each individual offender, the fundamental concern in sentencing is the punishment deserved for the crime and not whether more or less crime reduction is achieved by incarcerating that particular individual; so false-positives in predicting individual high-rate offenders are not an issue. There is in the aggregate, however, the potential for more or less crime reduction through incapacitation associated with the general policy for that offense. To the extent that appropriate target offenses can be found, the policy considered here has the potential to accommodate desert, or retributive, concerns with utilitarian crime control achieved through incapacitation.

A. Empirical Bases for Using Criminal Career Patterns to Differentiate Offenders

Statistical evidence is beginning to accumulate that characterizes the criminal careers of large numbers of adult offenders. In particular, estimates are now becoming available for the intensity of criminal activity by active offenders (reflected in individual arrest rates and crime rates) and for the duration or length of criminal careers. In addition to aggregate averages, the estimates of criminal career activity have been disaggregated to explore variations in offending with variables like age, prior criminal record, crime type, and time period (reflecting history or cohort differences).[21] From this research, new insights into the similarities and differences in criminal careers are emerging.

Blumstein and Cohen (1979, 1982) have analyzed the arrest histories of adults arrested in Washington, D.C., and in the state of Michigan to estimate individual arrest rates while free. Based on the attributes of the offender, separate arrest rates were estimated by cohort, offense specialties, and race of the offender and by the offender's age and number of prior arrests at the start of each year in the arrest history. This produced a multidimensional array of offense-specific mean arrest rates. The patterns of variations in arrest rates associated with crime type, cohort, age, race, and prior record were then examined using standard multivariate statistical techniques. The results indicate some strong similarities in individual arrest rates across age and race.

If the chance of arrest for a crime does not vary systematically by age or race, the stability found for arrest rates should also apply to individual crime rates. There is little direct empirical evidence on the variation in arrest risk for different demographic groups. However, some indirect evidence for the assumption that they are independent is available in results reported by Hindelang (Hindelang 1978, 1980, 1981; Hindelang, Hirschi, and Weis 1979). Hindelang finds close consistency between the attributes of *arrestees*—particularly their age, race and sex—as reported in the FBI's annual *Uniform Crime Reports* and the attributes of *offenders* as described by victims in the national victimization surveys. This consistency suggests that the chance of arrest for a crime is largely independent of these demographic attributes of offenders.

Further support for the stability of individual crime rates over age is found in the self-reported crime rates derived from the survey of California prison inmates. After controlling for individual offenses, Peterson and Braiker, with Polich (1980, p. 54) found that older offenders who were active in an offense reported committing that offense at the same rate as younger offenders. When different offenses were

[21]Age effects reflect changes in offending that occur during the career of an individual. These changes might be associated with maturation and declines in physical stamina as the offender ages. They would affect all offenders similarly regardless of when they were active. The time period effect reflects differences in criminality over time that are independent of age. These effects might arise from historical factors that affect all offenders similarly regardless of their ages. Or there might be cohort effects where different cohorts of offenders (i.e., groups of offenders who begin their criminal careers at the same time) have characteristically different offending rates. Such a cohort effect might reflect, e.g., the effects of being socialized at different times.

aggregated, however, the *total* crime rate for individuals decreased with age. This decrease with age in the total rate is associated with a decline in the number of different offenses that are committed by older offenders (see table 15).

The racial similarities in individual crime rates are illustrated in table 16. With the notable exceptions of robbery and larceny, individual crime rates for black and white offenders in their twenties who were active in the Detroit SMSA between 1967 and 1973 are strikingly similar. The racial differences for robbery and larceny are also evident in the rates for all index offenses together, where the mean individual crime rate for blacks is 33 percent higher than for whites. Excluding larceny, however, index rates for black and white offenders in Detroit are much closer, at about eight offenses per offender per year free. Furthermore, even when they exist, the racial differences in the individual crime rates of active offenders are much smaller than those observed in aggregate arrest statistics. In table 17, for example, the aggregate index arrest rates for nonwhite males in their early twenties

TABLE 15
Variations in Offending by Age from
Self-reported Crimes

Age*	Intensity Scale Score†	Total Offense Score‡	Number of Active Crime Types‖
Under 21	1.44	.64	4.61
21–25	1.42	.57	4.09
26–30	1.44	.49	3.29
Over 30	1.33	.35	2.70

SOURCE.—Peterson and Braiker, with Polich (1980, tables 27–29).

*Age at the midpoint of the three-year observation window prior to the present incarceration.

†Each offense respondent reported committing was assigned a score indicating whether respondent's crime rate in that offense was below the median (score = 1) or above the median (score = 2). Scores were then averaged over total number of offenses respondent was active in to yield "intensity scale score."

‡Each of eleven offenses studied was assigned a score reflecting respondent's level of activity in that offense. If the respondent reported that he never committed the offense, he was assigned a score of 0 for that offense. Respondents committing the offense at a rate below median were assigned a score of 1 for that offense; if their rate was above median, they were assigned a score of 2. Offense scores were then averaged over the eleven offenses in the study.

‖This is mean number of separate offenses respondent reported committing out of eleven different offenses studied.

60   Jacqueline Cohen

TABLE 16
Racial Differences in Free Crime Rates of Individuals Active in an Offense (Number of Crimes per Year Free per Active Offender)

Offense	Detroit SMSA* Whites	Blacks	Ratio of Blacks to Whites	Washington, D.C.†
Robbery	3.07	5.33	**1.74**	3.41
Aggravated assault	2.92	2.84	.97	1.72
Burglary	4.76	5.68	1.19	5.73
Larceny	4.47	9.50	**2.13**	10.88
Auto theft	8.93	10.27	1.15	2.98
Weapons	4.24	3.77	.89	4.02
Drugs	4.60	3.52	.77	8.00
Others	13.50	10.64	.79	10.42
"Index" total (without murder and rape)‡	10.46	13.91	**1.33**	12.51
"Index" total without larceny‡	7.99	8.60	1.08	6.58

NOTE.—The percentage of correctly identified offenders is shown in bold type.
*Blumstein and Cohen (1982).
†Blumstein and Cohen (1979).
‡Reported rates are averages for index offenses found for eight different "offender types." Criterion for "offender type" is having an arrest for offense of interest (e.g., "robbers" have at least one robbery arrest as adults). The eight individual crime types in the table identify eight different "offender types" averaged.

TABLE 17
Average Annual Index Arrests per 1,000 Population per Demographic Group in Pittsburgh between 1967 and 1972

Age	Males White	Nonwhite	Females White	Nonwhite
5–9	1.0	4.4	.1	.2
10–14	17.1	69.2	1.8	9.9
15–19	34.0	195.2	2.4	17.4
20–24	13.1	158.5	1.0	11.2
25–34	7.2	84.8	.7	7.6
≥35	1.6	13.6	.2	1.7

SOURCE.—Blumstein and Nagin (1975, table 2).

in Pittsburgh are twelve times those of white males the same age. This contrasts with ratios of two-to-one or less for active offenders in larceny and robbery in Detroit.

The observed differences in population arrest rates with age and race (like those evident in table 17) are more likely the result of differences in the *prevalence* of active offenders found within different demographic groups, rather than due to differences in the intensity of offending of active offenders. Further evidence for this conclusion with respect to race is provided in Blumstein and Graddy (1982).

In that study, prevalence measures the breadth of participation in arrests for index offenses found among males in large U.S. cities. To estimate prevalence, Blumstein and Graddy (1982) first estimate the chance of a first arrest for an index offense at each age using data on arrests for juveniles and young adults from the Philadelphia cohort (Wolfgang et al. 1972) and data on arrests for adults over age thirty found among adult arrestees in Washington, D.C. (Blumstein and Cohen 1979). Cumulating the chance of a first arrest at each age gives the prevalence of males in large U.S. cities who will experience at least one index arrest in their lifetimes. Arrest is found to be surprisingly prevalent for the limited set of serious offenses included among the index offenses. As many as one in every four males living in large U.S. cities can expect to be arrested for an index offense sometime in his lifetime.

Dramatic differences in prevalence for index offenses are found between black and white males in large U.S. cities. The estimated proportion of the population with at least one arrest for an index offense by age fifty-five was 51 percent for nonwhite males compared with only 14 percent for white males. Thus, nonwhite males are 3.6 times more likely than white males to be arrested for an index offense sometime during their lifetimes. The same study found no corresponding differences in the chance of recidivism among those who do engage in index offenses. The chance of rearrest for an index offense was between .85 and .90 for both white and nonwhite males.

Thus, variables that have long been thought to differentiate offenders sharply do not make much difference when appropriate controls are introduced—especially controls for being an active offender. At the same time, differences in offending have been found for type of crime charged and prior record. Table 18 summarizes the variations in criminal careers found in some preliminary analyses of Washington, D.C., arrestees. Arrestees for burglary and robbery include relatively high

TABLE 18
Variations in Criminal Career Patterns by Type of Offense

Offense	Percentage "Specialists" with ≥ 2 Prior Arrests Among All Arrestees*	Mean Individual Crime Rate for Active Offenders (Number Crimes per Year Free per Active Offender)		Mean Criminal Career Length for Eighteen- to Twenty-Year-Old Starters	
		For Individual Crime Type	Index Total† (Excluding Murder, Rape, and Larceny)	Total Career Length (Years)‡	Maximum Remaining Career Length in Years (Ages at Maximum)
Murder	7.9	N.A.‖	N.A.	9.6	7.9 (18–55)
Rape	9.9	N.A.	N.A.	5.9	6.6 (18–34)
Aggravated Assault	23.1	1.72	5.99	10.3	18.7 (21)
Robbery	28.5	3.41	7.12	4.9	7.2 (33–43)
Burglary	19.8	5.73	8.99	4.6	8.0 (33–43)
Auto Theft	15.3	2.98	7.48	3.9	6.2 (33–43)

SOURCE.—Cohen (1982).

*"Specialists" have a preponderance of arrests for same charge. About one-half of all arrests in a record, including the 1973 arrest, must be for current charge (Cohen, 1982, chap. 3).

†Index offenses include murder, rape, robbery, aggravated assault, burglary, larceny of more than $50, and auto theft.

‡Career length for offense is average period of time during offender's lifetime when that offense is committed.

‖Estimates of individual crime rates are not available for murder and rape because of small sample sizes for these offenses.

proportions of offenders who have prior arrests for the same offense and high rates of offending in these offenses. Aggravated assault arrestees, by contrast, also have a high proportion of offenders with prior arrests for the same offense, but they are characterized by low rates of offending in that offense.

There are also differences in career length, both with respect to type of crime and to the length of time already spent in criminal careers (Blumstein and Cohen, with Hsieh 1982). The approach to estimating career length derives from life-table analysis used to develop actuarial tables for expected lifetimes. The basic notion is to use the general fall-off in the number of arrestees that is observed with age as an indicator of dropout from criminal careers. In using this approach, however, there are factors other than dropout from criminal careers that may affect the number of arrestees of each age that must be controlled in the estimates. The age distribution of arrestees is first adjusted for the age distribution found in the general population to reflect the influence of variations in birth, death, and migration rates on the age distribution of arrestees. Also, differences in recruitment to and dropout from criminal careers for different birth cohorts are considered. Finally, in estimating expected lifetimes, age is a direct indicator of how long a person has lived so far. For criminal careers, using age as a proxy for time already elapsed in careers requires that we control for the age at which those careers began.

Blumstein and Cohen, with Hsieh (1982), apply this modified life-table approach to the age distribution of adults arrested in Washington, D.C., during 1973 to estimate expected total lengths of adult criminal careers and expected residual career lengths for individual index offenses. As indicated in table 18, careers are shortest on average for the property crimes of robbery, burglary, and auto theft. Also, while individual crime rates do not vary as offenders age, a very different pattern emerges for the residual length of criminal careers (i.e., the expected time remaining in a career after x years already spent in that career). In particular, the pattern of residual career length for robbery and burglary suggests that of offenders who have been criminally active since eighteen, those aged thirty-three to forty-three include the most persistent offenders, with the longest expected remaining careers in those crime types.

As indicated in table 19, persisters with long careers in robbery and burglary represented less than 3 percent of all adults arrested for robbery and burglary in Washington, D.C., during 1973. Nevertheless,

TABLE 19

Levels of Offending by High-Crime-Rate Persisters
in Robbery and Burglary in Washington, D.C., 1973

	Target Offense	
Offending Levels	Robbery	Burglary
Percentage of all adults arrested for target offense who started careers at eighteen and remained active at least fifteen years	2.8	2.9
Percentage of total "preventable"* adult arrests for target offense attributed to thirty–forty-year-old arrestees for that offense	8.3	16.1

*Arrests in 1973 are considered preventable if arrestee previously had a conviction for homicide, rape, robbery, aggravated assault, burglary, or auto theft and was thus previously subject to imprisonment.

these older persisters were responsible for larger portions of the total "preventable" arrests in these crime types;[22] they accounted for 8 percent of the preventable robbery arrests in 1973 and 16 percent of the preventable burglary arrests that year.

B. *Implications for Developing Aggregate Sentencing Policies*

The observed differences in criminal careers with respect to type of crime and prior record have implications for developing aggregate sentencing policies that can appreciably reduce crime through incapacitation. Aggregate sentencing policies of the sort proposed here fall somewhere between selective incapacitation and collective incapacitation as traditionally viewed. An aggregate sentencing policy avoids trying to make predictions about the expected future criminal behavior of any particular individual. Under an aggregate policy, individuals are sentenced solely on the basis of their present offense and, perhaps, their prior criminal record. Aggregate policies are thus similar to collective incapacitation policies, but they take advantage of the differences in offending patterns by offense and prior record in selecting the sentence for each offense and prior record category. Once identified, that

[22]In this analysis, arrests in 1973 are considered "preventable" if they were ever preceded by a conviction for homicide, rape, robbery, aggravated assault, burglary, or auto theft and thus subject to previous imprisonment. Since a previous conviction for a serious offense is required, all preventable arrests are attributed to persisters.

sentence is applied uniformly to all offenders convicted of that offense who fall within the relevant prior record category.

In the analysis of criminal career patterns in Washington, D.C., for example, convicted robbery and burglary defendants emerge as prime candidates for incapacitation. With their high rates of offending, they represent the best targets of incarceration for the purpose of preventing the largest number of future crimes. Also, the residual career length patterns for these crime types suggest that thirty-three to forty-three-year-old offenders who have been criminally active since age eighteen are good targets for incapacitation. These older persisters are least likely to end their careers during the period of incarceration. Earlier or later in robbery or burglary careers, there are many more offenders with very short careers who are likely to stop committing robberies and burglaries shortly anyway.

From the perspective of the offenders who are incarcerated, the greatest incapacitative potential for their crimes is in midcareer, after they have accumulated prior records. Those who persist to this point in robbery and burglary careers are more likely to continue their careers even longer. Largely informed by the sharp declines with age in aggregate arrest rates like those illustrated in figure 5, the conventional wisdom has been that older offenders (particularly those in their thirties) are more likely to be ending their criminal careers very shortly. The finding on residual career lengths, however, contradicts that conventional wisdom; offenders who persist in index crimes into their thirties may be few in number, but they appear to have the longest expected remaining careers.

The overall shortness of robbery and burglary careers also contributes to their incapacitative potential. At the point of maximum remaining careers, prison terms of only two years have the potential to avert from one-quarter to one-third of the expected remaining careers of six to eight years for offenders sentenced for burglary or robbery. To the extent that careers are not merely postponed by incarceration, this represents a potentially substantial reduction in crimes for those older persisters incarcerated under such a policy.

The actual magnitude of the incapacitative effects achieved by targeting incarceration on robbery and burglary can be estimated directly from the arrest histories of the 1973 Washington, D.C., arrestees (Cohen 1982, chap. 6). The basic method is to examine the past criminal records of the arrestees, looking for previous convictions, and then to determine whether the arrestees would have been incarcerated at the time of the

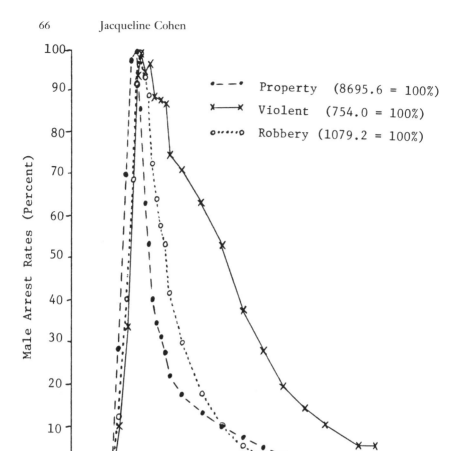

FIG. 5. Male arrest rates by age and type of crime in fifty-five large U.S. cities in 1970. Data include male arrests in cities with populations over 250,000 in 1970. Arrest rates for multiyear categories (e.g., 25–29) are noted at the midpoint of the category; arrest rates expressed as percentages of peak rates for each crime type. Property offenses include burglary, larceny, and auto theft. Violent offenses include homicide, rape, and aggravated assault. The peak rate for each crime type is expressed as arrests per 100,000 male population in the peak age category.

current 1973 arrest if they had been sentenced under alternative sentencing options at the time of the previous conviction. Assuming that alternative sentencing strategies would not have altered individual offending patterns significantly, the 1973 arrests of offenders who would have been incarcerated are considered preventable by the sentencing option. This provides an estimate of the portion of currently sampled arrests that would have been averted by alternative incarceration policies. To the extent that all offenders are vulnerable to arrest for their crimes and that arrestees with arrests averted are no more or less likely to be arrested than other arrestees, the proportion of arrests averted is also an estimate of the proportion of *crimes* that would be averted by the incapacitation strategy.

Table 20 reports the maximum potential crime reduction possible if life terms in prison were imposed after previous convictions. Two different sentencing strategies are compared, imposing prison sentences after any conviction and imposing prison sentences only after repeat convictions. The maximum incapacitative effects vary substantially for different target offenses. The potential reduction is greatest for robbery, burglary, and aggravated assault at 13–14 percent of current crimes prevented. When prison terms are restricted to repeat convictions, the maximum incapacitative potential is substantially reduced. Because of this limited crime reduction, the remainder of the discussion focuses on the "any conviction" sentencing strategy.

Figure 6 illustrates the differential crime reduction possible for prison terms of different lengths. When relatively short prison terms after any conviction are considered, targeting on convictions for robbery offers relatively larger crime reduction benefits than targeting on other of-

TABLE 20

Maximum Potential Incapacitative Effects (%) from
Life Terms Imposed on Different Offenses
(1973 Washington, D.C., Arrestees)

Target Offense	Sentence Imposed	
	Any Conviction	Repeat Convictions
Robbery	12.8	1.1
Burglary	14.2	4.2
Murder	7.9	...
Rape	3.6	...
Aggravated assault	13.7	3.3
Auto theft	8.2	2.0
Any "criterion"* offense	24.4	7.6

*The "criterion" offenses include murder, rape, robbery, aggravated assault, burglary, and auto theft.

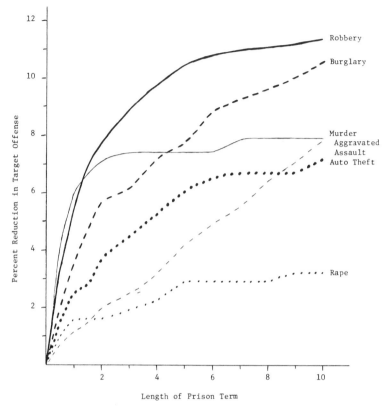

FIG. 6. Expected crime reduction from prison terms of varying length (in years) imposed after any conviction for different target offenses.

fenses. Minimum two-year terms imposed on all defendants convicted for robbery would result in an 8 percent reduction in robberies.

The figure also indicates the relative advantage in terms of crime reduction of short prison sentences. The marginal returns in added crime reduction decrease as sentence lengths increase. Smaller reductions in crime are achieved for each year added to prison terms. For robbery, an increase of from one to two years in prison terms achieves an additional 2.3 percent decrease in robberies. By contrast, the same one-year increase from five to six years in prison terms yields only an additional 0.3 percent decrease in robberies.[23] This finding is consistent

[23]Younger arrestees in 1973 have shorter prior adult careers in which to accumulate prior convictions. The differences in exposure time associated with the age distribution of arrestees could influence the results on incapacitative potential: a larger portion of

with general results from recidivism research, where it is found that if recidivism occurs, it is more likely to occur quickly.[24]

Aside from reductions in the target offense, prison terms for robbery also result in the largest reductions in criterion arrests generally. In addition to an 8 percent reduction in robberies, two-year prison terms after any robbery conviction would also prevent 3 percent of murders and rapes and 2 percent of auto thefts. This reduction in other offenses reflects the fact that persons convicted of robbery also engage in a variety of other offenses at reasonably high rates. This versatility in offending yields additional crime reduction beyond the target convicted offense.

All of the incapacitative strategies considered here involve increases in total prison population, as use of prison is expanded for one offense without corresponding decreases for other offenses. Figure 7 illustrates the trade-offs between prison increases and crime reduction associated with different sentencing policies. The most attractive policies are those in the lower-right-hand corner; they involve the smallest increases in prison population to achieve the largest crime reduction.

This figure suggests some directions in incarceration policies for purposes of achieving differential incapacitation. First, the relative advantage of shorter prison terms is apparent. For longer sentences, far greater increases in prison population are required to achieve each additional percent reduction in crime. There are also significant reductions in incapacitative benefits associated with a policy that limits prison terms to repeat convictions. At shorter sentences, the figure also dramatizes the strong dominance of any robbery convictions as a target

---

young people found among arrestees would increase the representation of short times to prior convictions. In this event, the decreasing returns in added crime reduction as prison terms increase in fig. 6 might simply reflect the age distribution of arrestees with more crime reduction evident for the much larger population of young arrestees and relatively little crime reduction for the much smaller group of older arrestees. To control for these differences in exposure time, the analysis was conducted separately within different age groups of arrestees in 1973. No similar decline in marginal crime reduction as sentences increase was found within any single age group. The decrease observed without controls for age apparently result from a combination of decreasing exposure time for younger arrestees and lower conviction rates (conviction/offender/time free) for older arrestees.

[24] The FBI Careers in Crime Program has followed individuals released from any point in the federal criminal justice system in 1963 and 1965. Federal Bureau of Investigation (1971) reports that of those persons rearrested within four years after release (63 percent of all releasees), 85 percent were rearrested within the first two years after release. In a study following a cohort of juveniles in Philadelphia until age eighteen, Wolfgang et al. (1972) obtained data on all juvenile arrests by members of the cohort. Our analysis of their data reveals that of 6,717 pairs of arrests, 88 percent of subsequent arrests occurred within two years of the previous arrest. For juveniles released from institutions, 92 percent of those arrested again were arrested within two years after release.

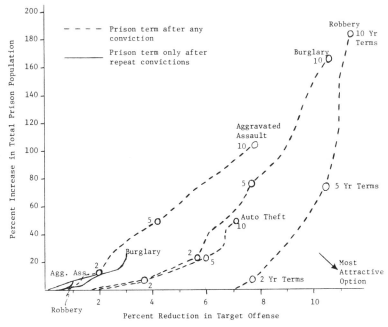

FIG. 7. Prison population increases and crime reduction from prison terms of varying lengths imposed after convictions for different target offenses.

for incapacitation. The same prison increases result in greater crime reduction when targeted on robbery convictions than on the other offenses. An aggregate policy of minimum two-year prison terms after any robbery conviction in Washington, D.C., has the potential to prevent 8 percent of robberies by adults at a cost of about a 7 percent increase in the total prison population in that jurisdiction.

The comparative advantage found for robbery convictions as a target for incapacitation is consistent with the analysis of variations in the size of incapacitative effects discussed above. There it was found that the potential for incapacitation is best where average individual crime rates or sanctions for a crime are already high (see Sec. IIE and App. B). As indicated in table 21, aside from murder, the expected prison term per arrest found in Washington, D.C., in 1973 was highest for robbery at just under one-half of a year incarcerated for every adult robbery arrest. At high sanction levels, large portions of offenders are already being incapacitated and the volume of crimes committed is already being reduced by current sentencing policies. The increment in sanctions, therefore, has the potential of large marginal effects on

TABLE 21
Expected Time Served per Arrest in
Washington, D.C., 1973

Offense	Number of Inmates, 1973*	Average Annual Number of Adult Arrests, 1971 and 1972†	Expected Time Served per Arrest (years)‡
Murder	274	212	1.29
Robbery	762	1,831	.42
Rape	68	234	.29
Burglary	246	1,226	.20
Auto theft	64	576	.11
Aggravated assault	129	2,086	.06

*U.S. Department of Justice (1976*b*, table 1: District of Columbia).

†Washington, D.C., Metropolitan Police Department (1971, 1972).

‡Expected time served per arrest for adults is estimated by dividing average daily prison population by number of arrests of adults.

remaining crime and small effects on the already substantial prison population.

These results illustrate the kind of analysis that can assess the comparative incapacitative effects of policies targeted on offenders convicted of different offenses and with different prior criminal records. Although promising from the perspective of developing a workable incapacitation policy, the available results are only preliminary and still very limited. Considerably more research, in the way of testing and validation in other settings, is required.

The present results derive primarily from the arrest histories of adults arrested in Washington, D.C., in 1973. Arrestees in that city are demographically unique and not representative of adult arrestees in other U.S. cities. As indicated in table 22, nonwhites are heavily overrepresented among Washington, D.C., arrestees, as they are in the general District population.[25] The results for Washington, D.C., thus may not

[25]In the 1970 census, the population of Washington, D.C., was 71 percent nonwhite compared with 12.3 percent nonwhite for the total urban population of the United States. Table 22 also indicates that eighteen- to twenty-four-year-olds are underrepresented among Washington, D.C., arrestees compared with arrests in U.S. cities. This difference

TABLE 22
Comparison of Washington, D.C., Arrestees with
Arrests in U.S. Cities in 1973

	1973 Washington, D.C., Arrestees (%)	1973 Index Arrests for Cities (excluding Larceny) (%)	
		Total	Persons ≥ 18
Race:			
White	8.1	55.3	N.A.
Nonwhite	91.8	44.7	N.A.
Sex:			
Male	89.7	92.5	91.6
Female	10.3	7.5	8.4
Age:			
<18	0.1	42.1	...
18–20	18.6	17.2	29.6
21–24	24.4	14.9	25.7
25–29	19.9	9.9	17.1
30–34	12.3	5.7	9.9
35–39	8.4	3.5	6.1
40–44	5.0	2.5	4.3
45–49	4.6	1.7	3.0
≥50	6.7	2.5	4.3

SOURCE.—Cohen (1982); Federal Bureau of Investigation (1974).

be generalizable to other U.S. jurisdictions, and analyses based on arrestees in other jurisdictions are needed.

There is also need for prospective validation of results that have so far been based entirely on retrospective arrest histories. Ideally, the data should include both past arrest histories and follow-up data on future arrests for the arrestees in the sampling period. The retrospective histories can be used to examine the variations in criminal careers by offense and prior record and to assess the incapacitative potential of alternative sentences applied to different target offenses. The prospectively observed careers of the same arrestees can then be used to validate the differences expected from the retrospective analysis. Similar results

is not accounted for by a similar difference in the general population. In the 1970 census, about 20 percent of the adult population (eighteen or older) in Washington, D.C., and in all urban areas of the United States were between the ages of eighteen and twenty-four. There is, however, a greater incidence of multiple index arrests for the same offender found among young adults (Cohen 1982, chaps. 3, 5). This age variation in multiple arrests would inflate the count of young adults among *arrests* compared to the count among arrestees.

in a variety of different settings would substantially increase the generalizability of the results.

C. Advantages of Aggregate Sentencing Policies

This analysis indicates the potential for developing aggregate sentencing policies that achieve differential reductions in crime and are at the same time consistent with concerns for justice and equity in sentencing. Such policies avoid many of the ethical and empirical problems that accompany use of individual-level predictions. To begin with, the severity of the sentence must be commensurate with the seriousness of the offense. Offenders are then subjected to the sentence only on the basis of convicted offense and prior criminal record. Moreover, the sentence is imposed uniformly within a category. No individual predictions of future criminality are employed, and thus the problem of false positives is avoided. Such sentences would be immediately acceptable from a modified just-deserts perspective. To accommodate a more restrictive view of just deserts that does not allow prior convictions to enter into the deserved punishment calculations, the aggregate policy could be reformulated to rely only on convicted offense.

Implementing the policy in Washington, D.C., would involve imposing minimum two-year prison terms on all adults convicted of robbery in that city. It is assumed that a two-year prison term for robbery would be widely viewed as aceptable from a just-deserts perspective. Such a policy would increase the expected prison stay per arrest for robbery from .42 to .50 years. An aggregate policy of this sort is attractive because the modification of current sentencing practices to impose deserved sentences more uniformly also results in other benefits, in the form of increased crime reduction. If the sentence necessary to achieve crime reduction were to fall outside the acceptable range, however, an aggregate policy that imposes that sentence would be vulnerable to many of the same problems already attributed to policies based on individual predictions.

Another consideration in evaluating aggregate policies is the relative magnitude of the benefits in crime reduction compared with benefits from more selective incapacitation policies that invoke individual-based predictions. In Washington, D.C., for example, an aggregate policy of two-year prison terms imposed after any adult robbery conviction had the potential to prevent 8 percent of the robberies by adults in 1973 at a cost of 7 percent increase in total prison population (Cohen 1982). Compare this with a reduction in armed robberies in California of 20

percent with an associated 2.5 percent increase in total prison population achieved through application of an individual-based selective
incapacitation policy, outlined in Greenwood, with Abrahamse (1982).[26]
The more selective policy led to more crime reduction and a smaller
increase in prison population. It is, nevertheless, possible to achieve
reasonable crime reduction through aggregate policies, while avoiding
the controversial ethical and empirical issues raised by individual-level
predictions of future criminality.

V. Conclusion

This review of research on incapacitation has highlighted a number of
problems in pursuing incapacitative strategies. Most important is the
recognition that the crime reduction benefits of any incapacitative strategy are inherently limited by the large number of offenders who have
no prior convictions. The crimes of these offenders could not have been
prevented by any incapacitation policy that requires a conviction before
imposing prison terms. Collective incapacitation policies that involve
uniform increases in the use of prison for a wide range of offense types
were found to have only modest impacts on crime while requiring
enormous increases in prison populations. By targeting incapacitation
more narrowly on career criminals or habitual offenders with their
higher rates of offending, selective incapacitation strategies offer the
possibility of achieving greater reductions in crime at considerably
smaller costs in terms of prison resources. The success of a selective
incapacitation strategy, however, depends critically on our ability to
identify the career criminals reasonably early in their careers.

For the purposes of incapacitation, career criminals are individuals
who can be expected to continue as high-rate offenders, to engage in
reasonably serious offenses, and to do so over a number of years into
the future. Under this definition, career criminals are characterized by
the intensity of their offending, the crime types they engage in, and
the length of their criminal careers. Until recently, these aspects of
criminal careers were measured only poorly, if at all. As a result, most
attempts to identify career criminals have used a wide variety of more

---

[26]The 10 percent increase in prison population cited in Greenwood, with Abrahamse
(1982, p. 79) is the increase in the size of the incarcerated population for robbery. In
California in 1980, convicted robbers accounted for 25 percent of the total prison population in that state (California Department of Corrections 1980). Applying this 25 percent
to the 10 percent increase in the robbery population represents a 2.5 percent increase in
the *total* prison population.

immediately accessible offender attributes in addition to official criminal record variables. These other prediction variables include personal demographics (especially age), psychological profiles, employment histories, and history of drug or alcohol abuse. These past prediction efforts, however, have been hampered by a number of ethical and empirical problems that seriously limit their ability to identify career criminals with any reasonable degree of accuracy.

A number of issues warrant consideration in any further pursuit of this sort of prediction research. Concern for predictive accuracy requires that attention be paid to improving internal and external validation of the prediction scales to assure an adequate basis for predictions. External validation on new samples is particularly important because of the potentially serious problem of shrinkage in accuracy as a scale is implemented more widely.

Furthermore, because data on self-reported crimes were available only for inmate samples, the most recent Rand scale focuses narrowly on the choice between jail and prison and on the lengths of terms for incarcerated offenders. A fuller view of the sentencing decision would also incorporate the decision whether to incarcerate or not. In extending the scope of prediction, the results on *inmates* cannot simply be generalized to all convicted persons. Inmates already represented a selective sample of convicted offenders, and the attributes associated with high-rate offending found among inmates may not be appropriate in distinguishing high-rate offenders at conviction. A scale that is to be applied at conviction should be validated on convicted offenders.

Finally, research should focus on self-reported high-rate offenders, first to assure the accuracy of the individual crime rates estimated for them, and second to seek identifying characteristics that might be more usefully applied in distinguishing them. As indicated by the presence of "past time incarcerated" as a predictor variable in the Greenwood scale, high-rate offenders tend to have been free on the streets for shorter times, and their annualized high rates are based on intense criminal activity in relatively short periods of time. A key question is whether that high rate of activity would have been sustained over longer periods if they had remained free. To the extent that the shorter period of intense activity reflects only a short-term spurt in crimes, the annualized rates would be overestimated. If it is confirmed that these offenders are indeed high rate, they can be examined in more detail to develop further insights into their distinguishing characteristics.

Recent research examining criminal careers directly has suggested the possibility of developing an alternative strategy to individual-level predictions for pursuing incapacitation. In particular, the emerging estimates for aspects of criminal careers such as individual crime rates and the length of criminal careers suggest that offense-related variables (i.e., the crime type of the current charge and prior criminal record) can be used to distinguish offenders who on average have high crime rates and long careers. The observed variations in criminal career patterns opens up the opportunity to develop sentencing policies that take advantage of the differential reductions in crime associated with different offenses. Such policies have the distinct advantage of relying only on offense-related variables in distinguishing sentences. These policies take a collective incapacitation strategy of aggregate sentences that are uniformly applied but focus it more narrowly on just those offenses with the greatest incapacitative potential.

Further research into criminal career patterns and their implications for identifying career criminals and developing aggregate sentencing policies in a broader range of settings, is required. This research should develop new estimates of individual arrest and crime rates and of the length of criminal careers. These estimates should be disaggregated to explore variations in career patterns with age, race, prior criminal record, crime type of the current charge, time period, and jurisdiction. These analyses will provide a basis for exploring the similarities and differences in individual career patterns in order to help identify the attributes of the most active offenders. Estimates based on retrospective arrest histories should also be subjected to prospective validation using future arrest experiences to assure that estimated career patterns do persist into the future.

The magnitude and variation of the incapacitative potential of alternative aggregate sentencing policies should also be explored in diverse settings. These estimates are best obtained by using the simulation approach in which the criminal records of the arrestees in a year are examined for past convictions. It can then be determined whether the arrestees would have been incarcerated at the time of the current arrest if they had been sentenced under alternative sentencing options at the time of previous convictions. This simulation approach does not rely on strong model assumptions like those underlying equation (1) and does not depend on any particular value of individual crime rates. The resulting estimates should then be confirmed through prospective follow-up of future criminal involvement for these arrestees.

Informed by the results of this further research on criminal careers, we may be able to develop workable aggregate sentencing policies based only on offense-related variables that have the potential to achieve differential crime reduction through incapacitation.

APPENDIX A

To estimate a lower bound on q_A, Greenberg combines data on the number of reported index crimes for the nation with an assumption about the proportion of virgin arrests (i.e., the first arrest for an offender). The basic relationship is that total index arrests in a year are just the sum of virgin index arrests and index arrests by recidivists,

$$Cq_A = V_I + rq_A VT ,$$

where:

- C = number of index offenses committed annually (reported and unreported);
- q_A = probability of arrest for an index offense;
- V = annual number of virgin arrests for nonminor offenses (including the index offenses, other larcenies, other assaults, arson, forgery, counterfeiting, fraud, embezzlement, possession of stolen property, weapons, narcotics, and gambling);
- V_I = annual number of virgin arrests for index offenses;
- r = annual rate of committing index offenses for all persons previously arrested for some nonminor offense;
- VT = number of nonvirgin, active criminals in any year (under steady-state assumptions with T = the expected length of criminal careers);
- A = number of persons arrested annually for nonminor offenses.

For q_A less than 1, $V_I q_A < V_I$ and $Cq_A > V_I q_A + rq_A VT$, to yield a lower bound on q_A of

$$q_A > \frac{rq_A VT}{C - V_I} .$$

A variable with empirical estimates is then included by dividing both numerator and denominator by the number of arrests for nonminor offenses, A, so that

$$q_A > \frac{rq_A T(V/A)}{(C/A) - (V_I/A)} . \tag{A1}$$

Estimates of $rq_A T$, C, A, V/A, and V_I/A are needed to estimate the lower bound on q_A. Using Blumstein and Larson (1969), Greenberg estimates $rq_A T$ as 2.5 index arrests in a career. The *Uniform Crime Report* for 1965 (Federal Bureau of Investigation 1966) reports 2.78 million reported index crimes and 5.03 million total arrests for a reporting population of 135 million. To obtain C, the total number of index offenses actually committed in the United States, the 2.78 million reported crimes must be scaled up to account for the police agencies not reporting to the FBI (covering about 59 million people) and for citizens not reporting to the police. Using 3 as the ratio of total crime to crime reported by the FBI, Greenberg estimates C as 8.34 million index crimes. Similarly, scaling up the number of arrests to the total U.S. population of 194 million and taking 27 percent for the proportion of arrests for nonminor crimes among all arrests, A is 1.94 million arrests.

Good empirical estimates are not available for the fraction of virgin arrests among all arrests for nonminor offenses (V/A), or for the fraction of arrests for nonminor offenses that are virgin arrests for index offenses (V_I/A). Nevertheless, some constraints can be placed on the values of these variables. The expected number of nonvirgin index arrests in a career (rq_AT) is estimated to be 2.5. Thus, the total number of index arrests in a career is no more than 3.5. Under steady-state assumptions, the total expected number of nonminor arrests in a career is given by $A/V = 1/(V/A)$. Since index arrests are included among nonminor arrests, the number of nonminor arrests in a career exceeds the number of index arrests. Thus, $A/V > 3.5$ and $V/A < 1/3.5 = 0.286$. Also, since $V_I < V$, $V_I/A < V/A$. With these constraints in mind, V/A and V_I/A are arbitrarily set at 0.25 and 0.20, respectively.

Substituting the numerical estimates of $rq_AT = 2.5$, $C = 8.34$ million, $A = 1.94$ million, $V/A = 0.25$, and $V_I/A = 0.20$ into equation (1), q_A must be greater than 0.15. For $rq_A = 0.5$, then r must be less than 3.33 in 1965.

APPENDIX B

This Appendix examines the effect of variations in the individual crime rate, r, and in the current level of incarceration on the magnitude of the incapacitative effect. The estimate of the incapacitative effect is given in equation (A1) as

$$I = \frac{rqJS}{1+rqJS}. \tag{B1}$$

In this relation, I is the incapacitative effect, or the proportional reduction in the individual crime rate, r, as a result of an incarceration policy where qJS is the expected time incarcerated for a crime.

The notion is that when an offender spends some time incarcerated during a year, his crime rate while free, r, applies only to the portion of the year when he is free. In this case, the offender's *effective* crime rate for the entire year, r^*, is only a fraction of the rate while free, r, with

$$r^* = r(1-I).$$

An offender, for example, may have a crime rate while free of ten crimes per year. If this offender is only free for six months of the year, however, his effective crime rate for the entire year is only five crimes per year—ten crimes per year during the half-year free and no crimes per year for the half-year incarcerated.

For a criminal population of size N, the total expected number of crimes committed in a year (C) is given by the product of the individual effective crime rate and the number of criminals:

$$C = r(1 - I)N = \frac{rN}{1 + rq\,JS}. \tag{B2}$$

Likewise, the total man-years in prison required annually (R) is obtained from the product of the expected prison stay per crime ($q\,JS$) times the total expected number of crimes committed:

$$R = Cq\,JS = \frac{rq\,JSN}{1 + rq\,JS} = I \cdot N. \tag{B3}$$

The elasticity of C or R indicates the responsiveness of crime or prison population to changes in imprisonment policy ($q\,JS$). In general, the elasticity of one variable (Y) with respect to another variable (X) is the percentage change in Y that is associated with a 1 percent change in X. This elasticity is given by

$$e_{Y,X} = \frac{dY}{Y} \Big/ \frac{dX}{X} = \frac{dY}{dX} \cdot \frac{X}{Y}.$$

The elasticity of total crimes, C, with respect to the imprisonment variable, $q\,JS$ (i.e., the expected man-years in prison per crime) is thus

$$\begin{aligned} e_{C,q\,JS} &= \frac{dC}{d(q\,JS)} \cdot \frac{q\,JS}{C} \\ &= \frac{-r^2N}{(1 + rq\,JS)^2} \cdot \frac{q\,JS}{C} \\ &= \frac{-rq\,JS}{1 + rq\,JS}. \end{aligned} \tag{B4}$$

Similarly, the elasticity of the total prison population, R, with respect to the imprisonment variable, $q\,JS$, is

$$\begin{aligned} e_{R,q\,JS} &= \frac{dR}{d(q\,JS)} \cdot \frac{q\,JS}{R} \\ &= \frac{rN}{(1 + rq\,JS)^2} \cdot \frac{q\,JS}{R} \\ &= \frac{1}{1 + rq\,JS}. \end{aligned} \tag{B5}$$

These elasticities can be combined to form a cost-benefit ratio reflecting the percentage change in prison population necessary to achieve a 1 percent decrease in crime. The cost-benefit ratio is

$$\frac{e_{R,q\,JS}}{e_{C,q\,JS}} = \frac{1}{1 + rq\,JS} \cdot \frac{1 + rq\,JS}{-rq\,JS} = -\frac{1}{rq\,JS}. \tag{B6}$$

The elasticity of total crimes (C) to changes in incarceration levels per crime ($q\,JS$) varies with the current values of the crime rate (r) and of the incarceration level ($q\,JS$). When the level of prison use per crime ($q\,JS$) is increased by 1 percent, the percentage reduction in total crime through incapacitation is greater at higher values for the current level of prison use (qJS) and for larger values of the individual crime rate (r) (eq. [B4]). The larger the current levels of these variables, the greater the expected reduction in total crimes from further increases in qJS.

This variation in the potential crime reduction from incapacitation is evident in several of the United States. In 1970 data on prison populations and reported crimes, there was wide variation in the use of incarceration in different states. In New York State, for example, qJS for index crimes was only .0076 (or about an eight in a thousand chance that an index crime would result in a one-year prison term), while in Mississippi qJS was .0593 (or more than a one in twenty chance of a one-year prison term for an index crime). The potential incapacitative gains from increasing qJS were quite different in these two settings. If the index crime rate for individuals was five crimes per year free in both states, doubling qJS would have resulted in only a 3.7 percent expected decrease in index crimes in New York compared with a 22.9 percent expected decrease in Mississippi. At a higher index crime rate of ten crimes per year free, the expected decrease in crimes would have been larger in each state, at 7.1 percent in New York and 37.2 percent in Mississippi.

Any increase in the imprisonment policy variable (qJS) also results in an increase in the prison population (eq. [B5]). In this case, the magnitude of the increase in prison population resulting from a 1 percent increase in qJS is smaller when qJS and r are already high. The larger the current level of these variables, the smaller the expected increase in prison population through further increases in qJS. For the illustrative states of New York and Mississippi in 1970, at $r = 5$, doubling qJS would have resulted in an expected 96.3 percent increase in the prison population for index offenses in New York State, and a 77.1 percent increase in Mississippi. The increases in prison population are somewhat lower at 92.9 percent in New York and 62.8 percent in Mississippi, if the index crime rate was larger at $r = 10$.

Combining the elasticities in equations (B4) and (B5) provides a cost-benefit ratio for incapacitation. This measure of the percentage increase in prison population necessary to achieve a 1 percent reduction in total crimes from incapacitation varies considerably with the current value of qJS (eq. [B6]). If the expected prison stay per crime is already high (say, above .05 for different values of r), the additional costs in terms of the percentage increase in the prison population required to achieve a 1 percent decrease in crime would not be unreasonable. Below $qJS = .05$, on the other hand, the increases in prison population associated with a 1 percent decrease in crime would be much larger. At an index crime rate of $r = 5$, the cost-benefit ratio for New York in 1970 involves a 26 percent increase in prison population for each 1 percent decrease in index crimes. In Mississippi, by contrast, with its already higher use of incarceration, the increase in prison population would have been only 3.4 percent for each 1 percent decrease in index crimes.

These variations in impact with the levels of r and qJS have implications for the size of the collective incapacitative effect that was estimated for different offenses and in different jurisdictions in tables 3 and 4 in the text. Crime reduction from collective incapacitation will be larger and prison population increases smaller where r or qJS are higher.

REFERENCES

Anderson, David C. 1982. "Whom to Throw the Book At." *New York Times*, October 21.

Avi-Itzhak, Benjamin, and Reuel Shinnar. 1973. "Quantitative Models in Crime Control." *Journal of Criminal Justice* 1:185–217.

Blumstein, Alfred, and Jacqueline Cohen. 1979. "Estimation of Individual Crime Rates from Arrest Records." *Journal of Criminal Law and Criminology* 70:561–85.

———. 1982. "Analysis of Criminal Careers from an Incapacitative Perspective." Work in progress under grant from National Institute of Justice. Pittsburgh, Pa.: Carnegie-Mellon University, School of Urban and Public Affairs.

Blumstein, Alfred, and Jacqueline Cohen, with Paul Hsieh. 1982. *The Duration of Adult Criminal Careers*. Draft report submitted to National Institute of Justice, August 1982. Pittsburgh: Carnegie-Mellon University, School of Urban and Public Affairs.

Blumstein, Alfred, Jacqueline Cohen, and Harold D. Miller. 1980. "Demographically Disaggregated Projections of Prison Populations." *Journal of Criminal Justice* 8:1–26.

Blumstein, Alfred, Jacqueline Cohen, and Daniel Nagin, eds. 1978. *Deterrence and Incapacitation: Estimating the Effects of Sanctions on Crime Rates*. Washington, D.C.: National Research Council, National Academy of Sciences.

Blumstein, Alfred, and Elizabeth Graddy. 1982. "Prevalence and Recidivism in Index Arrests: A Feedback Model." *Law and Society Review* 16:265–90.

Blumstein, Alfred and Soumyo Moitra. 1980. "The Identification of 'Career Criminals' from 'Chronic Offenders' in a Cohort." *Law and Policy Quarterly* 2:321–34.

Blumstein, Alfred, and Richard C. Larson. 1969. "Models of a Total Criminal Justice System." *Operations Research* 17:199–232.

Blumstein, Alfred, and Daniel Nagin. 1975. "Analysis of Arrest Rates for Trends in Criminality." *Socio-Economic Planning Sciences* 9:221–27.

Boland, Barbara. 1978. "Incapacitation of the Dangerous Offender: The Arithmetic Is Not So Simple." *Journal of Research in Crime and Delinquency* 15:126–29.

California Department of Corrections. 1980. *California Prisoners—1980: Summary Statistics of Felon Prisoners and Parolees*. Sacramento: California Department of Corrections.

Chaiken, Jan M. 1980. "Models Used for Estimating Crime Rates." Appendix C in *Doing Crime: A Survey of California Prison Inmates*, by M. A. Peterson and H. B. Braiker. Report R-2200-DOJ. Santa Monica, Calif.: Rand Corporation.

82   Jacqueline Cohen

Chaiken, Jan M., and Marcia Chaiken. 1982. *Varieties of Criminal Behavior.* Report to the National Institute of Justice, August. Santa Monica, Calif.: Rand Corporation.

Clarke, Stevens H. 1974. "Getting 'Em Out of Circulation: Does Incarceration of Juvenile Offenders Reduce Crime?" *Journal of Criminal Law and Criminology* 65:528–35.

Cohen, Jacqueline. 1978. "The Incapacitative Effect of Imprisonment: A Critical Review of the Literature." In *Deterrence and Incapacitation: Estimating the Effects of Criminal Sanctions on Crime Rates*, edited by A. Blumstein, J. Cohen, and D. Nagin. Washington, D.C.: National Research Council, National Academy of Sciences.

———. 1982. "Patterns of Adult Offending." Ph.D. dissertation, Carnegie-Mellon University.

Currie, Elliot. 1982. "Crime and Ideology," *Working Papers* 9(3): 26–35.

"Cutting Crimes Tied to Jailing of Busiest Criminals." 1982. *New York Times*, October 6.

Ehrlich, Isaac. 1974. "Participation in Illegitimate Activities: An Economic Analysis." In *Essays in the Economics of Crime and Punishment*, edited by G. S. Becker and W. M. Landes. New York: Columbia University Press, for National Bureau of Economic Research. Reprinted with corrections from *Journal of Political Economy* 81 (1973): 521–67.

Federal Bureau of Investigation. Various years. *Crime in the U.S.: Uniform Crime Reports*. Washington, D.C.: Government Printing Office.

Gottfredson, Michael R., Susan D. Mitchell-Herzfeld, and Timothy J. Flanagan. 1982. "Another Look at the Effectiveness of Parole Supervision." *Journal of Research in Crime and Delinquency* 19:277–98.

Greenberg, David F. 1975. "The Incapacitative Effect of Imprisonment: Some Estimates." *Law and Society Review* 9:541–80.

———. 1977. "The Correctional Effects of Corrections: A Survey of Evaluations." In *Corrections and Punishment*, edited by D. F. Greenberg. Beverly Hills, Calif.: Sage Publications.

Greenwood, Peter W., with Allan Abrahamse. 1982. *Selective Incapacitation*. Report to the National Institute of Justice, August 1982. Santa Monica, Calif.: Rand Corporation.

Hindelang, Michael J. 1978. "Race and Involvement in Common Law Personal Crimes." *American Sociological Review* 43:93–109.

———. 1980. "Sex Differences in Criminal Activity." *Social Problems* 27:143–56.

———. 1981. "Variations in Sex-Race-Age-Specific Incidence Rates of Offending." *American Sociological Review* 46:461–74.

Hindelang, Michael J., Travis Hirschi, and Joseph G. Weis. 1979. "Correlates of Delinquency: The Illusion of Discrepancy between Self-Report and Official Statistics." *American Sociological Review* 44:995–1014.

Hoffman, Peter B., and James L. Beck. 1980. "Revalidating the Salient Factor Score: A Research Note." *Journal of Criminal Justice* 8:185–88.

Johnson, Perry M. 1978. "The Role of Penal Quarantine in Reducing Violent Crime." *Crime and Delinquency* 24:465–85.

Lewin, Tamar. 1982. "Making the Punishment Fit Future Crimes." *New York Times*, November 14.

Lipton, Douglas, Robert Martinson, and Judith Wilks. 1975. *The Effectiveness of Correctional Treatment: A Survey of Treatment Evaluation Studies.* New York: Praeger Publishers.

"Lock Them Up." 1982. *Wall Street Journal*, October 8.

Marsh, Jeffrey, and Max Singer. 1972. "Soft Statistics and Hard Questions." Mimeographed. Croton-on-Hudson, N.Y.: Hudson Institute.

Martinson, Robert. 1974. "What Works?—Questions and Answers about Prison Reform." *Public Interest* 35:22–54.

Monahan, John. 1976. "The Prevention of Violence." In *Community Mental Health and the Criminal Justice System*, edited by J. Monahan. New York: Pergamon Press.

———. 1978. "The Prediction of Violent Criminal Behavior: A Methodological Critique and Prospectus." In *Deterrence and Incapacitation: Estimating the Effects of Criminal Sanctions on Crime Rates*, edited by A. Blumstein, J. Cohen, and D. Nagin. Washington, D.C.: National Research Council, National Academy of Sciences.

———. 1981. *Predicting Violent Behavior: An Assessment of Clinical Techniques.* Beverly Hills, Calif.: Sage Publications.

Moore, Mark H., Susan Estrich, and Daniel McGillis. 1982. *Report of the Project on Public Danger, Dangerous Offenders, and the Criminal Justice System.* Vol. 1. Draft report 2 to the National Institute of Justice. Cambridge, Mass.: Harvard University, Kennedy School of Government.

Morris, Norval. 1974. *The Future of Imprisonment.* Chicago: University of Chicago Press.

Palmer, Jan, and John Salimbene. 1978. "The Incapacitation of the Dangerous Offender: A Second Look." *Journal of Research in Crime and Deliquency* 15:130–34.

Pennsylvania Bureau of Corrections. 1981. *1980 Annual Statistical Report.* Camp Hill: Pennsylvania Bureau of Corrections.

Petersilia, Joan, and Peter W. Greenwood. 1978. "Mandatory Prison Sentences: Their Projected Effects on Crime and Prison Populations." *Journal of Criminal Law and Criminology* 69:604–15.

Peterson, Mark A., and Harriet B. Braiker, with Suzanne M. Polich. 1980. *Doing Crime: A Survey of California Prison Inmates.* Report R-2200-DOJ. Santa Monica, Calif.: Rand Corporation.

———. 1981. *Who Commits Crimes: A Survey of Prison Inmates.* Cambridge, Mass.: Oelgeschlager, Gunn & Hain.

Reiss, Albert J., Jr. 1980. "Understanding Changes in Crime Rates." In *Indicators of Crime and Criminal Justice: Quantitative Studies*, edited by S. Fienberg and A. Reiss. Washington, D.C.: Department of Justice, Bureau of Justice Statistics.

Robison, James, and Gerald Smith. 1971. "The Effectiveness of Correctional Programs." *Crime and Delinquency* 17:67–79.

Sechrest, Lee, Susan O. White, and Elizabeth D. Brown. 1979. *The Rehabilitation of Criminal Offenders: Problems and Prospects.* Washington, D.C.: National Research Council, National Academy of Sciences.

Shinnar, Reuel, and Shlomo Shinnar. 1975. "The Effect of the Criminal Justice System on the Control of Crime: A Quantitative Approach." *Law and Society Review* 9:581–611.

U.S. Department of Commerce. 1979. *Statistical Abstract of the United States, 1979.* Washington, D.C.: Government Printing Office.

U.S. Department of Justice. 1975. *Criminal Victimization Surveys in 13 American Cities.* Washington, D.C.: Government Printing Office.

———. 1976a. *Criminal Victimization Surveys in Chicago, Detroit, Los Angeles, New York, and Philadelphia: A Comparison of 1972 and 1974 Findings.* Washington, D.C.: Government Printing Office.

———. 1976b. *Census of Prisoners in State Correctional Facilities: 1973.* Washington, D.C.: Government Printing Office.

———. 1980. *Characteristics of the Parole Population 1978.* Washington, D.C.: Government Printing Office.

U.S. Department of Justice. Bureau of Justice Statistics. 1983. *Prisoners in 1982.* Washington, D.C.: Government Printing Office.

Van Dine, Stephan, John P. Conrad, and Simon Dinitz. 1979. *Restraining the Wicked: The Dangerous Offender Project.* Lexington, Mass.: Lexington Books.

Van Dine, Stephan, Simon Dinitz, and John P. Conrad. 1977. "The Incapacitation of the Dangerous Offender: A Statistical Experiment." *Journal of Research in Crime and Delinquency* 14:22–35.

———. 1978. "Response to Our Critics." *Journal of Research in Crime and Delinquency* 15:135–39.

Von Hirsch, Andrew. 1974. "Prediction of Criminal Conduct and Preventive Confinement of Convicted Persons." *Buffalo Law Review* 21:717–58.

———. 1976. *Doing Justice: The Choice of Punishments.* New York: Hill & Wang.

Washington, D.C., Metropolitan Police Department. 1971. *Annual Report 1971: Pt. II. Internal Report.* Washington, D.C.: Metropolitan Police Department.

———. 1972. *Annual Report 1972: Pt II. Internal Report.* Washington, D.C.: Metropolitan Police Department.

Wicker, Tom. 1982. "Making Things Worse." *New York Times,* July 9.

Williams, Kristen M. 1979. *The Scope and Prediction of Recidivism.* Washington, D.C.: Institute for Law and Social Research.

———. 1980. "Selection Criteria for Career Criminal Programs." *Journal of Criminal Law and Criminology* 71:89–93.

Wilson, James Q. 1975a. "Lock 'Em Up." *New York Times Magazine,* March 9.

———. 1975b. *Thinking about Crime.* New York: Basic Books.

———. 1977. "Changing Criminal Sentences." *Harpers Magazine,* November.

Wolfgang, Marvin E. 1978. "Overview of Research into Violent Behavior." Testimony to the Subcommittee on Domestic and International Scientific Planning, Analysis, and Cooperation of the House Committee on Science and Technology, 95th Cong., 2d sess.

Wolfgang, Marvin E., Robert M. Figlio, and Thorsten Sellin. 1972. *Delinquency in a Birth Cohort.* Chicago: University of Chicago Press.

Gordon Hawkins

Prison Labor and Prison Industries

ABSTRACT

Idleness is a leading characteristic of the American prison system. It is a feature so familiar to prison administrators and penologists that many accept it as inevitable. One need not share Calvin Coolidge's view of work as "the only means to manhood and the measure of civilization" to regard this situation as deplorable. Two explanations have been forcefully propounded and widely accepted. One is that a satisfactory solution to the prison employment problem is precluded by economic forces over which it is impossible to exercise control. The other is that lack of policy and determination rather than inexorable external constraints have been the crucial factors in the failure to use prison labor efficiently. Although the problem of prisoners' work and prison industry has commonly been viewed as peripheral to penal policy, it is in fact a key issue. The barriers to a rational solution to this problem are not impenetrable; effective political intervention is possible.

The prison labor problem is not confined to America. The 1955 United Nations report, *Prison Labor,* asserted: "International penitentiary congresses have debated the employment of prisoners since the middle of the last century; the general economic and social changes which have taken place throughout the world since have increased rather than diminished the urgency of this question, as shown by the fact that later international congresses devoted more and more time to complaints concerning idleness and competition. . . . Conversely, however, there are few aspects of prison administration on which specific information

Gordon Hawkins is associate professor of criminology and director of the Institute of Criminology at the University of Sydney. Norman A. Carlson, Daniel Glaser, James B. Jacobs, Franklin E. Zimring, and the editors of this volume commented on earlier drafts of this essay and helped to improve it.

is less evident in standard penological reference works or official reports" (United Nations 1955, p. ix).

The report covered thirty-eight countries. It found, inter alia, that complaints by free workers and entrepreneurs against unfair competition from prison labor had led, in most developed states, to the curtailment of productive output, the adoption of make-work expedients, and the organization of industrial operations "along deliberately archaic or economically inappropriate lines"; that vocational or trade training was "available only to a very small minority of prisoners"; that the employment of prisoners on public works was "very limited"; and that "the amounts paid to working prisoners are extremely small, with very few exceptions" (United Nations 1955, pp. 9, 37, 47 and 65).

Since 1955 no comparable international survey has been conducted and only desultory, scattered items of information have become available. There is nothing to suggest that the general situation has substantially changed or appreciably improved. The prison labor problem remains one of the central unresolved issues relating to the use of imprisonment as a penal method. This essay discusses principally the nature of that problem in America. It argues for the revival and implementation of the concept of the industrial prison where prisoners are employed in paid, productive work.

Section I demonstrates the central importance of prison industrial policy issues and deals with the way in which twentieth-century treatment ideology reinforced the long-standing tradition of opposition to, and neglect of, prison industries. Section II disputes the view that the prison labor problem is insoluble because "economic forces" preclude industrial development in prisons and argues that it is based on a perverse misreading of the historical evidence. Section III adduces evidence that the greatest obstacle to the rational organization of prison industry has been and continues to be the power of penal policy and principles, in particular the principle of less eligibility, rather than economic or fiscal factors. Section IV examines a number of internal and external factors commonly said to obstruct the development of efficient systems for the utilization of prison labor in profitable prison industries. It concludes that none of them represent real obstacles to the establishment of viable prison industries. Section V deals with the remuneration of prisoners and argues that prisoners' wages should parallel those paid for similar work outside prison. Section VI outlines the rationale for the organization of industrial prisons and defines the purposes to be served by effective prison work programs. Section VII, in conclusion, urges that an unusual opportunity is presented at this time for effective political intervention aimed at achieving the development of efficient prison industries and the profitable employment of prison labor.

I. Idleness and Inertia

According to article 23 of the United Nations' Universal Declaration of Human Rights, "Everyone has the right to work" (Brownlie 1981, p. 139). Although not all human beings are equally anxious to exercise that right, few would totally renounce it, even if it were not their only means of obtaining a livelihood. In *Civilization and Its Discontents*, Freud described work not only as a means of "fending off suffering" but also as "a path to happiness" and asserted that "[N]o other technique for the conduct of life attaches the individual as firmly to reality as laying emphasis on work; for his work at least gives him a secure place in a portion of reality, in the human community" (1962, pp. 26–27).

Ex cathedra pronouncements are no substitute for argument and evidence. But the development since the late nineteenth century of the technique of occupational therapy, including the introduction into hospitals of workshops and industrial programs, indicates that work is now generally recognized as salutary in the quite specific sense that it forms a valuable part of the treatment of both physical and severe mental disorders. There would today be little dispute that regular work (if coupled with protection against health hazards and occupational diseases) can help to promote and maintain health.

Moreover, the view that the significance of work and the extent of "self-realization" at work have greatly diminished as a result of industrial and technological development seems to rest on an idyllic conception of preindustrial society that bears little relation to historical reality. For the great mass of people, battling for survival in a subsistence economy is unlikely to have been an especially enriching experience.

For many people it is likely that much of the satisfaction obtained from work derives not so much from the nature of that work as from the fact that it is their major source of status and of a sense of adult independence. Conversely, unemployment creates childlike dependence on others. Also, most human beings are inclined by nature to companionship, and the opportunities for informal sociability with their fellows afforded by work are often a major component of its rewards. Possibly the most punitive aspect of the nineteenth century's "Separate" and "Silent" systems of prison discipline was that, although work was provided, both systems were designed to prevent congenial association between prisoners.

Today, by contrast, prisoners are far more likely to be able to associate freely than to be able to work. In recent years they have achieved some success in securing civil rights but not the right to work set out in the United Nations' declaration. Yet legally there is no reason to regard the prisoner's right to work as canceled unless the criminal law expressly provides otherwise.

The place of work in the prison community has always been problematic, although the significance of the nexus between work and imprisonment and the crucial importance of the problem of prisoners' work and prison industry have been recognized by penologists from Jeremy Bentham to Thorsten Sellin. In the two centuries separating the publication of the former's *A View of the Hard Labour Bill* (1778) and the latter's *Slavery and the Penal System* (1976), the importance of that problem did not diminish. Yet it has been neglected by penologists and policymakers, exacerbated by legislative restrictions, and a perennial frustration to prison administrators.

The long-term head of British prisons, Sir Lionel Fox, described the prisoner employment problem as "recurrently posed and left unsolved ever since serious attention was first given to it" (Fox 1952, p. 184). Despite this, surprisingly little attention was paid to it by criminal justice scholars and policymakers until very recently. Neither the 1967 President's Commission's *Task Force Report: Corrections* nor the 1973 National Advisory Commission on Criminal Justice Standards and Goals report *Corrections* devotes more than two pages (out of 222 and 636 pages, respectively) to the subject.

How is this neglect of a matter of such critical consequence to be explained? Somewhat paradoxically, a major factor in this latter-day indifference seems to have been the general acceptance in penological circles of the reformist or treatment approach to imprisonment. Prima facie there seems to be no reason why the development of purposeful and efficiently organized industrial programs in prisons should be impeded by the adoption of reformist principles. The place of work in a treatment regime was succinctly defined by Grünhut: "The object of prison labour in a rehabilitative program is twofold: training for work and training by work" (Grünhut [1948], p. 269; to like effect, see United Nations [1956], p. 72). The idea was simply that one way or another work should be an instrument of the restoration of offenders to a law-abiding life.

In theory the organization of efficient industrial programs seemed not merely to be consonant with the adoption of rehabilitative regimes in prison but to represent a valuable adjunct to that development. In practice, however, a less harmonious relationship prevailed. Arguments arose over the question of the priority of prison work over what were called "more direct treatment programs" (Sutherland and Cressey 1960, p. 526).

Arguments among practitioners in the workplace were translated into the theoretical arena, where the treatment ideology was dominant. Walter Reckless, in *The Crime Problem*, argued strongly for priority of treatment over industry. In future, he wrote, "work must be relegated to secondary importance, to be done when not interfering with the schedule of attitude and habit retraining. . . . [T]here must be no interference with the main business of the prison or reformatory—namely social re-education" (Reckless 1950, p. 439). Sutherland and Cressey said that while it "cannot be argued that prison labor has no rehabilitative effects . . . it is doubtful that labor is the most important activity which is, or could be, provided for the reformation of prisoners." Prison industries, they said, "become monsters which inmates must serve" (Sutherland and Cressey 1960, p. 527).

It should be said here that the hostile attitude of many penologists and penal reformers in America in both the nineteenth and twentieth centuries toward prison industries no doubt derived in part from revulsion at the exploitative character of the principal systems of convict employment. For example, one of the major systems was the lease system under which the state, in return for an agreed sum, abdicated almost all direct supervision and control of prisoners to contractors who agreed to take the prisoner, house, feed, and clothe him, and prevent his escape. This system, which continued in operation in some Southern states until the early 1920s, led to a degree of abuse and exploitation said to "rank with that of the old Egyptian taskmasters in the annals of Scripture" (Mohler 1925, p. 563).

A hostile attitude toward prison work was not confined to America. In Britain a similar approach prevailed. (See Great Britain Home Office 1960, p. 23; Howard 1960, p. 153; Cooper and King 1965a, pp. 8–9). More recently Richard Sparks, writing about "the extent to which profitable industrial work can be carried out in a prison," says, "Of course, even where such work is economically possible it may be that it should be subordinated to other things, such as the reform of offenders" (1971, p. 102). In the event, such subordination has been widely practiced. "Within the range of institutional activities available to a correctional inmate," wrote Dr. E. S. Lightman, "participation in an industrial programme has traditionally ranked among the least important. . . . [F]or many years prison industries have been primarily viewed as a residual activity, directed towards those inmates not involved in the more significant tasks of educational upgrading or vocational training" (1982, p. 36).

The attitudes of progressive penologists merely reinforced long-standing traditions. Opposition to productive labor by prisoners is as old as the penitentiary system itself. As early as 1801 the New York legislature passed restrictive legislation designed to reduce competition from prison industries (Lewis 1967, p. 48). The establishment of the successful and widely imitated factory system in Auburn Prison, New York, in 1823–24 initiated a century-long struggle culminating in federal legislation—the Hawes-Cooper Act (1929), 49 U.S.C. § 60, and the Ashurst-Sumners (1935) and Sumners-Ashurst (1940) Acts, 18 U.S.C. 1761, 49 Stat. 494 and 54 Stat. 1134—and legislation in some thirty states restricting the sale of prison-made goods. This "vast array of restrictions . . . crippled prison production and finally forced the abandonment of the open-market system of employing prisoners" (Flynn 1951, p. 239).

Nor did the shift from the open market to state-use markets put an end to opposition. Another piece of federal legislation, the Walsh-Healy Act 1936, 41 U.S.C. § 35, forbade the use of convict labor in connection with government contracts exceeding $10,000. State use was narrowly defined, and compulsory purchase statutes were ignored or evaded. Pressure from manufacturers, merchants, and organized labor combined with "the apathy or outright hostility of the public" led to a stagnant situation in prisons in the 1935–40 period described as "a slow motion picture, in which idleness, actual or thinly disguised, was the appalling, scandalous common denominator of prison life" (Flynn 1951, p. 241).

There followed a brief but instructive interlude. At the time of Pearl Harbor the situation in prison industry was "scandalous, baffling and demoralizing" (Barnes 1944, p. 3). Then in July 1942 President Roosevelt issued an executive order, entitled "Government Purchases of Prison-made Goods," which permitted the federal government to procure from federal, state, or territorial prisons any goods needed for the war effort (Exec. Order No. 9196, 7 Fed. Reg. 5,291 (1942)). The War Production Board set up, within its Government Division, a Prison

Industries Branch to implement this policy. No full account of what followed is available. But a 1944 War Production Board report, *Prisons in Wartime*, provides, along with martial "consciousness raising" (e.g., "Patriotism has swept through our penal institutions and has fired the hearts of our prisoners"), some relevant although regrettably ill organized and incomplete information regarding state prison production in that period.

The value of total state prison industrial production before Pearl Harbor averaged $15.5 million per year. The exact extent of the increase in production which followed the federal government initiative is not clear, but in the first half of 1944 state prisons produced nearly $18 million worth of industrial products for war use alone. The record in relation to agricultural production is equally striking. The value of state prison farm products increased by nearly 28 percent in 1942, compared with a 16 percent increase in farm production for the country as a whole. By 1943 prison farm production had been doubled, increasing from nearly $19 million in 1941 to nearly $38 million (Barnes 1944, pp. 2, 31, 97).

The report concludes with an expression of hope that "in the days after combat has ceased" there will not be a relapse "into the do-nothing era which will bring demoralization to prisoners, added administrative problems to prison officials and mounting tax burdens to the public" (Barnes 1944, p. 96). But in the aftermath of war President Truman revoked Roosevelt's order (Exec. Order No. 9859, 12 Fed. Reg. 3,557 (1947)), and there was a swift return to the idleness of prewar conditions (Flynn 1951, pp. 238, 244, 260).

Over twenty years later the most recent national commission to survey the American correctional system as a whole found that "only a few offenders in institutions have productive work." Once again attention was drawn to "the idleness characteristic of American corrections" (National Advisory Commission 1973, pp. 388, 584).

II. "Economic Forces" and Penal Policy

The historical record has induced some observers to regard the prison employment problem as insoluble. Rusche and Kirchheimer provided the classic statement of this view: "The house of correction reached a peak under mercantilism and gave great impetus to the development of the new method of production. The economic importance of the house of correction then disappeared with the rise of the factory system. . . . [T]he transition to modern industrial society, which demands the freedom of labor as a necessary condition for the productive employment of labor power, reduced the economic role of convict labor to a minimum" (Rusche and Kirchheimer 1939/1968, pp. 6–7). In short, as Thorsten Sellin summarizes, "[T]he demands of the labor market shaped the penal system and determined its transformation over the years, more or less unaffected by theories of punishment in vogue" (Sellin 1976, p. vii).

The explanation offered in this rather schematic account of the decline and dissolution of prison industry is not entirely clear. But Rusche and Kirchheimer indicate that the decisions and deeds of men were not significant factors in shaping the course of events which were the inevitable product of "social forces, above all economic and then fiscal forces" (1939, p. 5). Neither the irrelevance of human choice and action nor the inevitability of what is said to have happened are demonstrated; they are simply asserted. In fact, the notion of the human race being pushed around by "forces" is here merely a metaphor which bears little relation to what actually happened.

Rusche and Kirchheimer's analysis seemed plausible because it fitted the industrial situation in prisons at that time. There is no doubt that the introduction of restrictive federal legislation, the Hawes-Cooper Act of 1929 and the Ashurst-Sumners Act of 1935, and the subsequent state legislation were largely due to economic factors. The passage of such legislation obviously reflected the fact that the whole American economy was in a state of depression. It is true that "[t]he penal system of any given society is not an isolated phenomenon subject to its own special laws" (Rusche and Kirchheimer 1939, p. 207). It would be ludicrous to suggest that the organization and development of prison industry could be wholly insulated from the influence of economic developments in the world outside the walls.

But it is even more ludicrous to suggest that the state of the economy or economic forces wholly determine penal policy. The suggestion that "the transition to modern industrial society . . . reduced the economic role of convict labor to a minimum" (Rusche and Kirchheimer 1939, pp. 6–7) is plainly at variance with the historical record, as is the suggestion that the demise of the profit-sharing prison factories at the end of the nineteenth century in England was simply a matter of the operation of market forces.

Consider the first suggestion for a moment. In Britain the Industrial Revolution had been essentially completed by 1850 with that country solidly established as the world's greatest industrial power. But this did not put an end to the productive employment of prison labor; the reverse was the case. The Industrial Revolution did not halt outside the prison gates. Indeed, the nineteenth century saw a remarkable expansion of prison industry.

What happened is recounted in Sydney and Beatrice Webb's detailed history of English prisons under local government. They list the prisons at Wakefield, Preston, Manchester, Bedford, Chelmsford, Maidstone, Bodmin, Lewes, Warwick, Coldbath Fields, and Holloway among others as the scene of "the greatest manufacturing and trading developments." They describe them as follows:

> In the West Riding gaol at Wakefield, for instance, right down to 1878, the manufacture of mats of all kinds produced a gross revenue of £40,000 a year. Elsewhere clothes were made up for contractors: all sorts of brushes were manufactured for home and foreign markets; there were extensive boot and shoe manufacturers; and large sales were made of various other articles. Steam-power was often employed, and extensive machinery provided. "Trade Managers" as well as instructors (who acted as foremen) were engaged at substantial salaries, with additional bonuses dependent on the profits of the undertaking.

From these "most extraordinary developments of profit-making enterprise" both the staff of prisons and prisoners benefited.

> Governors and warders were also encouraged to promote the enterprise, to the inevitable detriment of prison discipline, by being themselves allowed to share in the profits. In some cases commercial travellers were employed to effect sales, and even agents in foreign countries. The prisoners were naturally encouraged to work by special bonuses and gratuities, and sometimes actually paid at piece-work prices. The trade managers, as well as the governors, were entrusted with these awards; and diligent prisoners were also given additional food, even to the extent, occasionally, of meals of hot mutton chops. [Webb and Webb 1922, pp. 197–98]

When we ask what put an end to these developments, it is clear that the elegant simplicity of the economic determinists' road map is a poor guide to the itinerary actually followed. It is clear that it was largely a matter of penal policy, in particular what the Webbs refer to as the "fetish of uniformity."

The policy of uniformity of treatment of prisoners was embodied in the Prisons Act of 1865. But the Home Office administrators were not in a position to implement it because the hundred or more local prisons were under the control of the County Justices and Municipal Corporations, many of whom believed firmly that prisons should be self-supporting. However, by the Prisons Act of 1877 (40 and 41 Victoria, chap. 21) the ownership and control of all the local prisons was vested in the home secretary.

This act did not in fact prohibit the employment of prisoners on productive work. The preamble to the section relating to labor says that the expense of maintaining prisoners might in part be defrayed by their labor. Nevertheless the Home Office "was plainly hostile to any development of industrial or remunerative labor," for the administration was convinced "that all efforts to make profit out of the prisoners' labor, by manufacturing goods for sale in the open market, inevitably led to gross inequalities in the treatment of prisoners" (Webb and Webb 1922, pp. 156, 196, 197, 204).

The Commissioners of Prisons appointed by the home secretary took the view that productive work which involved variable rewards to prisoners according to the nature of their employment was not consistent with the uniformity of deterrence at which they aimed. Accordingly, "[o]pportunity was taken to bring an end to the various profit-making enterprises of the local prisons. The bonuses and allowances to officers and prisoners were abolished and the foreign agents, the commercial travellers and most of the salaried trade instructors were dispensed with" (Webb and Webb 1922, pp. 205–7). But if it would be nonsense to argue that these events represent the operations of economic forces skillfully disguised as penological principles, it would be no less misleading to suggest that patterns of prison labor and the organization of prison industry are shaped wholly by the theories of punishment or penological principles which happen to be in vogue. Throughout prison history both economic and noneconomic factors have been interrelated in an extremely complex and variable fashion.

The present example is a case in point. Thus the preamble to the 1877 Prisons Act, while permitting "the exercise of and instruction in useful trades and manufactures," adds the rider, ". . . so far as may be consistent with a due regard on the one hand to the maintenance of the penal character of prison discipline, and on the other, to the avoidance of undue pressure on, or competition with, any particular trade or industry." It is clear from the Webbs' account that in the period 1865–77, Home Office administrators were not concerned only because the use of prisoners' labor led to inequalities in the treatment of prisoners and also to "practically unrestrained association among them." They were also worried about "what was becoming a matter of troublesome political agitation . . . complaints from employers and Trade Unions of the unfair competition of 'Prison Labour' " (Webb and Webb 1922, p. 196).

But to suggest that economic considerations were the predominant influence is perversely to misread the history of the prolonged controversy over penal labor in nineteenth-century England. For many of the protagonists economic considerations were not so much irrelevant as nonexistent. The attack on "the once-favourite panacea of profitable employment" at the beginning of the century was quite clearly grounded in penal theory. Neither George Holford, M.P. ("Work which is to produce profit will run counter to discipline and moral improvement"), nor Sydney Smith ("I would banish all the looms . . . and substitute nothing but the tread-wheel or the capstan, or some species of labor where the laborer could not see the results of his toil—where it is as monotonous, irksome and dull as possible") was in the least concerned about mercantile matters (Webb and Webb 1922, pp. 85, 88).

Moreover, at that time, before the takeover by the central government, the "irreconcilable divergences" which were manifest in theory were matched by an equal diversity in practice. "The whole field of prison industry ranged between institutions such as Coldbath Fields Prison, where a sternly punitive unproductive system of labour was enforced and those such as Wakefield, which aimed avowedly at fitting inmates for the pursuits of an industrious existence. Between these two extremes lay almost every kind of occupation" (Webb and Webb 1922, pp. 144–57).

In America, too, in the nineteenth century there was considerable diversity in the organization of prison labor; in a number of states (e.g., Arizona, Idaho, Delaware, Montana, Utah, and Wyoming) there were no convicts employed in productive labor at all (U.S. Department of Labor 1896, p. 443). The majority of prisons were operated on the contract system under which private contractors operated factories in prisons and paid the states for the convicts' labor. Through this system the Industrial Revolution and the substitution of machine industry for handicraft production entered American prisons and transformed prison industry. Many prisons became prosperous factories, and by the early 1870s eleven states defrayed the expenses of these institutions from the returns on the labor of their inmates (McKelvey 1977, pp. 94, 177).

The celebrated 1867 *Report on the Prisons and Reformatories of the United States and Canada* by Enoch Wines and Theodore Dwight, said to have had an impact on penal developments in America and Europe second only to John Howard's *State of the Prisons* (McKelvey 1977, p. 68), deplored the emphasis placed on production which caused the authorities to lose sight of the reformation of prisoners. The authors complain, "[W]e have had occasion to read hundreds of prison reports and other documents relating to prisons; and there are few of them whose perusal has not caused us pain. One string is harped upon *ad nauseam*—money, money, money. . . . Where one word is spoken for reformation, hundreds are spoken for revenue" (Wines and Dwight 1976, pp. 288–89). Wines, who was the most influential penal reformer of the period, denounced the contract system as perverting "the great work of the moral regeneration of the prisoners." "[T]his system of prison labor," he wrote, "opposes itself to all the great forces of reformation by which, if at all, the inmates of our prisons must be reclaimed, regenerated and reabsorbed into the mass of upright, industrious, and honourable citizens" (Wines 1968, p. 110).

The "determined attack upon the contract system by the prison reformers and penologists" (Mohler 1925, p. 561) was reinforced by attacks from both the new national trade unions and manufacturers. In 1878 a convention of hatmakers urged that "the chief purpose of imprisonment should be the reformation of the criminal" and demanded "the removal of machinery from prisons and employment of prisoners at hard labor only" (Hiller 1915, p. 256). In 1886 the Knights of Labor made a strong pronouncement against the competition of convict labor, and in the same year presidents of wagon factories and of shoe, furniture, and stove companies gathered in Chicago, organized the National Anti-Convict-Contract Association (Mohler 1925, p. 569, 570), and "frankly unveiled their interest in eliminating the unfair competition of their rivals" (McKelvey 1977, p. 120).

This kind of opposition is often seen as purely a matter of economic self-interest, but there was evidently also an element of what has been called "moral prejudice" (Mohler 1925, p. 572). Thus, in the labor unions there were those who felt that the "hard-working and honest mechanic is insulted by having felons put on an equal footing with him. The ranks of his trade are not filled with reputable and worthy men like himself, but with the outpourings of the penitentiaries, including thieves, robbers, murderers and villains of the lowest type" (American Prison Association 1887, p. 248).

As a result of combined attacks by penal reformers, trade unionists, and manufacturers, the value of goods produced under the contract system decreased from approximately $17 million in 1885 to approximately $8 million in 1895 (U.S. Department of Labor 1896, p. 446). A number of states, including Illinois, Massachusetts, New York, Pennsylvania, and South Dakota, abolished the contract system altogether (Mohler 1925, p. 579). Thus in America, as in England, we find that a combination of diverse factors at a particular juncture of circumstances led to the contraction of prison industries.

It is because penal history is so full of developments which cannot be shoehorned into a simplistic economic interpretation that Mannheim is able to give so many examples of developments in penal methods which "show no connection whatsoever with such [i.e., economic] factors" (Mannheim 1939, pp. 36–53). In this context perhaps the most notable of these is the Pennsylvania system and its analogues throughout the world. In this case it is clear that the absence of work for prisoners derived directly from a commitment to a specific body of penal principles originating in America and leading to a situation in which in "many of the larger European institutions a doctrinal adherence to the cellular system resulted in a lack of appropriate workshops and other facilities for industrial or agricultural work" (Grünhut 1948, p. 196).

There are two principal reasons why the organization and development of prison industry have often followed a course unrelated to trends in the national economy. The first is simply that, in terms of the production of wealth or the provision of goods and services, the amount of work done in prisons has never been of more than marginal and local significance. Moreover, even at the optimal feasible level of development it could never be more than that.

The point is not a new one. Elizabeth Fry made it in the early years of the penitentiary system. "[T]he benefit which society derives from the employment of criminals greatly outweighs the inconvenience which can possibly arise to the mass of our labouring population from the small proportion of work done in our prisons" (quoted in Fry 1951, p. 51). A century later the Gladstone Committee heard evidence that the conversion of *all* prisoners from nonproductive to productive labor "would only increase the interference of prison with outside labour in the proportion of 1 to 2,500" (Great Britain Home Department 1895, p. 22).

In 1940 it was reported that, compared with the corresponding branches of free industries, American prison workshops produced "goods of the total value of 0.38 per cent the output of the same trades in the community during the preceding year" (U.S. Department of Labor 1940, p. 24). In 1973, economist Neil Singer estimated that an expansion of work-release programs to accommodate some 375,000 prison inmates, out of an estimated 500,000 in custodial institutions, would represent an increase in the labor force of only 0.4 percent (Singer 1973*b*, p. 210). Such estimates are indices only, but they all point to the fact that even the fullest imaginable utilization of the productive capacity of prisoners would represent a minimal addition to the gross national product.

The second reason why prison industrial policy has, from the days of Bentham's Panopticon scheme, often developed independently of the outside economy is that prisons are primarily penal institutions, and even Bentham, who was extremely concerned about "pecuniary economy," never questioned that such considerations had to be subordinated to the other "several objects or ends of penal justice" (Bentham 1843, pp. 47, 174). It is this which explains why the history of punishment provides so many "instances when, for good or for evil, powerful ideas crossed and even superseded rational and economic considerations" (Grünhut 1948, p. 197).

In making social policy decisions it is usual for a great many factors to be taken into account. In relation to punishment policy in particular, it frequently happens that the decision-making process involves attention to a variety of principles: jurisprudential, ethical, political, economic, and some which are purely penal in that they derive from the nature of punishment itself.

One such principle—the principle of less eligibility—is one of the most potent ideas to have exercised influence on penal practice. It has also had so pervasive an effect in relation to the employment of prisoners that neither the past history nor the present predicament of prison industry can be understood if the operation of this principle is not taken into account.

III. The Principle of Less Eligibility

In his discussion, in *Inside the Whale*, of Henry Miller's novel *Tropic of Cancer*, George Orwell draws a distinction between "the Geneva language of the ordinary novel" and "the *realpolitik* of . . . everyday facts and everyday emotions" (Orwell 1940, p. 137). This contrast between Geneva language and *realpolitik* is nowhere more marked than in the field of punishment. It is most striking when one compares academic discussion of the theory of punishment with the "everyday facts and everyday emotions" one encounters in public reactions to crime and criminals.

There are a number of popular ideas or assumptions about punishment which have exercised a considerable influence on penal practice and yet rarely figure in the writings of those engaged in trying to meet "the need for a tenable justification for penal measures" (Walker 1980, p. viii). Indeed, when they are noticed they are mentioned only for the purpose of drawing attention to their inadequacy or their irrelevance to serious discussion. Thus, in *Struggle for Justice*, one of the best-known modern arguments for penal reform, the public is variously described as showing "a curious insensitivity" to the sufferings of prisoners, as thinking that "criminals are being treated too well," and as being "profoundly punitive." But what the authors refer to as "the perversity of adverse public opinion" is not seen as a matter for serious consideration (American Friends Service Committee 1971, pp. 47, 86, 94, 155).

Policymakers are more sensitive to the pervasiveness of such sentiments. Correctional administrators, too, often feel that they "cannot afford to get out of touch with the common sense of the community as a whole," and one of the most thoughtful of them identified a number of popular assumptions underlying public attitudes toward punishment. One of those assumptions, the principle of less eligibility, "the justness" of which is said to be "deeply ingrained in common thought about the treatment of convicted prisoners," is especially relevant here (Fox 1952, pp. 131–33).

The most authoritative formulation of the principle of less eligibility is that of the Webbs in their *English Poor Law Policy*: "That the condition of the able-bodied pauper should be less eligible than that of the lowest class of independent labourer." They derived it from what they refer to as a "dogmatic assertion" in a Royal Commission report in 1834 that the situation of the pauper should not be made "really or apparently so eligible as the situation of the independent labourer in the lowest class" (Webb and Webb 1910, pp. 1, 83). It is not difficult to understand why this principle, which was incorporated in the Poor Law Amendment Act of 1834, should be accepted as also applying to the penal system.

Indeed, it represented no more than a variant of an earlier prescription for penal discipline enunciated by Jeremy Bentham in his *Panopticon, or The Inspection House* (1791). In that work Bentham specified that "saving the regard due to life, health, and bodily ease, the ordinary condition of a convict doomed to a punishment . . . ought not to be made *more eligible* than that of the poorest class of subjects in a state of innocence and liberty." Or to put it, as Bentham did, even more briefly, "the lot of delinquents [should] not be raised above that of the innocent at large" (Bentham 1843, pp. 122–24).

Those concerned primarily with penal practice rather than penal philosophy most clearly assert the significance of the principle of less eligibility. Rusche and Kirchheimer refer to it as the "notion that the standard of living within the prison must be below the minimum standard outside" or as "the tendency against raising the prisoner's level of existence to that of the outside world." They describe it as "the leitmotiv of all prison administration down to the present time" (i.e., 1939) and as a principle which "no reform program has been willing to abandon" (1939, pp. 94, 151, 155, 159).

Similarly, Mannheim, writing in the late 1930s, observed that "it is becoming increasingly obvious that this old idea still represents the most formidable obstacle in the way of Penal Reform." He portrays penal administrators as engaged in a hazardous struggle to avoid any prisoner equivalence which would imperil society. "Every *deterioration* in the economic conditions of the *population at large*, as well as every *improvement* in *prison conditions* was bound to lead to an approximation of the conditions to an undesirable equality, which, according to common belief, would result in an explosion and in the collapse of the penal department of the social fabric" (1939, p. 59).

Thirty-five years later, Noel McLachlan, writing on progress in penal reform, found that "the old Poor Law principle of 'less eligibility,' the penal implications of which Mannheim drew attention to long ago, clearly still applies" (1974, p. 6). In *The Future of the Prison System*, published in 1980, the authors describe current, widely held, "considerable reservations about the standard of life that prisoners should be able to enjoy" as "best seen as a manifestation of the old Poor Law principle of 'less eligibility' " (King and Morgan 1980, p. 164).

It might be expected that the application of the principle in prisons would be most clearly exemplified in relation to such matters as physical comfort and food. "Food," wrote Bentham in this connection, "is the grand article" (1843, p. 123). And even nineteenth-century prison reformer Matthew Davenport Hill considered "the mischiefs that flow" from too liberal a jail diet to be "very fatal indeed" (Webb and Webb 1922, p. 133). But it will have required little managerial effort to ensure that food in prisons did not infringe the canon of less eligibility. In fact, it is not in relation to prison diet, but rather to prison industry, that adherence to less eligibility has had its most fundamental and enduring effect.

"Almost throughout its whole history prison labour has been denounced by trade and free labour as unfair competition" (Grünhut 1948, p. 225). Mannheim saw the principle as presenting "in the province of *Prison Labour* . . . the key to an understanding of what is one of the most depressing aspects of the penal problem" and also as representing "the greatest obstacle in the development of efficient methods of prison labour" (1939, pp. 75, 100). Even Rusche and Kirchheimer emphasized the persistence and potency of this principle in this context: "Prison labor remains a central problem. . . . The opposition is so strong both from the business world and from the trade unions that convict labor is generally limited. . . . Wages for convict labor are opposed on the same grounds as productive prison labor in general. Paying wages would mean placing such work more or less on the same level as free labor" (1939, pp. 152–53).

The contrast between Geneva language and *realpolitik*, between theory and practice, is strikingly exemplified in the relation between the prison labor problem and the question of less eligibility. We find Mannheim, at a time when "all progressive penal experts" were rejecting the notion of "an artificially contrived principle of less eligibility," saying that "belief in the justice and inevitability of the principle" was so deeply rooted in the community that the translation into practice of ideas contrary to it was not feasible (Mannheim 1939, pp. 70, 96). Similarly Fox, as chairman of the English Prison Commission, expressly repudiated the principle of less eligibility. It was, he wrote, "not [one of] the assumptions on which contemporary prison administration is based." Yet when he came to deal with the problem of work in prisons, "this central problem of prison administration," he recognized that a satisfactory solution to the problem was precluded by the operation of that principle (Fox 1952, pp. 130, 176, 184).

In America the most striking manifestation of the principle is in the substantial body of state and federal law which restricted prisoner employment, apart from the institutional maintenance work, to manufacturing goods for government use or to state public works. Although this restrictive legislation proliferated during the 1930s depression, the earliest laws of this type were introduced in 1801, and the 1930s legislation represented the culmination of a century-long campaign. What Mannheim calls the "obstinate resistance clothed in a passionate appeal" to the principle of less eligibility (Mannheim 1939, p. 96) is more than a mere reflex response to a particular set of economic conditions. Inevitably, though, passionate appeals to that principle are more audible in periods of economic recession.

Attempts have been made to interpret this principle as in some sense a function of the relations of production. It has been described as "the essential mechanism which locked the prison system into the changing class relations and forces of the nineteenth century . . . the key practical and ideological resolution to the critical problems of class discipline and control which arose in the eighteenth century and persisted for much of the nineteenth century" (Hogg 1980, p. 64). Even if this were a satisfactory account of the function of the less eligibility principle in the eighteenth and part of the nineteenth century, it utterly fails to account for its continued influence throughout the twentieth century.

What emerges from any serious examination of the history of prison labor is that frequently the determining factors are largely divorced from economic considerations. This is not to say that economic conditions are irrelevant. But opposition to prisoners doing work that *might* (even if only in theory) be carried out by free and honest citizens, or manufacturing goods that could be produced by private industry, is not a function of the trade cycle.

A significant example of the persistence of opposition to the employment of prisoners, even in a period of acute manpower shortage, occurred in Germany in the late 1930s. The government had passed decrees designed to secure systematic utilization of prison labor and ensure that prisoners should take their full share in the work of the Four Year Plan. Despite this, and despite the great scarcity of agricultural labor, worsened by the introduction of two-year military service, free peasants and farm laborers were vigorously opposed to the employment of prisoners on the land (Mannheim 1939, pp. 81–83). The peasantry's opposition was not based on economic self-interest. They badly needed assistance, for they had been deprived of their sons by military conscription. One of their principal objections was that it would have meant "a loss of social status to the free peasant and farm labourer if prisoners [were] allowed to do the same kind of work on the land" (Mannheim 1939, p. 83). Until it is recognized that it is the pursuit of policies reflecting considerations of this nature, rather than economic forces, which constitutes the principal stumbling block to the profitable employment of prisoners, the problem will continue to be misunderstood and unresolved.

IV. Other Aspects of a Rational Solution to
the Prison Labor Problem

The failure to develop efficient systems for the utilization of prison labor in prison industries is not due to the inherent intractability of the problem. Indeed, when the difficulties which are commonly said to stand in the way of its solution are analyzed it is clear that, taken singly, not one of them represents an insuperable impediment.

A. Internal Problems

1. *The Prison Work Force.*   Consider first what is frequently said to be "the most serious difficulty . . . the low working-ability of the average prison population" (Grünhut 1948, p. 223). Assertions about the inferiority of the prison work force are common in the literature, but, unlike Cesare Lombroso's claims (1912) about the poor physique and mental capacity of the criminal, they are never supported by evidence which can be subjected to critical examination. Nor is any such evidence available. The historical evidence is that when work and reasonable incentives are present the performance of the prison work force is at least as good as that of free human material. What we have here is an echo of the cry which is invariably heard in the community at large in times of economic recession and high unemployment: "The unemployed are the unemployable." The fact that the unemployed miraculously become employable when the recession ends passes unremarked.

There is one piece of historical evidence which graphically illustrates the tenuous character of this supposed obstacle to industrial development in prisons. In 1895 the Gladstone Committee report commenting on "the capacities of prisoners" said: "[The prison population] is of a low order of physical and mental development, it is constantly changing, and in short presents no favorable feature whatever for the development of industrial work" (Great Britain Home Department 1895, p. 22). This was written less than twenty years after the British prison administration had as a matter of deliberate policy forced the closure of flourishing prison industries throughout the country.

More recently, in America, the evidence available about the operations of the Free Venture prison industry programs (see below) lends no support to the notion that there is some intrinsic deficiency in the prison labor force. It has been found that productive abilities of prison labor are "comparable to similarly skilled employees in the world outside prison" (Schaller 1982, p. 12).

2. *Prison Industrial Operations.* The second most frequent objection to prison industries' development is the claim that they are grossly inefficient (Grünhut 1948, pp. 224–25; California State Assembly 1969, passim; Singer 1973*a*, p. 201). Outdated equipment, obsolete machinery, poor organization, and antiquated work methods are given as the causes of this situation in which, according to the 1967 President's Commission, "in many cases the prison-made goods are inferior in design and workmanship to those available from private firms; their delivery has been unreliable; and despite . . . cheap prison labor, the state may still charge more than the price of the products on the open market" (President's Commission 1967*b*, p. 55).

There are in fact three principal causes for the inefficient operation of prison industries, and none is inherent in the conditions of work in prisons. All are matters of policy which can be changed. In the first place, prison administrators faced with large-scale prisoner unemployment may sometimes be reluctant to take advantage of technological advances which might increase it. Therefore prison industrial operations frequently take the form of wasteful busywork programs. This has led to what a California Assembly Office of Research report on correctional industries called "the planned unreality of working conditions inside an industrial system *that must deliberately aim at inefficiency*" (California State Assembly 1969, p. 7; emphasis added).

In the second place, acquisition of advanced technology commonly requires substantial capital investment, which may not be available. It does not follow from this that the prison industrial system must aim at inefficiency, but rather that correctional industries will often have to be labor, rather than capital, intensive. In the third place, when efficiency is required it may not be achieved because industrial management personnel in prisons frequently have a low level of experience and competence. The kind of unqualified supervisory staff characteristic of "the typical prison industry" has been described as composed of "individuals trained as corrections officers with limited technical skills, no experience in a production environment and an unwillingness to relate to their subordinates as employees rather than as inmates" (U.S. Department of Justice 1981, p. 1). This situation has arisen because correctional authorities customarily follow the traditional practice of promotion within the service. They rarely recruit qualified persons from private industry to administer industrial programs. Here a change in policy, which would not require very substantial investment, is perfectly feasible.

3. *The Prison Workday.*   A third difficulty said to stand in the way of achieving free-world standards of productivity in penal institutions is the short workday, which in prison workshops and factories very seldom exceeds six hours and is generally much shorter (England 1961, p. 21). This is because of requirements relating to security and the demands of other institutional services and programs. However, this does not constitute an ineluctable obstruction. It has rarely been addressed seriously, simply because there has not often been any need to lengthen the hours of production.

When it is addressed, it is clear that it is an organizational problem which can be solved by giving industrial operations a degree of priority in prison schedules. In recent years many states have begun to deal with this problem by reorganizing meal services, introducing a "pre-order" system for commissary purchases, and rescheduling social worker and psychological activities to out-of-work hours. In these and other ways, by minimizing worker call-outs, they have moved toward securing hours of production comparable with free-world industry (Schaller 1981, pp. 225, 229–33).

B. External Problems

In addition to these internal obstacles, however, there are external factors which have presented persistent problems. These external factors are manifestations of the principle of less eligibility, in the form "of a law of non-competition" (Mannheim 1939, p. 76).

1. *The State-Use System.*   The confinement of prison industry to an exclusive state-use system need not lead, as it did in America in the 1930s, to the virtual elimination of the industrial prison (U.S. Department of Justice 1940, p. 34). In England in the same period it was also the case that work for prison purposes and for government departments was practically the whole of the work done in prisons (Great Britain Parliamentary Papers 1933, p. 17; 1935). Yet comparison of prisoner employment in Britain with that in America in 1939 revealed that "the percentage of prisoners productively employed varies between 74.2 in England and Wales and 43.5 in the United States, where one-fifth of all prisoners have no work at all. . . . England with a pre-war ratio of less than 10 per cent of prisoners without work, comes very near to the optimum of full employment" (Grünhut 1948, p. 200).

The explanation of these different results is simple and instructive. In America, as noted above, the government market was generally narrowly defined and "many seemingly broad laws" were "only pious expressions of goodwill." Moreover, although many American states adopted a compulsory system of state use, in practice "many compulsory-purchase statutes [were] easily evaded and others [were] just as easily ignored" (Flynn 1951, p. 244). But if state use were widely defined and compulsory purchase laws were strictly implemented, the government market should provide a very substantial outlet for prison productivity. The state, after all, is the biggest single consumer of all. The existence of big government entails the existence of a big market for products and services.

Twenty years ago it was estimated that, under a fully effective compulsory purchase state-use system, the total potential output of prison industries would meet the needs of only about 10 percent of that market. "On the average, if the correctional institutions could supply one-tenth of the total public institutional purchases in any year, all the able-bodied inmates could be put to work in productive enterprises. Thus a really effective state-use system could easily the solve the problem of prison labor and industry" (Barnes and Teeters 1959, p. 531).

Furthermore, the laws which restrict prison labor are, like all laws, subject to change. In 1951, it was said that "employment plans for today's correctional institutions must be formulated within the framework of the existing rules" (Flynn 1951, p. 245). But in recent years the rules have been changing. In December 1979, Congress passed an amendment (Justice System Improvement Act of 1979, P.L. 96–157, 93 Stat. 1167, 1215) to lift restrictions on the sale of state prison products in interstate commerce, to improve correctional industry operations, and to encourage public and private sector interaction. This amendment has been described as "the first thing to come along in 30 years that has any potential to significantly change the face of prison industries" (Pennsylvania Prison Society 1982, p. 2).

2. *Unfair Competition.* There have also been many changes in prison industry practices. The tradition of implacable opposition to prison industrial development on the part of private manufacturers is passing. Under the Law Enforcement Assistance Administration (LEAA) Free Venture prison industry program, and in some cases quite independently, private industry involvement in prison industry has begun to develop. In some states work is already being done inside prisons under contracts with private industry; in many others, legislation to allow private industry to set up shops within prisons or to allow prison industries to sell their products on the open market has been passed (Schaller 1981, pp. 223, 230–33). In all, twenty states have authorized

some form of private sector involvement with state prison industries (Auerbach 1982, p. 6).

The LEAA Free Venture model aims at the establishment of prison industries which are as similar as possible to their private sector counterparts. Free Venture industries are characterized by six principles: a full work week for inmate employees; wages based on productivity; private sector productivity standards; responsibility for hiring or firing inmate workers vested with industries staff; self-sufficient or profitable shop operations; and a postrelease job placement mechanism (Schaller 1982, pp. 4–5).

During 1979, LEAA provided funding to seven states which have sought to implement the Free Venture principles in their prison industry shops: Colorado, Connecticut, Illinois, Iowa, Minnesota, South Carolina, and Washington. A recent review of the demographics of Free Venture industries revealed that

> there were twenty-one shops employing 555 inmates. Inmates so employed may represent as much as two-thirds of the institutional population, as at Minnesota/Lino Lakes, or as little as 2 or 3 percent (Minnesota/Stillwater; Connecticut/Enfield). Worker turnover was generally high, and involuntary transfers accounted for much of the problem. Work hours generally ranged between six and eight hours per day; wages were between $.20 and $3.74 per hour, though the majority of shops paid less than $.50 per hour. Several shops used bonuses, good-time accumulation, and other nonwage incentives. . . . 43 percent of the shops showed a profit during 1979. Based on this and a series of other measures, 14 percent of the shops were rated "good" in terms of economic viability, while 24 percent were rated "poor." [Funke, Wayson, and Miller 1982, pp. 63–64]

There were wide variations in the implementation of each of the programs. In Minnesota, for example, there was heavy reliance on private industry contracts, and the prison industries performed services for private companies that had contracted with Minnesota Correctional Industries.

Phase Two of the federally supported program known as the Prison Industries Enhancement Program (PIE), a second pilot project for seven states, requires the actual involvement of private business in correctional industries. The best known of the PIE operations is Zephyr Products, Inc., in Leavenworth, Kansas. The plant, built by the city and leased to the company, makes sophisticated metal parts for missiles, radios, television sets, and self-propelled combines. It employs thirty-five inmates and pays them the prevailing wage plus bonuses and stock options every three months they are on the job. In the first year of operation Zephyr lost money, but now it is running at a profit. Inmate productivity matches that of private industry (Pennsylvania Prison Society 1982, pp. 2–3).

It has been suggested that there are two principal reasons for this change in attitude on the part of private enterprise. First, small private manufacturers who feared prison competition have been largely replaced by larger manufacturers and industrial conglomerates which have no reason to fear the very limited competition of the typically small production unit in a prison setting in one state. Second, in recent years American manufacturers have been placing their labor-intensive industrial operations in overseas locations where cheaper Third World labor forces can be employed. However, such factors as the increasing cost of overseas labor, the expense of relocation, and the shipping expenses involved have caused some manufacturers to recognize that American prisons, with their abundant supply of labor, are an attractive alternative to foreign-based production.

So it is conceivable "that in the future, prison manufacturing operations will pose a greater threat to Hong Kong and Seoul than they do to Detroit or Pittsburgh. Jeremy Bentham's principle of 'lesser eligibility' has thus been turned inside out, with American prison labor's status enhanced at the expense of the foreign worker" (Schaller and Sexton 1979, p. 4). Jeremy Bentham, who firmly believed in the profitable employment of prisoners, might have approved of this particular triumph of pecuniary interest over penological principle.

Opposition to prison industrial operations, particularly to the use of prison labor in the production of goods sold on the free market, has not been confined to manufacturers. Historically trade unions have played a significant role in bringing about the decline of prison industries. Union opposition has often taken the form of principled objections, not to prisoner employment, but rather to prisoner exploitation (Mohler 1925, p. 573). But more recently the unions' principal rationale has been that "a tax-subsidized industry should not be placed in a position that would cause unemployment for a tax-paying worker" (Funke et al. 1982, p. 24).

It has been said that union "views and tolerance of prison labor have softened over time" (Funke et al. 1982, p. 23). Insofar as this is true, it may in part reflect the fact that in the present state of prison industries there is little to alarm even the most fearful unionist. Participation in the PIE program requires that local union central bodies be consulted before initiation of a project, and the project may not result in the displacement of employed free-world workers.

C. Federal Prison Industries, Inc.

Evidence that none of the obstacles discussed above preclude the successful operation of prison industries may be found in the history of Federal Prison Industries, Inc.—or UNICOR, as it is now known— a self-sustaining corporation established by Congress in 1934 which has completed nearly half a century of profitable manufacturing operations and has always maintained a sound financial position. With an average of approximately 6,000 inmates (or one-quarter of the total population of the federal prison system) employed daily in 1980, UNICOR paid over $11 million in wages and awards to inmates and provided almost $2.8 million for vocational training programs out of gross value sales of $117 million from which the net income was in excess of $6.7 million.

Over 20,000 individual inmates had worked at one time during the year, and some penitentiaries contain large industrial complexes which have provided work for up to half of their populations. With eighty industrial operations in thirty-seven institutions producing more than forty different types of products and services for other federal agencies and departments, UNICOR has not achieved complete success in pursuing its mandated goals of providing the work necessary to prevent idleness within the prisons as well as job-related training for inmates, useful to them on release. But it has demonstrated that a diversified program of industrial operations to keep offenders constructively employed and provide occupational knowledge and experience can be developed in penal institutions (U.S. Department of Justice 1980, pp. 1–3; 1981, p. 6). It should be added that a major contributory factor in the success of UNICOR is the fact that it enjoys a diversified national market and is a mandatory source of supply for all federal agencies; neither of those conditions applies to state prison industries.

V. Prisoners' Wages

One area in which the influence of the principle of less eligibility has had dramatic illustration is that of prisoners' earnings. With few exceptions, incentives to work have for prisoners been so meager as to be risible. Those occasional "meals of hot mutton chops" mentioned by the Webbs were no doubt welcome, but they hardly represent a substitute for regular remuneration. In America in 1923 the free laborer earned 53 cents per hour, while the inmate earned 3 cents per hour. By 1972 the discrepancy had not grown significantly smaller: free laborers in all areas of manufacturing earned $3.33 per hour; inmates earned 13–25 cents per hour (Funke et al. 1982, pp. 15–16).

In 1973 the National Advisory Commission on Criminal Justice Standards and Goals recommended that "inmates should be compensated for all work performed that is of economic benefit to the correctional authority or another public or private entity. As a long-range objective to be implemented by 1978, such compensation should be at rates representing the prevailing wage for work of the same type in the vicinity of the correctional facility" (National Advisory Commission 1973, p. 387).

This recommendation was not entirely novel. The history of penal reform is a continuous register of unfulfilled objectives both short term and long range. More than twenty years earlier, at the Twelfth International Penal and Penitentiary Congress in 1950, it was resolved that "prisoners should receive a wage. The Congress is aware of the practical difficulties inherent in a system of paying wages calculated according to the same norms that obtain outside the prison. Nevertheless, the Congress recommends that such a system be applied to the greatest possible extent. From this wage there might be deducted a reasonable sum for the maintenance of the prisoner, the cost of maintaining his family, and, if possible, an indemnity payable to the victims of his offense" (Fox 1952, p. 442).

This proposal seems so entirely reasonable that the near universal failure to implement it requires some explanation. Yet there are reasoned objections to this kind of wage-payment policy which are quite independent of the less eligibility rationale. In view of this, the case for paying prisoners wages parallel with outside levels of remuneration will first be outlined briefly. This will be followed by a statement of the principal objections to any attempt to realize that conception.

The first argument for paying outside remuneration rates to prisoners is simply "the common human experience, that adequate earnings are a stimulus to work and a visible expression of its successful performance" (Grünhut 1948, p. 211). Even Freud, whose remarks on the beneficial nature of work were quoted above, admitted that "men are not spontaneously fond of work" and that the great majority of human beings can only be induced to submit to it "by a certain degree of coercion" (1961, p. 8). It is relatively rare that the required coercive force comes from interest in the nature of the work itself. For most people it is provided by normal economic self-interest. It is ludicrous to expect prisoners who may be "a negative selection with regard to ability and inclination for regular work" (Grünhut 1948, p. 223) to display a disinterested devotion to ill-paid enforced labor.

The second argument is aptly expressed in the assertion that "the wages paid to prisoners define to them the value of the work they are doing" (Freedman and Pappas 1967, p. 5). In practice the wages paid to prisoners in America and throughout most of the world are so niggardly that they serve only to disparage or depreciate any expenditure of energy and effort. Such dole payments do not stimulate industry or self-respect but lead inevitably to indolence and apathy. As a result, measured by such indices as absenteeism and productivity, the prison work force generally rates very poorly.

Another argument for paying prisoners at outside levels of remuneration is that this would neutralize trade union opposition to prison industry and the marketing of prison products. In this connection Braithwaite maintains that "[I]t is likely that most union opposition to prison industry would evaporate if prisoners were paid award wages and joined the appropriate union. Union opposition to work release, even during periods of high unemployment is non-existent precisely because the prisoners are becoming union members" (Braithwaite 1980, p. 1963). Significantly, the PIE program requires that the prisoner workers receive wages in connection with the work they do at the prevailing local wage rate, minus up to 80 percent of gross wages for taxes, room and board, family support, and victim compensation funds.

The PIE requirement represents the adoption of the policy recommended by the Twelfth International Penal and Penitentiary Congress in 1950. It is a policy which has been subjected to much criticism that applies generally to the conception of "an economic wage" for prisoners. The most forceful statement is Fox's critique of the 1950 Congress resolution, which is best discussed by dealing with each of his principal points seriatim.

The first point is that such a scheme would mean that after a complicated piece of bookkeeping, in which the prisoner would exercise no personal choice, he would be given the small weekly balance due to him, arbitrarily determined by the authorities. This process would be artificial and would bear no "realistic and comprehensible relation to real life" (Fox 1952, p. 462).

Yet it is an exaggeration to suggest that a situation in which the weekly balance available for free spending is small compared with gross income bears no relation to ordinary life. That is precisely the situation of the vast majority of wage earners in the outside world. The amount of freely disposable income available after such commitments as house-keeping, rent or mortgage payments, income tax, payments on the car and other credit purchases, health insurance, school fees, subscriptions, and savings have been met is almost invariably small (indeed, sometimes nonexistent) in the life of most free workers. And for most prisoners, despite the limits on personal choice and decision, the operation of a prison earnings scheme will, in this respect at least, bear a remarkably "realistic and comprehensible relation to ordinary life."

It should be said that if prisoners under such a scheme were expected to defray the full costs of incarceration the weekly balance available after the deductions might be even less than they receive today. But the proposal is for the deduction of "a reasonable sum for the main-tenance of the prisoner" and is not intended to meet the actual cost of his imprisonment. The prisoner, like other citizens, contributes to that cost through the taxation system.

The second major criticism is that a prison is the kind of community in which "absolute fairness between man and man" is essential for successful management; yet any earnings scheme involving rewards for industry and efficiency would inevitably result in inequality and in-equity. Moreover it would violate the "basic principle" that, subject to certain variations applying to defined groups in accordance with stated principles, "every prisoner should be treated alike in respect of the material conditions of life" (Fox 1952, p. 198).

With regard to the principle that every prisoner should be treated alike in regard to material conditions, it is in practice invariably subject to so many variations that it is difficult to see why further variations should create a major managerial problem. Inequity, inequality, and anomaly are inherent in all punishment. Imprisonment as a punishment does not fall equally on all subjected to it. The degree to which any particular conditions of confinement are afflictive varies inevitably with the personality and prior experience of each prisoner. And even if it were possible to transform penal institutions into enclaves of absolute isonomy, that intrinsic inequity would not diminish; it would, for many prisoners, be reinforced.

In outside industry the payment of rewards for diligence and skill is generally accepted. Arbitrary and discriminatory departures from that practice, on the other hand, frequently provoke conflict and discontent. There is no evidence to suggest, or reason to believe, that the existence of a security wall around a factory would produce a radical change in that aspect of industrial relations. Free Venture operations involving wage-rate differentials have not encountered difficulties in this connection (Schaller 1982, p. 13). All that is required is that such differentials, like other variations in the conditions of prison life, should be in accordance with recognized principles.

Fox's third major criticism relates specifically to prisoners' wage levels. He maintains that the prisoner, and possibly his family also, are maintained at the public expense, and "it is unlikely that the product of the prisoner's work approaches that expense in value." It follows that "any payment at all is by way of an act of grace." His conclusion is that as the purpose of the payment of prisoners is the contribution it makes to morale and discipline, then "the least amount necessary to effect that purpose is the most that the taxpayer should be asked to pay" (Fox 1952, pp. 199–200).

The cogency of this argument, however, rests on the premise that the value of the product of prisoners' work is minimal, and while this may currently be true in most cases, it is not a necessary truth. Moreover, while the logic behind a refusal to pay prisoners wages parallel with wages paid for similar work in the free world, on the ground that they are less productive, may be impeccable, as a policy it is ethically dubious. For, although there may be prisoners who, as Mark Twain put it, "dislike work even when another person does it," prisoners in present conditions are rarely in a position to increase the value of their work even if they want to.

If prison-based manufacturing enterprises are unproductive or unprofitable, that is principally a function of their management and organization or of the marketing of their products rather than of the attitude, ability, or effort of prisoners. It cannot, therefore, be advanced as a justification for preserving a wage system under which prisoners are paid only a negligible gratuity for their work. Fox's argument might be acceptable if the development of efficient and profitable systems for the utilization of prison labor and the payment of outside levels of remuneration had been shown to be unfeasible, but that is not the case.

In principle, there are no valid objections to the PIE requirement that prisoners should be paid at prevailing local wage rates minus appropriate deductions for room and board, family support, taxes, and victim compensation funds. In many cases, however, the fiscal situation may render this impossible. Although the evidence indicates that inmate wage incentives can increase worker productivity 50–100 percent, the gains from increased productivity may not offset the costs of the system change for some years (Funke et al. 1982, p. 124). Nevertheless, in such cases the other most common incentive for inmate work, sentence reduction by earned good time, may be adopted during the interim. Indeed, where determinate sentencing laws do not preclude it, inmates might usefully be allowed the option of taking the balance of their earnings in the form of good-time credits (Smith 1965; Williams and Fish 1971; Miller 1981; Funke et al. 1982; Sexton 1982).

It has been said that "the primary policy question that controls the inmate compensation issue is: what purpose(s) is/are intended to be served by having inmates work?" (Funk et al. 1982, p. 121). The next section will be devoted to answering this question.

VI. Controlling Principles

The President's Commission on Law Enforcement and Administration of Justice has recommended "correctional industries programs aimed at rehabilitation of offenders through instilling good work habits and methods" (1967b, p. 176). This is a proposition that has never enjoyed unquestioning acceptance or approbation. In the nineteenth century it was repudiated on the ground that the provision of useful and interesting work might, by making prisons insufficiently deterrent, actually increase recidivism. Currently prison work programs, including vocational training, are deprecated along with educational programs, psychotherapy, counseling, group therapy, etc., not because they are thought to have deleterious effects but because it is believed that they have no significant effects whatever.

Both logical and historical analysis teach the same lesson. That long ignored and grossly neglected American philosopher, Alexander Bryan Johnson, made the essential point as long ago as 1836: "The search after the unit is the delusion" (Johnson 1836/1947, p. 77). Prisons have always been multipurpose institutions.

The diversity of penal purposes has been reflected in the history of prison industries. Prison labor has been seen and used in a variety of ways: as a means of restitution for victims; as a means of achieving the economic self-sufficiency of prisons; as a means both of afflicting the offender and of achieving his moral reformation; as a disciplinary device or even an incapacitatory one; as a mitigating factor contributing to physical and psychological well-being; and as part of a training program designed to facilitate reintegration on release. Only rarely and in isolated cases has one purpose been dominant to the exclusion of all others.

Any attempt to develop or elucidate a contemporary rationale for the organization of a prison industries program must begin by recognizing that an adequate formulation will necessarily be multivalent. Also, because of the centrality of prison labor to prison discipline and to all correctional activities (Grünhut 1948, p. 196; Funke et al. 1982, p. 123), the principles determining inmate labor organization must correspond, or at least not conflict, with the controlling principles of the correctional system.

If we ask what purposes would be served by the performance of, and payment for, work by prisoners in our time, it seems clear that at least three basic principles are involved: economy, the right to work, and rehabilitation. They are not novel ideas, but neither is the concept of the industrial prison. It is necessary to restate them in the context of the revival of that concept.

With regard to economy no lengthy exposition is required. It is the most obvious and simplest principle. To Jeremy Bentham its importance seemed self-evident. It was something that "ought not to be departed from" any further than was necessary to secure such objects or ends of penal justice as deterrence, reformation, or incapacitation (Bentham 1843, p. 174). No doubt it seemed equally self-evident to the sponsors of the Auburn system, in the days before general acceptance of or acquiescence in the idea that convicted criminals should be supported in idleness by their victims and other fellow citizens.

It has been estimated that in prisons operated under the Auburn plan with private contractors employing the inmates, the income obtained was sufficient to meet 65 percent of prison expenses (Mohler 1925, p. 550). In the late 1820s and early 1830s, Connecticut, Massachusetts, and Maryland all registered substantial net earnings over all expenses from their industrial prison operations (Lewis 1967, pp. 132–33). Moreover, the income received by the prison authorities is said to have been "meager . . . compared with the profits earned by the contractors" (Funke et al. 1982, p. 10). As late as 1870, at the celebrated Cincinnati Congress on Penitentiary and Reformatory Discipline Dr. Enoch Wines of the New York Prison Association was still maintaining "that prisons can be made self-sustaining and at the same time reformatory; and all the more reformatory *because* they are self-sustaining" (Wines 1871/1970, p. 449).

Wines was supported by Amos Pilsbury, superintendent of Albany Penitentiary, who argued that "there is *morality* in making the prisoner feel that he must earn enough to pay for his own bread, and to pay me for taking care of him" (quoted in Wines 1871/1970, p. 449). But Congress resolved that "the desire to make a prison a source of revenue, or even self sustaining, should never be allowed to supersede those more important and ever-to-be-remembered objects—moral and religious improvement" (quoted in Wines 1871/1970, p. 569).

At the present time those ever-to-be-remembered objects have been, if not totally forgotten, certainly superseded, although not by the desire to make prisons self-sustaining. Yet it is hard to see why prisoners should not be expected, and through the efficient organization of prison industries enabled, to contribute to the cost of their maintenance in penal institutions. In his historic paper on "The Ideal of a True Prison System for a State," delivered at Cincinnati, Zebulon Brockway said that it was "too much to expect in our day that citizens generally will vote taxes upon themselves not only to provide suitable institutions for . . . criminals, but to support them in unproductive industry" (quoted in Wines 1871/1970, p. 59). Over a century later that expectation still appears egregious and the principle implicit in Brockway's statement unexceptionable.

The second basic principle, "the right to work," is a more recent conception. It is one of those economic, social, and cultural rights added, in the 1948 Universal Declaration of Human Rights, to the traditional political and civil rights derived from the eighteenth-century American and French bills of rights.

The Declaration does not impose any obligation on states to give effect to the rights listed in it. Nevertheless in a number of countries the law explicitly or implicitly guarantees prisoners the right to work. This is the case in Denmark, Norway, Sweden, and Mexico. In some others, for example, France, the Netherlands, and Switzerland, the right to work is recognized and reflected in administrative principles and practice although not guaranteed by law.

The notion that prisoners should be regarded as having a right to work preceded the Universal Declaration. Penologists have long argued that in a free society the forfeiture of personal liberty by imprisonment represents in itself a severe deprivation and a heavy penalty, whatever the conditions of captivity. To add to that deprivation the deprivation of work has been seen as constituting a gratuitous excess of cruelty. Grünhut cites a nineteenth-century German work on prison management which states that "a prisoner, as a human being, has a right to work. It is immoral to refuse it permanently and to condemn him to a long period of idleness" (Grünhut 1948, p. 198).

Over half a century ago, E. R. Cass, General Secretary of the American Prison Association, addressing a National Conference on the Reduction of Crime, said: "No greater cruelty can possibly be inflicted on prisoners than enforced idleness" (quoted in Robinson 1931, p. 2). More recently, it has been urged "on simple grounds of justice and equity" that in the context of prison labor "a principle of *greater* rather than *lesser* eligibility should be applied to the prison population" (emphasis added). In support of this contention it is said that when a person is sentenced to imprisonment the period in prison is assigned as "a just penalty for the wrong which has been committed." Prisoners "have a right to work and make a productive contribution to the nation equal to that of any citizen. Their punishment is confinement, not enforced idleness" (Braithwaite 1980, pp. 16–18).

The proposition that the state, whatever its responsibility may be in relation to ensuring the availability of employment generally, has a special responsibility in relation to prisoners answers the inevitable question, Why should prisoners work when honest citizens are unemployed? In this view, by imposing the penalty of imprisonment the state assumes certain obligations, and "it would forfeit the right to inflict punishment in the name of justice if it were to take a man from his place in society to enforced idleness within prison walls" (Grünhut 1948, p. 197).

Assertions of this nature are not irrebuttable. But it is notable that no justification has ever been offered for imposing on offenders compulsory unemployment in addition to the deprivation of liberty. It seems clear that at least part of the rationale for prison labor programs can be found in their representing a recognition of the prisoner's right to work.

Finally there is the question of rehabilitation. From the 1930s until the 1970s, the generally accepted, orthodox justification for the provision of work for prisoners was that lack of work would frustrate social adjustment and, more positively, that the provision of suitable work would actively assist rehabilitation. Criminologists and correctional administrators today are generally skeptical about the possibility of rehabilitation within prison. It is widely believed that the well-known review of evaluation studies by Lipton, Martinson, and Wilks (1975) demonstrated that none of the rehabilitation strategies which have been used in prisons were at all effective.

In fact the findings of *The Effectiveness of Correctional Treatment* have been misinterpreted. It is a survey of treatment evaluation studies, and what it principally shows is that most treatment evaluation studies, at least most of those included in the survey, were methodologically defective. The revelation that some claims about program effectiveness have been based on imperfect assessments does not justify the inference that "nothing works," any more than the discovery that an assayer had wrongly identified pyrite as gold would entitle us to infer that a gold mine had been exhausted.

Nevertheless, those seeking confirmation of the belief that "suitable employment is the most important factor in the physical and moral regeneration of the prisoner" (Great Britain Parliament 1933/34, p. 64) will find little gold in the meager supply of evaluative studies available. Reviewers of those studies have found either that the hope that prisoners will be rehabilitated by their work experience or by the acquisition of on-the-job skills is "not borne out by the evidence" (Taggart 1972, p. 56) or at best that the empirical evidence is "depressingly equivocal" and that "research findings in this area . . . are riddled with inconsistencies" (Braithwaite 1980, p. 29).

One of the best studies of work in prisons is the chapter on that topic in Daniel Glaser's *The Effectiveness of a Prison and Parole System,* and the conclusion of the section on prison work and recidivism is relevant here:

> For the minority who gain skills in prison at which they can find a postrelease vocation, prison work experience and training is a major rehabilitative influence. The above should be considered with the findings that: (1) prison work can readily provide the most regular employment experience most prisoners have had; (2) prior work regularity is more closely related to postrelease success or failure than type of work; (3) relationships with work supervisors are the most rehabilitative relationships with staff that prisoners are likely to develop. From this diversity it seems reasonable to conclude: Not training in vocational skills, but rather, habituation of inmates to regularity in constructive and rewarding employment, and anti-criminal personal influences of work supervisors on inmates, are—at present—the major contributions of work in prison to inmate rehabilitation. [Glaser 1964, pp. 258–59]

This guarded assessment of the contribution of work in prison to inmate rehabilitation seems reasonable. Higher claims commonly display a spectacular looseness of articulation between evidence and conclusions. Even this claim is largely intuitive, but here, as in relation to many other aspects of correctional practice, it is sometimes necessary to rely on intuition. Conrad, writing about the value of "a credible program of industrial employment" in prisons makes the point, "Some of the most obvious benefits of life are the least susceptible to rigorous scientific analysis. People of good sense and generosity sometimes have to rely on their instincts" (Conrad 1965, p. 50).

It should be added that the justification of the provision of employment for prisoners as possibly rehabilitative does not depend on belief in the rehabilitative ideal as the justifying purpose of imprisonment. This is important because in the contemporary debate on the purposes of imprisonment critical attacks on both the efficacy of, and the moral legitimacy of, rehabilitative programs (Rothman 1973; Morris 1974) have effectively undermined rehabilitation as the purpose of the prison sanction. Today both in theory and in practice the emphasis has shifted to incapacitation as the basis of incarceration policy, although this is not always explicitly acknowledged.

The incapacitative emphasis does not entail the abandonment of all programs that might be rehabilitative. Indeed, the reverse is the case, for this policy change provides even more justification for the application to prisoners of a policy of greater eligibility. The adoption of a policy which is based, as incapacitation is, on judgments about future behavior that will in many cases be mistaken imposes a moral obligation to expand rather than eliminate rehabilitation opportunities, although on a voluntary and facilitative rather than a compulsory or coercive basis. The organization of industrial operations in prison, which would enable incarcerated individuals to work at paid employment during their period of imprisonment, may be seen as one means of fulfilling that obligation.

These three principles—economy, the right to work, and rehabilitation—define the purposes to be served by having inmates work. It is reasonable that prisoners should make some contribution through their labor to the cost of their incarceration. The right to work conferred by article 23 of the Universal Declaration of Human Rights is not annulled by a sentence of imprisonment. The principle enunciated in *Coffin* v. *Reichard*, 143 F.2d 443 (6th Civ. 1944), cert. denied, 325 U.S. 887 (1945), that the convicted offender retains all rights which citizens in general have, except such as must be limited or forfeited to make it possible to adminster a correctional institution or agency, is relevant here. And it has been authoritatively stated, regarding the rights listed in article 23, that "the fact of becoming a prisoner does not cancel or suppress these rights" (Lopez-Rey 1958, p. 12). Finally, the fact that imprisonment in our time is used as an incapacitative measure imposes an obligation on the state to make available to inmates rehabilitative facilities, including the opportunity to engage in regular, remunerated work.

VII. In Sum

I have argued that the long-term failure to develop effective and profitable systems for the utilization of prison labor in prison industries is not due to the fact that economic forces impose inexorable constraints. The feasibility of developing productive prison industries has been demonstrated over the past forty years by the U.S. Federal Prison Industries, Inc. In more recent years the Free Venture prison industry programs have demonstrated that productive, profitable industrial operations are possible in American state prisons, and such developments have not been confined to Free Venture states.

The implementation, on a national basis, of the concept of the industrial prison would present economic problems. But the principal barrier over the years to the profitable employment of prisoners has been neither the conditions of the labor market, the prevailing mode of production, nor any other aspect of the economy. The principal barrier to a rational solution to the problem of prisoners' work and prison industry has been the persistent influence on penal policy of the principle of less eligibility.

How is it that this conception, far from being merely an anachronistic echo of the past, still "has a place in every debate about penal treatment, and has now become an almost ritual ingredient in such discussion" (Thomas and Stewart 1978, p. 73) strongly influencing contemporary penal practice? An adequate answer to that question would go beyond the limits of this essay and would require more attention than is commonly given to what have been called "the socio-psychological functions of punishment" (Rusche 1980, p. 11). Here I shall only point out that, despite the perennial potency of the less eligibility idea, it is not an immutable axiom proscribing any conceivable change in prison conditions. It is a relative concept which derives its meaning from a specific social context.

The desire to punish does not reflect an ineradicable atavistic appetite for cruelty. Both attitudes toward punishment generally and the interpretation of the principle of less eligibility have changed significantly over time. It is no longer generally felt that to be condign, punishment must necessarily be ferocious. Prison administrators today are not expected to ensure that the material conditions of prison life are in every respect worse than those enjoyed by "the lowest class of independent labourer." In many respects they are demonstrably worse and sufficiently miserable and dangerous to satisfy the most punitive citizen. But the task of achieving absolute conformity to less eligibility proved impossible to fulfill even "in the days when Bentham's principle was young and strong" (Fox 1952, p. 135).

It is difficult to understand why a policy which would reduce idleness and reduce the cost of incarceration by making prisoners contribute to those costs should be regarded as increasing the amenity of prison life to an excessive degree. At a time when the *real* cost of incarceration has been estimated at $50,000 per year over a ten-year sentence and $80,000 per year over a twenty-year sentence (Adelson 1978, p. 27; Coopers and Lybrand 1978, p. 22) the failure to provide productive activity for prisoners which could reduce correctional operating costs not only confers no benefit on the prisoners, it imposes a substantial burden on the public. Paradoxically, it is the citizen in his capacity as taxpayer who most feels the effect of the application of the principle of less eligibility in this context.

This fact provides the best hope for genuine and effective political intervention. Politicians are sometimes reproached with lacking the courage to reform the prison system, but they are endowed with no more courage than their constituents and they are unlikely to expend it in areas where there are no votes to be won. There is ordinarily little in prisons to interest those who seek to gain or retain power.

The public generally is disinterested and apathetic about penal matters, and the majority of citizens probably ask no more of prisons than that they provide what a recent United Kingdom Committee of Inquiry into Prisons referred to as "mere containment or custody" (Great Britain 1979, §4.2). At this time, however, more offenders are being imprisoned for longer periods than at any previous time in American history. In five years in the mid-1970s prison population increased by almost 50 percent, and a record annual rate of increase of 12.1 percent occurred in 1981.

Burgeoning prison populations and court intervention in correctional administration have produced soaring correctional costs. Prisons are enormously expensive to construct and operate. Each new maximum security cell costs (on a national average) $50,000; another $8,500 per year is spent to maintain each inmate (Abt Associates 1979). An unusual opportunity therefore arises to introduce changes which are not only rational and humane but also hold the promise of reducing costs.

The implementation of the industrial prison concept will of course involve transitional expenditures. The start-up costs arising out of the system changes required to initiate business-like prison industries might in many cases be obtained by involving private firms in prison industry operations. A bill, S. 1597, was introduced recently by Senator Robert Dole of Kansas to establish a federally chartered Prison Industries Corporation, with an appropriation of $750,000 per year, but planned to run mainly on private money.

It is intended that this corporation would have authority to obtain grants from and make contracts with individuals and with private, state, local, and federal agencies, organizations, and institutions. It would also award financial assistance by grant, contract, cooperative agreement, or loan (at low interest rates) to any correctional system proposing a project which fulfills the purposes of the act, serve as a clearinghouse for the exchange of information with respect to the purposes of the act, collect and disseminate information, and provide technical assistance.

If sufficient private sector capital is not forthcoming, it is difficult to think of a more appropriate investment for federal funds. Between 1968 and 1981 the federal government spent $8 billion through the Law Enforcement Assistance Administration on a "national war on crime." A recent, by no means wholly critical study of that operation estimated that about half the money was wasted, another quarter eaten up by costly overhead expenses, and "only twenty-five cents on the dollar was left as a *possibly* worthwhile investment" (Cronin, Cronin, and Milakovich 1981, p. x; emphasis added).

The expression "war on crime" is an inept metaphor and reflects a complete misconception of the specificity and complexity of the constituent elements of what is called "the crime problem." When, as in the case of this multibillion dollar experiment, the offensive consisted mainly of pouring funds into existing agencies to spend on "more of the same," it is scarcely surprising that the result was "a beleaguered, frustrated, and failed national effort" (Cronin et al. 1981, p. ix).

The national government's most useful role in improving the criminal justice system would be to encourage reform and system improvement as opposed to subsidizing the existing system. The revitalization of prison industries represents precisely the kind of innovative program to deal with a specific, clearly defined problem of national importance that a federal government should encourage and support.

REFERENCES

Abt Associates. 1979. "Conditions and Costs of Confinement." In "American Prisons and Jails." Vol. 3. Mimeographed draft. Washington, D.C.: National Institute of Justice.

Adelson, Marvin. 1978. "Correcting the Future." In "Future of Corrections." Mimeographed. Washington, D.C.: Department of Justice, LEAA, National Institute of Law Enforcement and Criminal Justice.

American Friends Service Committee. 1971. *Struggle for Justice: A Report on Crime and Punishment in America.* New York: Hill & Wang.

American Prison Association. 1887. *Proceedings of the National Prison Congress 1886.* Chicago: R. R. Donnelley & Sons.

Auerbach, Barbara. 1982. "New Prison Industries Legislation: The Private Sector Re-Enters the Field." Mimeographed. Philadelphia: American Institute of Criminal Justice.

Barnes, Harry Elmer. 1944. *Prisons in Wartime.* Washington, D.C.: War Production Board, Government Division.

Barnes, Harry Elmer, and Negley K. Teeters. 1959. *New Horizons in Criminology.* 3d ed. Englewood Cliffs, N.J.: Prentice-Hall, Inc.

Bentham, Jeremy. 1843. "A View of the Hard-Labour Bill" (1778). "Panopticon, or The Inspection-House" (1791). In *The Works of Jeremy Bentham,* edited by John Bowring. Vol. 4. London: Simpkin, Marshall & Co.

Braithwaite, John. 1980. *Prisons Education and Work.* Phillip A.C.T. Australia: Australian Institute of Criminology and University of Queensland Press.

Brownlie, Ian, ed. 1981. *Basic Documents on Human Rights.* 2d ed. Oxford: Clarendon Press.

California State Assembly Office of Research. 1969. *Report on the Economic Status and Rehabilitative Value of California Correctional Industries.* Staff report prepared for the Assembly Ways and Means Committee. Sacramento: Assembly Office of Research.

Conrad, John P. 1965. *Crime and Its Correction: An International Survey of Attitudes and Practices.* London: Tavistock Publications.

Cooper, M. H., and Roy D. King. 1965a. "Social and Economic Problems of Prisoners' Work." In *Sociological Studies in the British Penal Services,* ed. Paul Halmos. Keele: University of Keele.

————. 1965*b*. "Prison Work—but How?" *New Society* 6:8–10.

Coopers and Lybrand. 1978. *The Cost of Incarceration in New York City.* Hackensack, N.J.: National Council on Crime and Delinquency.

Cronin, Thomas E., Tania Z. Cronin, and Michael E. Milakovich. 1981. *U.S. v. Crime in the Streets.* Bloomington: Indiana University Press.

England, Ralph W. 1961. "New Departures in Prison Labor." *Prison Journal* 41:21–26.

Flynn, Frank T. 1951. "Employment and Labor." In *Contemporary Correction*, editor Paul W. Tappan. New York: McGraw-Hill Book Co.

Fox, Lionel W. 1952. *The English Prison and Borstal Systems.* London: Routledge & Kegan Paul.

Freedman, Marcia, and Nick Pappas. 1967. *The Training and Employment of Offenders.* Reference document. Washington D.C.: President's Commission on Law Enforcement and Administration of Justice.

Freud, Sigmund. 1961. *The Future of an Illusion.* New York: W. W. Norton. Originally published 1928.

————. 1962. *Civilization and Its Discontents.* New York: W. W. Norton. Originally published 1930.

Fry, Margery. 1951. *Arms of the Law.* London: Victor Gollancz. Originally published 1827.

Funke, Gail S., Billy L. Wayson, and Neal Miller. 1982. *Assets and Liabilities of Correctional Industries.* Lexington, Mass.: D. C. Heath.

Glaser, Daniel. 1964. *The Effectiveness of a Prison and Parole System.* New York: Bobbs-Merrill, Inc.

Great Britain, Home Department. 1895. *Report of the Departmental Committee on Prisons.* Command 7702. London: H.M. Stationery Office.

Great Britain, Home Office. 1960. *Prisons and Borstals.* 4th ed. London: H.M. Stationery Office.

Great Britain, Parliament. 1933. *Parliamentary Papers 1933/34.* Vol. XV. *Report of the Departmental Committee on the Employment of Prisoners. Part I.* 1933. London: H.M. Stationery Office.

————. 1979. *Report of the Committee of Inquiry into the United Kingdom Prison Services.* Command 7673. London: H.M. Stationery Office.

Grünhut, Max. 1948. *Penal Reform: A Comparative Study.* Oxford: Clarendon Press.

Hiller, E. T. 1915. "Labor Unionism and Convict Labor." *Journal of Criminal Law and Criminology* 5:851–79.

Hogg, Russell. 1980. "Imprisonment and Society under Early British Capitalism." In *Punishment and Penal Discipline: Essays on the Prison and the Prisoners' Movement*, edited by Tony Platt and Paul Takagi. Berkeley, Calif.: Crime and Social Justice Associates.

Howard, Derek Lionel. 1960. *The English Prisons.* London: Methuen.

Johnson, Alexander Bryan. 1947. *A Treatise on Language*, edited by David Rynin. Berkeley and Los Angeles: University of California Press. Originally published 1836.

King, Roy D., and Rod Morgan. 1980. *The Future of the Prison System.* Farnborough: Gower Publishing Co.

Lewis, Orlando F. 1967. *The Development of American Prisons and Prison Customs, 1776–1845.* Montclair, N.J.: Patterson Smith. Originally published 1922.

Lightman, Ernie S. 1982. "The Private Employer and the Prison Industry." *British Journal of Criminology* 22:6–22.

Lipton, Douglas, Robert Martinson, and Judith Wilks. 1975. *The Effectiveness of Correctional Treatment: A Survey of Treatment Evaluation Studies.* New York: Praeger Publishers.

Lombroso, Cesare. 1912. *Crime: Its Causes and Remedies.* Boston: Little, Brown.

Lopez-Rey, Manuel. 1958. "Some Considerations on the Character and Organization of Prison Labour." *Journal of Criminal Law, Criminology and Police Science* 49:10–28.

McKelvey, Blake. 1977. *American Prisons.* Rev. ed. Montclair, N.J.: Patterson Smith. Originally published 1936.

McLachlan, Noel. 1974. "Penal Reform and Penal History: Some Reflections." In *Progress in Penal Reform*, edited by Louis Blom-Cooper. Oxford: Clarendon Press.

Mannheim, Hermann. 1939. *The Dilemma of Penal Reform.* London: George Allen & Unwin.

Miller, Neal. 1981. "Inmate Labor Compensation Issues." Mimeographed. Washington, D.C.: National Institute of Corrections.

Mohler, Henry Calvin. 1925. "Convict Labor Policies." *Journal of Criminal Law and Criminology* 15:530–97.

Morris, Norval. 1974. *The Future of Imprisonment.* Chicago: University of Chicago Press.

National Advisory Commission on Criminal Justice Standards and Goals. 1973. *Task Force Report on Corrections.* Washington, D.C.: Government Printing Office.

Orwell, George. 1940. *Inside the Whale.* London: Victor Gollancz.

Pennsylvania Prison Society. 1982. "New Programs Work to Modernize Prison Industries." *Correctional Forum* (January), pp. 1–3.

President's Commission on Law Enforcement and Administration of Justice. 1967a. *The Challenge of Crime in a Free Society.* Washington, D.C.: Government Printing Office.

———. 1967b. *Task Force Report: Corrections.* Washington, D.C.: Government Printing Office.

Reckless, Walter C. 1950. *The Crime Problem.* New York: Appleton-Century-Crofts.

Robinson, Louis N. 1931. *Should Prisoners Work?* Philadelphia: Winston.

Rothman, David J. 1973. "Decarcerating Prisoners and Patients." *Civil Liberties Review* 1:8–30.

Rusche, Georg, and Otto Kirchheimer. 1968. *Punishment and Social Structure.* New York: Russell & Russell. Originally published 1939.

Rusche, Georg. 1980. "Labor Market and Penal Sanction." In *Punishment and Penal Discipline: Essays on the Prison and the Prisoners' Movement*, edited by Tony Platt and Paul Takagi. Berkeley, Calif.: Crime and Social Justice Associates. Originally published 1933 as "Arbeitsmarkt und Strafvollzug," *Zeitschrift für Sozialforschung* 2:63–78.

Schaller, Jack. 1981. "Normalizing the Prison Work Environment." In *Justice as Fairness: Perspectives on the Justice Model*, edited by David Fogel and Joe Hudson. Cincinnati: W. H. Anderson.

———. 1982. "Work and Imprisonment: An Overview of the Changing Role of Prison Labor in American Prisons." Mimeographed. Philadelphia: American Institute of Criminal Justice.

Schaller, Jack, and George E. Sexton. 1979. "The Free Venture Program: An Overview." In *A Guide to Effective Prison Industries*, vol. 1. Philadelphia: American Foundation.

Sellin, J. Thorsten. 1976. *Slavery and the Penal System*. New York: Elsevier.

Sexton, George E. 1982. "The Industrial Prison: A Concept Paper." Mimeographed. Philadelphia: American Institute of Criminal Justice.

Singer, Neil M. 1973*a*. "Incentives and the Use of Prison Labor." *Crime and Delinquency* 19:200–211.

———. 1973*b*. *The Value of Adult Inmate Manpower*. Correctional Economic Analysis Series. Washington, D.C.: American Bar Association Commission on Correctional Facilities and Services.

Smith, Kathleen J. 1965. *A Cure for Crime*. London: Duckworth.

Sparks, Richard F. 1971. *Local Prisons: The Crisis in the English Prison System*. London: Heinemann.

Sutherland, Edwin H., and Donald R. Cressey. 1960. *Principles of Criminology*. 6th ed. Philadelphia: J. B. Lippincott.

Taggart, Robert. 1972. *The Prison of Unemployment*. Baltimore: Johns Hopkins University Press.

Thomas, J. E., and Alex Stewart. 1978. *Imprisonment in Western Australia: Evolution, Theory and Practice*. Nedlands: University of Western Australia Press.

U.N. Department of Economic and Social Affairs. 1955. *Prison Labour*. New York: United Nations.

———. 1956. "Standard Minimum Rules for the Treatment of Prisoners." In *First United Nations Congress on the Prevention of Crime and the Treatment of Offenders, Geneva, 22 August–3 September 1955*. New York: United Nations.

U.S. Department of Justice. 1940. *The Attorney General's Survey of Release Procedures*. Vol. 5. *Prisons*. Leavenworth, Kans.: Federal Prison Industries, Inc., Press.

———. LEAA. 1981. *Impact of Free Venture Prison Industries upon Correctional Institutions*. Washington, D.C.: Government Printing Office.

———. UNICOR Federal Prison Industries, Inc. 1980. *Annual Report 1980*. Washington D.C.: Federal Prison Industries, Inc.

U.S. Department of Labor. 1896. *Bulletin Vol. I 1895–96. No. 5 Convict Labor*. Washington, D.C.: Government Printing Office.

———. Bureau of Labor Statistics. *Prison Labor in the United States*. 1886, 1895, 1905, 1914, 1923, 1940. Washington, D.C.: Government Printing Office.

Walker, Nigel. 1980. *Punishment, Danger and Stigma: The Morality of Criminal Justice*. Oxford: Basil Blackwell.

Webb, Sidney, and Beatrice Webb. 1910. *English Poor Law Policy*. London: Longmans, Green & Co.

———. 1922. *English Prisons under Local Government*. London: Longmans, Green & Co.

Williams, Vergil L., and Mary Fish. 1971. "Rehabilitation and Economic Self-Interest." *Crime and Delinquency* 17:406–13.

Wines, Enoch C. 1968. *The State of Prisons and of Child-saving Institutions in the Civilized World*. Montclair, N.J.: Patterson Smith. Originally published 1880.

———. ed. 1970. *Transactions of the National Congress on Penitentiary and Reformatory Discipline. Cincinnati 1870*. College Park, Md.: American Correctional Association. Originally published 1871.

Wines, Enoch C., and Theodore W. Dwight. 1976. *Report on the Prisons and Reformatories of the United States and Canada*. Montclair, N.J.: Patterson Smith. Originally published 1867.

Nicole Hahn Rafter

Prisons for Women, 1790–1980

ABSTRACT

Until recently, women's institutions and their inmates have received little
attention in the literature on prisons. This neglect in part stems from the
fact that over time women have comprised but a small fraction of the total prisoner population. Yet it is also the product of two common assumptions: that the development of the women's prison system and
experiences of its inmates closely resemble those of men; or that, if different, the evolution of the women's prison system and female experience
of incarceration are irrelevant to mainstream penology just because they
can shed little light on the nature of the prison system as a whole. Neither assumption is correct. During the first stage in the development of
the women's prison system (1790–1870), female penal units outwardly resembled male penitentiaries, but in some respects their inmates received
inferior care. During the second stage (1870–1935), strenuous and often
successful efforts were made to establish an entirely new type of prison,
the women's reformatory, in which women would receive care more appropriate to their "feminine" nature. Yet by institutionalizing differential
treatment, the reformatories legitimated a tradition of providing care that,
from our current perspective, was inherently unequal. In the third stage
(1935 to the present), the women's prison system continued to evolve in
ways which perpetuated the older traditions of differential treatment.
The women's prison system is not, then, merely a miniature version of

Nicole Hahn Rafter is associate professor of criminal justice, College of Criminal
Justice, Northeastern University.
This article partially reports the results of a study funded by grant 79-NI-AX-0039
from the National Institute of Justice, U.S. Department of Justice. Points of view or
opinions are mine and do not necessarily represent the official position of the U.S.
Department of Justice. Themes developed in this essay were introduced in Rafter (1982).
Subjects discussed in this essay will be further developed in a book to be published by
Northeastern University Press. For their comments on earlier drafts, I thank Robert S.
Hahn, John H. Laub, Sheldon Messinger, Norval Morris, Lloyd Ohlin, and Michael
Tonry.

that for men. Nor is the history of the incarceration of women irrelevant to understanding of the prison system as a whole. The older, questionable generalizations, however, may be safely replaced with another: despite variations in its causes and character, the fact of differential care of female prisoners has remained a constant across time in this country.

Until the early 1970s, women's prisons and their inmates were for the most part ignored by historians, sociologists, and specialists in criminal justice. Some writers evidently assumed that women's prisons and experience of incarceration were comparable to those of men and hence not areas which called for much separate investigation (e.g., Barnes 1930/1972). Others recognized major differences between men's and women's prisons but considered the latter irrelevant to mainstream penology because they had so little in common with the former (e.g., Robinson 1921, p. 126). In part, this neglect of women's institutions and their inmates flowed from the fact that women comprised but a small proportion of the total prison population. In 1978, only 4 percent of all state prisoners were women (Hindelang, Gottfredson, and Flanagan 1981, p. 492), and at times in the past the proportion has been even smaller. In part, the neglect has also been a result of the fact that until recently, most students of the prison system were male and hence more attuned to male than female experiences and issues.[1]

Since the early 1970s, however, the women's prison literature has expanded rapidly and in many directions. Flynn's 1971 discussion of special problems of female offenders, a harbinger of what was to come, was soon followed by a burst of publications. Singer (1973) protested bitterly against the inferior treatment accorded to female prisoners and against the criminal justice system's refusal at times to even recognize the existence of these women. Arditi and colleagues (1973) compiled a sobering catalog of patterns of sex discrimination in prisons throughout the country. Gibson's (1973) article of the same year, focused on the Wisconsin reformatory, took a first (if tentative) step toward historical research on women's prisons, and the year also saw publication of one of the first works in the area written for a broad audience (Burkhart 1973). Since then the literature has continued to thrive. It now includes a national survey of contemporary women's correctional programs (Glick and Neto 1977) and studies of such specialized aspects of female incarceration as utilization of legal aid (e.g., Alpert and Wiorkowski 1977),

---

1. There are exceptions: see, e.g., McKelvey (1936/1972); Lewis (1961); Ward and Kassebaum (1965); Giallombardo (1966).

relationships between inmate mothers and their children (e.g., Haley 1977), and biases in the delivery of health care to female inmates (Resnick and Shaw 1980). Hearings have been held at the federal level (U.S. House of Representatives 1979), and the General Accounting Office has published two devastating reviews of deficiencies in women's prisons (U.S. General Accounting Office 1979; U.S. Comptroller General 1980). In addition, we now have a detailed history of an important branch of the women's prison system, Estelle B. Freedman's *Their Sisters' Keepers: Women's Prison Reform in America, 1830–1930* (1981). Although Freedman's work deals for the most part with only one type of women's prison (the reformatory), it is the first study of the origins of women's prisons to appear in fifty years.[2]

This recent demonstration of interest in women's prisons and their inmates reflects the reawakening of feminism in recent years, especially the perception that the experiences of men and women may be quite different even when their structural positions are similar. The new interest is also a function of the fact that today there are simply more female researchers trained and available to investigate women's issues. Furthermore, social scientists are now aware that focus on low-rate groups (such as female or rural populations) may shed as much light on phenomena like the causes of crime and inmate social structures as did the traditional focus on high-rate (e.g., male, urban) groups (Hindelang 1979, p. 154; Laub 1980, p. 14).

Even though female prisoners comprise but a small proportion of the total prison population, arguably they compel attention through the sheer magnitude of their numbers: as of June 1982, over 17,000 women were under jurisdiction of state and federal correctional authorities (U.S. Department of Justice 1982, p. 2). A count of February 1978 had found yet another 10,000 women in jails (Hindelang et al. 1981, p. 482). Incarcerated women are not only numerous, they are becoming increasingly aware of inequities in their treatment and ready to litigate such matters (Potter 1978; U.S. Comptroller General 1980), a situation which suggests that we will see ferment in the management of women's prisons in the decades ahead.

Incarcerated women and the institutions which hold them command yet further attention because over time the women's prison system has differed in many respects from that for men. This system is not merely

2. For earlier versions, see Freedman (1974, 1976); the only other book-length treatment is Lekkerkerker (1931).

a small-scale replica of the male prison system. It differs radically along a number of key dimensions, including its historical development, administrative structures, some of its disciplinary techniques, and the experiences of its inmates. These contrasts contradict the usual view of "the" prison system as a monolith with a single history. The differences also have policy implications, demonstrating as they do the possibility of alternative approaches to punishment and reformation. Finally, they indicate a fruitful area for research into the history of women, particularly those working-class women most likely to become involved with the justice system.

This essay sketches the history of the incarceration of women, concentrating on the first two of three stages in the development of the women's prison system in the continental United States. During the first stage, spanning the years 1790–1870, separate penal units for women evolved as adjuncts to men's prisons and the *custodial model* of women's prison emerged, similar in many ways to penitentiaries for men. During the second stage, 1870–1935, there developed an entirely new type of women's prison, the *reformatory model*, and institutions of this type were established throughout the country. In contrast to the "masculine" custodial model, the reformatory had many "feminine" aspects, designed as it was around beliefs about fundamental differences between the sexes. During the third stage, extending from 1935 into the present, the custodial and reformatory models merged; this period also saw creation of a network of women's prisons in the South and West.

Space and time constraints force me to ignore local jails, federal prisons for women, and so-called coed prisons. Throughout I distinguish between *units* and *prisons*. I reserve *unit* to refer to quarters for women which, though to some degree separate from the main quarters of a male prison, were nonetheless geographically close to and administratively dependent on the latter. I use *prison* to refer to penal institutions for women which existed as separate and relatively independent entities. Some women's prisons remained physically close to a men's prison, with which they sometimes shared resources; others were geographically separate. I use *institution* to refer to either a penal unit or a prison. By *model*, I mean an ideal type, one to which no particular institution necessarily corresponded in all details.

As I discuss the development of the women's prison system, I refer to available secondary sources on women's prison history. However, this literature is scant, and most of it pertains to the reformatories established during the second stage. In large part, then, I perforce rely on original sources—annual reports of prisons and departments of correction, eyewitness accounts, studies by prison investigatory committees, and so on. Sections I, II, and III discuss the three stages in the development of women's prisons; Section IV identifies key areas for further research and suggests ways in which women's prison history may affect theory and policy.

While my primary purpose is to trace the development of the women's prison system, particularly during its first two stages, I am also interested in several comparative issues. The most important of these concerns male-female differences: occasionally I pause to ask, How did conditions for women differ from those of men? I am also able to make some within-group comparisons. Because the essay covers an extensive period of time, I am able to ask how the incarceration of women differed from one stage to the next in the development of the women's prison system. Because the essay covers the entire continental United States, I am also able to ask whether the incarceration experiences of women differed by region of the country. These within-group comparisons are given less emphasis than the exploration of male-female differences, and in no case am I able to discuss comparative issues in depth. They are worth raising, however, for they sensitize us to differences which traditional prison histories have often glossed over.

I. Origins of the Custodial Model: From 1790 to 1870

The period from 1790 to 1870 was characterized by the gradual establishment, within primarily male prisons, of separate quarters for female convicts. During this period, moreover, the first independent prison for women was founded—New York's Mount Pleasant Female Prison, an institution with its own enabling legislation and staff. And during this stage there developed the custodial model of women's prison unit that continues to affect the nature of women's prisons today.

A. The First Step: Physical Isolation of Female Prisoners

In the late eighteenth century, city lockups made little or no effort to separate prisoners by sex or according to the other criteria (such as age, race, and offense seriousness) by which prisoners have been classified and segregated in more recent times. For instance, the jail operated by Philadelphia at the corner of High and Third streets in the 1780s was reputed to have been an "abode of guilt and wretchedness" that held "in one common herd . . . , by day and by night, prisoners of all ages, colours, and sexes!" (Vaux 1826, p. 13). Discipline was poor to nonexistent in these Revolutionary War era city jails, a situation which led those who founded the first state prisons in the late eighteenth and early nineteenth centuries to insist on segregation of the sexes.

The earliest institutions for state prisoners consisted of large rooms in which a number of inmates were held together. They accomplished rudimentary classification by sex by isolating female prisoners in one or more rooms of their own. At Newgate, New York's first state prison, the rooms measured about twelve by eighteen feet and were considered "sufficient for the accommodation of eight persons." Women were held in rooms in the north wing "on the ground floor, and [had] a courtyard entirely distinct from that of the men" (New York Inspectors of State Prisons 1801, p. 18). In these first state prisons, then, women were separated from men. Their care seems to have been similar to that given to males, but this relative equality was not to remain the rule for long.

By the 1820s, penologists in the more populous states had grown dissatisfied with the large-room design. The arrangement did not prevent that communication between prisoners which reformers were coming to regard as a source of moral contamination, and it posed disciplinary and security problems. By the mid-1820s, the Walnut Street Jail in Philadelphia was said to have "become a school of corruption" due to "the contracted scale of its apartments and yards" and "the number of prisoners necessarily crowded together by day and by night" (Vaux 1826, p. 52). Thus states began to replace their earliest prisons with penitentiaries, larger and more secure institutions which consisted mainly of individual cells. As the penitentiaries opened, both men and women were transferred to them from the older structures. However, whereas men were now locked in individual cells, women usually continued to be held in a large-room type of arrangement for a number of years longer. In several states female convicts were sent to a large room on the second or third floor of the central, tower-like structure which served, on its ground floor, as entrance and administrative headquarters. At this point—when state penitentiaries began to open—for the first time sharp differences developed between the incarceration experiences of men and women.

New York's Auburn prison, first of the new Bastille-like penitentiaries to receive prisoners, illustrates the marked differences in the care of male and female convicts in such institutions. At Auburn, men were locked in separate cells at night, while during the day, after being marched to the yard to wash, they labored together in total silence. Work was interrupted twice a day by meals in a mess hall. Guards supervised the men closely and punished them harshly for rule violations (Beaumont and de Tocqueville 1833/1964, chap. 2). Female prisoners, on the other hand, were confined together in a single attic room above the institution's kitchen. For a number of years they had no matron but rather were "supervised" by the head of the kitchen below. Food was sent up to them once a day, and once a day the slops were removed. No provision was made for privacy or exercise, and although the women were assigned some sewing work, for the most part they were left to their own devices in the "tainted and sickly atmosphere" (New York Committee on State Prisons 1832, p. 9) of their crowded quarters. The wretchedness of their lot came briefly to public attention when one Rachel Welch, impregnated while in prison and severely flogged when she was about five months pregnant, later died (Lewis 1965, pp. 94–95). With the ensuing scandal, conditions improved somewhat, in part through the hiring of a matron. But when Harriet Martineau visited Auburn in the mid-1830s, conditions for the prison's women were still "extremely bad" (1838, p. 124). So long as women convicts continued to be herded into large rooms off in corners of mainly male penitentiaries, imprisonment was for them not only different from but also in many ways worse than for their male counterparts—more crowded, less sanitary, weaker in personnel and other resources. As Auburn's chaplain observed in 1833, "To be a *male* convict in this prison would be quite tolerable; but to be a *female* convict, for any protracted period, would be worse than death" (New York Auburn State Prison 1833, p. 17).

Eventually, women too came to be locked into individual cells, and as this happened the incarceration of women changed considerably in character. By the late 1830s a number of states, including New York, Ohio, and Pennsylvania, had abandoned the old, large-room plan and removed their female convicts to cells. With the change, care of women came once again to resemble that of men, especially in its physical aspects. From the point of view of the women who experienced the change, it probably had both advantages and disadvantages. Crowding was reduced (at least initially), and in their single cells the women now had somewhat more privacy. On the other hand, the shift to cellular housing in this period ordinarily brought higher security, greater isolation, more intense regimentation, and stricter discipline. The care of women was now more equitable, corresponding as it did more closely to that of men. However, in many respects it remained inferior.

Conditions for female convicts held in Ohio's penitentiary in the mid-nineteenth century illustrate ways in which the incarceration experience of women held in cells at this time approximated that of males while falling short of the latter in quality. Ohio was one of the first states to build a separate structure for its female convicts: in 1837 it erected a women's annex which backed onto the front wall of the state penitentiary in Columbus. The annex had its own yard, which meant that the women could get some exercise and fresh air. But now the women were isolated from whatever services (health, religious, educational) were available to the men in the main penitentiary. Little attention was paid to upkeep of their building, which deteriorated badly over time. Furthermore, as its population increased, the annex became overcrowded, for there was no way to enlarge the structure. Occasionally a compassionate and able woman was hired as matron, but the state's practice of awarding prison positions as political spoils frequently led, in the women's annex as in the adjacent penitentiary, to incompetent administrators (Victor 1887; Resch 1972). For the most part, then, Ohio's female prisoners endured very poor conditions. These generally resembled those of men held on the other side of the dividing wall; yet, because the women were more isolated and more easily ignored, their conditions tended to be even grimmer.

In rare cases, women held in cells of the early penitentiaries did not suffer such neglect. Pennsylvania's Eastern Penitentiary, at which women were held starting in 1836, provides a case in point. There good order seems to have prevailed in the female quarters at mid-century. In 1845 Dorothea Dix reported: "The Eastern Penitentiary has 20 women-convicts. This department I have often visited, and always found in order; neatness and good behavior appear to be the rule and practice of the prison; the exceptions being very rare. The matron is vigilant, and fills her station in a manner to secure respect and confidence. The women are chiefly employed in making and repairing apparel, and have full time for the use of books, and lessons which are assigned weekly by the ladies who visit the prison to give instruction" (1845/1967, p. 107).

The few such instances of relatively adequate care for female prisoners in the mid-nineteenth century were usually associated, as at Eastern, with the lady-visitor phenomenon. Prison visiting by middle-class women seems to have begun in England about 1815 when Elizabeth Fry first investigated and later undertook to improve the physical and moral condition of female prisoners. Fry and her circle managed to bring order and discipline to a previously disordered situation, arranging, for example, for the appointment of a matron at England's Newgate, for provision of employment and instruction of women con-

victs, and for a system of prisoner self-monitoring (Fry 1847). At about
the same time, middle-class women in the United States similarly began
to concern themselves with the plight of female prisoners. In Philadelphia, a group of eleven Quakers regularly visited the female convicts
incarcerated at Eastern Penitentiary. According to Dorothea Dix's account, "They make stated visits every Monday afternoon throughout
the year; and you may see them there seriously and perseveringly
engaged in their merciful vocation. Their care extends to the convicts
after the expiration of sentences. The ladies read the scriptures, furnish
suitable books for the prisoners, give instruction in reading, writing,
and arithmetic; and, what is of great value, because reaching them
through a direct influence, instruct them by conversation, suited to
their capacity" (1845/1967, pp. 61–62). From such mid-nineteenth-
century efforts, there developed a tradition of middle-class women's
involving themselves in the care of female prisoners, a tradition which
blossomed in the late nineteenth-century women's reformatory
movement.

At this point, we should pause in our inquiry into the nature of
female incarceration in the period 1790–1870 to ask another question:
Why, during this period, were women increasingly separated from
males, first in their own large rooms, later in large rooms on the pe-
ripheries of mainly male penitentiaries, and later still in their cellblocks?
What encouraged this mitotic process whereby female convicts were
gradually isolated into quarters of their own?

The answer lies in part with practical considerations and partly with
the nineteenth-century passion for classification (be it of flora or convicts) into subcategories. Practically, isolation of female prisoners was
an administrative convenience: it improved discipline and helped avoid
sexual scandals. Segregation of women did not prove to be a foolproof
method of birth control—male guards continued to carry keys to wom-
en's quarters (see, e.g., Indiana Senate 1869, p. 653). It did, however,
reduce the opportunity for communication between male and female
prisoners and, as matrons were hired, also reduced access to the women
by male guards. In a larger context, isolation of female convicts was
part of the broad process of differentiation and segregation of prisoners
into types that occurred throughout the nineteenth century (Barnes
1930/1972, chap. 8), beginning with delinquent children at the start of
the century (Schlossman 1977) and concluding, toward its end, with
the separation and differential treatment of prisoners considered mentally abnormal (Currie 1973, chap. 6).

That the treatment of criminal women followed and, later, to some degree paralleled that of delinquent children is a significant pattern in the development of the women's prison system, one that we shall have occasion to note again. At this point, however, it is important to observe that in the pre-1870 period, although women were separated from the general population of prisoners as children had been before them, the rationale did *not* lie (as it did toward the century's end) with an assumption that women were similar to children in their nature and needs. Quite the contrary: in the early and mid-nineteenth century the general opinion was that the female criminal was more depraved and hardened than the male. As Francis Lieber put it in 1833, "A woman, when she commits a crime, acts more in contradiction to her whole moral organization, i.e., must be more depraved, must have sunk already deeper than a man" (1833/1964, p. 11). Women were viewed as the moral force in society; once they fell into immorality, they were thought to jeopardize the very foundations of society. Thus Lieber claimed "that the injury done to society by a criminal woman, is in most cases much greater than that suffered from a male criminal" (1833/1964, p. 9). Similarly, Mary Carpenter wrote that "female convicts are, as a class, even more morally degraded than men" (1864/1969, p. 207). Connecticut officials declared themselves willing to take on an additional 450 male prisoners if they could rid themselves of five females (Rogers 1929, p. 519, n. 11; also see Lewis 1965, p. 159; Freedman 1981, pp. 18–20). Not paternalism but contempt informed the process by which female convicts were isolated into separate quarters of their own in early nineteenth-century prisons. This special disdain for—even horror of—the female criminal helps explain why, in this period, the care provided for such women was usually inferior to that of their male counterparts. Criminal women were considered even less deserving.

B. Mount Pleasant Female Prison:
The First Prison for Women

The initial step toward the establishment of a system of separate prisons for women was taken in 1835, when New York founded the Mount Pleasant Female Prison. This was the first and only penal institution for women established before the great era of prison construction that commenced in the late nineteenth century. Mount Pleasant is important in yet two other respects. First, several key years of its operation, during which it was managed by two remarkable women, exemplify the phenomenon mentioned earlier: when women from outside the walls actively involved themselves in the operation of penal units for women, conditions there often improved, sometimes dramatically. Second, Mount Pleasant provides a rather pure example of the custodial model of women's prison analyzed in the next section.

Like other women's prisons of the custodial type, Mount Pleasant was established primarily for practical reasons: New York ran out of other places to hold its female convicts. As we have seen, after the opening of Auburn, in 1817, some women were confined in its attic room. This space filled rapidly, however, and visitors publicized its many inadequacies. Meanwhile, the rest of the state's female convicts were held at the Bellevue Penitentiary in New York City.[3] There conditions were nearly as dreadful as at Auburn. Though separated at night, during the day the Bellevue women were herded together in a common room to sew and wash clothing for New York City convicts (New York Committee on State Prisons 1832, p. 9). Seldom (if ever) was a matron brought in to maintain order or tend to their needs. Technically these women were in the custody of Sing Sing, the new prison for men at Ossining. Sing Sing's inspectors visited Bellevue from time to time, finding the women's food inadequate, their accommodations unsanitary, and classification impossible (e.g., New York Mount Pleasant State Prison 1836, p. 5). Even these conditions might have been tolerated indefinitely had it not become clear that Bellevue officials would soon refuse to take any state women whatsoever. Faced with this prospect, the legislature initiated construction of a separate prison for women. Establishment of the Mount Pleasant Female Prison, then, was inspired more by practical considerations than by desire to uplift and reform.

Situated on the hill behind Sing Sing, overlooking the Hudson River, Mount Pleasant opened in 1839. According to a description of the late 1860s, it was "a handsome building, two stories high. . . . It has a front of fifty feet, with a Doric portico of imposing proportions, and a depth of one hundred and fifty feet" (Wines and Dwight 1867, p. 107). Its interior contained three tiers of cells with twenty-four cells in each tier. At the western end of the building, which had the best view, quarters for the matron were located. At the eastern end, within the inmates' area, was an elevated platform used for chapel services and

3. When New York's first prison at Newgate was closed in 1828, its men were sent to the new prison at Ossining and its women to the Bellevue Penitentiary (Young 1932, pp. 6, 15).

lectures. Below it was a nursery. In addition to the main building, the plant included a workshop and two separate punishment cells, each with its own yard. The women's complex was surrounded by a high wall. Mount Pleasant's cellblock plan and high level of security became typical of women's units of the custodial type.

Discipline quickly became a major problem at Mount Pleasant, due largely to overcrowding. Throughout much of 1843, when nearly eighty-five prisoners were being held in cells designed for seventy, the prison experienced a protracted riot. "Violent battles are frequent," according to a report for that year, "and knives have been known to be drawn among them [female prisoners]." The matron found it impossible to enforce the silent rule or prevent women from making contact with male prisoners at work in the nearby quarry (New York Mount Pleasant State Prison 1844, pp. 29–30, 202).

Punishments for disobedient convicts at Mount Pleasant, as at other women's units of the custodial type, were often severe, including strait-jacketing, solitary confinement, extended bread-and-water diets, and the "shower bath" that bombarded prisoners with water until they were close to drowning. Dorothea Dix was appalled by the punishment of gagging, "which seems to me shocking and extremely objectionable." One of Sing Sing's inspectors informed her that " 'the gag has been sometimes applied, but it has been only among the females that it has been rendered *absolutely* necessary!' " On the other hand, she learned that " 'in the women's prison, the lash is never used. There the punishments are confinement to their own cells in the main dormitory, or in separate cells, with reduction of food' " and, of course, gagging (Dix 1845/1967, pp. 13–14). Custodial women's prisons operated at later points in time abandoned some of these disciplinary mechanisms, but harsh discipline was frequently the rule—just as in many prisons for men.

Ultimate authority for management of Mount Pleasant lay with the Board of Inspectors of Sing Sing, but daily administration was left to the matron. Most of Mount Pleasant's matrons were unremarkable. Under them, the institution operated in the monotonous routine that became typical of custodial women's prisons. Inmates worked the entire day, mainly at sewing. Otherwise their program was minimal or non-existent, consisting at best of a Sabbath school.

One of Mount Pleasant's matrons, however, was outstanding—Eliza Farnham, supervisor of the institution from 1844 to 1847. She was aided by Georgina Bruce, assistant matron during part of Farnham's tenure. Together these two broke with many of the traditions of custodialism, demonstrating that care of female prisoners tended to improve when outside women involved themselves in penal affairs.

Farnham's experiments with methods to strengthen criminals morally were the most ambitious and innovative of their time, anticipating reforms of the late nineteenth century. A phrenologist, Farnham was convinced that if she could stimulate her prisoners with positive influences, their criminal tendencies would be overcome (Farnham 1846; also see Lewis 1965, 1971). To this end she introduced a program of education, personally instructed the women each morning, and provided books which they could take to their cells. Although she was a strict disciplinarian, Farnham rejected some of the harshest physical punishments of her day, tried to keep rules to a minimum, and abolished the rule of silence. In another departure from contemporary practice, she attempted to alleviate the grimness of the prison environment by introducing flowers, music, and visitors from the outside. Farnham also developed a system of prisoner classification. As a result of such efforts, women confined at Mount Pleasant during the Farnham-Bruce administration experienced conditions superior to those of males held at Sing Sing at the same time.

Farnham's reforms, however, were too radical for her contemporaries. Conservatives like Sing Sing's chaplain considered novel reading irreligious. Moreover, Farnham's abolition of the silent rule sowed dissension at the neighboring men's prison, where the rule still prevailed. Critics were also annoyed because, by providing time for instruction, Farnham did not keep her charges constantly at work; the effect, they argued, was to lower prison profits. (No doubt they were further irritated when she retorted that the profits of Mount Pleasant's Female Prison were low because its inmates, like women outside the walls, were paid less than men [New York Mount Pleasant State Prison 1847, p. 88].) Farnham's opponents publicly attacked her and her reforms (e.g., New York Mount Pleasant State Prison 1848). She fought back but eventually lost the struggle; in 1847 she resigned.

After Farnham's departure, the Mount Pleasant Female Prison reverted to patterns more typical of women's units within predominantly male institutions, even though it was relatively independent. The remainder of its history was one of decline. By 1859, overcrowding necessitated addition of another twenty-eight cells. This stopgap measure hardly sufficed, however, and by 1865, with a population of about two hundred, the prison's population was nearly double its capacity.

Overcrowding eventually led to a decision to close the women's prison entirely. In 1865 the legislature ruled that women from two judicial districts should be sent to local penitentiaries rather than to Mount Pleasant (Young 1932, p. 13), and about a decade later the institution's remaining prisoners were transferred to the King's County Penitentiary. So ended the first attempt to operate a separate prison for women. But while Mount Pleasant did not itself survive, it helped establish the custodial model of women's prison which outlived it by a century and is still a dominant type in female corrections.

C. The Custodial Model

To this point I have been describing both the incarceration of women in the pre-1870 period and the emergence of a particular type of penal unit for women. In what follows I analyze the custodial model in more detail, identifying key traits along five dimensions: (1) physical aspects and operating costs; (2) inmate characteristics; (3) administration; (4) discipline; and (5) programs.

1. *Physical Aspects and Operating Costs.*   Custodial prisons for women originated as units within the walls of state prisons for men. But in several respects, women's units departed from the architectural and custody practices of men's prisons. Little if any extra room was allotted for exercise or work: women were thought to have less need for recreation and less capacity for industrial labor; and their quarters, usually crammed into corners of men's institutions, could not be expanded. The burden of separation of the sexes, moreover, fell on the female departments. As Wines and Dwight explained, "Where prisoners of different sexes are confined in the same building or enclosure it is often necessary to impede light and ventilation by half closing windows, and by putting doors across passages which would otherwise be left open" (1867, p. 71). Such obstructions were placed on the smaller, usually women's units.

To cost-conscious officials, female convicts appeared to be a greater drain on resources than the men. Because they were few in number, their per capita costs were higher, especially when matrons were hired for their supervision. Chaplains, physicians, and other officials considered it bothersome to visit female departments after making their usual rounds (e.g., Indiana State Prison South 1874, p. 11). And because women were assigned to less productive labor (often to making and washing clothing for the men), their work was less profitable than that of male convicts (e.g., Dix 1845/1967, p. 108).

2. *Inmate Characteristics.* Custodial institutions for women received mainly felons. Women sentenced to New York's Newgate prison between 1797 and 1801 had been convicted of property offenses such as arson, burglary, forgery, and larceny (New York Inspectors of State Prisons 1801, p. 78). Most held at the Mount Pleasant Female Prison in the 1840s and 1850s had been convicted of property offenses, a few of crimes of violence (see, e.g., New York Mount Pleasant State Prison 1845, p. 26; New York Inspectors of State Prisons 1852, p. 230). Of the thirty-two women sentenced to the Tennessee State Penitentiary between 1840 and 1865, eighteen had been convicted of property offenses, nine of crimes of violence, and the rest of other felonies such as bigamy and perjury (Tennessee State Library and Archives, *Convict Record Book 1831–74*, Record Group 25, ser. 12, vol. 86). Vaux's Pennsylvania statistics cover both misdemeanants and felons, but even they show that in the period 1817–24 the overwhelming majority of women sent to Philadelphia's prison had been convicted of larceny; some others of violent crimes such as arson, assault and battery, and infanticide; very few had been sentenced for prostitution or other public order offenses (1826, pp. 70–75). Throughout the country in the pre-1870 period, when women were imprisoned for misdemeanors such as petty property crime and public order offenses, they (like male misdemeanants) were usually sent to local jails.

Although few data on female prisoners in this pre-1870 period have as yet been collected, those that are available give an idea of two other characteristics of women sent to custodial institutions: their age and race. The majority of such women were between twenty and thirty years old at the time of conviction, most of the others in their thirties.[4] The average age of women held in custodial institutions at any time tended to be high (relative to that of women in the reformatory prisons described in Sec. II), for those convicted of crimes of violence often served long terms.[5] As for race, there were sharp regional differences.

4. Some data on age are given by Vaux (1826, pp. 72–75). For the most part, however, this statement is based on my survey of published records pertaining to all independent prisons for women and the women's units which immediately preceded them and on a study of original prisoner registries from Ohio, New York, and Tennessee.

5. For example, one forty-four-year-old woman transferred in 1893 to the newly established New York State Prison for Women at Auburn had already served twenty-eight years of her life sentence. In the nineteenth century, even property offenders were sometimes sentenced to very long terms. Pardons were issued more frequently in the nineteenth century than today, however, and those with long sentences often did not serve their terms in full. Whether women were pardoned as frequently as men, and blacks as frequently as whites, remain open questions.

In the North in this period, female felons tended to be black. Even when outnumbered by whites, they were usually overrepresented in comparison to their proportion of the state's population as a whole. For instance, of the fifty-four women sent to the Philadelphia penitentiary in 1818, twenty-three were black (Vaux 1826, p. 71); and of thirty-eight women at New York's Bellevue Penitentiary in 1830, twenty-five were black (New York Mount Pleasant State Prison 1831, App. H, p. 34). A similar pattern did not prevail in the South in the pre–Civil War period, for slaves usually were punished by their owners. After the Civil War, however, prison populations became predominantly black in southern custodial units for women.[6]

3. *Administration.*   From about 1850 onward, daily operations at women's custodial institutions were supervised by matrons, women who lived within the walls and worked long hours for low wages. The main responsibility for and authority over such institutions, however, lay with officials of the neighboring prisons for men. The warden of the nearby men's prison hired the head matron and often her assistants as well. The women's unit rarely had a support staff of its own but rather was dependent for services on the chaplain, head teacher, and physician of the men's branch. Ultimate administrative authority over women's custodial institutions, moreover, fell to the states' boards of prisons; in the pre-1870 period these were exclusively male in membership and hence less attuned to the problems of female than of male convicts. The matrons of custodial prisons were seldom positioned to challenge the status quo: often they were older women, widowed and poorly educated, forced by necessity to accept unpleasant and poorly paid positions.

4. *Discipline.*   Women's custodial institutions approached discipline—rules, punishments, and routines—in a manner similar to that of the men's prisons with which they were associated. In general, the same standards were applied to women as to men, though with less consistency. Whether women were compelled to conform to the same rules was a function of one or more of three factors: the degree of overcrowding; the extent to which officials at the main penitentiary bothered to monitor activities in the women's unit; and the state's willingness to hire a matron.

6. Like earlier statements about age, these on race are primarily based on my survey and study of prisoner records referred to in n. 4 above.

Without supervision by a matron, female convicts could lead a riotous and even dangerous existence in their separate quarters. According to a report of the mid-1840s on the women's annex at the Ohio penitentiary, for example, its nine women gave more trouble than the institution's five hundred males: "The women fight, scratch, pull hair, curse, swear and yell, and to bring them to order a keeper has frequently to go among them with a horsewhip" (as quoted by Lewis 1922/1967, p. 263). Similarly, Dorothea Dix observed of the Ohio penitentiary, "There was no matron in the women's wing at the time I was there, . . . and they were not slow to exercise their good and evil gifts on each other" (Dix 1845/1967, p. 48). Former prisoner Sarah Victor later reported that "the knives had all been taken from the [Ohio Penitentiary's] female department, to prevent some refractory prisoners from cutting each other, which they had done, in a terrible manner, at times" (Victor 1887, p. 317).

On the other hand, some women held in custodial institutions experienced strict discipline. Beaumont and de Tocqueville said that "the experiment made at Wethersfield [Connecticut], where the women are, like the rest of the prisoners, subject to . . . absolute silence . . . , proves that the difficulty" of requiring silence of women "is not insurmountable" (1833/1964, p. 71). One New York women's prison enforced the silent rule into the twentieth century (Rafter 1982). Moreover, these prisons at times inflicted brutal punishments on uncooperative inmates. For example, in 1880 a new matron at the Ohio women's annex alluded, with some awe, to the harsh punishment employed by her predecessor, which she hoped never to use herself (Ohio Penitentiary 1880, p. 91).

There was, then, considerable variation in the degree to which inmates of custodial women's institutions were subjected to rigid discipline. Some institutions forced inmates to adhere to standards as strict as those imposed on males. Others, overcrowded or inadequately supervised, showed little concern with order. Laxity, however, was not necessarily preferable to rigorous oversight, for it sometimes went hand in hand with chaotic, dangerous, or brutal conditions.

5. *Programs.* Custodial women's institutions seldom took much interest in any program other than work. Insofar as they offered educational training at all, they provided it in the evening. Classes were taught, not by trained teachers, but by educated inmates.[7] Recreational

---

7. In the late nineteenth and early twentieth centuries, custodial prisons for women sometimes did hire teachers. These women, however, were usually supervised by the head teacher of the nearby prison for men.

programs tended to be even more impoverished. Because custodial women's institutions allocated space for little other than cells, their inmates often had no yard for exercise and no room other than the mess hall for attending religious services, meeting with visitors, or (when permitted) socializing with one another.

Work programs, in contrast, were often well developed. An industry organized along factory lines was operated by many units of the custodial type. In some, inmates produced clothing for the rest of the state's prisons; in others they caned chairs or otherwise finished off products manufactured in the neighboring prison for men. Although the tasks to which female convicts were assigned did not produce the profits of men's industries, they were expected to reduce operating costs. Women frequently labored eight or more hours a day, and they were sometimes paid a pittance for their work, money they could collect on release.[8] In all these respects, custodial institutions for women resembled prisons for men, which also ran industries, tried to defray costs with inmate labor, and paid inmates a small wage for their work.

Thus, the custodial model originated in the early penitentiaries of the northeastern and midwestern states. In the pre-1870 period, it also took hold in those southern states which, like Tennessee, built penitentiaries. By 1870, nearly every state had a female department, and New York had gone so far as to establish a separate women's prison. The treatment of inmates closely resembled that accorded to male convicts. But because there were relatively few female state prisoners and because these women were regarded as unredeemable, in important respects their care was inferior to that of males.

II. Emergence and Diffusion of the Reformatory Model, 1870–1935

As early as 1818, Elizabeth Fry conceived the idea which became the nucleus of the women's reformatory movement, the notion of a prison exclusively for women, administered by women, in which inmates would receive moral and domestic training (Fry 1847, 1:316–17). In retrospect we can detect muted notes of reformatory themes in the operation of the Mount Pleasant Female Prison during its Farnham years. Not until about 1870, however, did the reformatory concept take strong hold in this country, influencing the design of new institutions.

---

8. Women were however less frequently paid, and usually (perhaps always) they were paid in lesser amounts; see Rafter (1982), p. 250.

Thereafter it spread rapidly: for the next sixty-five years the reformatory was the predominant model in female corrections in the northeastern and north central regions. The twenty reformatories founded during this period established the stereotype of what is often, though erroneously, thought of today as the women's prison.

A reformatory is defined here as a prison for women, separate from and independent of an institution for men, which took deliberate steps to reform inmates through female-specific treatments. Table 1 identifies reformatories opened between 1870 and 1935. It omits institutions— the Vermont State Prison and House of Corrections for Women, opened in 1921, and the Rhode Island State Reformatory for Women, opened in 1925—which mixed the reformatory and custodial modes but in which the latter predominated. It also omits several reformatories which closed shortly after opening.

In both theory and design, the reformatory model was influenced by previously established institutions for children. (On relevant aspects of children's reformatories, see Reeves 1929; Mennel 1973; Schlossman 1977; Schlossman and Wallach 1978; Brenzel 1980). It was also much influenced by the first national convention of penologists and prison reformers that convened in Cincinnati in 1870 (Wines 1871, pp. 541– 47). The convention produced the famous Declaration of Principles that articulated the treatment (or "medical") approach that dominated corrections for the next century. On the basis of these principles, men's reformatories like Elmira were also established in the late nineteenth century. Reformatories for men and women shared some important characteristics, such as indeterminate sentencing structures, but the women's reformatory was a distinct type of institution. For example, men's reformatories like Elmira held felons, whereas women's reformatories generally aimed at the rehabilitation of misdemeanants (Lekkerkerker 1931, pp. 9–10). Men's reformatories did not break radically with prison tradition in their architecture and routines; women's reformatories were deliberately anti-institutional in their "cottage" architecture, and they dispensed female-specific types of treatment such as domestic training. Operated by and for women, female reformatories were decidedly "feminine" institutions, different from both custodial institutions for women and state prisons and reformatories for men. The women's reformatory, then, was a new phenomenon on the scene of adult corrections, an innovative effort to apply the 1870 Declaration of Principles specifically to the class of female petty offenders.

The reformatory model had a tremendous effect on the evolution of

TABLE 1
Reformatories Established for Women
in the United States, 1870–1935

Region and State	Original Name and Location	Date Opened
Northeast:		
Massachusetts	Reformatory Prison, Sherbon	1877
New York	House of Refuge for Women, Hudson*	1887
New York	Western House of Refuge, Albion	1893
New York	State Reformatory for Women, Bedford	1901
New Jersey	State Reformatory for Women, Clinton	1913
Maine	State Reformatory for Women, Skowhegan	1916
Connecticut	State Farm for Women, Niantic	1918
Pennsylvania	State Industrial Home for Women, Muncy	1920
North Central:		
Indiana	Reformatory Institution for Women and Girls, Indianapolis	1873
Ohio	Reformatory for Women, Marysville	1916
Iowa	Women's Reformatory, Rockwell City	1918
Kansas	State Industrial Farm for Women, Lansing	1918
Minnesota	State Reformatory for Women, Shakopee	1920
Nebraska	Reformatory for Women, York	1920
Wisconsin	Industrial Home for Women, Taycheedah	1921
Illinois	State Reformatory for Women, Dwight	1930
South:		
Arkansas	State Farm for Women, Jacksonville	1920
North Carolina	Industrial Farm Colony for Women, Kinston	1929
Virginia	State Industrial Farm for Women, Goochland	1932
West:		
California	Institution for Women, Tehachapi (female department of San Quentin, 1933–36)	1933

* Later became an institution for delinquent girls.

the women's prison system, affecting such diverse aspects of incarceration as architecture and sentence length. Its greatest impact lay in the area of treatment: women's reformatories established and legitimated a tradition of deliberately providing for female prisoners treatment very different from that of males. This tradition of differential treatment persists and is the source of many of the problems which plague the women's prison system today.

There is far more literature on reformatories than on custodial institutions, for in its heyday the women's reformatory was not merely an institutional model but a cause, a mission for the men and, more typically, women who struggled to generate public support for separate, reformative prisons for women. Not surprisingly, the literature produced by these advocates is intensely partisan. Promoters (e.g., Coffin 1886; Barrows 1910), reformatory superintendents (e.g., Johnson 1891; Davis 1911; Monahan 1941), and enthusiastic observers (e.g., Robert 1917; Rogers 1929), all wrote in support of the reformatory plan. One of the few exceptions to this rule of partisanship in the reformatory literature is Estelle B. Freedman's *Their Sisters' Keepers: Women's Prison Reform in America, 1830–1930* (1981), the first broadly focused and analytic study of the history of female corrections.[9] As its subtitle indicates, however, Freedman is more concerned with the women's prison reform movement than with the institutional history which is of primary interest here. In what follows, I integrate some of Freedman's findings and examples of the earlier partisan commentaries on women's reformatories into an overview of the women's prison system during its second developmental stage, one which extended from about 1870 to 1935.

I begin by identifying factors which contributed to the development of the reformatory, looking first at specific institutional contexts in which the new model emerged, second at factors in the wider social context that encouraged development and diffusion of the model. Next I analyze the reformatory model in terms of the five dimensions previously used to take the measure of custodial institutions; this subsection generalizes about the characteristics of reformatories as a group. I conclude by identifying reasons for the decline of interest in and eventual demise of the reformatory model in the 1930s.

In this section on the reformatories, as in the last on custodial institutions, we find examples of unequal treatment. The matter of differential care is more complicated in the case of reformatories, however, for such institutions were established for the explicit purpose of providing women with programs *superior* to those of custodial institutions (e.g., Barrows 1910, p. 167; Davis 1911, p. 45). Training was defined in gender-specific terms—instruction tailored to what was considered

---

9. SchWeber (1982) has recently produced an excellent analytic history of the first federal prison for women. There are a number of other sympathetic studies of women's reformatories in addition to those cited earlier in this paragraph; see, for example, Lekkerkerker (1931), Butler (1934), and Quarles (1966).

the childlike, domestic, and asexual nature of the true woman.[10] In the course of establishing prisons that would, proponents hoped, transform fallen women into true women, reformatory advocates institutionalized the double standard. From today's perspective, their efforts to save seem to have condemned their charges both to narrow programs and to care which, because it assumed adult women were childlike, was often infantilizing.

A. Origins of the Reformatory Model:
  The Institutional Context

Three institutional developments of about 1870 helped generate the new reformatory model of women's prison. First, a House of Shelter which opened in Detroit developed techniques that later became staples of reformatory treatment. Second, at about the same time an entirely independent, female-run prison for women was established in Indianapolis. Third, a national convention of penologists and reformers in 1870 formally endorsed the creation of separate, treatment-oriented prisons for women, thus giving a seal of approval and impetus to the nascent reformatory movement.

In the 1860s, Michigan held nearly all its state prisoners, male and female, in the fortress-like Detroit House of Correction, managed by Zebulon Brockway. There Brockway established, and operated between 1868 and 1874, a House of Shelter for women that McKelvey (1936/1972, p. 66) has quite rightly referred to as "in a sense the first women's reformatory in America." Brockway's inspiration for a separate unit in which women would receive special "feminine" care came during a visit to a school for delinquent girls. At the Lancaster, Massachusetts, institution Brockway observed two features which he later introduced into the operation of the shelter: a system of treating female delinquents as though they were members of "families" headed by motherly matrons; and the employment, as matrons, of "cultured" women who would provide role models (Brockway 1912/1969, p. 107). On his return to Detroit, Brockway built the shelter and hired, to oversee its operation, female assistants whom he hoped would "reclaim fallen women . . . through the sisterly care, counsel and sympathy of their own sex" (Detroit House of Correction 1869, p. 44). The "refined and virtuous

---

10. There are exceptions to this generalization. For example, some reformatories—particularly during their first years of operation—put inmates to work laying concrete walks, chopping ice for the icehouse, and farming. On the "true women," see Welter (1966).

women" (Brockway 1912/1969, p. 107) who managed the shelter were expected to create a context of family life in which inmates would "receive intellectual, moral, domestic, and industrial training" (Detroit House of Correction 1869, p. 7).

Methods of reform introduced at the House of Shelter soon became key elements in the reformatory plan: deliberate efforts to deal with female prisoners differently from males on the grounds of inherent differences between the sexes; the "familial" treatment of adult female prisoners and use of role models; and training aimed at reform. The same was true of other innovations with which Brockway experimented at the shelter—indeterminate sentencing and supervision of prisoners released early on parole, for example; the application of special, longer sentences to prostitutes (a misdemeanant group now incorporated into the state prisoner population); and a system of grading that rewarded good behavior with greater privileges. The shelter itself was short-lived (women were removed to provide more space for males), but its influence persisted. Channeled by Brockway through the conduit of the 1870 prison congress in Cincinnati, the correctional techniques which he and his chief assistant Emma Hall initiated in Detroit became a mainstream in female corrections.

At about the same time, scandals over forced prostitution of female prisoners at Indiana's Jeffersonville prison inspired a Quaker couple, Rhoda and Charles Coffin, to lead a movement for establishment of an entirely separate prison for women in Indianapolis. The institution which materialized in 1873 was the first entirely separate prison for women in the United States. Moreover, after an initial tug-of-war with an officious male member of the Board of Managers (Indiana Reformatory Institution 1877, pp. 51–54), the women who ran the new institution achieved complete administrative independence. Each of these characteristics—physical separation from a men's prison and an independent female administration—soon became a sine qua non of the women's reformatory.

In some respects, the Indiana Reformatory Institution fell short of what were to become, when fully formulated, reformatory ideals. For a while, for instance, it held girls in an adjacent (though entirely separate) unit; its original adult population consisted of felons rather than the misdemeanants later identified as the ideal reformatory population; and architecturally it more closely resembled the traditional prison than the cottage-dotted campuses of later reformatories. But in other respects, the Indiana institution pioneered in reformatory techniques. It insistently dealt with inmates in gender-specific ways, dressing them in gingham (rather than old-fashioned stripes) and serving meals at which "linen covers are spread over the clean tables, simple but attractive china makes the room attractive, and a vase of flowers is not considered too good for prison life" (Barrows 1910, p. 152). Moreover, the institution stressed creation of a familial atmosphere and the rehabilitative influence "of pure womanly examples" (Indiana Reformatory Institution 1874, p. 27), and it aimed at training inmates "to occupy the position assigned them by God, viz., wives, mothers and educators of children" (Indiana Reformatory Institution 1876, p. 27).

Those who designed the Detroit House of Shelter and the Indiana Reformatory Institution were to a large extent working in the dark; they had few examples to draw on as they strove to develop an entirely new type of prison for adults.[11] But it is also true that reform was in the air, as was demonstrated by the number and enthusiasm of the penologists and prison reformers who attended the 1870 convention in Cincinnati. Significantly, Zebulon Brockway was one of the central figures at this convention. For our purposes, most important among the principles endorsed by the convention was that calling for the classification of female prisoners into institutions of their own: "[T]here shall be . . . separate establishments for women" (Wines 1871, p. 543). This meeting was a major event in the origin of women's prisons of the reformatory type. The reformatory movement had begun slightly earlier, but the Cincinnati prison congress, by stamping it with official approval, gave the movement both respectability and momentum.

B. Origins of the Reformatory Model:
The Social Context

To identify the origins of the reformatory model is not to explain why it evolved and was adopted by many women's prisons founded in the late nineteenth and early twentieth centuries. Four factors were particularly influential: the desire of male wardens to rid themselves of female prisoners; the development of social feminism; the social purity movement; and the emergence of a new stereotype of the female criminal.

---

11. To some extent, they looked for guidance to the Irish system of prison management (Crofton 1871), which also influenced the design of men's reformatories; institutions for juvenile delinquents provided further inspiration. It is interesting to note that when Sarah Smith became first superintendent of the Reformatory Institution in Indiana, she visited the "penitentiary at Detroit [including the House of Shelter], the better to understand the workings of a model prison" (Indiana Reformatory Institution 1874, p. 15).

In the years after 1870, as in those before, one important source of pressure to create separate institutions for women came from wardens of predominantly male prisons. These administrators wholeheartedly advocated—indeed, sometimes begged for—removal of female convicts. The presence of women sometimes precipitated scandals, and wardens regarded the labor of women as "altogether unproductive" (Indiana State Prison South 1869, p. 7). Complaining of inconvenience, wardens throughout the country called for "wide separation" of the sexes (Wisconsin State Prison 1926, p. 36).[12]

Another, more positive force nurturing development and diffusion of the reformatory model was the movement since labeled "social feminism" (O'Neill 1969; Banner 1974, chap. 3). This movement involved middle-class women who, during the late nineteenth and early twentieth centuries, participated in a variety of reforms aimed at improving the lot of "the dependent and defective classes" and other underprivileged or disenfranchised groups. Some social feminists became active in suffrage, others in the settlement house movement and "child saving" (Platt 1977), yet others in women's prison reform. In contrast to radical feminists, who posed deeper challenges to the status quo, social feminists worked to ameliorate existing social arrangements. Instead of rejecting assumptions about gender differences, social feminists clung to and even amplified gender stereotypes, attempting to introduce domestic methods and values into the sphere of public policy. Indeed, such stereotypes were the vehicle on which they rode into public life, for, as Conway has pointed out, "Intellectually they had to work within the tradition which saw women as civilizing and moralizing forces in society" (1976, p. 309).

In connection with social feminism and its effects on women's prisons, Freedman's new study is especially useful. Freedman firmly locates agitation for women's reformatories within the broader context: "The establishment of separate women's prisons contributed to the larger process of female institution-building in the late nineteenth century. Prison reformers and other social feminists drew upon the ideology of women's separate sphere and gradually expanded its boundaries from the private to the public realm. By creating extradomestic female in-

12. While the wardens' pleas for relief from care of female prisoners contributed to the pressures that produced reformatories, the wardens often failed to achieve their own immediate aim. In a number of states, the laws establishing reformatories excluded felons, or at least recidivist and older felons, from the reformatory populations; hence these women remained in custodial units attached to state prisons for men.

stitutions—colleges, clubs, reform organizations, and even prisons—middle-class American women gained both valuable personal skills and greater public authority" (1981, pp. 46–47).

Freedman goes on to indicate the dangers intrinsic to this type of feminism: "Like the separate but equal racial ideology, however, social feminist strategy rested on a contradictory definition of equality. The nineteenth-century prison reformers did seek to expand women's rights. . . . But at the heart of their program was the principle of innate sexual difference, not sexual equality" (p. 47). For precisely this reason, social feminism not only encouraged establishment of separate prisons for women but also ensured that these institutions would help legitimate dual standards of treatments, one for men and another, inherently more restrictive, for women.

A third factor that created the supportive culture in which the reformatory movement flowered was the so-called social purity movement, also roughly spanning the period 1870–1930. Its leaders tended to come from the ranks of elite Yankee society; they included both men and women, and some simultaneously involved themselves in several social purity activities such as temperance and prison reform. Impelled by anxieties about alcoholism, immigration, prostitution, urbanization, venereal disease, and the like, the social purity movement generally sought to reaffirm and bolster traditional Anglo-Saxon standards (Feldman 1967; Pivar 1973; Schlossman and Wallach 1978; Connelly 1980). To a considerable extent, social purity leaders provided the reformatory movement with its ideological underpinning. In particular, they encouraged incarceration of prostitutes and other "immoral" women: to remove fallen women from sexual circulation was endorsed as a eugenic measure, one which, moreover, fitted nicely with Progressive interest in social engineering. Furthermore, the social purity movement stressed middle-class, Anglo-Saxon standards of propriety—standards that became institutionalized in reformatory discipline.

Finally, the reformatory movement was sustained by emergence of a new stereotype of the criminal woman that, in turn, the movement did much to promote. In the early and mid-nineteenth century, the female criminal had been considered thoroughly depraved and even less likely to reform than her male counterpart. Near the opening of the twentieth century, a second image began to emerge. No longer was the female criminal depicted as monstrous, masculine, and hardened beyond redemption. Rather, she was described as errant, led astray by white slavers, the victim of poverty, poor heredity, or heartless men. In short, the female criminal became a wayward girl—or, to use the favorite term of the time, a "delinquent" (see, e.g., Fernald et al. 1920; also see Freedman 1981, chap. 6). This new image was useful to reformers pressing the claim that they and other women were indeed capable of managing criminals. Moreover, their program of reformatory care meshed well with the image of the female offender as a childlike delinquent, in need of training rather than punishment.

These four factors do much to explain why the reformatory model evolved in the late nineteenth century and went on to shape the development of the prison system. But the reformatory movement did not meet with immediate success after the important events of about 1870 in Detroit, Indianapolis, and Cincinnati. Due to legislative reluctance to fund costly new institutions and endow women with administrative authority, women's prisons of the reformatory type were established quite slowly over the remainder of the nineteenth century. Other than the Indiana institution, only three were opened by 1900, one in Massachusetts and two in New York. However, those who founded and superintended these institutions were busy experimenting, refining the new model, and polishing formulations of reformatory ideals. Although the reformatory that opened in Massachusetts in 1877 conformed in many respects to traditional prison architecture, for example, it omitted the walls and offered a vigorous program of feminine activities (including dancing beneath trees in long white gowns). The House of Refuge opened a decade later at Hudson, New York, was the first adult institution to use the cottage plan, and thereafter reformatories allocated decreasing amounts of cell space in their central prison buildings while increasing the proportion of beds in the outlying cottages where inmates lived family style.[13] By the end of the nineteenth century, reformatory ideals had been articulated (for one classic statement, see Davis [1911]); what remained was more extensive implementation. This occurred rapidly in the early twentieth century: between 1901 and 1933, sixteen reformatories for women were opened in states across the country, primarily in the northeast and north central regions.

13. Though founded as an institution which could receive women between the ages of fifteen and thirty, Hudson later became an institution for girls only.

C. The Reformatory Model

In what follows, I describe the reformatory model in more detail, identifying its traits along the five dimensions used earlier to define the custodial model.

1. *Physical Aspects and Operating Costs.* Reformatories were usually located on large tracts of their own, sometimes several hundred acres of farmland. Most were constructed on the cottage plan, with a central administrative building. Around the administration building were grouped separate cottages, each with beds for twenty to fifty inmates. As one reformatory advocate explained in a passage applying to both adult and juvenile reformatories for females: "The idea of having small houses with little groups . . . was that each cottage should be a real home, with an intelligent, sympathetic woman at the head to act as mother. . . . It was believed that if small groups could be placed in cottages enough motherly women could be found to give them the sort of affection which would most surely help to redeem them" (Barrows 1910, p. 133).

In addition to creating the context for familial treatment, the cottage plan had other advantages which appealed to reformatory founders. It facilitated classification ("honor" inmates, for example, could be grouped together in one cottage, babies in another). Because each had its own kitchen and dining room, the cottage provided opportunities to hone inmates' domestic skills. Furthermore, the cottage symbolized the rural values held dear by the reformers, who associated the countryside and fresh air with betterment, the city with crime and corruption.

Reformatories proved costly to operate. Each cottage needed its own kitchen, dining room, and staff. Moreover, the farms often associated with reformatories required personnel and machinery. Due to such expenses, women's reformatories were usually the costliest penal institutions in their states.

Life in a women's reformatory was more comfortable than in custodial institutions for either men or women. Within the cottages, inmates sometimes had their own rooms, more spacious and homelike (though nonetheless secure) living units than traditional cells. Moreover, the reformatories were usually unwalled and in other ways low in security. Well-behaved inmates were occasionally granted freedom of movement among the buildings, and some superintendents organized picnics and nature walks over the often idyllic acreage of their institutions.

It is important not to idealize the physical advantages of the reformatories, however, or to equate these with overall improvement in the lot of female prisoners. Sprawling and inefficient, reformatory plants consumed funds which might otherwise have been funneled into programs. Moreover, their physical design was part and parcel of an effort that produced differential treatment. Inmates incarcerated in cottages, organized to dance on lawns in the dusk, and led on picnics and nature walks were being treated as children. They were being forced into the role of characters in a bourgeois fantasy of a bygone rural world, rather than being dealt with as adults in an industrializing, class-divided society. For their occasional advantages they paid a high price in status and, we can hypothesize, in self-image.

2. *Inmate Characteristics.*   Whereas inmates of custodial institutions were mainly felons, those of reformatories were usually misdemeanants or even less serious offenders. Developers of the reformatory plan aimed at rehabilitating women who, as Katherine Bement Davis put it, "led immoral lives or 'acted on impulse' " (1911, p. 46). Reformatory populations included women convicted of petty larceny, prostitution, and vagrancy and of even less serious offenses like "being in danger of falling into vice," "lewd and lascivious carriage," and "waywardness." Davis's study of the first thousand commitments to Bedford, the New York reformatory which she superintended, showed that 51.2 percent had been committed for offenses other than felonies or misdemeanors: " 'Other offenses' means common prostitute, frequenting disorderly houses and in danger of becoming morally depraved, habitual drunkard, soliciting on the public streets, etc. It should be said that out of the one thousand the number of those who have led sexually regular lives is almost negligible" (New York Bedford State Reformatory 1911, p. 56).

Not all reformatories were able to withstand pressures also to accept more serious offenders (Bedford, in fact, had admitted selected felons from the start), and as time went on, most were forced to squeeze out misdemeanants in order to make room for felons.[14] But, particularly in the early decades of the reformatory movement, some institutions were able to maintain the ideal of receiving only those petty offenders who, according to reformatory theory, were most susceptible to rehabilitative influences.

14. Those which did not were closed. For example, the California Institution for Women at Sonoma, a reformatory for selected misdemeanants, opened in 1922 only to close about a year later, and New York's State Farm for Women at Valatie, dedicated to care of older, repeat misdemeanants, closed in 1918 after several years of operation.

Thus women committed to reformatories, especially during these institutions' early years, often had no male counterparts in state-supported penal institutions in terms of their offenses. The state-run prisons for men which were called reformatories held young felons, not misdemeanants. Men who had committed crimes like fornication and drunkenness, if they were prosecuted at all, were at most punished with brief jail terms. Like correctional institutions for juveniles, women's reformatories brought under state control a population that previously had been ignored by the criminal justice system or else handled by cities and counties and treated more similarly to males.[15] The women who lobbied for and administered reformatories believed they were doing such offenders a service by providing for them special care. (See New York Hudson House of Refuge 1890, p. 10.) But in the course of doing good, they treated other women like children and perpetuated the double standard that required women to conform to more difficult moral rules than men and punished them if they failed to do so.

Not surprisingly, women committed to the reformatories tended to be young. During their early years, some reformatories had populations in which the majority of inmates were between sixteen and twenty-five years old. A few states went so far as to prohibit their reformatories from receiving women over thirty on the theory that older women were unlikely to reform. As we have seen, inmates of custodial institutions tended to be older.

Racially, too, reformatories differed in their populations from custodial institutions for women. Whereas disproportionate numbers of blacks were incarcerated in the latter, the former held mainly whites, particularly during the institutions' early years. Evidently judges were ready to save white women by committing them to reformatories but were reluctant to similarly save women of color, deeming the latter less worthy of rehabilitative efforts. Another factor which worked to exclude blacks was racial prejudice on the part of the institutions themselves. Two southern reformatories openly refused to receive black women during their first years of operation, and there are indications in admission ledgers of at least one northern reformatory that its early

15. Those who founded women's reformatories explicitly argued that such institutions were needed to hold minor female offenders for longer terms, stressing that "it would cost the State less in the end to take these girls and women and keep them long enough to train them so that a reasonable percentage could go out as respectable and self-supporting women" (Davis 1911, p. 45, quoting Josephine Lowell, founder of several New York state prisons for women).

administrators did not even consider the possibility of nonwhite commitments.[16] As time went on, black women were introduced into the
populations of the reformatories. However, they usually remained a
minority prior to 1935, and they were nearly always segregated by
cottage and program.

3. *Administration.* In contrast to custodial institutions, the reformatories were run entirely by women, and these women enjoyed high
degrees of administrative independence (cf. SchWeber 1982). Most states
required by law that their reformatory be superintended by a woman,
and some specified that she should hire mainly female staff. Thus not
only the guards but also the physician and head farmer were women
in some reformatories. This emphasis on female staff was in part a
result of the conviction (expressed most strongly by female reformers
themselves) that only other women could understand and deal with the
problems of female offenders. The emphasis also flowed from the concept of role models: about 1870 reformers began to endorse the theory
that, through example, proper women could encourage fallen women
to mend their ways.

The all-female nature of reformatory administrations had some obvious advantages for inmates. It eliminated the possibility of sexual
exploitation by male keepers, and it increased the likelihood that those
who operated the institutions would be sensitive to women's needs and
concerns. On the other hand, it is doubtful that such administrations
were as advantageous to inmates as the reformers claimed. Wide social
class differences divided the working-class women incarcerated in reformatories from the middle-class, sometimes highly educated women
who superintended them.[17] It is not clear that the administrators were
well prepared to understand the inmates' problems, particularly those
which related to social class, work, and independence. On the contrary,
it was in part the failure of the founders and administrators of reformatories to tolerate sexual and other mildly deviant behaviors of work-

16. The two southern reformatories were those of North Carolina and Virginia. The
northern reformatory was the Western House of Refuge at Albion; its intake ledgers
(now in the State Archives at Albany) leave space for the recording of information on a
large number of variables (including mental disabilities of the inmates' grandparents) but
none for race, thus indicating that only one race—the whites whom the institution did
in fact exclusively receive at first—was expected at the time the ledger format was
prepared. When in later years black women were received, "colored" was written at the
top of the ledger page.

17. The statement about the social class of inmates is based on as yet unpublished
data collected from the prisoner records of several reformatories. For information on the
social class of the reformers, see Freedman (1981).

ing-class women which led to the founding of reformatories in the first place. Moreover, the extent to which middle-class, college-educated administrators provided relevant role models for their charges (many of whom were being trained to be domestic servants) is also open to question. They encouraged propriety but certainly not upward mobility. Freedman (1976) has argued that the keepers, rather than the kept, profited from the reformatory movement's introduction of all-female administrations. Some middle-class women did benefit from the opening of positions in corrections to their sex. But for inmates the result was maternalistic care which, though well intentioned, was also morally intolerant, coercive, and condescending. Women held in custodial institutions, like male state prisoners, experienced nothing comparable to this intense moralism.

4. *Approaches to Discipline.* The innovative nature of the reformatory model was perhaps most clearly evident in its approaches to discipline. Two aspects of reformatory discipline are particularly noteworthy. First, the reformatories implemented the penology of rehabilitation in terms of gender roles, attempting to reform inmates by training them to be good wives, mothers, or domestic servants. Second, the reformatories developed a characteristic type of sentence, an indeterminate sentence of three years.

Women's institutions of the custodial type approached discipline in a manner similar to that of the men's prisons with which they were associated, albeit less consistently. Women's reformatories, in contrast, "feminized" prison discipline, stressing individualization of treatment, mildness in punishments, and a noninstitutional, homelike atmosphere. Discipline in women's reformatories was further congruent with the female gender role in its emphasis on sexual purity and its tendency to infantilize inmates. This translation of rehabilitation into feminine terms was very much influenced by the social feminist and social purity movements that themselves helped precipitate the reformatory movement.

Specific disciplinary practices within the reformatories were by and large derived from the concept of the institution as a substitute family. To the first superintendent of New York's Western House of Refuge, for example, the family system meant an "absence of rewards or penalties without any system of marking for conduct or misconduct." Like many other superintendents, she believed that the "female temperament" could not abide the "arbitrary rules" and stern punishments that characterized discipline in institutions for men (New York Western

House of Refuge 1899, pp. 16–17). Reformatories conceived of their charges as temperamentally close to children and punished them accordingly; priding themselves on underutilization of punishment cells, some chastised difficult inmates by sending them to their rooms. Although more punitive techniques eventually crept into the discipline of even the best reformatories, the ideal was a far cry from the disciplinary techniques of custodial institutions.

Another important difference between the two models lay in the area of sentencing. Women in custodial institutions received the same type of sentence as did men convicted of similar felonies; these sentences were determinate or indeterminate, depending on the historical period, and their length was linked to the seriousness of the offense. The sexes were treated with relative equality, then, in custodial institutions, and the principle of proportionality, according to which the punishment should fit the crime, prevailed.

Sentencing practices were quite different in women's reformatories. It is somewhat difficult to generalize on this point because the reformatories developed a variety of sentencing structures. However, there was a form of sentence typical of those reformatories that did not have to compromise their ideals. This was the indeterminate three-year sentence, a type unknown in custodial women's institutions, except at the Detroit House of Correction, where Brockway had written the original "three years law" applying to prostitutes (1912/1969, chap. 8). The indeterminate three-year sentence had no minimum. Prisoners could be released on parole at any time, but they could also be held for the three-year maximum if they failed to show signs of reformation. This type of sentence ignored the ancient principle of proportionality. Like the analogous sentence of some men's reformatories, it linked time served to prisoners' current behavior rather than the seriousness of their past offenses.[18]

In general, reformatory women spent less time in prison than did their custodial counterparts, for the latter were felons with longer sentences. But although the terms served by reformatory women were

18. The "pure" women's reformatory sentence was developed by the two New York state reformatories founded in the late nineteenth century at Hudson and Albion. Originally, women sent to these institutions could be held for up to five years (New York, *Laws of 1890*, chap. 238, §8). Some judges objected to the disproportionality involved in such lengthy sentences for women convicted of petty offenses, however, and in 1899 the maximum term was reduced to three years (*Laws of 1899*, chap. 632, §1). A five-year indeterminate sentence applied at the New York State reformatory for young men at Elmira, but that was a prison for felons.

usually briefer, they were arguably more severe in at least two senses. They were more severe in that, first, the principle of proportionality was abandoned by reformatories that adopted the three-year indeterminate (or a similar) sentence for what were often petty offenses. Some women who founded and managed reformatories argued that it was quite proper to ignore the principle of proportionality because their aim was not to punish but to treat—to retrain and reform, a process that required time (see n. 15). Other supporters of women's reformatories, those who subscribed to the principles of eugenics, argued that reformatory sentences should be totally indefinite so that genetically inferior women could be removed from sexual circulation (e.g., Glueck and Glueck 1934, pp. 309–10). No matter what the justification, up to three years (not to mention up to life) was a high price to pay for minor crimes.

The second sense in which reformatory sentences were more severe than those of custodial institutions lies in the fact that they legalized differential treatment of women. Men were sent to state prisons because they had committed felonies. Women could be committed to reformatories for misdemeanors or even lesser offenses. Similarly, men could not be required to serve up to three years for minor public order crimes. Women sent to reformatories were thus punished more harshly than men who committed the same types of offenses.

5. *Programs.*   Work programs in reformatories consisted mainly of training in cleaning, cooking, sewing, and waiting on tables. Although inmates of custodial institutions were also assigned to maintenance chores, the reformatories glorified such activities, even to the point of offering courses in them. One, for instance, set up a Cooking Department with worktables, sinks, and stoves so that inmates could be instructed in food preparation (New York Western House of Refuge 1918, p. 18). Many provided instruction in different types of knitting and sewing, courses which might culminate with production of one's "parole outfit." Such elaborate training in what the reformatories liked to call domestic science could not have been found in custodial women's prisons. The reformatories developed such vocational programs because they aimed at producing proper women who would, on release, assume positions as domestic servants or marry and become good wives. A New York report of 1927 on the Western House of Refuge explained that "no industries are maintained, but every inmate is taught to cook and care for a home. This is the most important thing in the work of the institution. Most of the girls when paroled go into homes where

this knowledge is necessary" (New York State Commission of Correction 1927, p. 87). Indeed, reformatories paroled large proportions of their inmates to positions as domestic servants. Parole could be revoked if the woman failed to perform satisfactorily.

In comparison to custodial institutions, reformatories developed strong programs in education and recreation. Women spent several hours daily in classrooms where they received instruction in such subjects as reading, penmanship, and personal health care. When not in class or on work assignments, they might be required to participate in outdoor sports, the production of a play, or choral singing. Such activities may have made reformatory life a richer (not to mention healthier) experience than that in custodial institutions. However, provision of these somewhat superior opportunities was inseparable from an institutional approach that treated women as unrefined youngsters.

The profile of "the" reformatory that I have drawn is perforce abstract, a type to which no specific institution corresponded exactly at any time. Certainly no actual reformatory continued to correspond to it as, over time, administrative realities began to temper idealism. In what follows, I qualify some of the preceding generalizations and explain why interest in the reformatory model eventually began to wane.

D. Diffusion, Decline, and Eventual Demise of the Reformatory Model

The movement to establish reformatories for women did not affect all regions of the country equally. It was strongest in the Northeast, where the social feminist and social purity movements also took strongest hold. Nearly every state in the Northeast established a reformatory, and New York founded three. Eight of the twelve states in the north central area also established reformatories. However, although the reformatory model had originated in the north central region (in the Detroit House of Shelter, the Indiana Reformatory Institution, and the 1870 Cincinnati prison convention), by the late 1870s leadership of the movement had passed to the northeastern states (see, e.g., van Wyck 1913, p. 94). Moreover, the north central institutions were seldom as successful as their eastern counterparts in achieving reformatory ideals: they tended to provide weaker programs; few made consistent use of the indeterminate sentence; only one placed an upper limit on the age of women who might be received; and several (such as the crowded, unambitious institution at Marysville, Ohio) made little effort to achieve reformatory aims.

The South was not entirely unaffected by the reformatory movement, for three institutions of this type were established in the region (in Arkansas, North Carolina, and Virginia). But in the southern reformatory movement, indigenous women's groups were less involved. The reformatory in Arkansas, for example, was established largely through the work of Martha P. Falconer, a visitor from the Northeast (Thomas 1930, p. 505). Southern reformatories were less likely than those of the North to be entirely separate from institutions for men; only one of the three adopted the cottage plan; none placed an upper limit on the age of women who might be received; and only one, in North Carolina, excluded felons. Their programs, furthermore, were thin. Significantly, the reformatories of Arkansas and North Carolina— the two which most closely resembled northern counterparts—were finally closed. Thus the women's reformatory movement was less extensive in the South and produced relatively weak institutions.

The West was even less affected than the South by the reformatory movement. Only California established a women's prison designed along reformatory lines, and that in 1929, when the movement had nearly run out of steam. The California Institution for Women took felons from the start, and after its first few years of operation it entirely excluded misdemeanants, the traditional reformatory population (Voight 1949, pp. 7–8, 11).[19] Moreover, this institution at Techachapi was so remote that in time it was abandoned as a reformatory for women, its population being relocated to Frontera in 1952.

Thus as a rule, the more distant a state was from the northeastern heart of the movement, the less interest it showed in establishment of a reformatory. Just as there was a geographical decline, so was there a falling off of interest in reformatory ideals over time: the goals, techniques, and even characteristics of inmates held in these institutions changed considerably over the sixty-five years spanned by the reformatory movement. Freedman (1981) has identified many of these changes: the "narrowing of reformers' visions" as they confronted the realities of prison management (p. 67); the shift in techniques from "feminine solicitude" to "more orthodox methods" of prison discipline (p. 72; also see pp. 73, 97); and the reformatories' "increasingly anachronistic" adherence to rural and domestic values as the nation developed

19. It is not clear that any misdemeanants were in fact committed to CIW; certainly felons predominated in its population from the start. In the nonreformatory states of the South and West, as in those of the other regions, female felons continued to be held in custodial units associated with prisons for men.

"an urban industrial economy" (p. 95). As time went on, moreover, the care that both women's and men's reformatories could provide declined in quality. They became overcrowded, and legislatures balked at funding expensive treatment programs. The tilt toward custodialism was encouraged by the eugenics movement, which led to demands that reformatories provide "permanent custodial care" for women with "inherent weaknesses . . . and defectiveness" (Kansas Women's Industrial Farm 1920, p. 6; also see Hahn 1980b). Despite their ideal of using only mild chastisements, some reformatories came to rely on harsh physical punishments (see, e.g., Kennedy [1921] and Freedman [1981], p. 99). More black women were committed as time went on, and in many states the seriousness of commitment offenses also increased as, faced with the need to deal with real offenders, judges were forced to forgo the luxury of sentencing to reformatories women guilty of offenses like being in danger of falling into vice. Actual vice came to command more attention than its mere threat.

The transformation of reformatory populations to include large proportions of felons marked the end of the reformatory movement. This transformation was in large part a product of financial need. Many reformatory states had also maintained a custodial, back-up unit for felons. As time went on, the expense of maintaining two women's institutions simply became too heavy. Significantly, it was about 1930, just after the start of a major economic crisis, that a number of states closed their custodial units, transferring their populations to reformatory grounds.[20] (Usually a new and more secure prison cottage was constructed for this group.)

Women's prisons that had begun as reformatories now changed character, perforce incorporating elements of the custodial model.[21] This debasement of the reformatory plan caused little dismay among members of the women's groups that traditionally had backed women's reformatories, however. By 1935, the women's reformatory movement had run its course, having largely achieved its objective (establishment

20. Ohio limited the population of its reformatory at Marysville to felons in 1929. In 1933, New York closed its State Prison for Women at Auburn, transferring its inmates to newly acquired property across the street from the Bedford reformatory. Similarly, Wisconsin, Nebraska, and Illinois closed the custodial units for women at their central state prisons in 1933, transferring the felons to their reformatories.
21. Of course, some reformatories had held both misdemeanants and felons from their time of opening; in these, elements of the two models had mixed from the start. However, even in these, as felons came to predominate in the population, the character of the institutions necessarily changed.

of separate prisons run by women) in those regions of the country most involved with Progressive reforms in general. Moreover, by the 1930s alarm over prostitution and venereal disease had abated (Connelly 1980), and the attention of penologists had begun to shift from rehabilitation of individuals to efficient management of the statewide prison systems (see, e.g., New York State Prison Survey Committee 1920). Thus, around 1935, states stopped building institutions according to the reformatory model, and the reformatory movement drew to a close.

With that movement's demise, inmates of prisons that had begun as reformatories no longer received the advantages associated with such institutions—concern to keep punishments mild, for example, and efforts to individualize treatment. Gone were the days of nature hikes over the reformatories' rolling hills. Women now had less freedom within the institutions, and security measures were intensified. Whatever benefits had accrued to inmates from the reformatory movement dwindled and disappeared. But there survived the reformatory legacy of differential treatment, a legacy which continued to manifest itself in infantilization of inmates and in the severer sentences to which women were liable.

III. The Third Stage, 1935–80: A Brief Overview of Recent Developments

The third stage in the development of the women's prison system is less clear-cut in character than the previous two, in part because no distinctive model or type emerged during this period, in part because regional patterns differed greatly. In what follows, I combine the chronological with a regional approach, looking at developments in the women's prison system in, first, the northeastern and north central states, then those of the South, and finally those of the West.

This third stage is covered in less detail than the earlier two, a limitation imposed not only by space but also by the quality of sources. It is more difficult to obtain information on recently established women's prisons than on those founded in the nineteenth century. Many nineteenth-century prisons published bulky annual reports brimming with details on inmates and management, and there are a number of types of documents that can be used to supplement these annual reports and check their accuracy. In contrast, contemporary prisons and correctional bureaucracies are chary of sharing information. No in-depth discussion of recent developments in the women's prison system can take place until researchers discover ways to circumvent the deficiencies in the currently available data.

A. *Development in the Northeastern and North Central States*

In terms of institution founding, there was almost no change in the women's prison system of the northeastern and north central states between 1935 and 1980. Only one new institution was established in this period—Michigan's Huron Valley Women's Facility, which opened in 1977.[22] The reason for this stasis is clear: due to the reformatory movement, states of these regions already had women's prisons.

That the quality of care provided in recent decades by these prisons fell far below that furnished to male prisoners in the same states has been thoroughly documented, as I noted in the introduction. Recent studies have identified some of the sources of this inequity, including the greater number of male prisoners and biases of male corrections officials. Another source was the merger, in the early twentieth century, of the custodial and reformatory traditions; pooling their disadvantages, they fed these into the subsequent operation of prisons which had begun as women's reformatories.

By 1935, most northeastern and north central states were sending female felons to the institutions that had originated as reformatories, and the idealistic reformatory movement had died of exhaustion. The former reformatories naturally began to incorporate aspects of the custodial model, including its tradition of less adequate care for female than for male prisoners. Even in the heyday of the reformatory movement, legislatures had often failed to allocate funds sufficient to support the ambitious rehabilitative programs, but now that the former reformatories held mainly felons, inadequacies in their facilities, programs, and staffs were even more easily ignored. Outsiders took little interest in the plight of female felons, and prison officials devoted the bulk of attention and resources to problems in men's institutions; thus inadequacies of women's prisons took low priority, just as they had in women's custodial institutions from the early nineteenth century. Other aspects of custodialism also worked to degrade the quality of care in

22. The Missouri State Penitentiary for Women was established as an independent institution in 1955. No more was involved than a few statutory and administrative changes, however, for the "new" institution was located in the buildings of the previous Women's Branch of the State Penitentiary. Because women had been held at that location at least since the 1860s, the prison established in 1955 does not qualify as a new institution.

the former reformatories in this post-1935 period—its more rigid approach to rules and punishments, for example, and its tradition of indifference to living conditions.

Many of the problems historically associated with the reformatory tradition, moreover, continued to affect management of institutions conceived in this tradition. Despite the growth of suburbs, the rural location of some women's prisons that had begun as reformatories remained troublesome, cutting inmates off from families and community resources. In addition, the former reformatories continued to have high overhead expenses due to their subdivision into a number of separate units. Even more significant were the original reformatories' social class prejudices and their resultant insistence on conformity to proper women's roles, biases which worked to perpetuate care which was moralistic and out of touch with the problems of working-class and minority women. For example, after 1935 as before, women's prisons attempted to cultivate inmate self-respect through encouragement of ladylike appearances; cosmetology courses and personal grooming programs played major roles in the curricula of such institutions. Lacking a tradition of industrial training, these women's prisons went on failing to prepare inmates for competitive jobs. Women continued to be called "girls" and in other ways as well were still subjected to the childlike treatment considered appropriate for female offenders. (For documentation of these and related problems, see Glick and Neto [1977] and Burkhart [1973].) It is in large part because of the tradition of differential treatment has such deep roots in the reformatory tradition that gender stereotyping remains a major problem in the administration of women's prisons (especially those which originated as reformatories) today.

Thus both the custodial and reformatory models, as they converged in the 1930s on the sites of former reformatories in the northeast and north central regions, brought to these institutions their own type of differential treatment of women.

B. Developments in the South

Seven separate prisons for women had been established in the south before 1935, and thereafter—at first glance—the development of the southern system of women's prisons seems to have been one of slow but steady growth.[23] One other institution was opened in the 1930s,

23. The seven southern prisons for women established before 1935 were Texas's Goree Farm (1910), Arkansas's State Farm for Women (1919), Alabama's Wetumpka State Penitentiary unit for women (1923, later moved to Julia Tutwiler Prison), North Carolina's

two each in the decades of the 1940s and 1950s, four in the 1960s, and five in the 1970s. But in actuality, the development of the women's prison system in the South was neither steady nor progressive. It was characterized instead by ad hoc solutions, frequent transfers of female populations from one inadequate location to another, and an absence of legislative involvement in provision for this group that led to a lack of legal standards and of checks on the authority of prison bureaucrats.

To understand the nature of developments in the South in the post-1935 period, it is necessary to step back a moment to get a longer-term view of the evolution of women's prisons in the region. After the Civil War, many southern states established or rebuilt some sort of penal institution for men in or near which female prisoners were also held. In some states, this was a penitentiary to which a custodial unit for women was appended and maintained until overcrowding forced establishment of a separate prison for women. The latter event, with few exceptions, occurred in 1930–80. This route of maintaining women's institutions as adjuncts to men's penitentiaries was taken, for example, by North Carolina, which held felons of both sexes together at the state prison at Raleigh until lack of beds forced removal in 1933 of the women to old prison buildings on the outskirts of town; over the years new buildings were added to the plant, and the North Carolina women's prison remains at the Raleigh location today. Similarly, Tennessee held its women prisoners in a series of custodial units near its central penitentiary until, in 1965, an overflowing female population led to establishment of a separate Prison for Women (Hahn 1980*a*). Unlike North Carolina, Tennessee built an entirely new institution for its female prisoners, but the process was basically the same one of splitting off from a men's penitentiary in these two and a number of other southern states.

Not all southern states built central penitentiaries, however. Some established prison farms or plantations, and in these states a different process brought separate women's prisons into being. Some states which operated prison farms began by renting women prisoners out to local

---

Industrial Farm Colony for Women (1927), Delaware's Women's Prison (1929), Virginia's State Industrial Farm for Women (1930), and North Carolina's Women's Prison (ca. 1933). However, the term "established" must be used somewhat loosely in the case of these and other southern prisons, for frequently establishment involved not legislative action but merely administrative fiat. Significantly, of the seven prisons just listed, only the three reformatories, in Arkansas, North Carolina, and Virginia, were formally established by legislative action.

farmers on a share system, mainly to work in the fields. Even in those states, however, women prisoners eventually were located at camps on the grounds of the state prison farm. Often they were moved from camp to camp for a number of years until they ended up in barracks which, enlarged and rebuilt over time, finally became the state's official women's prison. In general outline, it was this pattern of development—from farming out prisoners to establishing prison camps to an independent prison—that resulted in the first prison for women in Texas. (This prison, Goree, was supplemented in 1975 by another, more modern, women's institution.) Arkansas similarly shifted its female prisoners about until in 1951 it established a reformatory on the grounds of Cummins Farm.[24] In 1975, women were moved out of Cummins to a new women's unit at Pine Bluff, about thirty miles away.

Despite the many variations, the women's prisons established and operated in the South since the 1930s have shared two traits. First, as in the previous period, their populations were overwhelmingly black. Second, nearly all of these institutions conformed to the custodial model—often with a vengeance. They were usually more crowded than the women's institutions of other regions, in some cases appallingly so; and their programs were even weaker. Often crammed into unsanitary dormitories without the slightest opportunity for privacy, at times brutalized sexually, either abandoned to idleness or assigned to hard and at times crippling labor, women incarcerated in southern prisons in 1935–80 generally had poorer care than women prisoners in other regions during that time (see, e.g., Murton 1969). Their treatment seems to have been inferior to that of their southern male counterparts as well (see, e.g., Wheaton 1979). Like women in custodial institutions since the prison system began, those in the South in the post-1935 period were outnumbered by male prisoners. Hence they were neglected and underprotected, and their special needs were ignored.

C. Developments in the West

Until the 1960s, provision for female prisoners in the West remained at a stage out of which eastern states had begun to move about a century earlier. Only California had established a separate institution for women, and that only after a titanic struggle between women's groups and the

24. Despite its name, the Arkansas State Reformatory for Women at Cummins Farm was a purely custodial operation; even an Arkansas penal committee referred to it as "the so-called Reformatory for Women" (Arkansas Penitentiary Study Commission 1968, p. 3.18).

state prison bureaucracy (Monahan 1941). Other western states, having few female prisoners, continued to hold them in a central penal institution. Sometimes locked in a second-story room of the administration building, sometimes tucked away in a small annex of their own, these prisoners experienced the same disadvantages as had women held in the mid-nineteenth century in institutions like Auburn and the Ohio Penitentiary. Occasionally they were supervised by the warden's wife or a hired matron, but often they were left alone, vulnerable to each other and male staff. Because they were few in number, they did not seem to warrant the expense of special programs and equipment; yet they were isolated from the resources of the male population. As late as 1979, Montana and Utah were apparently still relying on the old solution of holding female state prisoners in small appendages to their central prisons for men.[25]

During the 1960s and 1970s, however, nearly all of the other western states created a women's prison system where none had been before by establishing seven separate institutions for women.[26] This sudden expansion was caused mainly by over-crowding and, frequently, decrepitude of the older units for women. Six of the seven new institutions (in Arizona, Colorado, Nevada, New Mexico, Oregon, and Wyoming) basically continued in the custodial tradition. They were larger than the previous custodial units for women and somewhat more independent in administration but otherwise not markedly different.

To judge from the scanty information available, the programs of these six new prisons for women were impoverished, gender stereotyped, and weaker than those offered in the same states' prisons for men. For example, in 1973 Nagel criticized neglect of industrial activities at Oregon's Women's Correctional Center: "Salem . . . has [only] small ironing and sewing rooms, the inevitable beauty shop, and the usual service activities" (p. 117). Several years later, a civil rights committee took this same women's prison to task for providing fewer educational

25. According to the American Correctional Association (1980, p. 139), in 1979 an average of eleven women were held at the Montana State Prison. However, different information on the situation of female prisoners in Montana appeared at about the same time in Potter (1978): "Montana's 12 women are divided between a separate Life Skills Center in Billings and a coed facility in Missoula" (p. 15). During the 1970s, Utah opened two work-release facilities for women. The American Correctional Association's *Directory* suggests, however, that Utah's female felons continued to be sent to the state prison until near the end of their sentences (1980, p. 233).

26. The only exception seems to be Idaho, which evidently held its few female prisoners at a coed unit opened in 1974 in Cottonwood (American Correctional Association 1980, p. 75).

and vocational programs and "fewer meaningful job opportunities" than Oregon's prison for men (Oregon Advisory Committee 1976, p. 37). While the details differed from state to state, the general picture for these six prisons was one of dreary routines and at best a few cosmetology and high school equivalency courses. Men's prisons in the same states offered richer programs, more services, and greater opportunities for furlough and work release.

The seventh of these recently established western prisons, Washington's Purdy Treatment Center, has been hailed as "the best women's prison in the country" (Potter 1978, p. 22). When it opened in 1971, Purdy consisted of "low brick and concrete buildings [that] face a landscaped and paved inner courtyard"; its architects were said to have "captured more of a community college atmosphere than that of a prison" (Horne et al., n.d., p. 2). In program, too, Purdy was in some respects innovative, providing separate apartments for women on work release, for instance, and encouraging contacts between inmates and their children.

In the design and operation of Purdy, we can perhaps detect the emergence (albeit tentative) of a third model of women's prison, one which rejects the traditions of both custodialism and the reformatory and might be called a *campus model*. During its first years, Purdy attempted to provide rehabilitative programs and to be sensitive to the special needs of women (thus rejecting the custodial tradition) and at the same time to avoid treating its inmates as children (thus turning its back on the reformatory model). Yet it is debatable whether Purdy achieved a radical break with the women's prison system's legacy of differential treatment. Although it was more varied than the programs of the custodial prisons of other western states, Purdy's program continued to emphasize interests traditionally associated with women—arts and crafts, cosmetology, and office skills. Moreover, its behavior management program has elicited scorn from inmates who, echoing an old theme in female corrections, have damned it as belittling and juvenile (Potter 1978, p. 24). Thus this seeming exception to the type of women's prison found elsewhere in the West, and in the country as a whole, may in fact not be much of an exception after all.[27]

27. A few other recently established women's prisons seem, like Purdy, to have begun by struggling to develop a new model, one which would involve modern buildings on

IV. Conclusion

A recent article in the *New York Times* pointed out that "the criminal justice system discriminates in two ways against women—for them and against them" (Bird 1979). In this sketch of the origins and evolution of the women's prison system, I have identified some of the historical roots of this double-edged inequity, discrimination against in the traditions of the custodial model, discrimination for in those of the reformatory model.

It will take much more research to bring the historical outlines of the women's prison system into clear focus. We need full-scale portraits of individual institutions, especially those founded since the 1930s; from these we can build toward more complete understanding of regional differences. Court records for specific cases and archives holding prisoner registries and case files can be used to establish inmate profiles and identify ways in which women reacted to incarceration. The relation between women's reformatories and institutions for juveniles calls for exploration, as does that between prisons and other institutions (such as mental hospitals) for women. Historical comparisons of the conviction offenses, sentences, and time served of men and women, and of black and white women, will shed light on issues such as offense patterns and differential treatment. More work also is needed on social factors that affected rates of female incarceration. Finally, the history of women's prisons must be better integrated with that of men's. Accounts of the penal system which ignore women distort our understanding of the evolution of women's prisons and of the prison system as a whole.

Once some of this work has been done, data on the incarceration of women can be used to test hypotheses about the functions of prisons. For example, Rothman has posited that the penitentiary was designed in response to a crisis of "disorder in the new republic," as an attempt to correct a perceived "faulty organization of the community" (1971, p. xix). Were the sources of this disorder associated mainly with men?

---

a campus-type site and that would avoid gender-stereotyped programs. Examples include the St. Gabriel prison opened in Louisiana in 1961 and the Women's Correctional center opened at Hardwick, Georgia, in 1976. But like Purdy, these other efforts to develop a new type of women's prison have by and large failed to achieve their potential, a failure due to overcrowding, underfunding, and persistence of gender stereotyping in program design. The warden of one such institution complained to me that she was unable to introduce more up-to-date programs because the state's correctional bureaucracy "funds the women's prison last."

If so, does this help explain why only one prison for women was established in Jacksonian America? If small numbers were the reason little attention was paid to female criminals during that era, we are still left with the question, Why were women in the early penitentiaries not fully subjected to the routines considered remedial for men? And why—as seems almost certainly to have been the case (Crawford 1835/ 1969, pp. 26–27; Lewis 1965, pp. 157–58)—were judges reluctant to sentence women to penitentiaries if these were viewed as institutions that could restore social stability? Similar questions might be asked of the revisionist historians who argue that penitentiaries and other nineteenth-century institutions were "weapons of class conflict or instruments of 'social control' " (Ignatieff 1981, p. 153). Why were women not included in this solution? And why, even when women were incarcerated and assigned to hard labor, was less effort made to exploit their work for profit?

While most such questions must wait till further information is available, enough is known of the women's reformatory movement to indicate that it, at least, will support the thesis that incarceration was economically useful to capitalism (Currie 1973; Foucault 1977). The thesis, however, will have to be restated, for where incarcerated males provided cheap labor, women's reformatories functioned to keep women *out* of the industrial labor force. On the other hand, the reformatory policies of domestic training and parole to domestic positions did help maintain a pool of cheap household help for middle-class women—the group who founded these institutions—and arguably these policies strengthened the gender-role divisions and family structure which undergirded industrial capitalism (Zaretsky 1976; Rafter, forthcoming).

Whatever other conclusions may be indicated by expansion of prison history and theory to include women, one will surely be that beliefs about gender have played a crucial role in the design of penal institutions and treatment of their inmates. Penitentiaries were designed for men. Given nineteenth-century beliefs about the nature of women (or, at least, white women), there could have been no widespread movement to subject women to the lockstep and lash. Although small numbers of female convicts were held in penitentiaries, they were treated differently in some respects just because they were women. The powerful influence of gender roles on prison design is best illustrated by the reformatory movement which, splitting into two tracks, produced very different institutions for men and women. And gender preconceptions continue to affect the nature of incarceration, contributing to a women's prison system which emphasizes role training.

Women's prison history has implications for policy as well as theory, indicating alternatives to current practices. Today, for example, there is growing concern to preserve the ties between incarcerated women and their children (Haley 1977). Lessons can be learned from the reformatories, many of which allowed prisoners to keep their infants. The past can also instruct when it comes to so-called coed prisons. Within the last several decades, a number of states and the federal system have returned to the nineteenth-century practice of holding women and men together (Anderson 1978). These experiments have increased the range of opportunities available to women, but due to women's own hesitancy or unwitting discouragement by staff, they may not use these opportunities to full advantage. As in the outside world, moreover, women tend to get in more trouble when there is illicit contact between the sexes (SchWeber 1980). History suggests that the potential benefits of coed prisons cannot be realized unless there are equal numbers of men and women and an administrative sensitivity to forces which push women toward the end of the line.

This leads to a third policy area, the current pressure for equal treatment of male and female prisoners. Differential treatment, over time, has been a product of unequal numbers as well as of gender-role assumptions. As Beaumont and de Toqueville pointed out in the early nineteenth century, "It is because they [female prisoners] occupy little space . . . that they have been neglected" (1833/1964, p. 72). If equal treatment is to be achieved or even attempted, the implications of the "numbers" problems will have to be faced. Equal treatment will necessarily involve much greater expenditure on female prisoners since it is more costly to operate institutions for relatively few. The current economic situation and crisis of overcrowding within prisons—not to mention nearly two hundred years of differential care—suggest that equal treatment of female prisoners will not be achieved in the foreseeable future.

REFERENCES

Alpert, Geoffrey P., and John J. Wiorkowski. 1977. "Female Prisoners and Legal Services." *Quarterly Journal of Corrections* 1 (4): 28–33.
American Correctional Association. 1980. *Directory 1980.* College Park, Md.: American Correctional Association.

Anderson, David C. 1978. "Co-Corrections." *Corrections Magazine* 4 (3): 33–42.

Arditi, Ralph R., Fredrick Goldberg, Jr., M. Martha Hartle, John H. Peters, and William R. Phelps. 1973. "The Sexual Segregation of American Prisons." *Yale Law Journal* 82:1229–73.

Arkansas Penitentiary Study Commission. 1968. *Report of the Arkansas Penitentiary Study Commission.* Little Rock: Arkansas Department of Corrections.

Banner, Lois. 1974. *Women in Modern America: A Brief History.* New York: Harcourt Brace Jovanovich.

Barnes, Harry Elmer. 1972. *The Story of Punishment.* 2d ed., rev. Montclair, N.J.: Patterson Smith. Originally published 1930.

Barrows, Isabel C. 1910. "The Reformatory Treatment of Women in the United States." In *Penal and Reformatory Institutions,* edited by Charles Richmond Henderson. New York: Charities Publication Committee.

Beaumont, Gustave de, and Alexis de Tocqueville. 1964. *On the Penitentiary System in the United States, and Its Application in France.* Carbondale: Southern Illinois University Press. Originally published 1833.

Bird, Maryann. 1979. "The Women in Prison: No Escape From Stereotyping." *New York Times* (June 23).

Brenzel, Barbara. 1980. "Domestication as Reform: A Study of the Socialization of Wayward Girls, 1856–1905." *Harvard Educational Review* 50:196–213.

Brockway, Zebulon Reed. 1969. *Fifty Years of Prison Service: An Autobiography.* Montclair, N.J.: Patterson Smith. Originally published 1912.

Burkhart, Kathryn W. 1973. *Women in Prison.* Garden City, N.Y.: Doubleday & Co.

Butler, June Rainsford. 1934. "A Study of Some Reformatory Systems for Women Offenders in the United States, with Particular Reference to the Industrial Farm Colony at Kinston, North Carolina." M.A. thesis, University of North Carolina at Chapel Hill.

Carpenter, Mary. 1969. *Our Convicts.* Vol. 1. Montclair, N.J.: Patterson Smith. Originally published 1864.

Coffin, Mrs. C. F. [Rhoda]. 1886. "Women's Prisons." In National Prison Association, *Proceedings for 1885.* Boston: Geo. E. Crosby & Co.

Connelly, Mark Thomas. 1980. *The Response to Prostitution in the Progressive Era.* Chapel Hill: University of North Carolina Press.

Conway, Jill. 1976. "Women Reformers and American Culture, 1870–1930." In *Our American Sisters: Women in American Life and Thought,* edited by Jean E. Friedman and William G. Shade. 2d ed. Boston: Allyn & Bacon.

Crawford, William. 1969. *Report on the Penitentiaries of the United States.* Montclair, N.J.: Patterson Smith. Originally published 1835.

Crofton, Sir Walter. 1871. "The Irish System of Prison Discipline." In *Transactions of the National Congress on Penitentiary and Reformatory Discipline,* edited by E. C. Wines. Albany, N.Y.: Weed, Parsons.

Currie, Elliott Park. 1973. "Managing the Minds of Men: The Reformatory Movement, 1865–1920." Ph.D. dissertation, University of California, Berkeley.

Davis, Katherine Bement. 1911. "A Reformatory for Women." *Ohio Bulletin of Charities and Correction* 2:43–48.

Detroit House of Correction. 1869. *Seventh Annual Report of the Officers of the Detroit House of Correction . . . 1868.* Detroit: Free Press Book and Job Printing House.

Dix, Dorothea Lynde. 1967. *Remarks on Prisons and Prison Discipline in the United States.* 2d ed. Montclair, N.J.: Patterson Smith. Originally published 1845.

Farnham, E. W. 1846. Notes and illustrations to M. B. Sampson, *Rationale of Crime and Its Appropriate Treatment: Being a Treatise on Criminal Jurisprudence Considered in Relation to Cerebral Organization.* From the 2d ed. New York: D. Appleton.

Feldman, Egal. 1967. "Prostitution, the Alien Woman and the Progressive Imagination, 1910–1915." *American Quarterly* 19:192–206.

Fernald, Mabel Ruth, Mary H. S. Hayes, and Almena Dawley. 1920. *A Study of Women Delinquents in New York State.* New York: Century.

Flynn, Edith Elisabeth. 1971. "The Special Problems of Female Offenders." In National Conference of Corrections, *Proceedings, December 5–8, 1971,* pp. 113–17.

Foucault, Michel. 1977. *Discipline and Punish: The Birth of the Prison.* New York: Pantheon Books.

Freedman, Estelle B. 1974. "Their Sisters' Keepers: An Historical Perspective on Female Correctional Institutions in the United States: 1870–1900." *Feminist Studies* 2:77–95.

———. 1976. "Their Sisters' Keepers: The Origins of Female Corrections in America." Ph.D. dissertation, Columbia University.

———. 1981. *Their Sisters' Keepers: Women's Prison Reform in America, 1830–1930.* Ann Arbor: University of Michigan Press.

Fry, Elizabeth. 1847. *Memoir of the Life of Elizabeth Fry with Extracts from her Journal and Letters,* edited by two of her daughters, in 2 vols. Philadelphia: J. W. Moore.

Giallombardo, Rose, 1966. *Society of Women: A Study of a Women's Prison.* New York: John Wiley & Sons.

Gibson, Helen E. 1973. "Women's Prisons: Laboratories for Penal Reform." *Wisconsin Law Review* 1973, pp. 210–33.

Glick, Ruth M. and Virginia V. Neto. 1977. *National Study of Women's Correctional Programs.* Washington, D.C.: Government Printing Office.

Glueck, Sheldon, and Eleanor T. Glueck. 1934. *Five Hundred Delinquent Women.* New York: Alfred A. Knopf.

Hahn, Nicolas Fischer [Nicole H. Rafter]. 1980*a.* "Female State Prisoners in Tennessee: 1831–1979." *Tennessee Historical Quarterly* 39:485–97.

———. [Nicole H. Rafter]. 1980*b.* "Too Dumb to Know Better: Cacogenic Family Studies and the Criminology of Women." *Criminology* 18:3–25.

Haley, Kathleen. 1977. "Mothers behind Bars: A Look at the Parental Rights of Incarcerated Women." *New England Journal of Prison Law* 4:141–55.

Hindelang, Michael J. 1979. "Sex Differences in Criminal Activity." *Social Problems* 27:143–56.

Hindelang, Michael J., Michael R. Gottfredson, and Timothy J. Flanagan, eds. 1981. *Sourcebook of Criminal Justice Statistics—1980.* Washington, D.C.: Government Printing Office.

178   Nicole Hahn Rafter

Horne, Jim, Hazel Robinson, Lora Stonefeld, and Martha Wandel. N.d. "Female Recidivism in Washington from 1966–1976." Unpublished manuscript. Seattle: University of Washington.

Ignatieff, Michael. 1981. "State, Civil Society, and Total Institutions: A Critique of Recent Social Histories of Punishment." In *Crime and Justice: An Annual Review of Research*, vol. 3, edited by Michael Tonry and Norval Morris. Chicago: University of Chicago Press.

Indiana Reformatory Institution for Women and Girls. 1874, 1876, 1877. *Report of the Indiana Reformatory Institution for Women and Girls.* Indianapolis: Sentinel Co.

Indiana Senate. 1869. *Indiana Senate Journal*, March 3, 1869. Indianapolis: Alexander H. Conner, State Printer.

Indiana State Prison South. 1869. *Annual Report of the Officers and Directors of the Indiana State Prison, South.* Indianapolis: Alexander H. Conner, State Printer.

————. 1874. *Annual Report of the Directors and Officers of the Indiana State Prison, South. December 15, 1873.* Indianapolis: Sentinel Co.

Johnson, Ellen C. 1891. "Discipline in Female Prisons." In National Prison Association, *Proceedings for 1891*, pp. 137–43.

Kansas Women's Industrial Farm. 1920. *Second Biennial Report of the Women's Industrial Farm . . . for the Two Years Ending June 30, 1920.* Topeka: State Prison.

Kennedy, John S. 1921. "Report to the Governor relative to the Investigation and Inquiry into Allegations of Cruelty to Prisoners in the New York State Reformatory for Women, Bedford Hills." In New York State Commission of Prisons, *Annual Report for 1920.* Ossining, N.Y.: Sing Sing Prison.

Laub, John. 1980. "Criminal Behavior and the Urban-Rural Dimension." Ph.D. dissertation, State University of New York at Albany.

Lekkerkerker, Eugenia Cornelia. 1931. *Reformatories for Women in the United States.* Batavia, Holland: Bij J. B. Wolters' Uitgevers-Maatschappij.

Lewis, Orlando F. 1967. *The Development of American Prisons and Prison Customs, 1776–1845.* Montclair, N.J.: Patterson Smith. Originally published 1922.

Lewis, W. David. 1961. "The Female Criminal and the Prisons of New York, 1825–1845." *New York History* 42:215–36.

————. 1965. *From Newgate to Dannemora: The Rise of the Penitentiary in New York, 1796–1848.* Ithaca, N.Y.: Cornell University Press.

————. 1971. "Eliza Wood Burhans Farnham." In *Notable American Women 1607–1950*, vol. 1, edited by Edward T. James, Janet Wilson James, and Paul S. Boyer. Cambridge, Mass.: Harvard University Press, Belknap Press.

Lieber, Francis. 1964. "Translator's Preface." In G. de Beaumont and A. de Tocqueville, *On the Penitentiary System in the United States, and Its Application in France.* Carbondale: Southern Illinois University Press. Originally published 1833.

McKelvey, Blake. 1972. *American Prisons: A Study in American Social History Prior to 1915.* Montclair, N.J.: Patterson Smith. Originally published 1936.

Martineau, Harriet. 1838. *Retrospect of Western Travel.* Vol. 1. London: Saunders & Otley.

Mennel, Robert M. 1973. *Thorns and Thistles: Juvenile Delinquents in the United States, 1825–1940.* Hanover, N.H.: University Press of New England.

Monahan, Florence. 1941. *Women in Crime.* New York: Ives Washburn.

Murton, Tom. 1969. *Accomplices to the Crime.* New York: Grove Press.

Nagel, William G. 1973. *The New Red Barn: A Critical Look at the Modern American Prison.* New York: Walker & Co.

New York Auburn State Prison. 1833. *Annual Report of the Auburn State Prison* [for 1832]. N. Y. Sen. Doc. no. 20.

New York Bedford State Reformatory. 1911. *Tenth Annual Report of the Board of Managers . . . for the year ending September 30, 1910.* N.Y. Sen. Doc no. 23.

New York Committee on State Prisons. 1832. *Report of the Committee on State Prisons.* N.Y. Sen. Doc. no. 74.

New York Hudson House of Refuge. 1890. *Annual Report of the Board of Managers . . . for Year Ending September 30, 1889.* Albany: James B. Lyon (Ass. Doc. no. 50).

New York Inspectors of State Prisons. 1801. *An Account of the State Prison or Penitentiary House, in the City of New-York.* New York: Isaac Colling & Son.

————. 1852. *Fourth Annual Report of the Inspectors of State Prisons of the State of New York.* N.Y. Sen. Doc. no. 35.

New York Mount Pleasant State Prison. Various years. *Report of the Inspectors of the Mount Pleasant State Prison.* N. Y. Sen. Docs., 1831 (no. 3), 1836 (no. 23), 1844 (no. 20), 1845 (no. 9), 1847 (no. 5).

————. 1848. *Report of the Minority of the Late Board of Inspectors of the Mount Pleasant State Prison.* N.Y. Sen. Doc. No. 17.

New York Western House of Refuge for Women. 1899, 1918. *Annual Report.* N.Y. Ass. Doc. no. 25, (1899), 20 (1918).

New York State Commission of Correction. 1927. *Annual Report for 1927.*

New York State Prison Survey Committee. 1920. *Report.* Albany: J. B. Lyon.

Ohio Penitentiary. 1880. *Annual Report of the Directors and Warden for the Year 1880.* Columbus: G. J. Brand & Co.

O'Neill, William L. 1969. *Everyone Was Brave: The Rise and Fall of Feminism in America.* Chicago: Quadrangle Books.

Oregon Advisory Committee to the U.S. Commission on Civil Rights. January 1976. *Civil and Human Rights in Oregon State Prisons.*

Pivar, David J. 1973. *Purity Crusade: Sexual Morality and Social Control, 1868–1900.* Westport, Conn.: Greenwood Press.

Platt, Anthony M. 1977. *The Child Savers: The Invention of Delinquency.* 2d ed., enlarged. Chicago: University of Chicago Press.

Potter, Joan. 1978. "In Prison, Women Are Different." *Corrections Magazine* (December), pp. 14–24.

Quarles, Mary Ann Stillman. 1966. "Organizational Analysis of the New Jersey Reformatory for Women in Relation to Stated Principles of Corrections, 1913–1963." Ph.D. dissertation, Boston University.

Rafter, Nicole Hahn. 1982. "Hard Times: Custodial Prisons for Women and the Example of the New York State Prison for Women at Auburn, 1893–1933." In *Judge, Lawyer, Victim, Thief: Women, Gender Roles, and Criminal*

Justice, edited by Nicole H. Rafter and Elizabeth A. Stanko. Boston: Northeastern University Press.

————. Forthcoming. "Chastising the Unchaste: Social Control Functions of a Women's Reformatory, 1894–1931." In *Social Control and the State: Comparative and Historical Essays*, edited by A. Scull and S. Cohen. Oxford: Martin Robertson.

Reeves, Margaret. 1929. *Training Schools for Delinquent Girls*. New York: Russell Sage Foundation.

Resch, John P. 1972. "Ohio Adult Penal System, 1850–1900: A Study in the Failure of Institutional Reform." *Ohio History* 81:236–62.

Resnik, Judith, and Nancy Shaw. 1980. "Prisoners of their Sex: Health Problems of Incarcerated Women." In *Prisoners' Rights Source Book: Theory, Litigation, and Practice*, vol. 2, edited by Ira P. Robbins. New York: Clark Boardman.

Robert, Jeanne. 1917. "The Care of Women in State Prisons." In *Prison Reform*, edited by Corrine Bacon. New York: H. W. Wilson.

Robinson, Louis N. 1921. *Penology in the United States*. Philadelphia: John C. Winston.

Rogers, Helen Worthington. 1929. "A History of the Movement to Establish a State Reformatory for Women in Connecticut." *Journal of Criminal Law and Criminology* 19:518–41.

Rothman, David J. 1971. *The Discovery of the Asylum: Social Order and Disorder in the New Republic*. Boston: Little, Brown.

Schlossman, Steven. 1977. *Love and the American Delinquent: The Theory and Practice of "Progressive" Juvenile Justice, 1825–1920*. Chicago: University of Chicago Press.

Schlossman, Steven, and Stephanie Wallach. 1978. "The Crime of Precocious Sexuality: Female Juvenile Delinquency in the Progressive Era." *Harvard Educational Review* 48:65–94.

SchWeber, Claudine. 1980. "Beauty Marks and Blemishes: The Co-ed Prison as a Microcosm of Integrated Society." Paper read at 1980 meeting of the Academy of Criminal Justice Sciences, Oklahoma.

————. 1982. " 'The Government's Unique Experiment in Salvaging Women Criminals': Cooperation and Conflict in the Administration of a Women's Prison." In *Judge, Lawyer, Victim, Thief: Women, Gender Roles and Criminal Justice*. Edited by Nicole H. Rafter and Elizabeth A. Stanko. Boston: Northeastern University Press.

Scott, Joseph F. 1910. "American Reformatories for Male Adults." In *Penal and Reformatory Institutions*, edited by Charles Richmond Henderson. New York: Russell Sage Foundation, Charities Publication Committee.

Singer, Linda R. 1973. "Women and the Correctional Process." *American Criminal Law Review* 11:295–308.

Thomas, David Y. 1930. *Arkansas and Its People: A History, 1541–1930*. Vol. 2. New York: American Historical Society.

U.S. Comptroller General. 1980. *Women in Prison: Inequitable Treatment Requires Action*. Washington, D.C.: Government Printing Office.

U.S. Department of Justice, Bureau of Justice Statistics. October–November 1982. "Prisoners at Midyear 1982," Bulletin NCJ–84875. Washington, D.C.: Department of Justice.

U.S. General Accounting Office. 1979. *Female Offenders: Who Are They and What Are the Problems Confronting Them?* Washington, D.C.: Government Printing Office.

U.S. House of Representatives, Committee on the Judiciary. 1979. *Hearings Before the Subcommittee on Courts . . . ,* 96th Cong. 1st sess., pts. 1 and 2 (October 10 and 11).

Van Wyck, Mrs. Katherine. 1913. "Reformatory for Women—Wisconsin's Outstanding Need." In Wisconsin Conference on Charities and Corrections, *Proceedings, October 5–8, 1912.* Madison: Democrat Printing Co.

Vaux, Roberts. 1826. *Notices of the Original, and Successive Efforts, To Improve the Discipline of the Prison at Philadelphia and To Reform the Criminal Code of Pennsylvania: With a Few Observations on the Penitentiary System.* Philadelphia: Kimber & Sharpless.

Victor, Mrs. Sarah Maria. 1887. *The Life Story of Sarah M. Victor. . . .* Cleveland: Williams Publishing Co.

Voight, Lloyd L. 1949. *History of California Correctional Administration from 1930 to 1948.* San Francisco: n.p.

Ward, David A., and Gene G. Kassebaum. 1965. *Women's Prison: Sex and Social Structure.* Chicago: Aldine Publishing Co.

Welter, Barbara. 1966. "The Cult of True Womanhood." *American Quarterly* 18:151–74.

Wheaton, Liz. 1979. "Rewarding Neglect: A New Women's Prison." *ACLU Women's Rights Report* 1 (3): 5–6.

Wines, E. C., ed. 1871. *Transactions of the National Congress on Penitentiary and Reformatory Discipline.* Albany, N.Y.: Weed, Parsons.

Wines, E. C., and Theodore W. Dwight. 1867. *Report on the Prisons and Reformatories of the United States and Canada.* Albany, N.Y.: Van Benthuysen & Sons.

Wisconsin State Prison. 1926. *Twenty-second Biennial Report of the Wisconsin State Prison for the . . . Period ending June 30, 1926.*

Young, Clifford M. 1932. *Women's Prisons Past and Present and Other New York State Prison History.* Elmira Reformatory: Summary Press.

Zaretsky, Eli. 1976. *Capitalism, the Family, and Personal Life.* New York: Harper Colophon.

Donald J. West

Sex Offenses and Offending

ABSTRACT

The extent to which the law should concern itself with the regulation of consensual sexual activities is a subject of continuing controversy. Dramatic differences exist between countries in regard to law and practice concerning abortion, adultery, prostitution, homosexuality, pornography, and the age of consent. In many countries the numbers of reported sex offenses and prosecuted sex offenses have decreased in recent years, most noticeably for crimes, such as consensual sexual intercourse with under-age girls, where there is no complaining victim. Consensual acts account for a substantial proportion of recorded sex crimes. In England and the United States, however, there has been a significant increase in the minority of serious, assaultive sex crimes, notably forcible rape. Children and young persons are involved as participants or victims in a high proportion of sex offenses. Studies of offenders point to the existence of subgroups with very different characteristics. Many offenders, once caught, are never reconvicted. A small minority, especially among exhibitionists and pedophiles, are persistent recidivists. Aggressive, assaultive sex offenders tend to be young, poorly socialized, of low socioeconomic status, and with conviction records for nonsexual crime. Child molesters are less often criminal and rarely violent. Many are social inadequates who choose children because they are easy to persuade rather than from a true pedophiliac fixation. Some of the most violent offenders are motivated by frustration and anger more than by lust. Many sex offenders, especially those lacking in social skills, afflicted with some unwanted deviant fixation, or emotionally frustrated in their sexual relationships, have problems for which treatment techniques, both behavioristic and psychotherapeutic, have been developed. While it may be difficult to validate effectiveness in terms of long-term reduction in recidivism, there are

Donald J. West is professor of clinical criminology and director, Institute of Criminology, University of Cambridge.

practical and humanitarian reasons for developing more treatment facilities and diverting more cases from prison.

The role of the criminal law in relation to the control of sexual behavior is a popular subject for criminological discussion. The great variations in the sexual mores of different cultures, the strange disparities between public postures and private conduct, the involvement of political and religious groups in heated argument about sex law, the plurality of sexual attitudes and behaviors in contemporary society, the high proportion of "victimless" crimes among sex offenses, and the ambiguous adjectives (such as "indecent" or "corrupting") used in the legal definitions of sex crimes all contribute to the complexities of the debate.

The right of citizens to be protected by the criminal law from unwanted or forcible sexual intrusion is everywhere acknowledged. Vaginal penetration against a woman's consent, and forcible sexual assaults on persons of either sex, are clear instances of victimization, liable to cause all kinds of harm, including unwanted pregnancy, loss of virginity, social embarrassment, physical injury, venereal infection, and psychological trauma. Some scope for dispute remains concerning the gravity of sexual assaults in relation to other crimes. Is it right, for example, that sexual intercourse accomplished by threat of violence should attract, as it does in England, a maximum penalty, the same as for murder—namely, life imprisonment? It has also become a matter of controversy that in many jurisdictions a wife cannot charge her own husband with rape because, by virtue of the marriage contract, she is deemed to have agreed to allow him free sexual access. If he makes unreasonable sexual demands, she can complain of cruelty and in extreme cases of assault, but the charge of rape is not open to her.

It is when the law seeks to do more than prevent deliberate harm's being done to other people that most controversy begins. The upholders of liberal values make frequent reference to the famous aphorism of John Stuart Mill in his essay *On Liberty* (1947, p. 6) in which he declared that, at least for mature persons, the only warrant for the exercise of power over any member of a civilized community against his will is to prevent harm to others. A clear echo of this occurs in a well-known phrase from the report of the Departmental Committee on Homosexuality and Prostitution set up in England under the chairmanship of Sir John (later Lord) Wolfenden (1957). It states (§61): "Unless a deliberate attempt is to be made by society, acting through the agency of the law, to equate the sphere of crime with that of sin, there must remain a realm of private morality and immorality which is, in brief and crude terms, not the law's business." The law's proper functions are (§13–14) "to preserve public order and decency, to protect the citizen from what is offensive or injurious and to provide sufficient safeguards against exploitation and corruption of others, particularly those who are specially vulnerable because they are young."

Opposed to the libertarians are those who believe that the law should uphold the moral consensus of society independent of utilitarian considerations. Lord Devlin (1965, p. 13), for example, suggests that "society is justified in taking the same steps to preserve its moral code as to preserve its government and other essential institutions. The suppression of vice is as much the law's business as the suppression of subversive activities." He criticizes unlimited tolerance of private sin. One person drunk in his home every night may matter little, but if too many followed that bad example the social effects would soon require legal intervention. Other jurisprudential authorities, including H. L. A. Hart (1963), have argued against use of criminal law to enforce current moral standards. Society does not depend on the preservation of a changeless, unitary moral system, and the law risks loss of credibility by supporting mores of the past.

For example, attitudes to prostitution have fluctuated considerably over time, as have the legal measures of control considered appropriate. An American study first published early this century (Woolston 1921) concluded that "so long as personal indulgence is regarded as merely a matter of individual concern, we shall continue to develop prostitutes, their patrons and panderers." A more recent study (James 1976) concluded, "As long as the definition of the 'normal' male sex role is broader than that of the 'normal' female sex role, there must be 'deviant' women to take up the slack." These contrasting attitudes led to equally contrasting legislative proposals: the first author wanting more active intervention, more suppressive policing, the establishment of reformatories and detention homes for the women, and severer penalties for their patrons; the second author strongly disapproving of attempts to use the law to eliminate prostitution. Reforms necessary to accommodate such changing values become difficult if the law seeks to adhere to an absolute standard of morality.

Another difficulty with the Devlin position is the problem of identifying a moral consensus on matters of contemporary controversy, such as abortion, prostitution, pornography, adultery, and homosexuality. The "harm to others" criterion appears philosophically and operationally preferable, but the problem of assessing harm remains. Adultery is arguably harmful, insofar as it may lead to broken homes, but is not treated as crime by most Western countries, although Greece has only recently decriminalized it and it remained a criminal offense in Italy until 1978. In both these countries the penalties were directed primarily to the female offender. The president of the Court of Appeal in Saudi Arabia recently explained that an adulterous woman commits such a serious offense against her family and her unborn child that flogging and stoning to death are appropriate punishments (UN Social Defense Research Institute 1980).

The Wolfenden Committee, while advocating decriminalization of consensual adult homosexual acts, recommended stricter controls on prostitutes and harsher penalties for soliciting. The latter proposals were swiftly translated into law, but the decriminalization of male homosexuality did not take place until 1967 in England and Wales, 1980 in Scotland, and 1982 in Northern Ireland. This last change was forced by a successful appeal to the European Court of Human Rights by an aggrieved citizen of the province who complained that the law breached Article 8 of the European Convention for the Protection of Human Rights and Fundamental Freedoms, which declares that everyone has the right to respect for his private and family life (Eur. Court H. R., Dudgeon case of 22 October 1981, Series A no. 45). In the United States, half the jurisdictions have decriminalized consensual homosexual acts between adult males, but in many parts of the world, including Mexico, New Zealand, Eire, the Soviet Union, and wherever Islamic law prevails, these remain crimes, and in Iran a number of men have been executed recently for homosexual offenses.

Another area of disagreement about the scope of the law concerns the control of the sexuality of the young, which may be justified on moral, utilitarian, or protectionist grounds. The age a girl must reach before it becomes legal for a man to have sexual intercourse with her varies considerably. In the United Kingdom it is sixteen, but it was once only ten (19 Eliz. 1, chap. 7 [1575–6]), and it remained as low as twelve until 1875 (Stafford 1964). In France, Sweden, and Denmark it is fifteen, in West Germany and Yugoslavia fourteen. In the United States, in those jurisdictions that specify an age of consent (governing such crimes as "statutory rape" and "carnal knowledge of a juvenile") the age varies from twelve in Oregon, through fourteen in Missouri, Washington, Georgia, and Hawaii, to eighteen in California, Idaho, and Wisconsin. Some jurisdictions make a distinction between cases of contact of an adult with a child or adolescent and cases involving only contacts between young persons. In the United Kingdom both situations are treated by statute as "indecent assault," leaving those responsible for bringing prosecutions to exercise discretion in what one hopes will be a fair and reasonable manner.

Another matter on which widespread cultural differences exist is the issue of obscene public displays. Many countries of the Third World regard disapprovingly the laissez-fair attitude toward pornography that has developed in the West in recent years. In some Eastern countries the act of kissing is considered obscene and cannot be portrayed in films. Censorship is often strict. In Sri Lanka, for example, a film will not be permitted to be shown publicly if it deals with the relations between the sexes in such a manner as to "suggest that illicit sexual relations are ordinary incidents of life and not to be reprobated" or to "depict directly or plainly . . . indelicate sexual situations . . . [or] scenes suggestive of immorality" (personal communication from secretary, Public Performance Board of Sri Lanka, 1982). Sex perversion or any reference to it is forbidden. In complete contrast, Scandinavian censors are generally unconcerned about the explicit depiction of heterosexual intercourse so long as it is not associated with acts of violence.

As moral values have changed so have theories about the causes of disapproved sexual behavior. There is, of course, a general trend in criminology to analyze the causes of crime in economic and social terms rather than in terms of personal idiosyncrasy or abnormality. Sex offenses that were once regarded, almost by definition, as evidence of psychopathic traits are now considered in the same way as more ordinary forms of misbehavior. For example, the older literature on female prostitution, much influenced by psychoanalysis, was preoccupied with the peculiarities of the women, their supposed frigidity, their unconscious desire to punish or castrate the male, their latent lesbianism, or their vain search for the love they could not find in the parental home (Rolph 1955; Glover 1957). It was supposed that no ordinary woman, unless driven from home or coerced by a procurer, would contemplate a career of prostitution. Recent thinking, backed by empirical study, suggests otherwise. Many of those who take to a life of prostitution appear to do so without undue persuasion, regarding it as a sensible, short-term money-making enterprise that contrasts favorably with the boring drudgery of low-paid feminine employments. Their personal motives are arguably less interesting and less mysterious than the way they learn the tricks of the trade, organize protection against harassment by authorities or clients, and integrate into the community of pimps, call-girls, and streetwalkers. Modern surveys of prostitutes and their activities are more or less unanimous that the profit motive is the major influence, that most of the women make a rational decision when they join the profession, and that they are not as a group noticeably dim-witted, neurotic, sexually frigid, and man-hating (Gebhard 1969; Winick and Kinsie 1971; James 1977; Cohen 1980; Cunnington 1980).

The demedicalization of much variant sexual behavior has been officially accepted in a number of contexts. Many states have repealed their sexual psychopath laws. In the United Kingdom, the most recent Mental Health Act (1983) specifically states that sexual deviation alone is insufficient grounds for classification as a psychopath. In 1973 the American Psychiatric Association resolved to delete homosexuality from its list of mental disorders, subsequently adopting "ego dystonic homosexuality" to include only those individuals who complain, either because weak or absent heterosexual arousal interferes with desired relationships or because a sustained pattern of unwanted homosexual arousal causes them distress (American Psychiatric Association 1980).

Such official reactions are in part a response to the rise of pressure groups representing the interests of social deviants themselves and claiming that their particular minority preference is neither immoral nor pathological. Best known are the homosexual groups. These have a long history dating back to the campaigns of liberal sexologists of a century ago, such as Havelock Ellis and Magnus Hirschfeld, but under the guise of "gay liberation" and similar movements they have become widely recognized only in the last twenty years. On a smaller scale, female prostitutes have also tried forming "collectives" to organize demonstrations and demand an end to repressive laws. Less well known are the organizations formed by transsexuals, such as the Beaumont Society in England and the Erickson Foundation in the United States, which are concerned, among other matters, with the law and practice governing genital surgery. There are even semiclandestine and much-harassed groups which circulate propaganda about the benefits of allowing children to have sexual contacts with adults. These include the Paedophyle Information Exchange (PIE) in England (O'Carroll 1980) and the North American Man-Boy Love Association (NAMBLA) in the United States and Canada. Some of the original leaders of PIE have been imprisoned (Plummer 1981) and some of the NAMBLA leaders have been tried for offenses against children and possession or distribution of child pornography. Sexual deviants whose conduct is not necessarily illegal have also started to form self-help groups. The Mackintosh Society, for example, exists to help fetishists who feel embarrassed, puzzled, or isolated on account of their sexual quirk (Gosselin and Wilson 1980).

Awareness of these manifestations of sex variant behavior is necessary not only to decide how far the criminal law should concern itself with sexual matters but also as a background to an understanding of behaviors that are clearly antisocial and never likely to be decriminalized. Philosophical discourse on the control of ethically problematic activities such as attempted suicide, euthanasia, abortion, pornography, homosexuality, and underage sex is not likely, in itself, to resolve all the issues of criminal law. The practical criminologist can make an important contribution through empirical inquiry into the nature and effects of sexual deviations, the social consequences of legislation and sentencing practices, the analysis of public attitudes, and the investigation of means and prospects of changing unwanted patterns of sexual behavior. Control by means of the criminal justice system is costly in terms of damaging side effects, such as hurting victims and innocent family members, as well as in terms of the financing of police, courts, and prisons. In deciding when and how to invoke the criminal law, its cost effectiveness in comparison with that of alternative forms of social control should be considered. These are matters for criminological inquiry undeterred by populist polemics.

Bearing in mind the issues of cultural relativity and changing standards outlined in this introduction, the succeeding sections attempt to summarize what is systematically known about sex offenses, their occurrence, sources, and treatment. Section I reviews official, published statistics on sex offenses. Section II describes studies of offenders and leads into Section III, which discusses possible causes of their behavior. Section IV looks at the problems from the side of the victims, while Section V deals with treatment. The essay concludes with a few thoughts on criminal justice policy.

I. The Pattern of Recorded Sex Crimes

Other than offenses arising out of prostitution, sex crimes are almost entirely male crimes. Certain offenses, such as (in England) "indecent exposure of the male person with intent to insult a female" are so defined in law as to apply only to males, and some illegal male behavior, notably private homosexuality, is not defined as criminal if committed by a female. Nevertheless, the sexist bias of the law apart, the kinds of behavior that give rise to most public concern, notably violent sexual assaults or predatory sexual molestation of children outside the home, are in reality nearly always committed by males.

For the purpose of this discussion, sex crimes can be roughly divided into the normal (or pseudonormal) and the deviant. The behavior of the first group is criminal only because the female partner was non-consenting or too young. The behavior of the second group is deviant because it involves acts that the average man would not find sexually gratifying. Contacts with prepubertal children, sex contacts with other males, "flashing" of the penis at women or girls in public places, making obscene telephone calls, or inflicting injuries on the sexual partner are all examples of deviant offenses. Because of the ambiguities in the legal labeling and recording of offenses, which do not necessarily show the ages of the victims involved (see below), it is difficult to give precise estimates, but a substantial proportion of sex offenses by males fall into the deviant category. The number of persons in England and Wales found guilty or cautioned for various sex offenses in 1981 is shown in table 1. It can be seen that the vast majority of offenders are male and that a majority of prosecutions concern deviant activities. This is an important consideration when it comes to deciding how to deal with offenders.

As with other kinds of crimes, the more serious sex offences are rarer than the less serious ones. In England and Wales in 1981, 1,068 reported rapes and attempts accounted for only 5.4 percent of all serious sex crimes known to the police (United Kingdom 1982, table 2.8). In the United States, where aggressive crimes of all kinds are much more frequent, arrests for forcible rape account for about a third of all arrests of males for sex offenses other than prostitution (Federal Bureau of Investigation 1981, table 27). The annual incidence of reported forcible rapes and attempted rapes per 100,000 inhabitants in the United States was 37.2 in 1980, some eighteen times the corresponding figure for England and Wales (United Kingdom 1982, table 17).

In most countries the totality of sexual crime recorded by police has not greatly changed in recent years. In England and Wales sex crimes known to the police have actually decreased from 23,621 in 1971 to 19,424 in 1981 (United Kingdom 1982, table 2.8). In the United States, arrests of males for sex crimes (other than rape or prostitution) increased by a modest figure of 12.2 percent in 1980 compared with 1971, whereas in the same period arrests for aggravated assaults increased by 47.5

percent and for forcible rape by 48.5 percent (Federal Bureau of Investigation 1981, table 27).

TABLE 1
Numbers of Persons Found Guilty or Cautioned for the
Main Categories of Indictable Sexual Offenses in
England and Wales, 1981

Category	Number	Percentage
Rape, indecent assault on a female, unlawful sexual intercourse with underage girls	5,384	58.1
Buggery, indecent assault on a male, indecency between males	2,566	27.7
Soliciting males	919	9.9
Gross indecency with a child	247	2.7
Incest	143	1.5
Total	9,259	100

Source.—United Kingdom, Home Office (1982).
Note.—The very common offense of indecent exposure, being nonindictable, is not included in these statistics.

In countries such as Denmark where the incidence of reported sex crimes has fallen, changes in the law or in prosecution practice may be largely responsible. In England, the largest reduction in reported offenses has occurred in the category of "unlawful sexual intercourse" with girls slightly under the legal age of consent, that is, aged between thirteen and sixteen. This is an offense in which the police exercise considerable discretion in deciding whether to prosecute, especially if the age gap between the girl and the offender is not very great.

In both England and the United States, however, recorded offenses of rape, unlike the less serious sexual offenses, have increased significantly. In England and Wales, recorded rapes and attempted rapes increased from 784 to 1,068, that is, by 36.2 percent, from 1971 to 1981 (United Kingdom 1982, table 2.8). Even so, this percentage increase was less than for general crimes of violence against the person, which more than doubled in the same period.

Rapid fluctuations in the number of recorded crimes may reflect changes in police activity more than change in behavior in the community at large. An alternative method of assessing trends in crime is by means of victim surveys. The annual National Crime Survey conducted for the Federal Bureau of Justice Statistics, based on inquiries from persons aged twelve or over in a representative sample of 60,000 households across the United States, has yielded evidence suggesting that the actual increase in rapes (as indeed of many other crimes) has been less than the increase shown in police statistics. Victim surveys are, of course, subject to their own particular sources of bias (Skogan 1981), but even so they do provide good reason for interpreting with caution the more dramatic fluctuations in police statistics. The number of forcible rapes and attempted rapes per 1,000 of population, as assessed from victim reports to the National Crime Survey, increased only slightly, from a rate of 1.0 in 1973 to 1.1 in 1979 (i.e., from 156,000 in a population of 164 million to 192,000 in a population of 178 million). Even in this large survey sample, the increase in rape victimization rates from 1973 to 1979 (13.7 percent) was not statistically significant. Over the same period the increase of 6.1 percent (from 32.6 to 34.5 per thousand) in the estimated rate of victimization by crimes of personal violence of all kinds, although proportionately smaller, was statistically significant (U.S. Department of Justice 1981, 1980). The proportion of rapes reported to the survey inquirers but not to the police has remained virtually unchanged, at approximately half. This seems to tell against the idea that increased reporting accounts for the increases recorded by the police. Perhaps the police, responding to the consciousness-raising efforts of the women's movement, are giving complainants greater credibility and sympathy and recording a higher proportion of reported incidents as true rapes.

Although rape is a crime taken very seriously by police and public the statistical returns have still to be treated with some reserve. Chappell et al. (1977), noting the high incidence of rapes in Los Angeles compared with that in Boston, found that in Los Angeles even such incidents as bottom pinching were being recorded as forcible rapes. One consequence of the keen interest taken in rape by criminologists is that there are available analyses of police records that reveal the substance behind the numbers and legal labels. The findings show that many rapes are neither so violent nor so unpredictable as popularly supposed. Surprise attacks on strange women carried out with extreme ferocity occur all too often but are not representative of the majority of rapes. Many are so-called contact cases in which some sort of social interaction precedes the crime (Amir 1971; Katz and Mazur 1979, ch. 9). A recent survey of rapes recorded over a period of five years by six English county police forces showed that the commonest sequence was a social encounter between a young couple followed by a period of drinking together, after which they would go off somewhere, perhaps on a car ride or a visit to one or the other's room, giving the male the opportunity to insist on sexual intercourse with force or threats if necessary. Most of the offenses (87 percent) were by a lone male; three-fifths were by an assailant whom the victim knew and could name. Some physical force was used in four-fifths of the cases, but in only 5 percent was there an injury sufficient to require any medical attention (Wright and West 1981).

It is only fair to point out, however, that in some cities street attacks by strangers appear commoner than the findings of Amir in Philadelphia or Wright in England would lead one to expect. An analysis by Chappell and Singer (1977) of 704 complaints of forcible rape or attempted rape made to the police in New York City over a one-year period showed that some three-quarters of the attacks were by total strangers and that a third of all initial encounters between rapists and their victims took place either on a public street or in a park or similar open space. The incidence of serious violence in the course of rapes was also high in New York, with 15–20 percent of victims requiring some hospital treatment for injuries. It may be, of course, that in New York the less serious crimes go unrecorded, but if so the true incidence of rapes must be extraordinarily high.

Most of the injuries sustained in rapes are occasioned by battering as the offender tries to subdue a struggling victim. In an important minority of cases, however, victims, even when prepared to submit, are subjected to gratuitous insults, humiliations, and cruelties, as if the object of the attack were to vent anger as much as to obtain sexual satisfaction. Sex murders, that is, killings in the furtherance of a rape attempt, killings to satisfy sadistic lust, and killings to ensure the victim cannot report what happened are very exceptional. Children because of their physical vulnerability, prostitutes because of their frequent exposure, and promiscuous homosexuals who pick up strangers are all at some degree of risk. Fortunately, even in these groups the risk remains small. Homicide records in England contain a very small number of sex-related murders, something like ten or twelve out of an annual total of five hundred or more murders known to the police (Gibson and Klein 1969).

Annual statistics of sex offenses known to the police, or numbers of persons prosecuted, give no information about the circumstances of sex offenses or the criminal careers of sex offenders and tell one nothing about the victims. Because sex offenses in England were being considered by the Criminal Law Revision Committee (1980), the Home Office Research Unit carried out a survey, based on information in police files. They analyzed all serious sex offenses that had led to a conviction in England and Wales in the year 1973 (Walmsley and White 1979). For the first time, a clear picture of the business of the English courts in relation to sex offenses became available.

One of the prime concerns of the Home Office inquiry was to assess how many crimes were consensual activities rather than assaults in the true sense. They classed behavior as consensual only "where the documentary sources gave clear evidence to that effect," discounting cases where a young victim "submitted out of fear or mere obedience." They also discounted cases in which the victims were under the age of ten, making no attempt to assess consent below that age. The outcome was surprising. A substantial number of offenders, 18 percent, had been involved with children under ten, and 39 percent had been involved with nonconsenting victims, but this still left as many as 43 percent whose offenses were with fully consenting partners. Clearly, the law was being used not merely for the suppression of unwanted sexual intrusion, but also very largely for the suppression of activities considered immoral—notably, indecent behavior with youngsters or homosexual indecencies in public places, usually public lavatories.

Another feature that came to light was the high proportion of the offenders' partners or victims who were children or young persons. In the case of the 709 males in the sample convicted of unlawful sexual intercourse with a minor, all the girls involved were necessarily under sixteen, the legal age of consent, but so were 70 percent of the victims of 2,551 offenders convicted of indecent assault on a female, 32 percent of the victims of 321 men convicted of rape, and 73 percent of the victims of 129 incest offenders. Only a minority of the 2,478 homosexual offenders, less than a third, were convicted for offenses with victims or partners under sixteen. As many as 80 percent of the homosexual offenders whose victims or partners were over ten had engaged only in consensual behavior, the corresponding figure for the heterosexual offenders being 34 percent.

A great many sex offenses, especially of the consensual variety, come to light through police observation or detection or through complaints from disapproving third parties, but the "dark figure" of unreported incidents must be enormous. This means that conviction records of sex offenders are not necessarily a sound indication of actual behavior. Nevertheless, certain important generalizations are possible.

Many sex offenders appear before the courts on one occasion only and are never reconvicted. In a study of a large English sample of sex offenders, Radzinowicz (1957, table 53) reported that 84 percent of the 1,919 offenders studied, and 90 percent of aggressors against females of sixteen or older, were not reconvicted of any sex crime during a follow-up period of four years in freedom. In a large Danish study in which the records of 2,934 sex offenders were followed for periods of from twelve to twenty-four years, only about 10 percent were reconvicted of a sex crime (Christiansen et al. 1965). This optimistic outlook needs some qualification. As Christiansen pointed out, certain types of offender, notably exhibitionists and pedophiles, are more likely to be reconvicted than others, and offenders convicted on two or more occasions carry a very greatly increased risk of further convictions. The population of known sex offenders has a somewhat bimodal distribution, with a large number of one-time offenders and a significant minority of persistent offenders. Another characteristic is that although the risk of reconviction for a sex offense may be low, it persists for many years. Soothill and Gibbens (1978) and Gibbens, Soothill, and Way (1981) followed for very long periods the criminal records of men convicted of rape or of offenses against young girls. They found that the cumulative reconviction rate, estimated in a five-year follow-up, doubles when offenders are followed for twenty-two years.

Many sex offenders appear to be law abiding in other respects, but some of them, particularly those guilty of aggressive, nonconsensual behavior, are very likely to have a record of convictions also for property offenses or nonsexual violence. In the Home Office survey, for example, 73 percent of the men convicted of rape had a previous conviction of some sort, although only 22 percent had a previous conviction for a sexual offense (Walmsley and White 1979, app. E). Gebhard et al. (1965), in a large survey based on imprisoned sex offenders in Indiana and California, found that about half had been convicted for sex offenses only. In contrast, the vast majority of the men guilty of aggressive sexual attacks, expecially attacks on minors, had convictions for nonsexual offenses. The more serious and violent the sex crime, the more likely the offender was to have a criminal record for crimes other than sex offenses. Of course, sexual misconduct may be more readily detected once a man has become known to the police in other connections, but this scarcely suffices to account for the very considerable overlap between sexual and nonsexual delinquency among the more serious and more persistent offenders.

Among recidivist sex offenders, as Gebhard et al. were able to demonstrate, the predominant tendency was to repeat the same kind of offense, child molesters continuing to behave indecently with children, exposers continuing to expose and aggressors to aggress. No systematic escalation with time from the less serious to the more violent types of sex crime was evident. That is not to say, of course, that escalation does not sometimes occur. Some persistent rapists have been peepers and exposers in their earlier years, but exposers and peepers are fortunately commoner than rapists and escalation is for the exceptional few (West, Roy, and Nichols 1978).

To sum up, reported sex crimes include a substantial proportion of consensual, "victimless" incidents involving homosexual behavior or activities with minors. Reported offenses of these kinds have been decreasing in most countries in recent years. Seriously aggressive heterosexual assaults account for only a small minority of recorded sex crimes, but they are relatively more frequent where there is a high incidence of crimes of nonsexual violence. For the generality of sex crimes, reconviction rates are low, although the risk persists over many years. There is some evidence that recent increases in rape statistics may be at least in part attributable to changes in reporting and recording. Crimes of sexual deviance are distinguishable from crimes of sexual aggression, the latter being more closely linked with generalized criminality, for reasons that will become more evident when the characteristics of offenders are discussed in Section II.

II. Studies of Offenders

Many deviant sex offenders, such as exhibitionists and child molesters, seem different from ordinary criminals. They are generally unaggressive and nonviolent toward their victims, and often appear timorous and unassertive in everyday life. There are more older offenders among them and individuals from higher income groups are not unusual. At the same time, social inadequates and social isolates are to be found in considerable numbers, especially among the child molesters. Many of these offenders admit that they have sexual problems for which they would like help (Mohr, Turner, and Jerry 1964; Groth and Birnbaum 1978; Rooth 1980).

In contrast, men who commit aggressive attacks on young women are themselves predominantly young, typically from the lower socioeconomic stratum, likely to have delinquent characteristics and an arrest record for nonsexual crimes, and unlikely to view themselves or to be considered by others as psychologically abnormal (Gebhard et al. 1965). If committed to prison, their crimes, unlike those of child molesters, do not arouse the animosity of fellow inmates. They adjust rather easily to the criminal subculture of the prison, but this only goes to show that their life-style and attitudes are not representative of either the statistical average or the ideal norm. However, some of the features of their offenses, such as the clustering of incidents at weekends and in the late evening, and the differing incidence according to ethnicity and social class, point to the influence of social mores as much as, if not more than, individual propensities (Dietz 1978).

It has been suggested that the features of apprehended sex offenders reflect to some extent the relative ease with which certain types of individual can be picked up and convicted rather than characteristics that have a necessary link with sexual crime. That is less likely to be true of the more seriously aggressive offenses which provoke determined efforts at detection and prosecution. The U.S. National Crime Survey obtained victims' judgments as to the age and race of rape assailants. Based on these reports it was estimated that the rape-offending rate of eighteen-to-twenty-year-old blacks was double that of older males, and the rate for eighteen-to-twenty-year-old blacks was over five times that of white males in the same age group (Hindelang 1981). Since these findings were in keeping with the stereotype of the rapist derived from police reports, it seems probable that the latter do in fact provide a substantially correct profile (Hindelang and Davis 1977).

In regard to the more private and less readily reported offenses, such as consensual incest or indecencies with children, which are not infrequently committed by persons of respectable social status, the offenders who fall into the hands of the police are less likely to be representative. This was glaringly obvious when consensual homosexual activity between adults in private used to be a matter for an occasional prosecution. The apprehended homosexuals tended to be persons who had fallen foul of the police for other reasons or persons whose recklessly flaunting behavior called unfavorable attention to themselves. In addition to their homosexual orientation, they were likely to be deviant in personality and socially maladjusted, features which are now recognized to be uncharacteristic of large numbers of homosexuals who live happily in the community without coming to the attention of the authorities (West 1977, pp. 31–34).

Pressure of deviant sexual impulses is often a crucial, but not necessarily the only, factor in offending. For example, whether an impulse to touch a child sexually is put into action will depend not only on the strength of the desire, but also on the strength of the individual's adherence to the social and legal code. As with more ordinary crimes, the temptation will be greater if the offender has no particular social status, no family attachments, and no worthwhile job to lose if he is found out. The claim made by many sex offenders that they were intoxicated at the time is by no means always a purely self-exculpatory invention. In other words, the criminogenic circumstances common to most crimes are still operative even when the main motive is to satisfy a deviant sexual desire.

Surveys of men convicted of different kinds of sex crime show clearly that, even where the more deviant types of offenses are concerned, sociopsychological problems other than or in addition to aberrant erotic interests are frequently in evidence. For example, in the large Indiana survey (Gebhard et al. 1965, table 107) only a small proportion, not more than 10 percent, of the men imprisoned for sexual acts with children under twelve, or minors under sixteen, admitted a preference for children or youngsters under sixteen as sexual partners. The vast majority had apparently resorted to children because their desires for older partners were for one reason or another frustrated. Rather similar conclusions have been reached in other studies, although the proportion of child molesters primarily attracted to children rather than using children as substitutes is usually higher than 10 percent. For example, Groth and Birnbaum (1978) examined 175 men convicted of sexual assault against children. They classified 47.4 percent as "fixated" on children, on the grounds that since adolescence they had been primarily or exclusively attracted to the young. The majority, however, were deemed to have regressed from an established sexual orientation toward mature partners, and in fact three-quarters of the regressed men were or had been married.

An interesting point about these results was that although 31 percent of the "fixated" category and 16 percent of the regressed category had been involved with boys, or with both boys and girls, there were no instances of men regressing from a primary attraction to other adult males into pedophilia. The homosexual offenses were committed either by regressed heterosexuals or, more commonly, by men who had always had a pedophiliac orientation. This result fits in with the observations from other sources. First, molesters of small boys, although fewer in number than molesters of girls, tend to be more persistent and recidivistic in their offenses, presumably because they are more likely to have a primary fixation. Second, male homosexuals who are attracted to their age peers are well known for the high valuation they place upon the bodily attributes of mature masculinity. This has been confirmed by phallometric assessments of the sexual arousal of adult-oriented heterosexual and homosexual males to erotic pictures of subjects of various ages. Whereas both groups show some responsiveness to child subjects, the homosexuals' responses "appear substantially lower than that of the normal heterosexual" (Freund 1981). The idea that the average homosexual is a greater risk to children than the average heterosexual would seem to be incorrect.

It is important from the standpoint of management and treatment to recognize how often force of circumstances, or conditions that frustrate attempts to find normal sexual outlets, influence the commission of deviant offenses. This becomes especially obvious in prisons and other closed, sex-segregated institutions where adults begin to participate in homosexual activities who would never do so in conditions of freedom. Circumstances liable to produce sexual frustrations are easy to identify. Adolescence, a phase when experimental acts of voyeurism, homosexuality, exhibitionism, and sexual molestation are especially prevalent, is also a time when the conflict between heterosexual passions and social restraints is at a peak. Some males are convicted for the first time late in life for resorting to children. Often this results from a dwindling or loss of marital sex at a time of life when diminished attractiveness and failing confidence and potency prevent the acquisition of new partners. Among some compulsive exhibitionists offenses are noticeably more frequent at times of stress, especially stress caused by marital discord (Hackett, Saber, and Curran 1980). The mentally retarded, as a group, are particularly vulnerable to involvement in minor sexual delinquencies, and this doubtless reflects the difficulties and frustrations in obtaining approved sexual partners occasioned by their social handicaps.

In regard to aggressive offenders against mature females, one school of thought emphasizes how much they have in common with nonsexual offenders. They consist predominantly of badly brought up, poorly socialized and generally delinquent young working-class males. Others emphasize a different aspect, namely, the deviant or dysfunctional sexuality that prevents some aggressive offenders from obtaining erotic satisfaction from consensual heterosexual intercourse or from obtaining emotional satisfaction in close relationships with the opposite sex (Groth 1979).

It is often argued that the phenomenon of rape is simply an expression of the unequal status of men and women in society. Anthropological evidence suggests that communities where the level of violence is high, where women have low status, and where premarital sexual relationships are prohibited tend to have many rapes (Sanday 1981). In contemporary society themes of rape are common enough in the sexual fantasies of normal men, and this is supposed to be the result of having absorbed the culturally accepted identification of ideal masculinity with dominance and aggression, so that every male is a potential rapist, or would be if there did not exist contradictory taboos about the use of violence and cruelty. Indeed, one survey found that a substantial percentage of American males believed they might rape if they found themselves in circumstances in which they would not be punished (Malamuth 1981).

Investigations of actual rape offenders, however, have shown that at least some of them have characteristics not fully explained by the adoption of a culturally supported macho stance. Intensive explorations of the sexual fantasies of rape offenders indicate that although many of them are maximally excited by ideas of consensual intercourse, for some violence and subjugation are necessary in order for them to achieve full sexual arousal (Abel et al. 1978). However this condition of sadism arises, the inability to obtain full satisfaction without violence is a sexual deviation the presence of which has definite implications for the treatment of these offenders.

Sadistic lust, sexual dysfunctions, or lack of socially acceptable outlets are not the only reasons for aggressive sexual offenses. Attitudes and emotions that impede the establishment of harmonious relations with the opposite sex play an important part. Rapists committed to institutions tend to be repeat offenders for whom the shock of detection has not brought to an end the urge to attack women. Many such men have extensive heterosexual experience in marriage or with girlfriends, but their relationships are turbulent, unsatisfying, even violent. "They tend to experience women negatively as hostile, demanding, ungiving and unfaithful" (Cohen et al. 1971, p. 229). McCaldon (1967) identified a group among imprisoned rapists who are definite misogynists with strong feelings of masculine inadequacy and failure. Their behavior represents "a struggle versus the overwhelming superiority of females, a hostile proof of one's masculinity." Seymour Halleck (1971, p. 191) wrote: "Many rapists are individuals who are plagued with doubts about their own masculinity. . . . In his attacks upon women [the rapist] both

conquers his fears and confirms their inferiority." After having close
contact with a series of serious, repetitive rape offenders who were
undergoing deep psychotherapy, I reached a similar conclusion. "The
man who has an urge to rape is often the man who feels at a disadvantage
with women. He doubts his attractiveness as a mate, he fears exploitation, he doubts his sexual proficiency or he is afraid of being cheated
and so becomes demanding or jealous" (West, Roy, and Nichols 1978,
p. 125). In their sexual assaults these men avenge themselves on innocent
strangers for real or imagined rejections, treachery, or insults to their
masculine pride experienced at the hands of women they have known.
Any actual defect or uncertainty in sexual performance exacerbates
their paranoid sensitivity. A significant proportion of attempted rapes
are not completed because the man's potency fails rather than because
the women's resistance cannot be overcome. Furthermore, pronounced
bisexual tendencies, which may give rise to anxiety for reassuring demonstrations of manhood, are surprisingly common among convicted
rapists.

These suspicious, hostile feelings toward women seem always to have
their roots in very disturbed upbringing and unhappy experiences in
childhood. Emotional maltreatment and parental repressiveness and
hostility toward developing sexuality are as important in this context
as overt brutality, rejection, or neglect. While retrospective inquiries
into the early histories of individual rapists help to give meaning to
apparently irrational attitudes, such psychodynamic interpretations are
rarely specific enough to provide empirically testable hypotheses. There
are too many examples of men with similarly disturbed upbringings
and warped thinking who do *not* become rapists for these factors to
provide a complete explanation. The psychodynamic observations are
useful, however, as a basis for therapeutic discussions aimed at changing
attitudes.

The matter is further complicated by the rather similar psychody-
namics discernible among relatively minor offenders, such as exhibitionists, whose fantasies during their deviant rituals are of successfully
shocking or frightening women or of overwhelming them with a display
of impressive masculinity. Men who resort to such covert and devious
ways of expressing their feelings are likely to be lacking in assertiveness
at home and resentful of the dominant character of their wives (Rosen
1979; Rooth 1980).

One variety of aggression arises from hatred of sexuality rather than
from uncontrolled sexual impulses. Peter Sutcliffe, the so-called York-

shire Ripper, who recently terrorized the town of Leeds, was in the habit of waylaying women he believed to be prostitutes, not to take advantage of their services, but in order to stab or bludgeon them to death. He was a schizophrenic whose hallucinatory voices commanded him to fulfill a divine mission to rid the world of such women. A less pathological manifestation of rather similar hatred is the phenomenon of "queer bashing," when gangs of young thugs visit the cruising grounds of homosexuals in order to beat up men thought to be sexual deviants.

When desire is concentrated totally on some deviant target, with actual impotence or complete uninterest toward approved sex objects, then pressure toward the commission of offenses becomes very strong, since the only alternative sexual outlet is solitary masturbation to deviant fantasy or pornography. When homosexual acts by males were punished severely, even to the extent of the death penalty, there were always substantial numbers prepared to risk everything for the sake of satisfying the sexual appetite. Today, when sexual indecencies with small boys attract extreme opprobrium, it is noticeable that highly respected members of society are willing to take similar risks (Gerassi 1966). Not only that, but some men organize their whole existence, their work, their living arrangements, and their friendship networks entirely around their commitment to the pursuit of boys (Rossman 1979). Some exhibitionists are so compulsive that imprisonment and the loss of job, wife, and family makes no impression on their repeated offending (Bluglass 1980).

Notwithstanding the compulsive element apparent in many deviant offenders, there is evidence that some offenders can be diverted from antisocial habits. A striking natural experiment occurred in Denmark when the liberalization of the obscenity laws led to a suddenly increased availability of pornography. A remarkable decrease in recorded sexual offenses against children ensued, which did not appear to be due to any change in the condemnatory attitudes of the public or the likelihood of cases being reported to the police (Kutchinsky 1973). A further decrease took place a few years later when pornography featuring children became available. These observations strongly suggested that many child molesters, both those using children as substitutes for adults and those fixated on children, were prepared to satisfy themselves by masturbating to appropriate pornography instead of risking the commission of a serious crime. There was no corresponding decrease in rapes and assaults on mature females. Two speculative reasons for this have been suggested. First, as already mentioned, some rapists are specifically motivated to cause women suffering and so could not be satisfied by pornography. Second, surveys of convicted rapists have shown that a higher proportion of them than of other prisoners or volunteer "controls" say they had no exposure to pornographic materials at adolescence (Goldstein and Kant 1973). Rapists tend to have had sexually inhibited upbringings and to be relatively unimaginative in sexual outlook and fantasy, regarding anything other than actual intercourse as uninteresting.

III. The Causes of Deviant Sexual Behavior

Since a substantial proportion of all sex offenses result from attempts to satisfy deviant sexual inclinations, it is relevant to consider how deviant fixations come about and whether they can be changed. Unfortunately, knowledge on this topic remains uncertain and controversial. A great deal has been written, particularly about the origins of a homosexual orientation, but the more this question is explored the more complicated it appears.

One topic of theoretical dispute is the extent to which adult sexual behavior is the outcome of individual learning and how much it depends on innate neurological programming. If learning is the key, then peculiarities of parenting, cultural pressures, early sexual experiences, or difficulties in establishing appropriate heterosexual contacts might each be the main determinant. If a flaw in neurological programming is the answer, then genetic factors, cerebral dysfunctions, or neuroendocrinological disorders might be responsible. Explanations in terms of faulty learning, which leave open the possibility of corrective relearning, are generally more favorable to the notion of therapy aimed at modifying sexual proclivities.

The nature-nurture dichotomy is, of course, an oversimplification, since human development requires both. In lower mammals sexual behavior is relatively rigidly fixed by neurophysiological processes. Periodic fluctuations in hormone levels determine the timing of the estrous phase during which the female becomes receptive and gives out signals, by scent and posture, which arouse the male to pursuit and mounting. Each member of the pair reacts automatically in ways that ensure the necessary mechanics of copulation are successfully accomplished. In primates, as in man, the routine is much less stereotyped and far more dependent on learning. Monkeys deprived of social interactions in early life, so that they cannot observe or practice copulation, develop into sexually incapacitated adults. If attempts at copulation occur at all, they may not achieve penetration. If the female

animal becomes pregnant, she may prove incompetent or disinclined
to carry out her life-supporting role when the baby arrives.

The human sexual scene is further complicated by the varied social
systems that regulate when, where, with whom, and in what manner
sexual behavior is approved or condemned. Our own social system is
peculiar in discouraging sexual behavior and sexual interest in the young,
while expecting immediate, skillful, discriminating, and effective arousal
and performance when marriageable age is reached. These expectations
are supported by an implicit assumption that appropriate sexual reactions are readily evoked when required in all normally constituted
persons by virtue of innate neurophysiological mechanisms that come
into play under the influence of hormones released at puberty. This
viewpoint, at least in this crude version, is scarcely compatible with
the actual behavior and feelings of young persons, the differences between cultures in the nature of the physical acts utilized to effect sexual
arousal and the age when overt sexual contacts are permitted to commence, or the strange reversals of sexual orientation that sometimes
occur quite late in life.

Human sexual responses are not governed in any direct way by
hormone levels. Administering hormones to an adult may increase or
decrease sexual arousability, but it does not alter a person's sexual
preferences or the nature of the sexual behavior he finds satisfying.
Estrogens and androgen antagonists decrease libido in males and are
used for that purpose to quell the impulses of chronic sex offenders.
Androgens tend to increase eroticism in both sexes. Spontaneous changes
in hormone levels, which occur during the female menstrual cycle, for
example, are probably connected in some way with arousability, but
the relationships are complex and reported observations inconsistent
(Money 1980). In other words, adult hormones activate preexisting
mechanisms but do not initiate them.

Recent evidence, however, suggests that there is in mammals a critical
phase of fetal development, which occurs after the physical attributes
of sex are clearly differentiated but before brain functions are stabilized.
A temporary disturbance of hormone levels at this stage may mascu-
linize an otherwise female brain or feminize a male brain. This can
result in the animal's developing normally in appearance and acquiring
normal adult hormone levels at puberty but evincing cross-sex behavior,
such as mounting by female rats and lordosis by male rats. An analogous
mechanism has been postulated to explain the development of homosexuality in humans (Dörner 1976; MacCulloch and Waddington 1981).

In spite of the technological advances in methods of measuring hormone levels in blood and plasma, comparisons between samples of adult heterosexuals and homosexuals have failed to yield consistent differences (Tourney 1980). However, it has been claimed by Dörner and his co-workers that a test of the function of the hypothalamic pituitary complex (that is the area of brain concerned with sex differentiation) reveals a difference between homosexual and heterosexual males. Homosexuals respond to an injection of conjugated estrogens with an initial decrease followed by an overcompensatory increase of pituitary luteinizing hormone, a pattern of response characteristic of normal females but not of heterosexual males. From this it is deduced that the brains of male homosexuals have been feminized during early development so that in adulthood the normal levels of circulating hormones potentiate homosexual instead of heterosexual arousals.

Dörner's theory and his test have yet to be confirmed. However, even if they were established, the mechanism involved could hardly amount to more than a predisposing factor. There is good evidence, for instance, from identical twins discordant for sexual orientation (West 1977, pp. 80–83) that life experiences are also important determinants. Whether or not one accepts the fanciful ideas about incest guilt and castration fears propagated by Freudian analysts, there seems little doubt that many individuals with peculiarly deviant sexual interests, including some homosexuals, have been exposed to sexually repressive, anxiety-provoking styles of child rearing that have blocked or inhibited ordinary heterosexual learning and indirectly encouraged substitute outlets.

Some deviant sexual interests, rubber fetishism, for example, are such that they could only be acquired through life experience. There is no doubt that almost any stimulus can be eroticized. Physiological responses of arousal are initially somewhat indiscriminate. Almost any emotional excitement or mechanical stimulation suffices to induce erection in young boys. Some sociologists argue that cultural expectations are almost entirely responsible for developing the link between orgasmic response and heterosexual intercourse. On this view, erotic responsiveness is harnessed to social needs through the contexts in which it is encouraged or discouraged and the social meanings and values ascribed to the different situations in which it may occur (Gagnon and Simon 1974).

Behavioristic psychological theory takes an intermediate position. The existence of programmed reflex arousal to primary sexual stimuli is not contested, but it is acknowledged that a wide range of secondary stimuli may acquire equal power to arouse by virtue of conditioning by association. On this view, early homosexual experiences, especially if reinforced by repetition in subsequent masturbation fantasies, would be expected to be an important factor in the development of a permanent homosexual orientation (McGuire et al. 1965). Empirical observation, however, suggests that the sequence of events is more complex. The recollections of homosexual adults (Bell, Weinberg, and Hammersmith 1981) suggest that marked sexual preferences often develop before the opportunity for sexual contacts occurs. A misfit, discernible in early childhood, between an individual's temperament or interests and his expected gender role is often predictive of homosexual orientation as an adult (Zuger 1978, 1980). Furthermore, extensive and precocious homosexual experiences are by no means incompatible with exclusive heterosexuality in adulthood.

Evidence from twin studies suggests that genetic predisposition may play some part in the development of even such odd habits as transvestitism and flagellation rituals (Gosselin and Wilson 1980, p. 106). Moreover, in the case of some fetishists and transvestites, a causal connection with cerebral dysfunction centered in the temporal lobe has been suggested (Epstein 1961), but the association might be partly accounted for by the social handicaps caused by psychomotor seizures and prolonged medication (Money and Pruce 1977). However that may be, predisposition cannot be the overriding factor in sexual deviations. Learning from experience, especially in early life, through the emotional and symbolic meanings attached to body contact behavior, is crucial to the sexual development of humans. In some primitive cultures it was obligatory for males up to a certain age to participate fully and exclusively in homosexual relationships, after which the heterosexual activity became equally obligatory (Carrier 1980). Neither simple physical conditioning nor biological predisposition can satisfactorily explain such culturally ordained shifts. For many sexual deviants the ritual which affords prime satisfaction is often the reenactment of a complex situation, such as being caned on the buttocks by a person dressed in an academic gown, which is clearly a fantasy construction built up from some long-past experience.

Once established, erotic rituals may be continually reinforced by practice and fantasy elaboration. Psychodynamic interpretations elicited in the course of psychotherapy suggest that nonsexual meanings can be incorporated into and further reinforce sexual fantasy. A sadomasochistic ritual may be something more than a reawakening of a childish pleasure from spanking; it may satisfy a socially inadequate person's dreams of domination over or revenge on the opposite sex. An exhibitionist's ritualistic exposure, derived perhaps from the memory of erotic sensations provoked by a young sister admiring his genital equipment, can be translated into a reassuring fantasy of power to shock and impress women in a way he could never hope to do in real life.

As with so many aspects of human behavior the causative factors are multiple, and some truth can be found in most of the current theories. Physical opportunities and cultural or subcultural supports for deviant behavior play an important part, but certain determining influences appear to originate in the individual's early experience and personal development. Each case of deviant behavior, therefore, has to be examined on its merits, for what may be an important motive or driving force in one case may not be the same in another, although the behavior appears superficially similar. The topic will be taken up again in relation to the varieties of treatment that may be appropriate. Before discussing the control and treatment of deviant behavior, however, it is necessary to consider in the next section the interactions between the offenders and the individuals defined as their victims.

IV. Sex Victimology

Criminological research into the role of the victim is particularly relevant to the study of sexual crime, since such a large proportion of offenses either involve only consensual participants or are committed under circumstances in which there is a serious conflict of evidence about how the misconduct was initiated. Furthermore, unlike crimes of violence resulting in observable and measurable injury, most sexual assaults or molestations are held to be damaging to the victim psychologically or morally rather than physically. The nature and extent of such damage is difficult to assess and open to much dispute.

One of the most difficult and contentious issues revolves around the damage that may be caused to children through sexual contact with an adult. It has lately become widely recognized that the asexuality of children is a myth of relatively recent origin (Ariès 1962), that evidence for the so-called latency period is lacking (Goldman and Goldman 1982), and that some cultures permit sexual contacts with or between children without apparent harm (Ford and Beach 1952; Money et al. 1977; Constantine and Martinson 1981). Nevertheless, because children in our society are traditionally shielded from knowledge or experience of sexuality, premature contacts of the gentlest kind can be very frightening. The cases that come before the courts represent a tiny and biased selection from the totality of such activities in the community, and they probably give an exaggerated impression of the seriousness of such events. That, certainly, was the opinion of Kinsey and his collaborators, derived from questioning supposedly representative samples of white Americans. Reports from females in the Kinsey survey of their sex experiences before the age of thirteen with persons at least five years older than themselves were analyzed by Gagnon (1965). Of a total of 4,441 females presented with basic questions, 1,075 (24 percent) reported such an experience. A smaller number, 1,200 females, were questioned more intensively, and of these, 333 (28 percent) reported a total of 400 such incidents, only 6 percent of which had been reported to the police at the time and 21 percent of which had never been mentioned to anyone prior to the research interview. Of the 333 victims, a majority of 257 (77.2 percent) reported no more than a single "accidental" incident, such as a man exposing in the street or a casual act of indecency by a stranger or acquaintance with no prior buildup of social interaction. A further forty-five (13.5 percent) reported more than one accidental incident. A small minority, less than 5 percent, of the victims of accidental incidents had been subjected to forcible molestation. The remaining thirty-one victims (9.3 percent) reported extended or repeated contacts. Five of these thirty-one reported having been subjected to preparatory coercion, but twenty-six admitted that they had collaborated through a provoked or mutual desire. The assailants of the five "coerced" victims were either their fathers or a male relative and in four of these cases nonforcible sexual intercourse took place. In four of these five coerced victims the events had begun when they were under six years of age. Otherwise most victims had been older, nine to twelve, at the time of their first or only experience. The vast majority described negative reactions at the time, mostly simple fright, but others, especially the collaborating victims, reported having had mixed feelings of anxiety and arousal and subsequent guilt. An interesting feature was that a majority of the victims (and a higher proportion than expected from questioning females who had not been victims) admitted prepubertal sex experiences with other children before the age when they first had contact with an adult. Sexual precocity probably increases a child's vulnerability to molestation by adults.

Only eighteen (5 percent) of the women who reported early sex victimization were considered by the interviewers to have serious sociopsychological difficulties. It is unclear whether this proportion exceeds expectations for an unselected sample of the population, but in any event only three of the eighteen women attributed their problems to their early sex victimization. It was significant, however, that four of the five who reported having been coerced preparatory to their offense were among the maladjusted adults. The conclusion to which these data pointed was to a general absence of long-term deleterious outcomes except in the case of the small number of coerced victims exposed to aggression over an extended period at the hands of a father or relative.

The Kinsey survey was based on a broad sampling of the population and provides what are still the best available estimates of child sex victimization (Gagnon 1965), although it may be that persons who volunteer to discuss such topics are untypical. However, more restricted surveys conducted since have yielded essentially similar findings. For example, a survey of mothers involved in child abuse, which utilized a control group of 500 "normal women" in New Mexico, found that 24 percent of the normal group had experienced some kind of stressful sexual incident by the age of eighteen and that 3 percent of them had had experience of sexual contact with or exposure by a male relative, usually a father, stepfather, or uncle, before they had reached thirteen years of age (Goodwin 1982, p. 160).

Landis (1956), using a questionnaire addressed to students taking classes on marriage and the family (all of whom were said to have cooperated willingly), found that 35 percent of the girls reported having had one or more sex experience with an adult. The 360 positive replies that were analyzed described 531 incidents. Since only 53 percent of these girl victims reported that their (presumably first) experience took place before age thirteen, the incidence of prepubertal victimization works out a little less than in the Kinsey study. Over half the reported encounters were with exhibitionists and over a quarter consisted of sexual fondling. Only 1.9 percent were rapes or attempted rapes, although in a further 8.5 percent there was some interest in or attempt at coitus. Only 1.5 percent were lesbian approaches. The commonest response of the girls at the time was to leave the scene, and the commonest emotional reaction was one of fright or shock.

Although 30 percent of the girl victims in the Landis survey felt they had been temporarily affected emotionally, only 3 percent thought they had sustained permanent emotional damage. However, the small minority who had been subjected to aggressive attacks, that is, rape or attempted rape, were much more likely to describe emotionally damaging effects. The victimized girls, particularly the 169 girls who had had sexual contacts in circumstances in which they may have initiated or collaborated in the behavior, included a smaller proportion of virgins.

A more recent questionnaire survey (Finkelhor 1979) again utilized American students who were taking classes in sociology, psychology, or other subjects for which such an inquiry might seem relevant. Some 18 percent either declined to cooperate or did not complete the childhood sex questions, but of the 530 completed replies from females 11.3 percent reported having had, before reaching the age of thirteen, at least one sex experience with an adult of at least eighteen years of age. The inclusion of two other categories of experiences, that is, children under thirteen with adolescents under eighteen but at least five years older than the girl, and girls of thirteen to sixteen with adults at least ten years older, brought the incidence figure up to 19.2 percent. The fact that the sample came from a relatively privileged section of the New England population may have been responsible for the incidence figures being lower than in the Kinsey survey.

Analyzing all three categories of experience together, the mean age at the time of the (presumably first) incident was 10.2 years. Girls in their immediate prepubertal years, ten to twelve, were much the most vulnerable. Most of the experiences (60 percent) were single occurrences, but when repeated they tended to continue for some time (average duration thirty-one weeks). The commonest types of experience were genital fondling (38 percent) or an encounter with exhibitionism (20 percent). Only 4 percent of the experiences involved sexual intercourse. There were just a few (ten) incidents of lesbian approaches by adult women to young girls (Finkelhor 1979, p. 79). Hardly any of the girls said they had initiated the incidents themselves, most of them (58 percent) felt afraid, and 66 percent remembered their experiences with negative feelings. Although many of them recalled some positive aspects, such as pleasurable sensations and enjoyment of affection, feelings of guilt and helplessness predominated. Most of the victims told nobody at the time, and for many the survey was the first occasion when they had ever mentioned their experiences. The kinds of experiences which evoked the most negative feelings were those in which the offender was aggressive or used force, in which the offender was the girl's own father, and in which the age gap between victim and offender was particularly great. Possible connections between any current psychological difficulties and childhood sex experiences were not investigated.

Whereas surveys prove that young girls quite commonly have some sex experience with an adult without its apparently producing any more damaging effect than temporary anxiety or annoyance, clinical experience of the minority of cases of child sexual abuse which come to the notice of courts and the social services shows that some do involve serious and occasionally lasting upset (Lukianowicz 1972; Browning and Boatman 1977; Beezley and Kempe 1980; Goodwin 1982). This seems to be more closely related to the amount of tension in the family than to the actual sex incidents themselves. Sometimes it is unhappiness in the home that causes affection-seeking behavior in the child and so makes her vulnerable. Often, however, the tension is provoked, or preexisting tension greatly exaggerated, when the sexual misconduct of a family member comes to light, especially if, following repeated interrogations and perhaps a cross-examination of the child in court, her father or a near relative is taken away to prison or she is herself sent to a children's home (Gibbens and Prince 1963). In most cases however, even where there is initial manifest disturbance, the children outgrow these reactions and make a satisfactory adjustment (Burton 1968). In one long-term follow-up of sexually abused children involved in court cases, who were investigated some twenty to thirty years later, all but eight out of the sample of fifty-four were considered "well adjusted" (A. Rasmussen, writing in 1934, cited in Burton [1968]). Considering that twenty-one out of fifty-four had come from homes in which a parent was absent or inadequate, and thirteen of the fifty-four girls had formed a steady relationship with the adult offender, the result was remarkable confirmation of the resilience of most children in the face of experiences that might be expected to have serious effects.

Incest with a father appears to be potentially the most damaging type of early sex experience. Now that problems of sex can be talked about more openly, women have come forward to publicize the fact that they have been incest victims and that their whole lives have been blighted by the experience. Their evidence is perfectly credible, for undoubtedly some child incest victims are terrorized or pressured into compliance. They may suffer dreadfully from shame and guilt when they reach an age to realize how strongly such behavior is condemned and yet feel helplessly trapped by family ties and fear of exposure. What remains problematic is the frequency of these malignant situations in comparison with the relatively benign instances that produce minimal long-term ill effects.

One of the main worries about girls being subjected to sexual approaches from adults is that they may find the experiences so aversive that future heterosexual relationships will be spoiled. Public concern about boys in similar situations with adult males centers somewhat inconsistently on an opposite risk, that of being seduced into homosexuality. Both the Landis (1956) and Finkelhor (1979) surveys covered male as well as female child victims. Landis found that almost as many males as females recalled a childhood sex approach by an adult, but that was largely because the survey included experiences at adolescence, when boys become more likely to experience such incidents. In Finkelhor's sample 8.6 percent of males reported at least one experience, four-fifths with adult men, one-fifth with adult women. Both surveys reported that boys were less worried at the time than girls, more likely to be involved with adults outside of the home and family, and less likely to report the incident to anyone at the time. Finkelhor noted that unwilling boys were more likely than girls to resist with force. On the other hand, incidents with boys, especially those which continue over any length of time, are more likely to involve collaboration. Finkelhor noted that boys' experiences with adult women were less common than their experiences with men but were recollected with less negative feelings. The occasional encounters of girls with adult women were also recalled less negatively than their experiences with men.

Surveys, either retrospective (Landis 1956; Gibbens 1957; Schofield 1965) or by follow-up (Doshay 1943), have found no evidence that boys' experiences of sexual approaches by adult males are likely to result in a homosexual orientation. For some boys or girls, however, especially those involved with other members of the family, the experience can be very upsetting and cause anxiety about becoming homosexual (Goodwin 1982). Where boys' relationships with older men take place in the context of an ongoing, loving relationship it has been suggested by some writers that the effects may be more beneficial than harmful, providing emotional support and educational experience, on the lines of "Greek love," without necessarily affecting sexual orientation (Guyon 1950; Eglinton 1971; O'Carroll 1980; Wilson 1981).

One indisputable source of harm in adult-child sexual relations is pregnancy arising from incest. If the baby is not aborted and attempts are made to bring it up within the family, the ambiguous relationships can be a source of continued stress. Moreover, the risk of producing a genetically impaired offspring appears to be considerable (Adams and Neel 1967; Carter 1967; Seemanova 1971).

The influence of feminist writers has attracted a great deal of attention to the topic of rape victimology (Schultz 1975). In order to qualify as an offense, sexual molestation of mature females is necessarily non-consensual. In addition to the physical unpleasantness and sometimes considerable brutality involved in a sexual assault, the victims feel peculiarly humiliated, even degraded, by the gross nature of the intrusion. They have reason to fear further consequential damage, notably unwanted pregnancy, venereal infection, irrational criticism or rejection from jealous husbands or boyfriends, and loss of reputation. The belief dies hard that raped women are partly to blame for placing themselves in a position where such a thing could happen. Most rapes occur in the absence of witnesses, and unless some injury has been sustained it can be just one person's word against another that the woman did not give consent. Rape complainants often feel that their evidence is challenged unsympathetically or dismissed too readily by prejudiced male policemen. The police may feel obliged to adopt a critical stance in order to see whether the testimony will stand up in court against hostile cross-examination on behalf of a defendant desperate to avoid long imprisonment.

The classic survey of rapes in Philadelphia by Amir (1971) caused much resentment because he reported evidence for what he called "victim precipitation." The choice of words, implying some positive or even culpable action by the victim, was unfortunate. Victim vulnerability might have been more apt. Although it may be true that a lone female hitchhiker places herself at some risk, she cannot be assumed to be soliciting an attack any more than the householder who leaves a window unfastened can be assumed to want a burglary. In both situations it is the aggressor who takes advantage of the victim's relatively defenseless position.

Surveys reveal the high incidence of sexual harassment of female employees by men in authority over them (C. Brodsky 1976; Evans 1978) and the high incidence of actual or near rape of students out on dates with boyfriends (Schultz 1975, p. 77). It appears that being sexually experienced increases rather than diminishes the risk of being forced unwillingly (Kanin and Parcell 1977). Such findings highlight the inherent ambiguity of sexual situations and the clash of values and expectations between males and females leading to breakdowns in communication. Culturally supported myths about the naturalness of male dominance and female submission may promote sexual attitudes and conduct that offend women, but prevailing macho attitudes are inadequate to account for the more compulsive and brutal sexual assaults that no section of society would condone.

The victim's best strategy in the face of a threatened rape has been a topic of some research (Brodsky 1976). Unsurprisingly, fierce verbal attack and determined physical resistance serve to discourage many assailants, but a dangerous minority of aggressive men are aroused all the more by such a response. Calm talk, reasoning, and appeals to sympathy are sometimes effective in defusing both anger and sexual frustration.

The feminist movement has had a salutary influence on the treatment of complainants by both police and courts. Changes have been introduced to prevent irrelevant cross-examination about sexual experience with men other than the offender, to prevent attacks on the character of the witness, to modify rules of corroboration, to accommodate the special circumstances of rape cases, and to define nonconsent with greater realism. The establishment of rape crisis centers for giving aid, comfort, and advice to victims has probably increased reporting and has certainly improved the standards of both medical examinations and police interrogation of complainants. Furthermore, the publicity given to feminist views cannot have failed to reduce belief in the "myths" to which they so strongly object.

V. Treatment

The need to institute practical measures for dealing with known sex offenders brings into sharp focus the uncertain state of knowledge, the lack of comprehensive theory, and the peculiar difficulties of obtaining essential research data on sexual behavior. Acts condemned by law or morality may be secretly condoned and practiced by large but unknown numbers in the population. When accidentally exposed the behavior may seem more exceptional and deviant than in fact it is. Owing to the low detection rate and the reluctance to report embarrassing occurrences, the true incidence of offending remains largely unknown.

Disapproved sexual practices that for one person seem mere casual indulgence, open to modification voluntarily or by means of ordinary penal deterrents, for others may represent their only sexual outlet or in some cases a truly compulsive craving over which they have little control. In some instances, sexual offenses may come about, like other forms of lawbreaking, through situations of temptation coupled with a certain amount of subcultural support, whereas in other cases they may be closely associated with, or a by-product of, severe distortions of personality or generalized social maladjustment.

Quantitative evaluations of the relative incidences and overlaps between these different patterns as they exist in the community at large are simply not available. Direct observation is not feasible and valid self-report data of sufficient depth and honesty from representative samples are virtually unattainable. The analysis of treatment needs can only be based on the highly selected populations of convicted offenders referred for examination. This has to suffice as a guide for penal practice, but cannot be used for generalizations and theories about the sexual behavior of a whole society.

Ordinary criminal offenders such as burglars and car thieves rarely think that there is anything the matter with them that requires treatment, but among sex offenders, especially those with deviant inclinations, many are well aware that they have problems that the average man does not have to face. Some offenders have no wish to change their habits, but others would be only too glad to be able to do so, and it is in the interest of society that they should receive whatever help offers a reasonable chance of success. Specialized treatment being a scarce and expensive commodity, the community has a right to ask if it is cost effective. Rehabilitative treatment schemes for nonsexual offenders have come under fierce attack in recent years from critics who point out that few, if any, treatment programs in the penal system have been proved effective by vigorous scientific evaluation, whereas many have been shown to have no detectable effect (Brody 1976; Sechrest, White, and Brown 1979). The outcome of treatments for sex offenders has so rarely been evaluated critically that opinions, either favorable or skeptical, remain largely unsupported.

The clearest criterion of success would be a reduction in the rate of reconviction, but there are great obstacles to the application of this criterion in practice. In order to show that treatment reduces the already low rate of reconviction of sex offenders, either it must be dramatically successful or the sample must be very large before a statistically significant result can be expected. Because reconviction risk persists over many years it takes a very long time to judge the long-term results of treatment. In view of the secretive nature of sexual misconduct and the low detection rate, reconviction data can provide only a crude measure. Given sufficiently large-scale and long follow-up these problems could be overcome, but even more serious are the practical difficulties in obtaining properly matched control groups of untreated offenders. Random allocation of every other case to either treatment or no treatment is rarely possible in the face of legal, administrative, and ethical objections. Those who run treatment programs for sex offenders are necessarily selective in the kinds of offenders they are prepared to include, and the range of cases from which they can select depends on whether the source of referrals is a community service, the criminal courts, or prison authorities. After every effort has been made to find similar cases for comparison, some suspicion must always remain that an effect apparently attributable to treatment might have been due to selection.

Although the long-term effectiveness of treatment in reducing sexual recidivism has as yet to be conclusively demonstrated, there is good evidence for short-term changes. Improvement in social skills can be demonstrated (Crawford and Allen 1979), and lessened sexual arousal to inappropriate stimuli can be verified with the penile plethysmograph (Freund, Chan, and Coulthard 1979). Unfortunately, such beneficial changes are not necessarily lasting or generalizable to real-life situations after the offender is released from the treatment facility. One of the therapist's greatest problems in dealing with offenders in a penal setting is his minimal contact with or control over those features of the client's living situation that favor a recrudescence of deviant behavior. The motives of offenders during incarceration and their responsiveness to therapeutic manipulation may change dramatically once they are at liberty and exposed to temptations.

Treatments for sex offenders take four main forms: therapy on the mental health model, behavior modification, life skills training, and hormone manipulation (Brodsky 1980; Brodsky and West 1981). Programs based on these methods are in operation in the United States and have been the subject of at least two comprehensive surveys (Brecher 1978; Delin 1978). A welcome feature of some of these projects is a lessening of rigid theoretical commitments to one particular approach and a willingness to invoke a variety of techniques according to each client's unique set of problems.

Treatment on the mental health model operates on the assumption that behavior can be changed through self-revelatory discussion of intimate feelings and personal problems, utilizing techniques of psychotherapy, group therapy, therapeutic community, and social work. The aim is to bring about beneficial insights into how aberrant habits develop, the motivations which they serve, and the undesirable consequences of continuing them. This in turn promotes desire for change, aids the development of more acceptable social attitudes and life-styles, and helps to break down the inhibitions that stand in the way of obtaining sexual satisfaction in conventional ways. The relationship that develops between client and therapist is arguably at least as important as the intellectual content of the discussion. Even therapists who are opposed to the mental health model on theoretical grounds still make use of personal contact and discussion to inspire motivation and confidence in their clients.

Behavior modification utilizes much the same methods and principles whether the clients are patients with anxieties and phobias (Rachman and Teasdale 1969), ordinary delinquents (Trasler and Farrington 1979), or sexual deviants (Bancroft 1974; Gelder 1979). Deviance is attributed to faulty learning and thought to be modifiable by suitable conditioning routines. Aversive methods make use of repeated electric shocks or aversive thoughts induced when the client becomes aroused by a picture or story representing a deviant sexual situation. In time the client begins to lose interest in the deviant stimulus or even to develop a definite repulsion. Feelings of shame are sometimes used for aversive purposes. The offender, most often an exhibitionist, is made to demonstrate his deviant ritual to a critical audience who may make derisory comments (Serber 1970).

Aversive techniques do nothing directly to promote appropriate behavior in place of the suppressed activities. Positive conditioning, based on reward, now finds greater favor among therapists. The techniques attempt to establish a link between approved sex thoughts and pleasurable orgasm (Keller and Goldstein 1978). The simplest procedure is to encourage the client, perhaps with the aid of suitable erotica, to use his imagination to create nondeviant fantasies during masturbation. The technique has been used with apparent success in helping some aggressive rapists to become more responsive to ordinary sexual situations where the pleasure is mutual and the behavior reciprocal (Marshall, Williams, and Christie 1977). Another technique, called "shaping," uses erotic slides during masturbation. As orgasm approaches a picture of a less deviant character is substituted so that the pleasurable sensation becomes linked with more acceptable thoughts. For some inhibited deviants, actual practice in sexual intercourse with sympathetic female therapeutic aides who can guide and help him to overcome his anxieties (referred to in the jargon as "in vivo desensitization") is sometimes effective but encounters numerous ethical problems and is also unlikely to succeed in changing an exclusive lifelong homosexual orientation. It is probably attempted more often than the sparse reports in the literature suggest (Kohlenberg 1974).

Education and training in life skills and sexual knowledge is used to overcome the shyness, ignorance, inadequacy in heterosexual situations, and fears of rebuff, ridicule, or impotence that are frequent problems among sex offenders (Crawford and Allen 1979; Groth 1979). Equally important for some offenders is training in self-control, the disciplining of antisocial impulses, and the avoidance of situations of temptation. Rooth (1980) reports success in treating exhibitionists by planned avoidance of trigger situations and the use of a diary to aid recognition of dangerous moods or precipitating events.

Hormonal manipulations are used to suppress libido or induce impotence. The most drastic method, surgical castration (Brown and Courtis 1977; Heim and Hursch 1979), apart from legal and ethical objections, is not quite so certain in its effects as commonly supposed. Some castrates remain sexually responsive for long periods. Among those who become impotent libido is not necessarily totally abolished and aggressive tendencies may be unaffected. Self-medication with substitute hormones can reinstate potency. Nevertheless, statistically very significant reductions in sexual recidivism have been demonstrated in long follow-up studies of castrated men (Ortmann 1980).

Substantial doses of estrogens are demonstrably effective in reducing both libido and potency and can be administered in the form of slow release implants that remain effective for some months. A significant decrease in postrelease reconvictions has been claimed for prisoners so treated (Field and Williams 1970). Unwanted side-effects, such as nausea, permanent and disfiguring breast enlargement, and thrombosis, seriously reduce the utility of this treatment. Cyproterone acetate has similar results with fewer side-effects. It combats the action of natural male androgens and also reduces androgen secretion by blocking the production of pituitary gonadotrophin. It induces sterility and impotence, but both are said to be reversible even after prolonged administration. It is normally given orally in tablet form requiring regular doses, the effect of which can be monitored by blood tests of testosterone levels. A depot injection lasting about twelve days is in use in Germany. The drug is not without complications. Breast enlargement has been reported and lassitude and depression are not uncommon complaints. The drug is not available in the United States, but other antiandrogens have been found effective in reducing unwanted sexual cravings (Berlin and Meinecke 1981).

Clearly, the long-term use of suppressant medication is justified only in serious cases. It is unsuitable for married offenders or if the establishment of an acceptable sex life is a realistic goal. It can be used on a temporary basis to reduce sexual tension while the offender undergoes other forms of treatment. Its application to prisoners involves the problem of establishing true consent, but if a man cannot otherwise be released and wants to have it, he should perhaps be allowed the choice.

Sex offenders have to be treated very often under difficult circumstances. They rarely present themselves of their own accord. They are likely to see a therapist only if they are remanded for medical examination by the court that convicts them. There are exceptions, especially among men in favorable social positions who have much to lose and who have an appreciation of therapeutic ideas, but for many who find themselves before a court the primary objective is to try to avoid a punitive sentence, either by persuading the doctor to take them on as a patient or by convincing him that their misbehavior was an isolated aberration unlikely to be repeated. The circumstances are not conducive to an honest interchange. If the offender does not see a therapist until he gets into prison the situation becomes still worse, with both therapist and client under adverse pressures. The organization of most penal establishments is highly regimented in the interests of security and strict discipline. The open admission of personal shortcomings and frank discussion of deviant impulses which are essential to treatment breach the inmate code of noncooperation with the authorities. Men who participate risk retaliation from fellow inmates. Sex offenders, who are already a much despised group, fear to incur this additional risk. From the standpoint of the prison officers, the selection of the most unpopular characters for special treatment and seemingly special privileges must appear subversive. Prisoners who opt for treatment may be suspected of trying to curry favor to secure release on parole. Finally, the fact that imprisoned sex offenders can have no access to the opposite sex means that practice in heterosexual relationships, which is an essential part of some treatments, is effectively ruled out. For all of these reasons treatment is best carried out away from prison, in a mental health facility or, even better, provided the risks are not too great, with clients living free in the community.

In view of the multiplicity of problems found among sex offenders a treatment facility intended to be used as an alternative to imprisonment or fine must be somewhat versatile as regards its methods if it is to be of help to a significant proportion of the clientele of the courts. It must also be realistic in its assessments of the sort of case it can cope with effectively. One program that appears to fulfill these requirements satisfactorily is operated by Western State Hospital, Washington. This facility makes use of a sexual psychopath law in force in the state of Washington which empowers the courts to commit sex offenders to hospital. They are committed initially for a thorough assessment, which can last up to ninety days. If they are found by the therapists to be suitable for the regime the court can commit them for treatment. Initially they are confined to the hospital wards, but usually for somewhat less time than they would be likely to spend in prison under sentence, after which they are allowed gradually increasing periods at liberty under supervision until finally released into the community with a requirement to report back at stated intervals. The phased release begins only after the sentencing court has received favorable reports from the therapists and given its consent. If reassuring reports are not forthcoming the court can substitute a punitive sentence for the treatment order. This formal and public procedure helps to motivate cooperation and is a safeguard against abuse by either the offender or the authorities.

The Washington regime runs on a "guided self-help" principle. The chief therapeutic activity is participation in intensive discussion groups at which the offender is required to present before his peers and the therapist a very frank and truthful autobiography, including a full account of his sociosexual relationships, fantasies, and offending behavior. He must also take part in the work assignments and social and recreational activities of the therapeutic community and learn to live in intimate proximity to others who know about his problems and oversee his reactions with a sympathetic but critical eye. The aim is to promote in the offender recognition of the hurtfulness of his behavior, an understanding of how his offenses come about, and an acceptance of responsibility for changing his ways. Practice in breaking down social isolation and developing more constructive relationships is considered essential. The offender has to demonstrate before a sophisticated audience real progress in all these respects before he is eligible to commence the first steps toward release.

The regime is meant primarily for men whose sexual misconduct stems from poor socialization or inability to sustain fulfilling adult relationships, rather than for those whose prime problem is a deviant fixation. Nevertheless, exercises in orgasmic reconditioning by manipulation of masturbation fantasies are encouraged in selected cases. Most of the clients are adults in their twenties or thirties with a history of repeated sex offenses and consequently a high risk of recidivism. The great majority of their victims are young females or children. A recidivism rate of 22 percent in a follow-up period of from one to twelve years has been reported (Saylor 1980), which is considered significantly less than expected for the type of client concerned. Unfortunately, as with so many promising treatment programs, there is no adequate control group with which to compare this statistic. A somewhat similar scheme, accepting more desperate cases and treating them under conditions of high security, has been in operation in a penitentiary hospital in British Columbia (West, Roy, and Nichols 1978). According to the psychiatrist responsible (Chuni H. Roy, personal communication, 1982) none of the men released after completing the treatment has been reconvicted of a sex offense, which seems remarkable in view of their previous recidivistic records. If, however, as is likely to happen sooner or later as substantial numbers of offenders pass through, a serious offense by a released patient attracts notoriety and unfavorable comment in the media, public confidence may be lost and the whole scheme sacrificed. This nearly happened on more than one occasion in Washington state. Critics rarely stop to consider whether, without the treatment efforts, incidents of a similar kind following release from ordinary imprisonment might not be still more frequent.

Occasionally, a controlled study has appeared to show a reduction in sexual recidivism as a result of treatment. Peters and Roether (1968) reported a research with sex offenders on probation. A series of ninety-two men given group psychotherapy was compared, during a two-year follow-up, with a control group of seventy-five untreated cases. The reconviction rates for sex crime were 1 percent and 8 percent, respectively.

Even in the absence of a satisfactory control group, a statistically valid assessment can be obtained in respect of highly recidivistic offenders, such as exhibitionists, by comparing the frequency of offending before and after treatment. Wickramasekera (1976) published an account of an aversive routine which he applied with dramatic success to sixteen chronic, compulsive sexual exhibitionists whose exposing habits had been going on from four to twenty-five years at a rate of from one to twenty exposures a month. They were followed up after treatment for periods of from three months to seven years, checks being made in police records and with relatives as well as from the patients' own reports. There were no relapses whatsoever.

The technique included taking a full history of the frequency, circumstances, and individuals present at the exposing incidents and extracting an account of the associated fantasies and masturbation habits. These topics had then to be openly discussed with persons most closely concerned, such as wife, parent, or lawyer. This was followed by a session in front of a one-way mirror and a video camera, and in the presence of observers of both sexes, in which the therapist would order the patient repeatedly to pull out his penis and go through his usual masturbation ritual. Each time he did so the patient had to reply to pointed questions from the observers asking about what he usually thinks and feels on these occasions, what he thinks about the sight of his body in the mirror, what he imagines the observers are thinking about him, and so on and so forth. After a session lasting forty minutes the patient is said to be "frequently in tears, trembling and nauseous." Some patients were made to go through repeat sessions. The video recordings were used to display to other cases who were thought unwilling or unfit to undergo the treatment except vicariously.

Wickramasekera did not claim to cure all exposing offenders in this way. Obviously he had to have highly motivated and cooperative clients. He selected men who were introverted, anxious, moralistic, and nonassertive (a common combination in such cases) but avoided sociopathic types who indulged their inclinations without guilt or worry. An essentially similar method was used by Jones and Frei (1977), who treated fifteen male exhibitionists with a mean duration of exposing of seven years and a frequency of exposing of from eight to twelve times a month. They were followed up for from nine months to five years. In a majority of cases, ten out of fifteen, their previously intractable behavior was completely eliminated; in the rest it was substantially reduced in frequency.

The use of treatment under coercion for sex offenders raises difficult and emotive issues. Every therapist prefers to deal with clients motivated of their own free will to cooperate fully, but in reality many sex offenders, like many alcoholics, are prepared to undertake treatment only when under some external pressure. Some therapists decline to treat individuals who do not present themselves spontaneously of their own volition, but others recognize that an initial reluctance or ambivalence on the offender's part sometimes changes, once contact has been established, to wholehearted participation.

The Washington state treatment scheme described earlier is a coercive system insofar as it operates under a law permitting commitment for an indefinite period of treatment of persons deemed "sexual psychopaths." On the other hand, since the hospital is prepared to receive only those motivated to cooperate with the regime, and since the deprivation of liberty for those admitted is probably shorter and the conditions certainly more pleasant than in prison, offenders are advantaged rather than disadvantaged by being deemed "psychopaths." That is not the case in all states operating mentally disordered sex offender statutes. Monahan and Davis (1982), in an examination of how such systems work in practice, point out that the less serious offenders, who would otherwise serve relatively short sentences in jail, tend to be deprived of liberty longer by being deemed "disordered," whereas the more serious offenders, who would otherwise serve long terms in state prisons, tend to obtain earlier release. Lawyers being aware of these differentials, the prosecution and defense put forward or oppose such pleas according to the likely sentence if the man were not disordered.

Mentally disordered sex offender statutes have been much criticized and many states have repealed them. They have rarely fulfilled the ideal of selecting on the basis of treatment needs. In practice, as Monahan and other commentators (Konecni, Mulcahy, and Ebbesen 1980) have pointed out, the determining criteria for selection tend to be previous convictions for sex offenses rather than any more sophisticated psychological assessment. Moreover, it is not clear from such follow-up studies as have been reported that sex offenders deemed disordered are reconvicted any less often than those given determinate sentences, but a firm conclusion on this is impossible because properly controlled comparisons are so difficult to achieve. The absence of specific treatment programs and in many cases the absence of any definable disorder susceptible to treatment are additional sources of criticism. The concept of indeterminate detention loses credibility in the absence of firm criteria for "cure" or for when an offender is no longer a risk.

In addition to placing the sex offender in an institution that is (or should be) therapeutically oriented, one of the advantages of a mental health commitment is that the offender, especially if he is a child molester, runs less risk of being attacked by fellow inmates. In Canadian and American prisons, especially during riots, murders of sex offenders by other prisoners have occurred. In Canada, the Dangerous Sexual Offender (DSO) statute (since replaced, by §687 of the Canadian Criminal Code, with a wider definition of dangerous offender) enabled selected cases to be retained indefinitely in penitentiaries rather than in hospitals and led to some extreme brutalities. These were all the more horrendous in view of the fact that many of the DSOs had never been physically violent (Greenland 1977).

England has never had a disordered sex offender statute, but under the more general rubric of "psychopathic disorder" some serious sex offenders have been dealt with by hospital orders instead of imprisonment. The Mental Health Act of 1983, however, specifies that sexual deviation alone shall no longer be grounds for a diagnosis of "psychopathy." Moreover, in serious cases a sentence of "life imprisonment," which means indefinite detention pending a decision by the home secretary and the parole board to order release, is available to the judges and is not infrequently invoked. For less serious cases submission to treatment, either as an outpatient or in hospital, can be ordered by the court as a requirement of probation (under the Powers of the Criminal Courts Act of 1973, §3). The condition has to be explained to the offender and he must agree to it voluntarily before the order can be made, but once having agreed he commits a further offense if he fails to cooperate. From a legal and administrative standpoint this system is ethically less objectionable than most and admirably flexible in conception, since the only qualification for entry is medical evidence that treatment is required and is available. Unfortunately, the statute does nothing to provide the treatment facilities appropriate for sex offenders, which are sadly lacking in Britain's hard-pressed National Health Service. The need in England as elsewhere is less for law reform than for an integration of treatment facilities and proper assessment procedures with the legal provisions already available.

VI. Concluding Thoughts on Policy

In a criminological context treatment means how offenders are dealt with by the criminal justice system, not just the application of medical model techniques. Prevailing policies are in various respects unsatisfactory. In the first place, the law is arguably too all-embracing. Only in exceptional circumstances should consensual sexual activities, homosexual or heterosexual, be treated as crime. Certainly, the criminal law is an ineffectual and unnecessary blunderbuss for the control of adolescent sexuality. Since the number of underage pregnancies exceeds prosecutions for sexual intercourse with a minor (Farrell 1980) it is obvious that the laws are being applied in a patchy and unjust manner in response to complaints by third parties. In some contexts, such as the Indecency with Children Act, a child is defined in English law as a person under fourteen. For many purposes this is probably more realistic than the higher ages fixed by most jurisdictions for protecting females from their own sexual inclinations (Schultz 1980).

Sexual contacts between children and adults are dealt with as if the behavior were rarer and more damaging than is in fact the case. All too often the child is victimized more by the police and court interrogations, by local publicity, or by the breakup of the family if a relative is implicated than by the offense itself. The offender needs to be curbed or treated, but not at the cost of unnecessary damage to the child. In California, a system of staying prosecution when an adult member of the family has sexually abused a child, on condition he submits to treatment, appears to work well and to result in many more cases coming to light and being satisfactorily resolved (Giarretto 1980). A system of confidential reporting of child sex abuse to a medical authority operates in Holland, which likewise successfully avoids unnecessary prosecutions.

Where prosecutions are unavoidable, much can be done to protect the child from further trauma. Scandinavian countries employ specially trained police to interrogate child victims and in some circumstances permit recordings of these interviews to be heard as evidence at the trial (Libai 1975). Instead of leaving the task to the police, Israel employs experienced youth interrogators who are given exclusive authority to question children about suspected sex abuse and where necessary to veto their appearance as witnesses in court. In the latter event, the interrogators' written reports may be passed to the prosecution and used in evidence (Reifen 1973). Short of infringing the offender's constitutional rights to cross-examination of his accuser, various compromise proposals have been put forward (Libai 1975). One would be to have a preliminary informal hearing of the child's evidence by an investigatory judge. This could be recorded on videotape and played back to the jury later, obviating the need for further cross-examination in most cases. A further protection would be a ban on publication of the child's identity or that of the offender if the latter is a relative.

In the prosecution of rape cases victims are badly served by jurisdictions that (as in English law) define the offense as nonconsensual vaginal penetration by the penis. Some brutal sexual attacks involving anal intercourse or fellatio or manual penetration can be worse than conventional rape. Some jurisdictions, Michigan and Nebraska for example, have introduced degrees of sexual assault to include a wider variety of behaviors by both males and females and to grade the severity of the intrusion. Fixing a very severe penalty for rape regardless of the extremely varied circumstances of the crime is also counterproductive. It discourages guilty pleas, makes juries think twice about pronouncing a verdict against the defendant, promotes plea bargaining, and encourages stressful challenges to the complainant's evidence.

The widespread use of imprisonment for nonviolent sex offenders is hard to justify. Most of these men are more pathetic than dangerous and stand in need of treatment and welfare rather than punishment, which can be more readily accomplished in a facility in the community. Inside penal institutions they are the butt of harassment and sometimes sexual assault. In the English system many of them appeal to be put under "Rule 43," which means that they are segregated for their own protection and may spend protracted periods in virtual solitary confinement. Imprisonment has to be available as a last resort for the uncooperative and recalcitrant, but even without such a penalty the social consequences of a conviction for a sex offense act as a powerful deterrent.

For the common assaultive offender who is typically young, somewhat antisocial but not sexually deviant, and statistically unlikely to repeat a sex offense, there may be no need for anything more than the usual deterrents available to the criminal justice system, although some of these individuals might benefit from training in sociosexual sensitivities and skills. The more extreme or dangerously repetitive aggressors, especially those with unusual psychopathology, call for a more intensive effort. They are usually detained for long periods, but nearly all are released sooner or later. The community has an interest in demanding that any treatment that might reduce the risk of reoffending should be made available. Therapeutic approaches are carried out more easily in a specialized hospital unit, but if it has to be done in prison then the process is best started as soon as possible after the offender is received into prison and before he is submerged in an antagonistic subculture. A policy of this kind, however, can only be effective if a sound working relationship exists between the authorities responsible for treatment and those in charge of the conditions of custody, the timing of release, and the arrangements for postrelease supervision. Collusion between therapists and authorities responsible for custody has been much criticized on ethical grounds (Brodsky 1979), but it can operate to the benefit of both society and the offender.

REFERENCES

Abel, Gene G., Edward B. Blanchard, Judith V. Becker, and A. Djenderedjian. 1978. "Differentiating Sexual Aggressives with Penile Measures." *Criminal Justice and Behavior* 5:315–32.
Adams, Morton S., and James V. Neel. 1967. "Children of Incest." *Paediatrics* 40:56–62.
American Psychiatric Association. 1980. *Diagnostic and Statistical Manual of Mental Disorders.* 3d ed. Washington, D.C.: American Psychiatric Association.
Amir, Menachem. 1971. *Patterns in Forcible Rape.* Chicago: University of Chicago Press.
Ariès, Philippe. 1962. *Centuries of Childhood.* New York: Vintage Books.
Bancroft, John. 1974. *Deviant Sexual Behavior: Modification and Assessment.* Oxford: Clarendon Press.
Beezley, Mrazek P., and C. Henry Kempe, eds. 1980. *Sexually Abused Children and Their Families.* New York: Pergamon Press.
Bell, Alan P., Martin S. Weinberg, and S. K. Hammersmith. 1981. *Sexual Preference.* Bloomington: Indiana University Press.
Berlin, Fred S., and Carl F. Meinecke. 1981. "Treatment of Sex Offenders with Antiandrogenic Medication: Conceptualization, Review of Treatment Modalities and Preliminary Findings." *American Journal of Psychology* 135:601–7.
Bluglass, Robert. 1980. "Indecent Exposure in the East Midlands." In *Sex Offenders in the Criminal Justice System*, edited by Donald J. West. Cropwood Conference Series. Cambridge: Cambridge University Institute of Criminology.
Brecher, Edward M. 1978. *Treatment Programs for Sex Offenders.* Washington, D.C.: Government Printing Office.
Brodsky, Carroll M. 1976. "Rape at Work." In *Sexual Assault*, edited by Marcia J. Walker and Stanley L. Brodsky. Lexington, Mass.: D. C. Heath.
Brodsky, Stanley L. 1976. "Prevention of Rape." In *Sexual Assault*, edited by Marcia J. Walker and Stanley L. Brodsky. Lexington, Mass.: D. C. Heath.
———. 1979. "Ethical Standards for Psychologists in Corrections." In *Who Is the Client?* edited by John Monahan. Washington, D.C.: American Psychological Association.
———. 1980. "Understanding and Treating Sexual Offenders." *Howard Journal* 19:102–15.
Brodsky, Stanley L., and Donald J. West. 1981. "Life-Skills Treatment of Sex Offenders." *Law and Psychology Review* 6:97–168.
Brody, S. J. 1976. *The Effectiveness of Sentencing.* Home Office Research Unit Study no. 35. London: H.M. Stationery Office.
Brown, Robert S., and Richard W. Courtis. 1977. "The Castration Alternative." *Canadian Journal of Criminology and Correction* 19:157–69.
Browning, Diane H., and Bonny Boatman. 1977. "Incest: Children at Risk." *American Journal of Psychiatry* 134:69–72.
Burton, Lindy. 1968. *Vulnerable Children.* London: Routledge & Kegan Paul.

Carrier, J. M. 1980. "Homosexual Behavior in Cross-cultural Perspective." In *Homosexual Behavior*, edited by Judd Marmor. New York: Basic Books.

Carter, Cedric O. 1967. "Risk to Offspring of Incest." *Lancet* 1:436.

Chappell, Duncan, Gilbert Geis, Stephen Schafer, and Larry Siegal. 1977. "A Comparative Study of Forcible Rape Offenses." In *Forcible Rape*, edited by Duncan Chappell, Robley Geis, and Gilbert Geis. New York: Columbia University Press.

Chappell, Duncan, and S. Singer. 1977. "Rape in New York City: A Study of Material in the Police Files and Its Meaning." In *Forcible Rape*, edited by Duncan Chappell, Robley Geis, and Gilbert Geis. New York: Columbia University Press.

Christiansen, Karl O., Mimi Elers-Nielson, Louis Le Maire, and George K. Stürup. 1965. "Recidivism among Sexual Offenders." In *Scandinavian Studies in Criminology*, Vol. 1, edited by K. O. Christiansen. London: Tavistock.

Cohen, Bernard. 1980. *Deviant Street Networks*. Lexington, Mass.: Lexington Books.

Cohen, Murray L., Ralph Garafolo, Richard B. Boucher, and Theoharis Seghorn. 1971. "The Psychology of Rapists." *Seminars in Psychiatry* 3:307–27. Reprinted 1977 in *Forcible Rape*, edited by Duncan Chappell, Robley Geis, and Gilbert Geis. New York: Columbia University Press.

Constantine, Larry L., and Floyd M. Martinson, eds. 1981. *Children and Sex: New Findings, New Perspectives*. Boston: Little, Brown & Co.

Crawford, David A., and J. V. Allen. 1979. "A Social Skills Training Programme with Sex Offenders." In *Love and Attraction: Proceedings of an International Conference*, edited by Mark Cook and G. Wilson. Oxford: Pergamon Press.

Criminal Law Revision Committee. 1980. *Working Paper on Sexual Offences*. London: H.M. Stationery Office.

Cunnington, Su. 1980. "Some Aspects of Prostitution in the West End of London in 1979." In *Sex Offenders in the Criminal Justice System*, edited by Donald J. West. Cambridge: Institute of Criminology.

Delin, Bart. 1978. *The Sex Offender*. Boston: Beacon Press.

Devlin, Patrick. 1965. *The Enforcement of Morals*. London: Oxford University Press.

Dietz, Paul E. 1978. "Social Factors in Rapist Behavior." In *Clinical Aspects of the Rapist*, edited by Richard T. Rada. New York: Grune & Stratton.

Dörner, Günter. 1976. *Hormones and Brain Differentiation*. Amsterdam: Elsevier Scientific Publishing Co.

Doshay, Lewis J. 1943. *The Boy Sex Offender and His Later Criminal Career*. New York: Grune & Stratton.

Eglinton, J. Z. 1971. *Greek Love*. London: Neville Spearman.

Epstein, A. W. 1961. "Relationship of Fetishism and Transvestitism to Brain and Particularly to Temporal Lobe Dysfunction." *Journal of Nervous and Mental Disease* 133:247–53.

Evans, Laura J. 1978. "Sexual Harassment: Women's Hidden Occupational Hazard." In *The Victimization of Women*, edited by Margaret Gates. Beverly Hills, Calif.: Sage Publications.

Farrell, Christine. 1980. "Sexual Attitudes and Behavior of Young People." In *Changing Patterns of Sexual Behavior*, edited by Walter H. Armytage, Robert Chester, and John Peel. London: Academic Press.

Federal Bureau of Investigation. 1981. *Crime in the United States: Uniform Crime Reports*. Washington, D.C.: Government Printing Office.

Field, Leopold H., and Mark Williams. 1970. "The Hormonal Treatment of Sex Offenders." *Medicine, Science and the Law* 10:27–34.

Finkelhor, David. 1979. *Sexually Victimized Children*. New York: Free Press.

Ford, Clellan S., and Frank A. Beach. 1952. *Patterns of Sexual Behaviour*. London: Eyre & Spottiswoode.

Freund, Kurt. 1981. "Assessment of Paedophylia." In *Adult Sexual Interest in Children*, edited by Mark Cook and Kevin Howells. London: Academic Press.

Freund, Kurt, S. Chan, and R. Coulthard. 1979. "Phallometric Diagnosis with 'Non-Admitters,' " *Behavior Research and Therapy* 7:451–57.

Gagnon, John H. 1965. "Female Child Victims of Sex Offenses." *Social Problems* 13:176–92.

Gagnon, John H., and William Simon. 1974. *Sexual Conduct: The Social Sources of Human Sexuality*. London: Hutchinson Publishing Group.

Gebhard, Paul H. 1969. "Misconceptions about Female Prostitutes." *Medical Aspects of Human Sexuality* 3 (March): 24–30.

Gebhard, Paul H., John H. Gagnon, Wardell B. Pomeroy, and Cornelia V. Christenson. 1965. *Sex Offenders: An Analysis of Types*. New York: Harper & Row.

Gelder, Michael. 1979. "Behavior Therapy for Sexual Deviations." In *Sexual Deviation*, edited by Ismond Rosen. 2d ed. Oxford: Oxford University Press.

Gerassi, John. 1966. *The Boys of Boise: Furor, Vice, and Folly in an American City*. New York: Macmillan Publishing Co.

Giarretto, Henry. 1980. "Humanistic Treatment of Father-Daughter Incest." In *The Sexual Victimology of Youth*, edited by Leroy G. Schultz. Springfield, Ill.: C. C. Thomas.

Gibbens, Trevor C. N. 1957. "The Sexual Behavior of Young Criminals." *Journal of Mental Science* 103:527–40.

Gibbens, Trevor C. N., and Joyce Prince. 1963. *Child Victims of Sex Offences*. London: Institute for the Study and Treatment of Delinquency.

Gibbens, Trevor C. N., Keith L. Soothill, and C. K. Way. 1981. "Sex Offences against Young Girls: A Long-Term Record Study." *Psychological Medicine* 11:351–57.

Gibson, Evelyn, and Samuel Klein. 1969. *Murder 1957–1968*. Home Office Research Studies no. 3. London: H.M. Stationery Office.

Glover, Edward. 1957. *The Psychopathology of Prostitution*. London: Institute for the Study and Treatment of Delinquency.

Goldman, Ronald, and Juliette Goldman. 1982. *Children's Sexual Thinking*. London: Routledge & Kegan Paul.

Goldstein, Michael J., and Harold S. Kant. 1973. *Pornography and Sexual Deviance*. Berkeley: University of California Press.

Goodwin, Jean. 1982. *Sexual Abuse: Incest Victims and Their Families*. Boston: J. Wright.

230   Donald J. West

Gosselin, Chris, and Glenn Wilson. 1980. *Sexual Variations*. London: Faber & Faber.

Greenland, Cyril. 1977. "Psychiatry and the Dangerous Sexual Offender." *Canadian Psychiatric Association Journal* 22:155–59.

Groth, A. Nicholas. 1979. *Men Who Rape: The Psychology of the Offender*. New York: Plenum Publishing Corp.

Groth, A. Nicholas, and H. Jean Birnbaum. 1978. "Adult Sexual Orientation and Attraction to Underage Persons." *Archives of Sexual Behavior* 7:175–81.

Guyon, René. 1950. *Sexual Freedom*. New York: Alfred A. Knopf.

Hackett, T. P., F. A. Saber, and William J. Curran. 1980. "Exhibitionism." In *Modern Legal Medicine, Psychiatry and Forensic Medicine*, edited by William J. Curran et al. Philadelphia: F. A. Davis.

Halleck, Seymour L. 1971. *Psychiatry and the Dilemma of Crime*. Los Angeles: University of California Press.

Hart, Herbert L. A. 1963. *Liberty, Law and Morals*. London: Oxford University Press.

Heim, Nikolaus, and Carolyn J. Hursch. 1979. "Castration for Sex Offenders: Treatment or Punishment?" *Archives of Sexual Behavior* 8:281–304.

Hindelang, Michael J. 1981. "Variations in Sex-Race-Age-Specific Incidence Rates of Offending." *American Sociological Review* 46:461–74.

Hindelang, Michael J., and Bruce L. Davis. 1977. "Forcible Rape in the United States: A Statistical Profile." In *Forcible Rape*, edited by Duncan Chappell, Robley Geis, and Gilbert Geis. New York: Columbia University Press.

James, Jennifer. 1976. "Motivations for Entrance into Prostitution." In *The Female Offender*, edited by Laura Crites. Lexington, Mass.: D. C. Heath.

———. 1977. "Prostitutes and Prostitution." In *Deviants: Voluntary Actors in a Hostile World*, edited by Edward Sagarin and Fred Montanino. New York: Silver Burdett.

Jones, Ivor H., and Dorothy Frei. 1977. "Provoked Anxiety as a Treatment of Exhibitionism." *British Journal of Psychiatry* 131:295–300.

Kanin, Eugene J., and Stanley R. Parcell. 1977. "Sexual Aggression: A Second Look at the Offended Female." *Archives of Sexual Behavior* 6:67–76.

Katz, Sedelle, and Mary A. Mazur. 1979. *Understanding the Rape Victim: A Synthesis of Research Findings*. New York: John Wiley & Sons.

Keller, D. J., and A. Goldstein. 1978. "Orgasmic Reconditioning Reconsidered." *Behaviour Research and Therapy* 16:299–301.

Kohlenberg, R. J. 1974. "Treatment of a Homosexual Pedophiliac Using in Vivo Desensitisation: A Case Study." *Journal of Abnormal Psychology* 83:192–95.

Konecni, Vladimir J., Erin Maria Mulcahy, and Ebbe B. Ebbesen. 1980. "Prison or Mental Hospital: Factors Affecting the Processing of Persons Suspected of Being 'Mentally Disordered Sex Offenders.' " In *New Directions in Psychological Research*, edited by Paul D. Lipsitt and Bruce D. Sales. New York: Van Nostrand Reinhold.

Kutchinsky, Berl. 1973. "The Effect of Easy Availability of Pornography on the Incidence of Sex Crimes: The Danish Experience." *Journal of Social Issues* 29:163–81.

Landis, Judson T. 1956. "Experiences of 500 Children with Adult Sexual Deviants." *Psychiatric Quarterly Supplement* 30:91–109.

Libai, David. 1975. "The Protection of the Child Victim of a Sexual Offense in the Criminal Justice System." In *Rape Victimology*, edited by Leroy G. Schultz. Springfield, Ill.: C. C. Thomas.

Lukianowicz, Narcyz. 1972. "Incest." *British Journal of Psychiatry* 120:301–13.

McCaldon, R. J. 1967. "Rape." *Canadian Journal of Corrections* 9:37–59.

MacCulloch, Malcolm J., and John L. Waddington. 1981. "Neuroendocrine Mechanisms and the Aetiology of Male and Female Homosexuality." *British Journal of Psychiatry* 139:341–45.

McGuire, R. J. et al. 1965. "Sexual Deviations as Conditioned Behavior: A Hypothesis." *Behavior Research and Therapy* 2:185–90.

Malamuth, Neil M. 1981. "Rape Proclivity." *Social Forces* 37:138–57.

Marshall, W. L., S. M. Williams, and M. M. Christie. 1977. "The Treatment of Rapists." In *Perspectives on Rape*, edited by C. B. Qualls. New York: Pergamon Press.

Mill, John Stuart. 1947. *On Liberty.* New York: F. S. Crofts. Originally published 1869.

Mohr, Johann W., R. E. Turner, and M. B. Jerry. 1964. *Pedophilia and Exhibitionism.* Toronto: University of Toronto Press.

Monahan, John, and Sharon K. Davis. 1982. "Mentally Disordered Sex Offenders." In *Mentally Disordered Offenders: Perspectives from Law and Social Science*, edited by John Monahan and Henry J. Steadman. New York: Plenum Publishing Corp.

Money, John. 1980. *Love and Love Sickness: The Science of Sex, Gender Difference, and Pair Bonding.* Baltimore: John Hopkins University Press.

Money, John, J. E. Cawte, G. N. Bianchi, and B. Nurcombe. 1977. "Sex Training and Traditions in Arnhem Land." In *Handbook of Sexology*, edited by John Money and M. Mustaph. Amsterdam: Elsevier.

Money, John, and Gloria Pruce. 1977. "Psychomotor Epilepsy and Sexual Function." In *Handbook of Sexology*, edited by John Money and H. Mustaph. Amsterdam: Elsevier.

O'Carroll, Tom. 1980. *Paedophylia: The Radical Case.* London: Peter Owen.

Ortmann, Jørgen. 1980. "The Treatment of Sexual Offenders: Castration and Antihormone Therapy." *International Journal of Law and Psychiatry* 3:443–51.

Peters, Joseph J., and Herman A. Roether. 1968. "Group Psychotherapy of the Sex Offender." *Federal Probation* 32, no. 3:41–45.

Plummer, Ken, ed. 1981. *The Making of the Modern Homosexual.* London: Hutchinson Publishing Group.

Rachman, Stanley, and John Teasdale. 1969. *Aversion Therapy and Behaviour Disorders.* London: Routledge & Kegan Paul.

Radzinowicz, Leon, ed. 1957. *Sexual Offences.* London: Macmillan Publishers.

Reifen, David. 1973. "Court Procedures in Israel to Protect Child-Victims of Sexual Assaults." In *Victimology: A New Focus 3*, edited by Israel Drapkin and Emilio Viano. Lexington, Mass.: D. C. Heath.

Rolph, Cecil H. 1955. *Women of the Streets.* London: Secker & Warburg.

Rooth, Graham. 1980. "Exhibitionism: An Eclectic Approach to Its Management." *British Journal of Hospital Medicine* 23:366–70.

Rosen, Ismond. 1979. "Exhibitionism, Scopophilia and Voyeurism." In *Sexual Deviation*, edited by Ismond Rosen. 2d ed. Oxford: Oxford University Press.

Rossman, G. Parker. 1979. *Sexual Experience between Men and Boys*. London: Temple Smith.

Sanday, Peggy R. 1981. "The Socio-cultural Context of Rape: A Cross-cultural Study." *Journal of Social Issues* 37:5–27.

Saylor, Maureen. 1980. "A Guided Self-Help Approach to the Treatment of the Habitual Sex Offender." In *Sex Offenders in the Criminal Justice System*, edited by Donald J. West. Cropwood Conference Series. Cambridge: Institute of Criminology.

Schofield, Michael. 1965. *The Sexual Behavior of Young People*. London: Longman Group.

Schultz, Leroy G., ed. 1975. *Rape Victimology*. Springfield, Ill.: C. C. Thomas.

———. 1980. "The Age of Consent: Fault, Friction, Freedom." In *The Sexual Victimology of Youth*, edited by Leroy G. Schultz. Springfield, Ill.: C. C. Thomas.

Sechrest, L., S. O. White, and E. D. Brown, eds. 1979. *The Rehabilitation of Criminal Offenders*. National Research Council Report. Washington, D.C.: National Academy of Sciences.

Seemanova, E. 1971. "A Study of Children of Incestuous Matings." *Human Heredity* 21:108–28.

Serber, M. 1970. "Shame Aversion Therapy." *Journal of Behavior Therapy and Experimental Psychiatry* 1:217–26.

Skogan, Wesley G. 1981. *Issues in the Measurement of Victimization*. U.S. Department of Justice no. NCJ-74682-June. Washington, D.C.: Government Printing Office.

Soothill, Keith L., and Trevor C. N. Gibbens. 1978. "Recidivism of Sexual Offenders: A Re-appraisal." *British Journal of Criminology* 18:267–76.

Stafford, Ann. 1964. *The Age of Consent*. London: Hodder & Stoughton.

Tourney, Garfield. 1980. "Hormones and Homosexuality." In *Homosexual Behavior*, edited by Judd Marmor. New York: Basic Books.

Trasler, Gordon, and David P. Farrington, eds. 1979. "Behaviour Modification: Symposium." *British Journal of Criminology* 19:313–448.

United Kingdom. Home Office. 1982. *Criminal Statistics, England and Wales, 1981*. Command 8668. London: H.M. Stationery Office.

United Kingdom. Home Office. 1981. *Criminal Statistics, England and Wales, 1980*. Command 8376. London: H.M. Stationery Office.

U.N. Social Defence Research Institute. 1980. *The Effect of Islamic Legislation on Crime Prevention in Saudi Arabia*. Rome: U.N. Social Defense Research Institute.

U.S. Department of Justice. 1980. *Criminal Victimization in the United States: Summary of Findings of 1978–79; Changes in Crime and of Trends since 1973*. Washington, D.C.: Government Printing Office, September.

U.S. Department of Justice. 1981. *Criminal Victimization in the United States 1979*. Washington, D.C.: Government Printing Office, September.

Walmsley, Roy, and Karen White. 1979. *Sexual Offences, Consent and Sentencing.* Home Office Research Study no. 54. London: H.M. Stationery Office.

West, Donald J. 1977. *Homosexuality Re-examined.* London: Gerald Duckworth & Co.

West, Donald J., Chuni Roy, and Florence L. Nichols. 1978. *Understanding Sexual Attacks.* London: William Heinemann.

Wickramasekera, I. 1976. "Aversive Behavioral Rehearsal for Sexual Exhibitionism." *Behavior Therapy* 7:167–76.

Wilson, Paul R. 1981. *The Man They Called a Monster.* Camperdown: Cassell Australia.

Winick, Charles, and Kinsie, Paul M. 1971. *The Lively Commerce.* New York: Quadrangle/New York Times Publishing Co.

Wolfenden, John. 1957. *Report of the Committee on Homosexual Offences and Prostitution.* Command 247. London: H.M. Stationery Office.

Woolston, Howard B. 1921. *Prostitution in the United States.* New York: Century Publishing Co.

Wright, Richard, and Donald J. West. 1981. "Rape: A Comparison of Group Offences and Lone Offences." *Medicine, Science and the Law* 21:25–30.

Zuger, Bernard. 1978. "Effeminate Behaviour in Boys from Childhood: 10 Additional Years of Follow-Up." *Comprehensive Psychiatry* 19:363–69.

———. 1980. "Homosexuality and Parental Guilt." *British Journal of Psychiatry* 137:55–57.

David Biles

Criminological Research in Australia

The first European settlement in Australia in 1788 was essentially for the purpose of establishing a penal colony to ease the crowding of English prisons. With such a criminologically relevant beginning, it might have been expected that the systematic study of crime and criminals would have been established early in the development of the nation, but such was not to be the case. Only in very recent years has there been any detailed study of Australia's convict ancestry, and very little of this could be described as criminological in its focus. An exception is the biography of an early penal reformer, Alexander Maconochie, by the late Sir John Barry (1958) of the Supreme Court of Victoria. This work is widely regarded as the first serious contribution to Australian criminology, but it was preceded by *The Habitual Criminal* (Morris 1951) and some studies of Australian police systems. The dearth of criminological talent until recent years is probably best illustrated by the fact that the first two editions of a monumental tome on all aspects of Australian society (Davies and Encel 1965/1970) made no mention of crime, delinquency, prisons, or criminal justice.

Even today Australia cannot claim to have an especially large community of scholars engaged in teaching or research in criminology, though there has been significant growth in the past twenty or thirty years. In the last five years, however, there has been a slight decline in the strength of most research centers. This growth and subsequent decline are sketched in this essay. Section I describes the major research institutions, Section II assesses the extent of governmental influence

David Biles is assistant director (research), Australian Institute of Criminology, formerly Senior Lecturer in Criminology, University of Melbourne.

on research priorities, Section III summarizes recent research trends, and the conclusion offers a speculative glimpse at future directions.

I. Major Research Institutions

The number of major research institutions devoted to the study of criminal justice is small enough for them all to be mentioned in this essay. They are outlined below in the order in which they were established.

A. *Melbourne University Criminology Department*

This department, the first of its kind in Australia, was established in 1951 with a Board of Studies chaired by Sir John Barry. The department from 1953 offered a single undergraduate course in criminology. In 1958 Stanley Johnston was appointed full-time head of the department, and since 1960 a postgraduate diploma in criminology has been offered. By the late 1970s the department comprised one reader, one senior lecturer, and four lecturers, but in 1981 the senior lecturer who resigned was replaced by a senior tutor, a significant downgrading of faculty strength. In 1982 the department enrolled 180 undergraduate students, seventy graduate diploma students, twelve master's degree candidates, and three doctoral candidates.

Even though Melbourne University Criminology Department has been predominantly concerned with teaching, it has had a notable research output. Major research areas have been: juvenile offenders (Challinger 1977*a*), shoplifting (Challinger 1977*b*), child welfare administration, automobile theft, and various aspects of police administration (Milte and Weber 1977). The department has also provided the secretariat for the Australian and New Zealand Society of Criminology for nearly the whole of the period since its formation in 1967. The society publishes a quarterly journal, *Australian and New Zealand Journal of Criminology*, which is widely circulated in the region and overseas. Even though for most of its fifteen years this journal has used the criminology department as its base, the Melbourne faculty have no responsibility for it; the editor and assistant editor are appointed by the executive of the society.

B. *Sydney University Institute of Criminology*

After lengthy discussions between the government of New South Wales and the University of Sydney, in 1959 the government made a grant to the university to enable the establishment of an institute of criminology within the University's faculty of law. The then dean of the faculty of law, Professor K. O. Shatwell, became the institute's first director, and four other appointments were soon made including a criminologist, a psychiatrist, and a statistician. The position of a full-time psychiatrist has been lost in recent years. An elective subject in penology has been offered to undergraduate law students since 1961, but since 1965 four graduate level courses lead to a master's degree in law and four undergraduate courses lead to a diploma in criminology. The latter is taken mostly by police officers and other persons employed in criminal justice agencies. In recent years approximately a hundred students have enrolled for the diploma each year, and all law students at bachelor's and master's level have optional criminology subjects available to them.

The research interests of the institute faculty have covered a number of fields. The work of the present director, Gordon Hawkins, in penology is probably the best known outside Australia (e.g., Hawkins 1976). Other works have focused specifically on the practice of criminal law in New South Wales (Roulston 1975) and reviewed the issues underlying the law-and-order debate (Ward and Woods 1972). Institute faculty have also produced a comprehensive survey of police organizations and public attitudes to the police in Australia and New Zealand (Chappell and Wilson 1969) and two editions of a widely used book of readings on Australian criminal justice (Chappell and Wilson 1972, 1977).

No other universities in Australia undertake graduate teaching or research in criminology, but a number of law schools and sociology departments offer optional subjects at undergraduate level. Some colleges of advanced education also offer such courses.

C. Australian Institute of Criminology and Criminology Research Council

The most recent significant development in Australian criminology was undoubtedly the passage in 1971 of the Commonwealth of Australia's *Criminology Research Act 1971* by the federal parliament. This act was prepared after extensive negotiations between the federal government and the governments of the six states. The act created the institute, funded solely by the federal government and controlled by a board of management, and a funding agency, the Criminology Research Council, funded jointly by the federal and state governments, the latter contributing on a per capita basis.

The institute is an independent statutory authority whose functions are: "(*a*) to conduct such criminological research as is approved by the Board; (*b*) to communicate to the Commonwealth and the States the results of research conducted by the Institute; (*c*) to conduct such seminars and courses of training or instruction for persons engaged, or to be engaged, in criminological research or in work related to the prevention or correction of criminal behaviour as are approved by the Board; (*d*) to advise the Council in relation to needs for, and programmes of, criminological research; (*e*) to provide secretarial and administrative services for the Council; (*f*) to give advice and assistance in relation to any research performed wholly or partly with moneys provided out of the Fund; (*g*) to give advice in relation to the compilation of statistics relating to crime; (*h*) to publish such material resulting from or connected with the performance of its functions as is approved by the Board; and (*i*) to do anything incidental or conducive to the performance of any of the foregoing functions" (*Criminology Research Act 1971*, s.6).

The institute is controlled by a board of management, half of the membership of which is appointed by the federal attorney-general, the other half being elected by the Criminology Research Council, a body dominated by state representatives. Thus a balance of federal and state interests is maintained in the work of the institute, but if a serious clash of interests occurred the federal view would prevail as one of the federal appointees to the board is the chairman and he has a deliberative and casting vote. No such conflict has yet occurred.

The structural arrangements for balancing national and local interests in criminal justice as far as the institute and council are concerned are illustrated diagrammatically in figure 1. These arrangements are unique in that they provide for financial and policy input from all Australian governments (except the recently created government of the Northern Territory, which has not yet sought full statehood) without undue influence coming from any single source. The institute therefore works with and for all governments, and its priorities are determined by discussions between senior institute staff, mostly recruited from university positions, and the official representatives of the state and federal governments.

The first permanent director of the institute, William Clifford, was appointed in 1975. He was formerly the director of the Crime Prevention and Criminal Justice Section of the United Nations and has done much to establish the international reputation of the institute and its

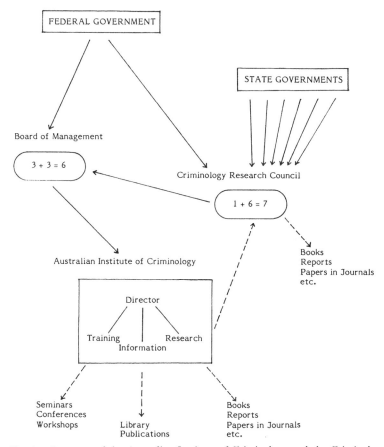

Fig. 1.—Structure of the Australian Institute of Criminology and the Criminology Research Council.

work. In mid-1983 the institute itself had a staff of thirty-one, including seven academic researchers, training officers, librarians, publications officers, and administrative personnel. Six years earlier the institute had fifty-nine staff members; the reduction was brought about by federal government cuts in public expenditure. The total institute budget in 1982–83 was approximately US$1.1 million and that of the council was US$100,000. The institute has the largest criminological library in Australia, its training staff conduct from twelve to fifteen seminars or workshops each year, and its publications staff produce quarterly newsletters and information bulletins as well as numerous books, research reports, and seminar proceedings. The work of the institute's research staff will be outlined later in this essay but it is worth noting at this point that their academic backgrounds include law, sociology, psychology, and statistics/computing.

In its first eleven years of operation the Criminology Research Council provided funds for over a hundred separate research projects, the grantees all being individuals or organizations other than the Australian Institute of Criminology. Just over half of the recipients of research grants have been on the staff of universities or tertiary institutions, but many grants have also been made to criminal justice agencies and a small number to private organizations and individuals. The relatively low level of funds available (US$100,000 per year) was the same in 1982 as it was in 1972. This has meant that the average grant has been a little over US$10,000 and the council has been forced to exclude operational projects which include the provision of program staff or resources, but the council has provided research staff to evaluate new projects. The council has also declined to provide funds for research which in its view should be routinely undertaken by operational agencies. The council has endeavored to identify innovative areas of research, the results of which would be applicable beyond the actual research location. Probably its most successful grants have been to academics whose salaries have been met by their universities and for whom a small injection of funds provides research assistance, computing time, and limited capacity for travel. In these cases a grant from a national agency is often seen as a matter of some status, and it also imposes some degree of external discipline in ensuring that the research is completed.

An analysis of the research topics funded by the council reveals that studies related to criminal behavior and the correction of offenders have attracted considerably more attention and funding than other areas of criminology. Relatively small numbers of grants have been made, for example, in the areas of community attitudes to crime and justice, the criminal law, or the operation of police or court systems. In the earlier years in particular, many of the studies merely described juvenile or other classes of offenders, or attempted to evaluate the effectiveness of particular correctional measures. In more recent years, however, attention has been directed to a much broader range of issues and more sophisticated evaluations have been conducted. It is difficult and perhaps invidious to make comparisons between research projects on a wide range of topics, but among those completed with council funds which have evoked wide interest are an evaluation of the Tasmanian work order scheme (Mackay and Rook 1976), a survey of gun ownership and gun control policy in Australia (Harding 1981), a study of the criminological consequences of the Hobart Bridge collapse (Whelan, Seaton, and Dax 1976), and a history of the West Australian prison system (Thomas 1978).

As a matter of policy a distinction has been drawn between the types of research that are appropriate for council funding and those which are more appropriate for the institute itself to undertake. The Board of Management of the institute and the Criminology Research Council have both agreed that projects of a local or regional character, which may involve primary data gathering by interview, observation, or questionnaire, are generally more appropriate for council funding than for the institute itself, while the institute is best suited to projects which are national and comparative in orientation and will generally make use of secondary data sources. Thus the institute is more likely to examine particular criminal justice practices in the six states and two territories, while council-funded projects are more likely to concentrate on particular practices in specific locations.

D. New South Wales Bureau of Crime Statistics and Research
Established in 1971 within the State Department of the Attorney-General, this body quickly earned a reputation for producing useful research reports. The first director of the bureau, Tony Vinson, later was chairman of the Corrective Services Commission of New South Wales for two years before he accepted his current university chair in social work. With a professional staff of five or six and an equivalent number of support staff, since 1974 the bureau has published annual reviews of higher and lower court statistics in New South Wales. It has also published short research reports on a wide range of topics, and in recent years it has undertaken evaluations of reforms in the law with respect to bail, homicide, sexual assaults, and the decriminalization of public drunkenness. Since its establishment the bureau has published more than sixty reports of various kinds.

E. South Australian Office of Crime Statistics
Using the model of New South Wales, this office was established in 1978 with the immediate object of producing up-to-date quarterly reports of police, court, and correctional statistics for South Australia. This has been done since 1978, and South Australia is the only jurisdiction to publish up-to-date data on all aspects of criminal justice.

From 1980 the office has also published more detailed analyses of lower court statistics every six months and occasional research reports on specific topics. The staff of the office comprises only two professionals and two support staff, and yet it has been singularly successful in producing useful information. The first director of the office, Peter Grabosky, also chaired a government committee which produced a major report on the victims of crime in 1981 (Committee of Inquiry on Victims of Crime 1981).

F. Other Research Institutions

Inevitably, criminological research in Australia is not totally confined to the institutions outlined above, and from time to time other bodies and organizations undertake or promote such research. Each of the states has one or more law reform bodies, and some of the reports coming from them incorporate considerable research material. One such body, the Criminal Law and Penal Methods Reform Committee of South Australia, chaired by Justice Mitchell, published four major reports over the period 1973–77 dealing with sentencing and corrections, criminal investigation, procedure and evidence, and the substantive criminal law (Criminal Law and Penal Methods Reform Committee of South Australia 1973, 1974, 1975, 1977). Of particular significance, however, is the Australian Law Reform Commission, chaired by Mr. Justice Kirby, which has produced major reports on a number of topics, the most criminologically relevant of which have been concerned with criminal investigation and the sentencing of federal offenders (Australian Law Reform Commission 1980). (Australia has no federal prisons and therefore offenders against the laws of the federal government, if imprisoned, serve their sentences in state prisons. This arrangement, which is provided for in the Australian constitution, raises profound questions of the relative desirability of uniformity of the treatment of offenders within and between jurisdictions.)

Other bodies, which occasionally promote criminological research, are the law foundations of each of the states. Of these, New South Wales Law Foundation has been most active. This body has occasionally provided supplementary funding to research originally funded by the Criminology Research Council, but in its own right this organization has either conducted or funded projects on a number of topics. Examples are studies of bail and pretrial release (Tomasic 1976), the failure of imprisonment to achieve its objectives (Tomasic and Dobinson 1979), and the delivery of legal services (Cashman 1981). Possibly the foun-

dation's most ambitious project was a national survey of judicial attitudes which it conducted in 1979 in cooperation with the Australian
Law Reform Commission as a part of the commission's study of the
sentencing of federal offenders. The results of this survey were included
in a long appendix to the commission's report (Australian Law Reform
Commission 1980) and outlined the responses of 350 judges and mag-
istrates (approximately 74 percent of the national total) to a broad range
of items included in a mailed questionnaire.

II. Government Influence on Research Priorities
Research in criminology anywhere in the world is likely to be subjected
to a greater degree of government influence than other academic disciplines because the incidence of crime and the operation of criminal
justice systems are of central concern to all governments. University
researchers in Australia, as elsewhere, are free to undertake such studies
as they choose, but if they need access to official data or records and
if they want their work to be seen as relevant to contemporary needs,
they are likely to expose themselves to some degree of government
influence. If government funding is being sought, the degree of influence of course becomes greater. This does not mean that all Australian
criminologists are government lackeys—some are the most trenchant
and vocal critics of criminal justice policies and practices—but it is well
to recognize the symbiotic relationship between those who administer
and those who research in the same field.

It could be argued that all research undertaken by the Australian
Institute of Criminology is directly influenced by the government because, as shown earlier, such research must be approved by the institute's Board of Management. In practice, however, the selection of
research projects within the institute is a matter of negotiation between
the researchers, the director, and ultimately the board, with the individual interests and talents of researchers being taken fully into account.
Only on very rare occasions has the board declined to approve, or
suggested modifications to, research proposals submitted to it. In March
1982 the board resolved inter alia as a matter of policy "that . . . subject
to the need to recognize the requirements of justice and the maintenance
of fundamental human rights . . . the basic objectives of research conducted by the Institute should be to provide research results of data
relevant to: (a) the reduction of costs associated with crime or with the
operation of the criminal justice system, or (b) the evaluation or improvement of the efficiency of the criminal justice system." The board

also resolved that in future it would require evidence of consultation with government agencies and other experts indicating support for research proposals before approval would be given. Thus access to agencies and data is assured and the relevance of the research is established before specific projects are undertaken.

The Criminology Research Council is explicitly required by statute "to examine, and determine the relative importance and urgency of, projects for which expenditure of moneys . . . may be authorized." As all members of the council are federal or state government officials, generally at very senior levels, this requirement may be seen as clear evidence of government influence on research priorities which applies not only to government employees but also to university researchers who seek funding from the council. In practice, however, as with institute research, the interests and talents of researchers are ultimately the most significant criteria. The council has only rarely overtly sought proposals in particular areas, and generally it has adopted a reactive stance, receiving applications and either approving or rejecting the request for funds or suggesting modifications to the research strategy or budget. In a country with a relatively small number of experienced researchers, this has seemed to be the most reasonable and appropriate stance to adopt.

Another area of government influence on research priorities is the annual Conference of Ministers in Charge of Prisons, Probation, and Parole representing all states and the Northern Territory. The institute has conducted a number of projects for this body, including studies of long-term prisoners (Wardlaw and Biles 1980), prison labor (Braithwaite 1980a), restitution programs (Scutt 1980), and rights and obligations in prisons (Clifford 1982a). In 1982 the ministers gave their approval to the institute's conducting a national census of prisoners in all Australian jurisdictions. This is the first census of its type in the country's history and will be repeated annually.

At the local or regional level, most police and correctional agencies have small research units which undertake projects or collect and analyse data considered necessary for government purposes.

III. Recent Research Trends
Only major research commitments of the Australian Institute of Criminology will be reviewed here, as most other major projects have been mentioned elsewhere.

A. Principles of Sentencing

Since its effective establishment in 1974 the research division of the institute has devoted a considerable proportion of its resources to studies of the principles in sentencing as enunciated by the higher criminal courts in their appellate jurisdiction. Several books, of interest to legal practitioners as well as researchers, have focused on the law and sentencing practice in different jurisdictions. This project was conceived and developed by a former institute staffer, Mary Daunton-Fear, whose two works (1977, 1980), dealing with Western Australia and South Australia, respectively, were supplemented by studies focused on Queensland (Newton 1979) and New South Wales (Potas 1980). A further study of sentencing in Victoria is being conducted by noninstitute researchers with Criminology Research Council support. Another study has dealt with the sentencing of aboriginal offenders (Daunton-Fear and Freiberg 1977). All of these works are essentially descriptive in nature in that they do not test specific hypotheses but seek to identify the principles that judges follow in determining sentences. Most of these books include some statistics of lengths of sentences imposed, but their focus is more analytical than empirical.

More recently, preliminary work has been undertaken on the factors associated with the sentencing of federal offenders convicted of importing or trafficking illegal drugs. This empirical work is using a computer to determine the relative significance of a large number of variables in the determination of the lengths of prison sentences. Preliminary results indicate relatively low levels of sentencing disparity between jurisdictions when all relevant factors are taken into account, but in those jurisdictions with high rates of drug offenses harsher penalties were generally imposed. It was found that a relatively small number of variables, such as type and quantity of drug and prior criminal record, were able to predict the sentence outcome with a high level of accuracy.

B. Crime Trends

One of the largest single projects undertaken by the institute was a study of crime trends over the period 1900–1976 (Mukherjee 1981). This study used statistics of appearances before higher and lower courts in all Australian jurisdictions for nearly eight decades as a basis for the expansion of relationships with other social, demographic, and economic data. This analysis tended to show that serious criminal behavior had remained relatively stable per unit of population, but since the

Second World War there had been very significant increases in minor and traffic offences. A by-product of this project was the publication of a data source book (Mukherjee, Jacobsen, and Walker 1981), which will be periodically updated. An earlier product of this project was a study of female criminality (Mukherjee and Fitzgerald 1981) which found little evidence to support the hypothesis that female crime rates were rising at a faster rate than male crime rates. Two smaller studies of crime trends (Biles 1979a, 1982a) have used data on offenses reported to the police over the period 1964–65 to 1979–80 in all Australian jurisdictions. Over this considerably shorter period of time the evidence suggests that most categories of serious crime have increased markedly. Within this period, however, there seems to have been a leveling off of most sorts of crime in the first half of the 1970s.

C. Victimization

In 1975 the Australian Bureau of Statistics conducted the first national crime victims survey in Australia with a sample size of over 18,500. Computing problems and staffing restrictions delayed the publication of the results of this survey until 1979 (Australian Bureau of Statistics 1979), at which time the bureau undertook a number of further analyses of the data at the request of the institute. This additional work enabled institute staff to prepare ten papers on various aspects of the results for publication in Australian and international journals. An overview (Braithwaite and Biles 1980a) summarized the findings, and another paper compared Australian data with the results of victimization studies in the United States (Braithwaite and Biles 1980b). These papers were extensively used in a South Australian government inquiry into the needs of crime victims. Further national crime victims surveys are planned by the Australian Bureau of Statistics, but it is doubtful if they will ever be conducted annually, as in the United States.

D. Corporate Crime

Australia is rapidly becoming recognized as one of the world leaders in research into corporate crime. Recent UN meetings have asserted that illegal activities by business corporations are more damaging and more costly than all individual crime and therefore should be the subject of more intensive investigation. The institute has endeavored to respond to this challenge by encouraging some of its leading researchers to work in this area. Two early institute publications (Hopkins 1978a, 1978b) examined the impact of prosecutions under Australian trade practices legislation on the subsequent behavior of businesses and the sociological sources of Australian monopoly law, while two later papers (Braithwaite 1979, 1980*b*) examined the transnational nature of offenses by large corporations. Current institute research into corporate crime is using interviews with executives in a number of countries as the basic research tool to investigate bribery, safety testing, fraud, occupational health, and other offenses. This work has resulted in the preparation of manuscripts for two books (Braithwaite, in press; Fisse and Braithwaite, in press) dealing with the international pharmaceutical industry and regulation through the use of adverse publicity. This technique has resulted in one preliminary report (Clifford and Braithwaite 1981).

E. Correctional Statistics

Since 1976 the institute has collected and published monthly data on the numbers of prisoners in the eight Australian jurisdictions. As there are no federal penitentiaries or county jails in Australia, it is relatively easy to obtain up-to-date and accurate data of persons in prison. With a general population of approximately 15 million, Australia has had just under 10,000 prisoners at any time in recent years. The national imprisonment rate is approximately sixty-six per 100,000 population, but there are very great differences between individual states and territories. These differences seem to have little or no relation to the incidence of crime (Biles 1979*b*, 1982*b*). (The national census of prisoners, referred to earlier, will facilitate comparisons of the structure as well as the size of the prison populations in each jurisdiction.) More recently the institute has also collected and published monthly data on the number of offenders on probation and on parole, and a comparison between these data and the imprisonment figures tends to provide no support for the assumption that the extensive use of probation and parole would be associated with low use of imprisonment (Potas and Biles 1979). Nationally there are about 20,000 offenders on probation and about 5,000 on parole at any time, but again rates of usage vary widely between jurisdictions. Research is continuing on explaining these differences and predicting future trends.

In addition to the research outlined in the preceding paragraphs, the institute has undertaken projects relating to police unionism, terrorism, domestic violence, drug use, juvenile justice, mentally ill offenders, prison classification, automobile theft, and a number of other topics. It also maintains close links with similar institutes and research organizations in other parts of the world.

IV. Future Directions

The future of criminological research in Australia, as elsewhere, depends to a very great extent on the state of the national economy and
the philosophical assumptions that are applied to control it. As long as
it continues to be assumed that it is necessary to restrict public expenditure in order to control inflation, government expenditure on
criminological research will remain limited, and this also applies to
universities and to criminal justice agencies themselves. Police and
correctional authorities, for example, who are struggling to provide
basic operational services are unlikely to invest in research and may
well be forced to cut their existing research capabilities. As I have
shown, most of the organizations in Australia specifically devoted to
criminological research have been reduced in size in recent years, and
no change is predicted in the immediate future.

Notwithstanding this bleak outlook, a number of positive signs can
be seen on the horizon of Australian criminology. First and foremost,
it must be said that the criminologists themselves have gained in competence and confidence and are being increasingly recognized in the
international community. Thus the productivity of Australian criminologists is probably higher now than ever before, and, provided they
are given some degree of support and encouragement (and provided
they do not all accept appointments overseas), this productivity is likely
to continue.

In more concrete terms, a future development of great significance
to Australian criminology will be the availability of more comprehensive
and reliable crime and criminal justice statistics. The Australian Bureau
of Statistics has been working for some years on the development of a
national classification of offenses (which is applicable to different legal
systems) and counting rules to be used by police, court, and correctional
authorities. This new system includes sixty-one separate offenses, which
can be compressed into twenty-five offense groups, and will replace
the series of seven selected offenses for which uniform data have been
available since 1964 (Biles 1982a). The first products of the new system,
which will be restricted initially to police statistics of offenses reported
and cleared, are expected to be available shortly. As other dimensions
of data are added, Australian criminologists will have available to them
a gold mine of information to be used for the identification and testing
of a range of hypotheses relating to all aspects of criminal justice.

Furthermore, Australia is an ideal site for such work. With its relatively homogeneous population and cultural heritage and only eight

jurisdictions with similar if not identical laws and criminal justice systems, Australia may be seen as a social science laboratory in which hypotheses can be developed for testing in more complex federal structures such as the United States. For example, the currently limited Australian criminal justice data suggest that automobile theft is inversely related to the level of automobile ownership (Biles 1977). This observation might lead to the conclusion that with increasing affluence and increasing automobile ownership the rate of theft might go down, but before such a conclusion can be seriously considered the basic correlation would need to be established in other countries, as it may turn out to be no more than an idiosyncratic twist of the Australian data. Numerous other hypotheses of this type can be generated in Australia for testing elsewhere.

Apart from future improvements in criminal justice statistics, an area of urgent need for further research relates to aborigines and their involvement with the criminal justice system. Aborigines are grossly overrepresented in all Australian prison systems (Clifford 1982b) and their general levels of social and economic deprivation are of widespread concern. Many studies and inquiries have examined these problems (e.g., Eggleston 1976), and recently the Board of Management of the Australian Institute of Criminology authorized the development of an information service concentrating solely on materials related to all aspects of aborigines and the law. A number of research projects examining specific aspects of this topic can be expected in the future.

Further development can also be expected in research into corporate and white-collar crime including such aspects as environmental pollution and industrial safety. We can also expect that research into all aspects of correctional administration will continue to expand as the public becomes more concerned about the costs and apparent ineffectiveness of imprisonment. No doubt some of this work will be undertaken by a small group of radical criminologists who, in association with ex-prisoners, have occasionally published their own journal, the *Alternative Criminology Journal*. This group, together with a rapidly growing number of feminist criminologists, is generally critical of the perceived timidity and caution of the established criminological community. These differences of ideology and orientation, with the inevitable tensions that they produce, will undoubtedly continue into the foreseeable future. In the immediate future, however, the small number of Australian criminologists have more than enough to do in pursuing the research activities outlined in this essay. Perhaps the one significant advantage of working in a relatively underdeveloped field is the fact that one need not look very far to find vast areas of criminal justice untouched by the hands of researchers. In Australian criminology, therefore, there is no need for researchers to jostle with each other in order to establish claims for their own piece of territory.

While Australian rates of reported crime and imprisonment remain relatively low by international standards, it is doubtful that there will be any significant upsurge of demand for more penetrating and costly criminological research. Sad as that might be for researchers, it is a situation which might be envied by law-abiding citizens in many other parts of the world.

REFERENCES

Australian Bureau of Statistics. 1979. *General Social Survey: Crime Victims May 1975.* Catalogue no. 4105.0. Canberra: Australian Government Publishing Service.
Australian Law Reform Commission. 1980. *Report No. 15: Sentencing of Federal Offenders.* Canberra: Australian Government Publishing Service.
Barry, Sir John. 1958. *Alexander Maconochie of Norfolk Island: A Study of a Pioneer in Penal Reform.* Melbourne: Oxford University Press.
Biles, D. 1977. "Car Stealing in Australia." In *Delinquency in Australia,* edited by P. R. Wilson. St. Lucia: University of Queensland Press.
———. 1979a. *The Size of the Crime Problem in Australia.* Canberra: Australian Institute of Criminology.
———. 1979b. "Crime and the Use of Prisons." *Federal Probation* 43:39–43.
———. 1982a. *The Size of the Crime Problem in Australia.* Rev. ed. Canberra: Australian Institute of Criminology.
———. 1982b. "Crime and Imprisonment: An Australian Time Series Analysis." *Australian and New Zealand Journal of Criminology* 15:133–53.
Braithwaite, J. 1979. "Transnational Corporations and Corruption: Towards Some International Solutions." *International Journal of the Sociology of Law* 7:125–42.
———. 1980a. *Prisons, Education and Work.* St. Lucia: University of Queensland Press.
———. 1980b. "Inegalitarian Consequences of Egalitarian Reforms to Control Corporate Crime." *Temple Law Quarterly* 53:1127–46.
———. In press. *Corporate Crime in the Pharmaceutical Industry.* London: Routledge & Kegan Paul.

Braithwaite, J., and D. Biles. 1980*a*. "Overview of Findings from the First Australian National Crime Victims Survey." *Australian and New Zealand Journal of Criminology* 13:41–51.

———. 1980*b*. "Crime Victimization in Australia: A Comparison with the U.S." *Journal of Crime and Justice* 3:95–110.

Cashman, P., ed. 1981. *Research and the Delivery of Legal Services.* Sydney: Law Foundation of New South Wales.

Challinger, D. 1977*a*. *Young Offenders.* Melbourne: Victorian Association for the Care and Re-Settlement of Offenders.

———. 1977*b*. *Studies in Shoplifting.* Melbourne: Australian Crime Prevention Council (Victorian Branch).

Chappell, D., and P. R. Wilson. 1969. *The Police and the Public in Australia and New Zealand.* St. Lucia: University of Queensland Press.

———. 1972. 2d ed., 1977. *The Australian Criminal Justice System.* Sydney: Butterworths.

Clifford, W. 1982*a*. *Rights and Obligations in a Prison.* Canberra: Australian Institute of Criminology.

———. 1982*b*. "An Approach to Aboriginal Criminology." *Australian and New Zealand Journal of Criminology* 15:3–21.

Clifford, W., and J. Braithwaite. 1981. *Cost-Effective Business Regulation.* Canberra: Australian Institute of Criminology.

Committee of Inquiry on Victims of Crime. 1981. *Report of Committee of Inquiry on Victims of Crime.* Adelaide: Australian Government Publishing Service.

Commonwealth of Australia. 1971. *Criminology Research Act 1971.* No. 15.

Criminal Law and Penal Methods Reform Committee of South Australia. 1973. *First Report: Sentencing and Corrections.* Adelaide: Government Printer.

———. 1974. *Second Report: Criminal Investigation.* Adelaide: Government Printer.

———. 1975. *Third Report: Court Procedures and Evidence.* Adelaide: Government Printer.

———. 1977. *Fourth Report: The Substantive Criminal Law.* Adelaide: Government Printer.

Daunton-Fear, M. W. 1977. *Sentencing in Western Australia.* St. Lucia: University of Queensland Press.

———. 1980. *Sentencing in South Australia.* Sydney: Law Book Company, Ltd.

Daunton-Fear, M. W., and A. Freiberg. 1977. " 'Gum Tree' Justice: Aborigines and the Courts." In *The Australian Criminal Justice System*, edited by D. Chappell and P. Wilson. 2d ed. Sydney: Butterworths.

Davies, A. F., and S. Encel, eds. 1965. 2d ed., 1970. *Australian Society, a Sociological Introduction.* Melbourne: Cheshire.

Eggleston, E. 1976. *Fear, Favour or Affection—Aborigines and the Criminal Law in Victoria, South Australia and Western Australia.* Canberra: Australian National University Press.

Fisse, B., and J. Braithwaite. In press. *Publicizing Corporate Crime.* Albany: SUNY Press.

Harding, R. 1981. *Firearms and Violence in Australian Life.* Nedlands: University of Western Australia Press.

Hawkins, G. J. 1976. *The Prison—Policy and Practice*. Chicago: University of Chicago Press.

Hopkins, A. 1978*a*. *The Impact of Prosecutions under the Trade Practices Act*. Canberra: Australian Institute of Criminology.

———. 1978*b*. *Crime, Law & Business: The Sociological Sources of Australian Monopoly Law*. Canberra: Australian Institute of Criminology.

Mackay, J. G., and M. K. Rook. 1976. *Tasmania's Work Order Scheme*. Report to Criminology Research Council.

Milte, K. L., and T. A. Weber. 1977. *Police in Australia: Developments, Functions and Procedures*. Sydney: Butterworths.

Morris, N. 1951. *The Habitual Criminal*. London: University of London.

Mukherjee, S. K. 1981. *Crime Trends in Twentieth-Century Australia*. Sydney: George Allen & Unwin.

Mukherjee, S. K., and R. W. Fitzgerald. 1981. "The Myth of Rising Female Crime." In *Women and Crime*, edited by S. K. Mukherjee and J. Scutt. Sydney: George Allen & Unwin.

Mukherjee, S. K., E. N. Jacobsen, and J. R. Walker. 1981. *Source Book of Australian Criminal & Social Statistics, 1900–1980*. Canberra: Australian Institute of Criminology.

Newton, J. E. 1979. *Cases and Materials on Sentencing in Queensland*. Canberra: Australian Institute of Criminology.

Potas, I. 1980. *Sentencing Violent Offenders in New South Wales*. Sydney: Law Book Company Ltd.

Potas, I., and D. Biles. 1979. "Australian Correctional Data: A Comparative Analysis." *Australian Institute of Criminology Newsletter* 6 (4): 14–15.

Roulston, R. P. 1975. *Introduction to Criminal Law in New South Wales*. Sydney: Butterworths.

Scutt, J. A. 1980. *Restoring Victims of Crime*. Canberra: Australian Institute of Criminology.

Thomas, J. E. 1978. *Imprisonment in Western Australia: Evolution, Theory and Practice*. Nedlands: University of Western Australia Press.

Tomasic, R. A. 1976. *Bail and Pre-Trial Release: Strategies and Issues*. Sydney: Law Foundation of New South Wales.

Tomasic, R. A., and I. Dobinson. 1979. *The Failure of Imprisonment: An Australian Perspective*. Sydney: Law Foundation of New South Wales.

Ward, P., and G. Woods. 1972. *Law and Order in Australia*. Sydney: Angus & Robertson.

Wardlaw, G., and D. Biles. 1980. *The Management of Long-Term Prisoners in Australia*. Canberra: Australian Institute of Criminology.

Whelan, J., E. Seaton, and E. C. Dax. 1976. *Aftermath—the Tasmanian Bridge Collapse: Criminological and Sociological Observations*. Canberra: Australian Institute of Criminology.

Anthony N. Doob

Criminological Research in Canada

The organization and funding of almost any area of research might be described, in the aggregate, as falling somewhere along a continuum from a highly planned, unitary, focused research program to an unplanned laissez-faire—even anarchistic—situation without an identifiable focus. Any single portion of this aggregate, for example, within a research institution or within a funding agency, might be expected to be located closer to the "unitary focus" end of the continuum than would be the aggregate. The issue that I explore in this essay will relate largely to the possibility of shifts in the aggregate, in Canada, in the direction of a more unitary focus.

Canada, like some other Western countries, both funds and carries out its social science research through a number of different mechanisms. The federal government is involved both through its granting council, the Social Sciences and Humanities Research Council, and two government departments, the Ministry of the Solicitor General and the Department of Justice. The provinces each have at least one ministry involved in criminal justice matters, and from time to time they fund specific projects having to do with their responsibilities. The provinces and federal government also support criminological research through their funding of the universities—direct in the case of the provinces and indirect in the case of the federal government. Criminological research centers, funded by the universities and by direct contributions from the federal government, now exist in seven Canadian

Anthony N. Doob is director, Centre of Criminology, University of Toronto.

universities. Finally, of course, private foundation support from organizations like the Donner Canadian Foundation has played an important role through sometimes large grants for research. For the most
part, these organizations act independently of one another.

In principle, one of the most open funding agencies is the Social
Science and Humanities Research Council (SSHRC), whose general
purpose is "to promote and assist research and scholarship." It is supposed to encourage "curiosity-oriented research" and thus provide a
"base of advanced knowledge in the universities." In the past decade
or so, there have been two important trends in funding from this source
that have had an impact on criminological research in Canada. The
first, and hardly unique, trend is toward an erosion of available funds
(a decline in real value by about 25 percent in the last decade). The
second, and in certain ways more insidious, trend is toward a higher
degree of centralized decision making in priority areas. The SSHRC,
ostensibly in order to increase its overall budget, recently developed
"strategic themes" with funds associated with each theme. The three
themes for 1982 were population aging, family and the socialization of
children, and human context of science and technology. These themes
appear to be related to social issues on which the government either
feels it would like research or can best tolerate research. The themes
do not easily accommodate most criminological research, though if they
are broadly interpreted, some research might be included. Thus juvenile delinquency research might be able to fit under "family and the
socialization of children" just as a study on the police, who seem to be
important users of modern technology, might be able to fit into the
"human context of science and technology." It would appear, though,
that the one agency in Canada whose mandate is most clearly to support
research deriving from the ideas of independent researchers is itself
embarked on a policy of spending a decreasing portion of its available
funds on independent research.

There are three other federal government organizations which have,
to varying extents, been involved in sponsoring criminological research—the Law Reform Commission of Canada, the Department of
Justice, and the Ministry of the Solicitor General. Until recently the
Law Reform Commission of Canada sponsored empirical research (on
such topics as the effects of jury unanimity), but lately it has taken the
position that in the area of criminal law and procedure it no longer
feels that "useful empirical research could be designed, implemented,
and evaluated in time to inform our [legal] research and recommen-

dations." Instead, the commission intends to rely on the research funded by the other two government departments.

Whether such a strategy will be successful is an open question. The problem, of course, is that the strategy of relying on other departments implies a level of coordination and cooperation that does not appear to exist. It is not that antagonism exists; rather, it is natural that a body such as the Law Reform Commission of Canada does and should have goals that are different from those more closely aligned to the political process. Indeed, given the goal of a measure of independence from the other government ministries, one wonders whether such a strategy will serve the commission well.

One of these other departments, the Department of Justice, has a relatively small but active research group (though they carefully avoid using the term "research" in describing their mandate) involved in both in-house and externally contracted research. The division of responsibility between the Department of Justice and the Ministry of the Solicitor General is at times vague, though the largest difference (from the point of view of those outside the federal government and interested in getting research funds) is that the Ministry of the Solicitor General, Canada, has most of the research funds at its disposal.

The Department of Justice has recently been involved in funding such projects as a comparison of different methods of delivering (federally subsidized) legal services (e.g., Brantingham 1981) and research on various aspects of the interface between psychiatry and the criminal process (e.g., Webster, Menzies, and Jackson 1982). The general area of sentencing in criminal courts, though theoretically a responsibility of a committee of both ministries, appears to have been left to or taken over by the Department of Justice.

The Ministry of the Solicitor General, Canada, is responsible for penitentiaries, parole, and the Royal Canadian Mounted Police, and sponsors the largest single portion of criminologial research done in Canada. The research division, staffed with about a dozen people who have higher degrees (some with a Ph.D.) in relevant social sciences, contracts out most of its research, though recently it has increased the amount of work that they are doing in-house. They describe their role as "to initiate, promote, and coordinate research to enable the Ministry to provide advice, and influence the development of strategies to reduce the social and economic costs of crime in Canada." This definition of their role is an interesting and important one, because it ties their research effort fairly clearly to immediate policy issues. How close the research must be to specific policy initiatives of the federal government has, not surprisingly, been an issue with a substantial number of university-based researchers in Canada.

The legislative responsibility for criminal law in Canada lies with the federal government, though the administration of criminal justice is the responsibility of the ten provinces. In other words, although the federal parliament passes changes in the criminal laws, the provinces have to deal with the effects of these changes. In addition, sentences of less than two years' imprisonment are served in provincially controlled and funded prisons, whereas sentences of two years or more are spent in federally controlled and funded penitentiaries. Thus the provinces have a strong interest in criminal justice and, to some extent, are involved in research on criminal justice matters. Generally speaking, it would appear that the concerns of the provinces are narrower than those of the federal government, though generalizations such as this are risky given the variation that exists across provinces. Notwithstanding this risk, it appears to me that provincial research usually deals with a very specific question, such as the effectiveness of particular programs. Though absolutely necessary from the point of view of effective use of public funds, such research rarely makes significant contributions to our understanding of broad questions and makes its contribution largely in the aggregate of accumulated findings.

Provincially funded criminological research is carried out both within the provincial government departments and through contracts with external organizations. Some provincial government departments, such as Ontario's Ministry of Correctional Services, have research groups located within the ministry itself which are responsible for both in-house studies and for contract research. Other provincial departments appear to rely completely on outside organizations for their social science research expertise.

As with many other countries, research in criminology is carried out in Canada by a mixture of public and private organizations. At the moment, there are about half a dozen criminological research centers associated with the universities whose mandates are largely to carry out research. As part of universities, they tend to be funded in large measure by their parent organizations, which are themselves dependent on the provinces for support. These centers have quite varied histories. The University of Toronto Centre of Criminology, for example, was created in 1963 as a research institution within the university; teaching, in the form of an M.A. program, first became a responsibility of the center in 1971. Simon Fraser University's Criminology Research Centre grew out of their Department of Criminology, which is a full-fledged department within the Faculty of Interdisciplinary Studies. The recently founded Atlantic Institute of Criminology associated with Dalhousie University in Halifax, Nova Scotia, was created as a result of interest both in the Atlantic region of Canada and in the Ministry of the Solicitor General, Canada, in having a university-based criminology center in eastern Canada. The federal government has aided this new institute for its first few years by providing over $100,000 per year in support (including the salary of a senior official of the Ministry of the Solicitor General, Canada, who will be spending two years at the institute). The other centers have similarly varied histories.

The criminological research centers have direct and continuing financial contact with the federal government through a system of "contributions" from the Ministry of the Solicitor General. The Centre of Criminology at the University of Toronto, for example, receives, at present, $105,000 annually in this way. Twenty percent of this amount is earmarked for the development of research manpower in criminological research and the other 80 percent can be used for any legitimate research-related purpose. The federal government has been making these contributions to the university research centers for about ten years. They originally were given only to the University of Toronto and the Université de Montréal, the oldest criminology research centers in the country. More recently they have expanded as other centers grew up in other universities. Originally conceived of as a method of ensuring university presence in criminological research, their purpose has been expanded to include the development of a research capacity in criminology in Canada.

Although the overall budget of the Centre of Criminology is quite small compared with other budgetary units within the university, this contribution from the federal government gives us more economic freedom than many much larger units. With university funds largely committed on an ongoing basis to permanent staff and research funds tied closely to specific projects, this contribution to criminological research by our federal government allows an enormous number of things to be done which otherwise would be impossible. Effectively, it is an untied research fund available for worthwhile projects which need additional funds, which are just starting, or which have difficulty attracting funds from normal sources. It does, of course, make us somewhat dependent on the federal government, but the form of dependence is, I think, mutually advantageous.

The private sector, through both large and small "consulting" firms, is also heavily involved in research related to criminology. Whether this involvement is functional is, of course, a fundamental question. There are some commentators who have strong reservations about the use of tax dollars in private sector research. Hackler suggests that while "increasing amounts of money are being invested in criminological research in Canada, . . . this investment will yield low dividends because it rewards commercialization rather than genuine scholarship" (Hackler 1979, p. 197). He further suggests that the incentive system in the private sector does not reward contributions to knowledge, rather that the rewards are for large short-term studies resulting from quickly produced proposals. The data and reports that result from this process often give superficial answers to questions that may not have deserved to be asked in the first place.

Given that most of the research being funded in criminology in Canada is justified because it might help to inform policy, it is perhaps instructive to look in more detail at the process by which this research is carried out. The problem for those interested in doing policy-oriented research in Canada is that often policy development, if it can be called that, occurs in response to apparently short-term problems. An issue will arise and an attempt will be made to "solve it" with some quickly gained knowledge. Waller (1979), for example, highlights two reports commissioned by the Ministry of the Solicitor General, Canada, on capital punishment, apparently as examples of reports prepared and distributed to help inform the policymakers. As head of the Research Division of the Ministry until 1979, Waller had a strong view of the importance of the timeliness of research: "The researcher contributing to policy making must be prepared to work within a pre-established timetable" (Waller 1979, p. 210). At the same time, he recognized the importance of a "longer-term approach, which enables . . . a better understanding of the underlying problems." The issue, and a source of strain between the government funding agencies and university researchers, is how one creates an appropriate mix between these two types of research.

I suspect that this issue is not one that is unique to Canada, and, in addition, I suspect that the various views held by different people in Canada could be matched in other countries. However, it is a fundamental issue, and I think it deserves some discussion. One serious problem with the short-term close relationship with policy is, of course, that one runs the risk of always being too late to inform policy. An interesting example of this problem in Canada occurred with respect to legislation designed to replace our 1908 juvenile legislation. The process of changing the legislation began in 1961; the bill including the new legislation was passed in 1982 and will come into effect sometime in the future. During the 1970s there were four separate sets of proposals for new legislation coming from government or from government committees. The effect of this on research on the processing of juveniles was that it was always too late to inform policy. For example, I was told in 1975 that some ideas I had for research were interesting, important, and relevant for policy but there really was no time to do the research because the bill would be introduced into Parliament later that year.

Aside from the fact that the estimates in this case for the introduction of legislation were off by about six years, it is probably naive in general to think that any legislation will solve an issue forever. Canada passed new legislation dealing with the preventive detention of dangerous offenders in the mid-1970s. Only the most optimistic politician would believe that this legislation could deal forever in a perfect manner with the issue of incarcerating those deemed to be dangerous to others.

An alternative funding strategy that has been popular in the Canadian federal funding agencies in criminal justice is to set priority areas for research, as has been discussed with reference to the Social Sciences and Humanities Research Council. The model is a simple one: those sitting in the center are presumed to be in a unique position to identify those areas where research is needed to inform policy. They then create a list of priority items, distribute this list, and then wait for proposals to arrive. The difficulty, of course, is that the priorities may not always be the most sensible ones. In addition, the priority-setting process may not reflect the realities of research. During the latter part of the 1970s, for example, the Research Division of the Ministry of the Solicitor General announced on an almost annual basis a different set of high-priority areas in which they were interested in funding research. Given the difficulty for most researchers in setting up sometimes large research programs and the problems of putting together proposals in order to meet these priorities, it appears that this procedure was not satisfactory either for the research community or for the government department. It is hard to hit a target that disappears as soon as it is aimed at.

More recently, the government funding agencies seem to be moving, officially at least, toward an even more directed system where requests for proposals are sent out to a selected group of research companies and universities. In some cases, there is an explicit preference stated for proposals from the private companies. In any case, the proposals are expected to fulfill aims defined and detailed centrally. Since some of these proposals involve large projects, the impact on the funding situation is large: funds allocated for these "megaprojects" are not available for other smaller projects which might have been suggested by the members of the research community. Such a centrally controlled mechanism is the logical extension to Waller's (1979) suggestion that "the policy developer must participate in identifying research priorities" (p. 206) in that the policymaker is, in many of these cases, determining the research priorities rather than simply participating in identifying them.

The definition of research as a result of this kind of process can itself change. For example, in early 1982, a request for proposals from those interested in studying "public expectations and satisfaction with police services" was sent out by the federal government's "Science Procurement Manager." In the context of government cutbacks of various services, including the cutback of police services in the eight provinces policed on contract largely by the federally controlled Royal Canadian Mounted Police, it is perhaps understandable that there was interest in spending $220,000 during a sixteen-month period on a project whose ultimate goal was, among other things, to provide "specific guidelines and procedures concerning the use by police forces of the instruments and procedures to measure public expectations and satisfaction with police services and for relating the resulting information to the planning and evaluation of police services." Whether such a project should be considered to be "research" or a form of management tool is a moot point. It is unlikely, however, that a package of instructions for an RCMP detachment commander to use to measure public expectations in a community would normally be the kind of thing that would be published in a research-oriented journal.

If the definition of what is research is vulnerable to changing definitions, so also are other aspects of the research process. Hackler (1982) has written about what he describes as the "auditor" model of research where not only is the research question defined centrally, but the control of the research process is central. Thus decisions are made to engage external researchers in a research project, but the central funding agencies feel it to be in their interests to audit the program as it progresses. This tendency may be greatest in the case of the large megaprojects referred to earlier. In one of these projects, for example, a study ostensibly on the impact of the new juvenile delinquency legislation, six research sites were chosen across the country and contracts for the data collection were written with six separate organizations. Because it was decided that the same data would be collected in all research sites, all decisions had to be made and coordinated centrally. Many reservations have been expressed in Canada about such projects generally and about this one in particular. One basic question is whether an interrupted time-series design with only two points in time being sampled (without any kind of comparison group) can really inform anyone about the impact of a new law. Most experienced researchers would probably have come up with quite a different design; in this case there was no opportunity for input at the crucial stages from the research community. Hence the design cannot answer the questions that were used to justify a large allocation of funds to the project. It is interesting to note in this case that one senior ministry official openly admitted to me that the study could not accomplish the goals that were cited to sell it to the government, but he did feel it could be justified in other, unspecified ways.

All organizations sometimes appear to be making bizarre decisions, and another way of considering what is "really" happening is to see what happens when organizational rules are challenged. Thus one can ask what occurs when an apparently good idea is suggested from outside the organization. Fortunately, and perhaps not surprisingly, rules and procedures in our federal agencies appear to be less rigid than they are made out to be. With reasonable people, the rules may even be made to serve the more general goal of informing policy and doing interesting research. Compared to the United States, Canada is a small country. One effect of this is that many if not most members of the research community know one another and know those in government who are responsible for decisions about research. And, fortunately, most of these government officials are intelligent reasonable people. Interesting ideas may be difficult for them to deal with if they do not fit into the priority system but the ideas are not impossible to accept. One way to deal with the problem of an interesting, important "low-priority" idea is to stretch the notion of what the priority means. Research on "victims" (our current fad) can mean almost anything, including the obvious things such as victim services and victim compensation, crime control/

prevention (since that is avoiding being a victim), private policing and private justice systems (since they represent responses outside of the criminal justice system by potential victims), and even the views of victims and potential victims (which together form the "general public") about various aspects of the criminal justice system. The definition of research on victims does not have to be broad, but it appears that those in government departments are willing to view a topic in its broadest sense if they are convinced that the topic is important.

At the same time that the government departments appear to be moving officially toward a more controlled and narrow view of the research process, there are signs (or at least words) which would suggest an opposite movement. Some high-ranking government officials have been talking recently about a program involving the allocation of a portion of the funds in their department to policy-related research, the ideas for which would originate in the university research community. The notion behind such a program would be to support research related to issues which, although not listed as being of high priority, would probably turn out to be relevant to policy. In this way policymakers would have a chance at having basic information available for use when the issue later was seen as important. The idea would be that the university research community would have an opportunity to make arguments about the importance of a topic for federal funding, a procedure not explicitly allowed for in the present system. After seeing the value of such programs as the Ministry of the Solicitor General's "contribution" program, such a program could easily be justified as being a way of profiting from the expertise of the research community in identifying important areas. Perhaps, then, the future of criminal justice research funding in Canada will involve both trends simultaneously: a shift in some research toward more central control and a shift in other areas toward a more decentralized model. At this point it is hard to tell. It is clear, however, that the structure of the funding of research in Canada is changing. Only time will tell whether the changes will lead to a more productive funding structure.

REFERENCES

Brantingham, P. 1981. *The Burnaby, British Columbia, Experimental Public Defender Project*. Ottawa: Department of Justice.

Hackler, J. 1979. "The Commercialization of Criminological Research in Canada." *Canadian Journal of Criminology and Corrections* 21:179–99.

———. 1982. "Conflicting Funding Strategies Hurting Research." *Canadian Association of University Teachers Bulletin* 29 (3): 20–22.

Waller, I. 1979. "Organizing Research to Improve Policy: A Perspective from Canada." *Journal of Research in Crime and Delinquency* 16:196–217.

Webster, C. D., R. J. Menzies, and M. A. Jackson. 1982. *Clinical Assessment before Trial: Legal Issues and Mental Disorder.* Toronto: Butterworth.

John Croft

Criminological Research in Great Britain, with a Note on the Council of Europe

Criminological research is a recent event in the history of the social and behavioral sciences in the United Kingdom. Its practice on any significant scale is a feature of the last quarter of a century, although the roots of this development were laid half a century ago and may be traced back even further. At the time of writing—May 1982—the main source of support for criminological research comes from government funds, and more than half of all the research workers engaged full-time in this pursuit are employed by official agencies. The account that follows reflects this perspective. And, since any speculation about the likely direction of research is determined in some degree by the past, attention will be given to those strands which, woven together, not only make up the present pattern but are likely to influence the future design.

I. Organization and Funding

The Home Office is one of the most ancient departments of state, its modern form originating in 1782. The home secretary is responsible to Parliament for a variety of subjects concerned with law, order, and protective services and also with broadcasting, ethnic relations, and immigration. With the lord chancellor, the home secretary shares responsibility for the criminal justice system in England and Wales.[1] The Home Office, therefore, deals with the police, the lower courts, the

John Croft is the former head of the Home Office Research and Planning Unit.

[1] To be precise, this responsibility is shared with the law officers of the Crown, namely, the attorney general and the solicitor general. The law officers of the Crown for Scotland are the lord advocate and the solicitor general.

probation and after-care service and the prisons, and with the development of criminal and of penal policy generally. While some of its functions correspond to those of the U.S. Department of Justice and its agencies, it combines most of the activities that in many countries are the concern of separate ministries—namely, of the interior and of justice. The home secretary, by virtue of acts of Parliament, has statutory authority to carry out and commission research. These powers to carry out research were first granted in the Criminal Justice Act 1948. In Scotland, the secretary of state has a wide range of functions. Those for criminological research are discharged through the Scottish Home and Health Department. There are separate arrangements for Northern Ireland.

The Home Office, in its research and planning unit, employs at the time of writing (1982) some fifty staff engaged full-time on research; in addition, both the scientific research and development branch and the prison psychological service have a number of scientific officers and psychologists working on the evaluation of certain aspects of policing and prison regimes, respectively. In Scotland, the central research unit allocates half a dozen research officers to the Scottish Home and Health Department. In Northern Ireland, a handful of research workers is concentrated in the policy planning and research unit of the Department of Finance. In addition to the cost of maintaining these intramural capabilities, the Home Office disburses (in round figures) annually £600,000 by way of extramural grant for criminological research and the Scottish Office £100,000: the recipients of these monies are for the most part universities.

As regards institutions of higher education, the picture is more diffuse. Most criminological research is carried out in universities and, to a much lesser extent, polytechnics.[2] Much of this activity is undertaken by individual workers, of whom, while no accurate tally exists, the number is relatively small and scattered among British universities. The identifiable concentration is to be found in institutes, centers, or departments in five universities, namely, Cambridge, Edinburgh, Lon-

[2]There are forty-nine universities in the United Kingdom and a large number of polytechnics and colleges which constitute a substantial part of the higher education system. Faculty members are paid by their universities and not out of Home Office grants. In addition to the three established full professorships of criminology, a few persons hold personal appointments and thus the title of professor. There are also two established readerships, at London and Oxford, respectively. Although the bulk of research is concentrated in comparatively few centers, criminology is taught in quite a few universities, of which Cardiff, Hull, and Southampton deserve mention.

don, Oxford, and Sheffield. Only in Cambridge, Edinburgh, and Sheffield are fully fledged chairs of criminology recognized: in these universities and elsewhere one or two ad hominem appointments are to be found. In terms of research these universities are preeminent. Nevertheless, the number of persons involved full-time in research (as distinct from teaching) is not large. The Cambridge Institute of Criminology (1982), for example, has seven faculty members, whose duties of course include teaching at under- and postgraduate levels, but only four research associates; in addition there are eight students working full-time on doctoral theses and a small number of persons engaged on short-term fellowships. The Oxford Centre for Criminological Research (1981) has only one faculty member but about ten research assistants, all of whom are dependent for support on extramural grants. At the Sheffield Centre for Criminological and Socio-Legal Studies (1982), the number of research fellows and others engaged on full-time research does not appear to exceed nine. These facts—and there are difficulties in defining what is meant by someone engaged full-time in criminological research—are given for the purposes of illustration only and to emphasize the point that for every academic researcher in the United Kingdom, there is at least one researcher—and in all probability rather more than one—employed within government. And when it is appreciated that most of those research workers in universities are funded by government grants for specific projects, the dominance of criminological research by official resources in the United Kingdom will be apparent.

To complete the picture, it must be emphasized that—unlike the United States of America, for example—research institutes independent of both government and universities are relatively rare in the social sciences; none of those few that exist is involved in criminological research. The Social Science Research Council, established in 1965 almost a decade later than the specialist institutions set up in the Home Office and at Cambridge, devotes a tiny fraction of its current budget of about £20 million to criminological research; and although the council funds a small number of units established in universities, including one for sociolegal studies at Oxford, none is concerned with criminological studies as such. Furthermore, the private foundations, which in the years following the Second World War did invest a certain amount of funds in research on crime and delinquency, reduced their commitment when the government establishments developed in the later 1950s. Thus only a small amount of money is now forthcoming from that source, and not in any event on a continuous basis.

It is important to understand how this situation has come about if any assessment is to be made of present possibilities and future trends. Before the 1930s criminological research in the United Kingdom—despite a strong tradition of empirical enquiry in the social sciences stretching far back into the early nineteenth century—was neglected, exceptions to this indifference being represented by the work of Burt, East, and Goring in the previous decade and that before the First World War. With the arrival in England of Grünhut, Mannheim, and Radzinowicz, and the subsequent establishment at Oxford, at the London School of Economics and Political Science, and at Cambridge of criminological teaching, research—albeit on a very modest scale—was started. However, it was only after the war that the Home Office, confronted with a rise in crime generally and in juvenile delinquency in particular, began to support criminological research on a regular basis. In 1957 the Home Office set up its own unit for the purpose. A year or so later saw the inauguration, with a grant from the Wolfson Foundation, of the Institute of Criminology at Cambridge. These important developments are well documented in Hood (1974) (notably, in articles by Antilla, Butler, and Lodge in that volume). They set the scene, as it turned out, for the next quarter of a century; and the pattern then established persists, with but minor modification, at the present day. The rationale for this policy was enshrined in a government White Paper published in 1959, and some of what it had to say about research is worth quoting in full:

> Delinquency cannot be dealt with effectively without more knowledge of its causes and a more accurate measurement than we have at present of the success of the various forms of treatment. It is now widely recognised that in this field research is as essential as in the fields of science and technology.
>
> Research is not necessarily best conducted by official agencies. The outlook, training and environment of the academic worker give him advantages in some kinds of research over the staff of a Government Department. On the other hand, a Department in daily practical touch with the realities of penal treatment, and with contacts and access to data not available to outside workers, has its own distinctive contribution to make. The work that is being done and planned is therefore being shared between academic and official agencies working closely together. In this new

advance, the Home Office has taken a lead. It has set up a Research Unit and assists from its [funds] research work being done elsewhere.

Research into the causes and prevention of delinquency is confronted with problems which are immense both in range and complexity. The causes of crime are varied; heredity, environment and the unpredictable influences to which the individual may be subjected all play their part. Although much is being done, there are no easy answers to these problems and progress is bound to be slow. The difficulties are not so great with research into the use of the various forms of treatment and the measurement of their results, since this is concerned with matters that can be analysed more precisely. It is therefore on constructive work in this part of the field that special emphasis is being put.

The next section deals with the implications of these sentiments for the content and methodology of research insofar as their substance was influenced by official pronouncements. As far as the structure of the research establishment was concerned, the injection of public funds together with the rapid expansion of the government's own capability was to have a substantial effect in that, within a short time, most of the research carried out at Oxford and Cambridge and, to an extent, elsewhere was supported by grants from official resources. This state of affairs was not to be disturbed for some ten years. The turning point was the National Conference on Teaching and Research in Criminology held at Cambridge in 1968, which led to the National Deviancy Conference in York and, to quote Wiles (1976), the "renaissance in sociological criminology in Britain." These events, which epitomized the birth of radical criminology in the United Kingdom,[3] were to have a considerable impact on teaching and to a lesser degree on research. But it was also significant that for the first time the dominance of official funding of research was questioned. Despite criticism, reechoed recently by Brusten in a collection of papers by the European group (Brusten and VanOutrive 1981), and the flight on the part of some radical criminologists from empiricism and the consequent need for

[3]It would be too simplistic to suggest a direct causal link. In the late 1960s there was some dissatisfaction with what might be described as the more orthodox tradition of British criminology. This gave rise to a break-away group initially to be identified with a younger generation of teachers mostly located in the newer universities that had received their charters after the war. The radical criminologists disavowed empiricism as an epistemological position, but there are now signs that they have not totally abandoned empirical research.

support from public funds, this virtual monopoly, however, remained unbroken. It is only now, in the context of the economic constraints on funding for the social sciences as a whole, that a brake is being put on the heady expansionism of the sixties and seventies. These issues, which go deeper than questions of structure and organization, will be taken up again below.

II. Content and Methodology

The tradition of research in the social sciences in the United Kingdom is empirical and positivist; in criminology this tradition has been tinged with a flavor that is interdisciplinary, correctional, and reformist. Historically, inquiry into the state of crime was associated with organizations concerned with penal reform and scientific advancement, such as the Howard League for Penal Reform and the Institute for the Scientific Treatment of Delinquency (from the title of which the word "scientific," once the point had been established, was dropped and the word "study" substituted). Despite the buffeting received at the hands of radical sociology, "British criminology," as Sparks (1982) remarks, "still remains predominantly eclectic, pragmatic and multi-disciplinary: it has no dominant intellectual orientation, and is virtually unconcerned with explanatory theory."[4]

It is apparent that English empiricism was reinforced by the grafting of Continental scholarship represented by the advent of Grünhut, Mannheim, and Radzinowicz some fifty years ago; the German and Italian schools upon which they drew were after all positivist in outlook. The statement in the government White Paper quoted above was not seen, therefore, to be at variance with this intellectual orientation, even if it contained a strong hint that public funds would not be spent on theoretical studies but would be devoted to what were identified as practical problems. In the long run, of course, these practical problems were not to be solved—or at best were to be solved in a way unlikely to appeal much to the authorities—but the story of how penal policymakers eventually had to accept the negative findings of research on treatment, much of it produced by the Home Office unit, need not detain us here. The main point is that the assault on orthodox criminological research by the new criminology—which drew largely on the

[4]This is somewhat of an exaggeration. Works by Trasler and Walker, among others, dealing with the explanation of criminal behavior may be cited in contradiction of Sparks's statement.

sociology of deviance, phenomenology, and symbolic interactionism (together with a good measure of Marxist dialectic) and of which the best-known exposition was first set out by Taylor, Walton, and Young (1973)—hardly deflected it from its course. In examining developments in research on juvenile delinquency over the last fifteen years, Parker and Giller (1981) somewhat ruefully confirm that conclusion.

Nevertheless, somewhere around the early 1970s, a subtle change took place in the content and to an extent the methodology of research. Clarke and Cornish (1983), in their apologia for government research, record the abandonment of a medico-psychological model for a "more complex choice formulation of criminal behaviour" that is reached by way of a situational perspective. Dispositional accounts of behavior in terms of personality variables are superseded by theories of social learning and of interaction. It is fair to say that research which concentrates on the solution of problems is likely to be parsimonious in the use of theoretical concepts. When it was discovered that sentencing, treatment, and, latterly, policing are not the easy way to crime control, then some reappraisal both of the objectives of research and of how one went about it was inevitable. Although those who run systems of criminal justice and are responsible for law enforcement can be expected to be concerned primarily with the efficiency and effectiveness of those measures—and this is still a paramount concern in government funding of research—the emphasis has shifted from a focus on crime and criminals to the analysis of the institutions of criminal justice, such as the police and the criminal process, as much as with individuals caught up with the criminal law. In this sense the influence of sociology, and particularly the growth of sociolegal studies, has drawn attention to social, economic, and political issues; evaluation in quantitative terms alone has given way to evaluation in both quantitative and qualitative terms without abandonment of a basic adherence to scientific method.

What, then, might the proverbial man from Mars—or rather, in the light of the findings (negative again) of modern science, a man from outer space—identify as the main characteristics of contemporary criminological research in the United Kingdom? He would observe that researchers, brought up in a tradition of empirical studies influenced rather more by psychiatry and clinical psychology than by law and—until recently—sociology, were carrying out work for the most part with a pragmatic orientation. This would be reflected in the main learned journal devoted to the subject, the *British Journal of Criminology*, the first issue of which (as the *British Journal of Delinquency*) appeared in 1950. This work was rarely on a large scale but often consisted of small area studies using relatively small samples. It tended to be concentrated in five academic centers of excellence complemented by government units of some capacity which, since they controlled the source of funds, subtly influenced the program and direction of research. He might also notice the absence of research on any significant scale of a sociobiological kind, the apparent disregard (with isolated and distinguished exceptions) of research on the economic aspects of crime (especially those embedded in the social structure of the alternative society), and the relative lack of attention given to violent crime, including terrorism. He might also comment on the lack of empirical research with any strong legal orientation and an inclination to eschew close involvement in much theoretical endeavor.

There are, however, some positive features of British criminological research which might strike the informed observer just as forcibly. Sparks (1982), commenting on the period 1955–70, identified five broad areas within which a substantial number of projects could be comprised, namely, studies of patterns of officially recorded crimes and officially defined criminals, the content and effectiveness of punishments and treatments, prediction methods, regimes and organization of penal institutions, and decision making by agents of the penal system. Sparks went on to remark on the pragmatic character of the bulk of this research, which was regarded primarily as a weapon in the "war against crime." He also commented on its untheoretical character, which has led it to ignore the debates about *politique criminelle* that have occupied criminologists in continental Europe for the past hundred and fifty years. The pressing problems of the penal system and the growing recognition of the importance of research for policymaking seem to have combined—despite an academic community to some extent divided over the issue of radical criminology—to maintain much of what might be described as mainstream or traditional criminological research on course, even granted the disillusion of the 1970s with statistics of officially recorded crime and the failure to identify potential criminals and to reform actual criminals. So much research continues on such traditional subjects as abnormal offenders, the evaluation of legislative measures—for example, the Criminal Justice (Scotland) Act of 1980; the handling of juveniles and young offenders, a particular concern in Northern Ireland, no less than in England and Wales; and "hardy annuals" such as drugs, sex, and to an extent drink. But there are some new features to be discerned on the landscape, and these may be categorized as follows:

1. Growing interest, among historians as well as criminologists, in the history of criminal justice. This has manifested itself in a school which has developed beyond the confines of legal history, as may be perceived from Bailey's review (1980).

2. The growth of police research, stimulated by the Royal Commission on Criminal Procedure (1981), which in the space of two or three years expended some £250,000 on research.

3. The attention given to crime prevention, not only as a function of policing but also in its social and environmental setting. As an adjunct to this, the victims of crime are now the subject of more research, notably by the British crime survey which is being carried out in England, Wales, and Scotland.

4. Law-and-order issues in politics and the press. Associated with this dimension is the study of discrimination and disadvantage in criminal justice with reference to the West Indian and Asian ethnic minorities.

5. The development of comparative research which attempts to study the effects of legal processes and penal measurements as between Britain and certain Continental countries (in preference, it seems, to more distant countries sharing the common-law tradition).

Some of these new features are in their infancy, and whether they will flourish or their growth be stunted is a matter of speculation. There are fashions in criminology as much as in anything else, but one has the impression that the scope, if not the scale, of criminological research has expanded within the last decade. Whether this trend will be maintained forms the subject of the next section.

III. Contemporary Issues and Trends

My views on what I have described as the technological management of criminological research in the English context may already be known to some readers (Croft 1981). There is now, perhaps, no longer any need to stress the importance of research for policymaking. And even if among some policymakers there is still an expectation, originally generated by social scientists some thirty years ago but now abandoned, that criminological research will solve the problems that beset the penal system, realists have adjusted their utilitarian perspective to new horizons. Certainly the concern with the efficiency of systems and their effectiveness will always loom large in political and administrative assessment of criminal justice but, in a democracy, more account is now taken of public attitude and tolerance. It is more clearly understood that research defines, often negatively, the scope of possible action, especially if that action is constrained by considerations of cost and public accountability, as is usually the case. So research is beginning to be perceived as setting the limits to legislative and practical measures and of identifying options for the more economical and fruitful disposal of limited resources.

The proposition that the advancement of knowledge rests with the scientific community needs to be tempered by the realization that the resources for that advancement are not under the direct control of scientists. In the United Kingdom they lie with government and, short of a great accretion of wealth to independent foundations, this monopoly is unlikely to be broken. The point at issue, therefore, is an institutional one: How does the scientific community have a say in the disbursement of whatever resources may be available, and how can it influence the size of these resources? In the United Kingdom the research councils, operating under a system of peer review, are the vehicle for the allocation of resources for scientific research. In the instance of criminology, however, the Social Science Research Council has so far made few grants for criminological research but has been content for the Home Office and the Scottish Office between them to make as generous provision as circumstances allowed. In Northern Ireland very limited research in criminology exists outside government, and the universities and polytechnics there have neither received nor (perhaps) sought such stimulus.

It is considerations such as these that must prompt government departments to ask themselves what business they are in and for those departments, in conjunction with the research councils and the scientific community at large, to ascertain whether there is a need for basic or fundamental research in criminology for which existing resources are either inadequate or at present directed to other purposes. The answer to the first question is unequivocal; government needs research for the formulation of policy and judges that the size of its intramural capabilities and extramural funds are by and large adequate and suited to the purpose in hand. The answer to the second question is not so apparent, for a variety of reasons. First, there is no great clamor on the part of the scientific community for increased resources in a discipline where the distinction between applied and basic research is somewhat artificial. Second, there is no national forum whereby such needs can be recognized, although the reorganization of the committee structure of the Social Science Research Council may facilitate this. Third, as has already been mentioned, criminological research in the United Kingdom is more inclined to the pragmatic than the theoretical, and theoreticians—and particularly the new radical school of criminology—have not demanded resources for empirical work on any considerable scale to substantiate theory. Nevertheless there are areas—such as the history of criminal justice, intergenerational studies based on sizable cohorts, examination of the social structure of penal and other institutions, and further (and painstaking) investigation of some of the classical problems of criminology such as deterrence—which seem to deserve some backing but which, because of the long-term commitment required, are unlikely to appeal so readily to the purveyors of funds normally allocated for purposes with a more immediate return.

There is, so far as can be discerned, no impending crisis in criminological research in the United Kingdom. The wounds inflicted by the radical attack have not festered, and if they have not entirely healed, the patient has by inoculation gained a degree of immunity. Because of, and in spite of, this, criminological research is healthier, if perhaps a trifle complacent. The government capabilities have maintained a considerable, if not altogether recognized, output of solid work while being forced by both economic constraint and intellectual assault to reappraise their role and objectives. If government influence pervades research priorities, and there is no immediate prospect of a diminution of such influence, power is liberally exercised; but it would do no harm, and indeed some good, if some rival source of power could be established, not for the sake of unconstructive competition but to provide an alternative focus for the intellectual consideration of research strategies together with some means for their tactical implementation.

IV. Conclusion

At the most generous estimate there are one hundred and fifty workers engaged full-time in criminological research in government units and academic institutions in the United Kingdom. Some £3 million is expended annually to this end; the bulk of this sum comes from government sources. The dominant tendency, encouraged by official patronage, is for studies to have an empirical in preference to a theoretical emphasis. The achievement of the government units, and the scientific credibility they have established for themselves, are generally recognized abroad and held up as a model for such capabilities elsewhere: radical criminologists, however, would not share this view. Academic centers of excellence have their own distinctive attributes but, being multidisciplinary like the government units, are neither sharply differentiated nor highly specialized within the limits of the discipline itself.

It is not easy to identify a distinctive British criminology. The general approach is now more social than clinical or legal. Despite Continental influences at a formative period, criminological research in the United Kingdom tends to draw heavily on the product of North American studies. Whether the balance will be redressed in favor of the Continental orientation will depend on Britain's relationship with the rest of Europe, to which the next section of this essay is devoted, as against the pull of the language shared in common with its Transatlantic connection. It is clear, however, that British research workers are sympathetic to the traditions of empirical inquiry wherever they may be found.

V. The Council of Europe

The Council of Europe (1977) is an association of states, at present numbering twenty-one, and has as its aim "to achieve a greater unity between its Members for the purpose of safeguarding the ideals and principles which are their common heritage and facilitating their economic and social progress." Its northernmost member is Norway and its southernmost is Malta; its membership stretches from Iceland in the west to Turkey in the east. Its secretariat is based at Strasbourg on the eastern border of France and the Federal Republic of Germany. Its involvement in the prevention of crime and the treatment of offenders is discharged through the European Committee on Crime Problems, which first met in 1958. Certain countries (e.g., Finland) have been accorded observer status, along with various international organizations, both governmental and nongovernmental; observers from Canada, Israel, the United States of America, and occasionally from the socialist countries of eastern Europe are normally invited to attend conferences.

The European Committee on Crime Problems recognized the importance of the contribution that research could make not only to the advancement of knowledge but also to the planning of member states' criminal policies, and in 1963 a Criminological Scientific Council was established. This event is recorded by Antilla in Hood (1974). At the time that I am writing, the membership of this council consists of seven persons holding senior academic posts or senior appointments in the administration of research from France, the Federal Republic of Germany, Italy, the Netherlands, Norway, Spain, and the United Kingdom. Criminological activities, which are fully described by Tsitsoura (1981), include the following: organization of criminological conferences or colloquia; work by subcommittees or small committees of research workers; commissioning of reports from consultants; conducting inquiries into matters of criminological interest; award of individual or coordinated fellowships to criminological research workers; and publication of a bulletin for the exchange of information on criminological research projects.

At a rough calculation, the scientific program costs upward of £50,000 a year to maintain. It consists of at least one conference attended by some fifty experts each year, and this may be supplemented by the holding of a seminar like that held in 1981 on crime prevention. The conferences or colloquia—which in recent years have been concerned with subjects as diverse as economic crime, public opinion on crime and criminal justice, the role of the police in crime prevention, the maltreatment of children, comparative trends in crime, and sexual behavior and attitudes—may in turn lead to the implementation of further activities which are pursued in an administrative legal context, assisted by expert consultants, in select committees.

It is important to make the point that the European Committee on Crime Problems initiates little original research in the sense of the collection and analysis of empirical data. Most of the work it commissions, and the volume accumulated in the course of almost twenty years' endeavor is not inconsiderable, is in the form of critical reviews of research drawn from a wide range of activity in different countries and many languages. For example, the Norwegian Institute for Alcohol Research has recently completed a review of international research on the relationship between alcohol consumption and crime. These reviews are eventually published in reports of the proceedings of conferences or are otherwise incorporated into the final reports of committees. There are exceptions to this method of working, for example, the coordinated fellowship program whereby a small number of scholars from different member states working closely together have tackled in depth subjects such as the role of the school in the prevention of juvenile delinquency, professional and organized crime, and female criminality. The difficulties of collecting and comparing data drawn from differing legislative and administrative systems are so great that such exercises have not been an unqualified success.

In this connection it must be appreciated that, although it is assisted by a competent and well-informed secretariat drawn from the directorate of legal affairs, the European Committee on Crime Problems has no research capability at its direct disposal and no facilities for the central collection and processing of statistical data. The main collective contribution that European criminologists are able to make, therefore, can be identified as: (1) the pooling of knowledge derived from research on particular subjects of topical interest; (2) the dissemination of this information among scholars, policymakers, and penal administrators (in this regard, there is liaison with other parallel activities of the Council of Europe in the fields of education, social welfare, employment, and the environment); and (3) the application of scientific knowledge to policy and practice (detailed in Ferracuti [1979]). Given that a primary task of the Council of Europe is to harmonize the legislations of member states relating to penal law, procedure, and administration, the scientific program does ensure that this activity is informed by the results of research, and machinery exists at various levels to facilitate this. For the purpose of planning the program, for example, the Criminological Scientific Council and the Bureau (consisting of five members elected by the European Committee on Crime Problems for the purpose of managing business) meet together twice a year with officials of the directorate of legal affairs. This said, it is legitimate to ask whether, if this forum did not exist, exchanges between research workers would not take place at any rate, with or without the presence of those responsible for criminal policy and administering systems of justice. It is probable that such exchanges would continue on an ad hoc basis among the four larger countries, the Scandinavian states, and the three Benelux countries in one way or another, but the smaller and relatively more remote countries would probably lose the benefit of the contact afforded by Strasbourg. There are also some political, but not primarily scientific, questions affecting possible overlap with other international organizations located in various European centers. In scientific terms, the issue is whether criminological research in a European context can build further on the foundation laid over the last twenty years and develop the utilitarian concept that has been established, and which could be a model for other parts of the world, in terms of inaugurating a research facility with the potential for carrying out international comparisons. Given the present state of the art, however, and the economic constraints afflicting so many Western nations, this vision is not likely to be realized in the ninth decade, at least, of this century.

REFERENCES

Antilla, I. 1974. "The Foundation of Cooperation in European Criminological Research: Sir Leon Radzinowicz and the Criminological Scientific Council at the Council of Europe." In Hood 1974.
Bailey, Victor. 1980. "Crime, Criminal Justice and Authority in England: A Bibliographical Essay." *Bulletin of the Society for the Study of Labour History* (Spring 1980).
Brusten, M., and L. VanOutrive. 1981. "The Relationship between State Institutions and the Social Sciences in the Field of Deviance and Social Control." In European Group for the Study of Deviance and Social Control 1981.
Butler, Lord, of Saffron Walden. 1974. "The Foundation of the Institute of Criminology in Cambridge." In Hood 1974.
Cambridge University. 1982. "Report of the Director of the Institute of Criminology to Its Advisory Council for the Meeting on 27 May 1982." Unpublished.
Clarke, R. V. G., and D. B. Cornish. 1983. *Changing Perspectives in Crime Control: British Research in a Government Context.* Albany: SUNY Press.
Council of Europe. 1977. *Activities in the Field of Crime Problems, 1956–1976.* Strasbourg: Council of Europe, European Committee on Crime Problems.
Croft, John. 1981. *Managing Criminological Research.* Home Office Research Study no. 69. London: H.M. Stationery Office.
European Group for the Study of Deviance and Social Control. 1981. *State Control on Information in the Field of Deviance and Social Control.* Working Papers in European Criminology no. 2. Bremen: European Group for the Study of Deviance and Social Control.
Ferracuti, F. 1979. "The Co-ordination of Research and the Application of Its Findings in the Field of Criminal Policy." Mimeographed. Strasbourg: Council of Europe.
Home Office. 1959. *Penal Practice in a Changing Society: Aspects of Future Development* (England and Wales). Command 645. London: H.M. Stationery Office.
———. 1982. *Home Office Research and Planning Unit Programme, 1982–83.* Mimeographed. London: Home Office.
Hood, Roger, ed. 1974. *Crime, Criminology and Public Policy: Essays in Honour of Sir Leon Radzinowicz.* London: Heinemann.
Lodge, T. S. 1974. "The Founding of the Home Office Research Unit." In Hood 1974.
Oxford University. 1981. "Report for 1979–81." Mimeographed. Oxford: Centre for Criminological Research.
Parker, H., and H. Giller. 1981. "More and Less the Same: British Delinquency Research since the Sixties." *British Journal of Criminology* 21 (3): 230–45.
Royal Commission on Criminal Procedure. 1981. *Report.* Command 8092. London: H.M. Stationery Office.
Sheffield University. 1982. "Annual Report 1980–81." Mimeographed. Sheffield: Centre for Criminological and Socio-Legal Studies.

Sparks, R. F. 1982. "Criminology in Britain." In *The International Handbook of Contemporary Developments in Criminology*, edited by E. H. Johnson (in press).

Taylor, I., P. Walton, and J. Young. 1973. *The New Criminology: For a Social Theory of Deviance*. London: Routledge & Kegan Paul.

Tsitsoura, Aglaia. 1981. "Un quart de siècle d'activités dans le domaine des problèmes criminels." *Revue internationale de criminologie et de police technique* 34 (3): 253–68.

Wiles, P. 1976. *The New Criminologies: The Sociology of Crime and Delinquency in Britain*. Vol. 2. London: Martin Robertson.

Josine Junger-Tas

Criminological Research in the Netherlands

The Netherlands, a small country with about 14 million inhabitants, has eight full-fledged universities, three institutes of higher technology, and numerous schools for higher professional training in social work, nursing, physiotherapy, and the like. Although two universities were founded and originally supported by the churches and their members (Nijmegen's Catholic University and Amsterdam's Protestant University), all are now financed entirely by the state and all university personnel are civil servants. Traditionally each university has had a criminological institute or department with teaching and research functions.

Funding for social science research comes from three sources. The first is the universities themselves. In the furtherance of their research mission, the universities have traditionally been expected to fund at least some of the research of their faculties. Until the 1980s, the universities fulfilled this function adequately, and many full professors and their staffs have enjoyed the luxury of pursuing their own research interests and hobbies without having to consult university colleagues or to fit their projects into an overall faculty or departmental research program.

Special foundations such as the Dutch Foundation for Pure and Fundamental Research are the second funding source. Other foundations that regularly support social science research include the Foundation for Educational Research. Although they are private organizations, these foundations are supported by state money. The foundations are huge bureaucratic organizations, and requests for funding are generally

Josine Junger-Tas is scientific counsellor, Scientific Research and Documentation Centre, Ministry of Justice, Netherlands.

not acted on for at least a year. Members of grant review committees represent different research traditions and conceptions of science and different organizational and political interests. Disciplinary and organizational politics are not irrelevant to funding decisions, and it helps to have allies on the relevant committee or to have one of the committee members take an aggressive interest in a proposal. Besides these large foundations, there are a large number of private funds. The most important are the Queen Juliana Foundation, the Prince Bernhard Foundation, and the Children's Stamp Fund. The private funds provide subsidies for experimental projects in the social field as well as for research.

The government itself is the third major funding source. Many researchers believe that the foundations do not function altogether satisfactorily. Partly in consequence, many social scientists seek funding directly from specific government departments such as the Ministry of Social Affairs, the Ministry of Culture and Social Work, the Ministry of Education, and, in the case of criminological research, the Ministry of Justice. Relatively large sums were available from government departments for external research and, in the years of affluence, which extended until well into the seventies, scientific standards and research requirements were not highly demanding and financial support for research was relatively easy to obtain. One could say that up until recently all was for the "best in the best of all possible worlds" for academic researchers. Everyone "did his own thing," and the quality of the research varied.

Government support for social science research has been expanding since the seventies. In 1974 the Dutch government spent 48 millipercent of its gross national product on social science research, including university research, which means an increase of 50 percent with respect to 1970. (For comparative purposes, in France this proportion was 34 millipercent, or +2 percent; in England 10 millipercent, or +70 percent; and in Germany 19 millipercent, or +12 percent.) In 1982, the Dutch government spent a total of Fl 163 million on social science research, again including the direct funding of university research. It is impossible to know how much of this money is spent on criminology research. However, the Ministry of Justice spends about Fl 5 million a year on research: Fl 3 million on its own research center, Fl 1 million to fund outside research in the field of criminal justice, and Fl 1 million to fund juvenile delinquency and child protection research.

Criminological research in the Netherlands has traditionally been theoretical and nonempirical. Until 1966 all professors of criminology had a penal law background and little or no experience in empirical social research. This may help to explain their lack of interest in practical social problems and criminal policy issues, although more generally Dutch academic tradition has had a certain disdain for such down-to-earth concerns.

However, change was introduced into Dutch criminological research with the appointment in 1967 of W. Buikhuisen, a psychologist, as professor of criminology at Groningen University. Buikhuisen's doctorate had been an empirical study of marginal youth groups, such as the English teddy boys (Buikhuisen 1965). Buikhuisen has had great interest in criminal policy matters and believes that social science research can be relevant to policymakers and can assist them in trying to solve social problems. Under Buikhuisen the Groningen Criminological Institute undertook a series of studies that introduced empiricism and a certain practical orientation into criminological research.

Typical research projects included (1) a number of studies on alcohol consumption and its effects on perception and driving under the influence of alcohol; personality characteristics of drunken drivers; recidivism of drunken drivers (Buikhuisen et al. 1968; Buikhuisen and Jongman 1972); (2) evaluations of police campaigns to improve car safety (Buikhuisen and van Weringh 1969); (3) studies of drug use among school populations (*Nederlands Tijdschrift voor Criminologie* 1972); and (4) a considerable number of studies on dark number criminality and dismissal policies (Buikhuisen et al. 1969; Jongman and Smale 1972*a*, 1972*b*). Most of these studies concluded with a discussion of the policy ramifications of the findings and many contained specific policy recommendations.

The weakness of these early Groningen studies, which elicited the criticism of academic colleagues, lies in general in a lack of theoretical underpinnings. But it is unarguable that Buikhuisen gave a new impulse to criminological research in the Netherlands. In the 1970s, the Ministry of Justice enlarged its documentation center and created within it a new research center. In 1974 Buikhuisen became general research consultant to the minister and director of the new center.

This essay reviews the organization of criminological research in the Netherlands and briefly describes current research trends. Section I describes the organization of government research, especially in the Ministry of Justice's research center. Section II is an overview of current

research in the universities and in government. The conclusion discusses the respective roles of university and government research in
the Netherlands.

I. The Government and Criminological Research
The Ministry of Justice was the first governmental department to create
its own research center. The essential reason is that government officials
increasingly felt the need for scientifically based advice and recommendations that, for a variety of reasons, the universities could not or
would not supply. Van Dijk's (1981) historical account of the creation
of governmental research centers offers the following analysis. The
construction of the welfare state in the 1950s and 1960s entailed an
expansion of the tasks of all government agencies. The police and the
judicial authorities were allotted a variety of social service tasks in
addition to their responsibilities for maintaining order. Increased emphasis was placed on police efforts directed at resocialization, social
prevention, and service delivery. It was gradually realized that many
questions related to crime and the public order were not just legal
matters but constituted social problems of a much wider scope. At the
same time, questions arose about the efficiency and effectiveness of the
criminal justice system as a whole, and in particular of specific sub-
systems such as the police, probation, the prison system, and the child
protection system. With the realization that the simple continuation of
the system was not sufficient, but that criminal policymaking was needed,
came the need to evaluate the functioning of the constitutive elements
of the criminal justice system.

But why, it may be asked, did not the government simply ask the
universities to do more contract research? Van Dijk mentions three
factors that operated to create governmental skepticism of university
research and led to the search for other solutions. The first factor was
the growing popularity in the sixties and seventies of "critical" criminology. Its proponents did not want simply to change criminal policy
but wished to abolish the whole criminal justice system. They did not
believe in changing the system "from within"; they had a deep mistrust
of all government officials and did not want to collaborate with them.
So they were not interested in research questions aimed at improving
and humanizing the system. As in other countries, this critical orientation led to a series of important studies on, for instance, the selectivity
of judicial intake procedures (Jongman 1971; Jongman and Smale 1972b)
and the effects of institutionalization on juveniles. Unfortunately, the

mutual distrust between members of the criminal justice system and academic researchers made constructive collaboration between them very difficult.

A second factor, to which I have already alluded, is the pronounced theoretical orientation of Dutch universities. Researchers have traditionally been interested mainly in testing abstract theories, which are often of little immediate relevance to practical issues. This tendency has made policymakers extremely skeptical about the usefulness and practical relevancy of most of the traditional criminological research.

The third factor mentioned by van Dijk is more practical: university researchers are often less concerned about schedules and deadlines than are government officials. A report that is delivered six months late may be too late to have any practical relevance for policymakers.

Other well-known factors contribute to the gap between university researchers and policymakers. Academics often translate policy issues so as to integrate them into some existing theory. The result may be that the issues are transformed in a way that makes them unrecognizable to practitioners. The same is true for the research results, which may be presented in a form that is hard for practitioners to penetrate. This may be due to esoteric language and technical jargon, or to the elaborateness and length of reports. Finally, the recommendations often form the weakest part of the study. Of course, this is a delicate issue because recommendations, implying value judgments, can never be abstracted directly from research results. Unfortunately, academics sometimes are so little informed about practical constraints and realities of the criminal justice system that their policy recommendations are often phrased as vague generalities and lack specificity and directness.

When the Ministry of Justice research center was reorganized in 1974, it was heavily attacked by the university establishment. This continued for several years. There were two major lines of argument: (1) the center was not independent, so the research, its results, and its recommendations would be biased; and (2) the ministry's need for policy-relevant findings would produce scientifically weak research— mere "fact-finding" empiricism without any theory.

A. *The Independence of Government Research Centers*

The independence of a government research center is of course an important issue. Questions about guarantees for the center's independence have been directed in parliament to the Minister of Justice. Several official guarantees do exist and are supported by the minister. One of the most important is the prompt publication of all research reports and the issuance of a press release when a study is published. Moreover, researchers are free to write papers and articles in professional journals, in which they can elaborate their views on research or policy matters. Also, the research program for the upcoming year is published annually and presented to parliament, and all research reports are sent to the members of the standing committee of justice in parliament. Finally, the *Research Bulletin of the Ministry of Justice*, a review of ongoing research in the center, as well as in the university criminological institutes, is published annually in English and sent all over the world.

Although these devices to publicize and disseminate the center's work do enhance its independence, there remain insidious dangers that threaten the independence of government researchers. One is closeness of policymakers to researchers: if researchers are not careful, they can find themselves adopting "official" perspectives and end up "sitting in the chair" of the policymakers, accepting their problem definitions and research priorities. Another consequence of this closeness is that researchers may become concerned about financial considerations and political feasibility in making recommendations: these matters, although not irrelevant, are not the responsibility of the researchers and should not be their concern. Political choices, policy priorities, and management decisions cannot be made by researchers. Yet another danger is that researchers' perspectives will narrow toward conducting research only on issues of immediate importance.

Finally, it must be acknowledged that informal pressures are often employed to influence the final texts of potentially controversial studies before they are released. Sometimes these pressures are concerned with matters of language and style, for instance, when certain findings or conclusions are stated in ways considered too extreme or too colored. When this is the case the obvious solution often is a more careful or objective wording. But in some cases the findings themselves are considered too painful to be published, and subtle pressures can be exerted (How did you get these results? What method did you use? Was not something wrong with the measures taken?) not to include them in the report. In this respect the center is not prepared to compromise and accede to policymakers' wishes, because the center's credibility and its very raison d'être are at stake.

However, it is naive to expect that one battle won means the issue is settled for once and for all. It will be an endless battle, for the issues are such that pressures will continue to be exerted to keep certain disagreeable truths from being published.

B. The Credibility of Government Research Centers

The second line of objections to establishment of a government research center concerns the scientific quality of the research and the apprehension that governmental research will be theoretically and methodologically weak.

It should be kept in mind that policy research and university research have different objectives. Where academic research often attempts to test theory or to accumulate scientific knowledge, policy research aims to inform policymaking and thus to promote policy change. So, of course, criminological theory considerations are of less relevance here than to research questions whose policy relevance is less immediate.

Policy problems rarely present themselves in simple and clear-cut forms, but nearly always as complex, multifaceted problems that are related to a number of other questions. Therefore, as Coleman noted, it is advisable to use a differentiated methodological approach (Coleman 1972). A good example of this approach is a recent evaluation study of Dutch basic police training (Junger-Tas et al. 1979a, 1979b). The research included an observation study of police performance, the interviewing of police recruits and police officers using structured interview schedules, survey research among the Dutch population, and open interviews of high police officials. The weakness of the study resided in its sampling procedures and problematic generalizability, but its strength appeared to be the differentiated approaches and the exceptional consistency of the results of the different substudies.

It is, however, clear that scientific requirements of quality and integrity must be upheld by any research center if its work is to be useful. If standards gradually lower, the foundations and the ultimate justification of the existence of a policy-research center would be undermined. This is one of the reasons why the center has established a continuing relation with the division of social science methodology and data-theory development of Leiden University.

It must be conceded that work pressures are high in the research center, and little allowance is made for theoretical reflection. But this also depends on the interests and qualities of individual researchers. Policy research does not by definition exclude theory construction, and several lines of theoretical development are being pursued at the center. One is based on the systematic victimization studies, like the American

National Crime Survey. New lines of inquiry and of theory formation are being developed (van Dijk and Steinmetz 1981). Another line of development is the testing and extension of social control theory from the perspective of judicial intervention in cases of delinquency (Junger-Tas et al. 1983).

The existence of a governmental criminological research center is based on various assumptions, the most important of which is that the objectives of general criminal policy are reasonably consistent and knowable and that there is a general consensus on the proposition that the principal aim of the criminal justice system is to protect the life, rights, and goods of the individual citizen and to preserve the state as a state of law. A second assumption is that the institutions of the criminal justice system are characterized by a reasonable consistency of objectives and functioning.

From these assumptions it follows that one of the important functions of a governmental research center is the testing and evaluation of the criminal justice programs in terms of whether, and to what extent, they contribute to the realization of the stated objectives.

A third assumption is that the use of rational methods, as embodied in the scientific approach, will help to achieve a better coordination between means and aims, that we elect to be a scientific society—as Coleman put it, "a society that uses scientific methods to change itself."

II. Recent Criminological Research in the Netherlands

Space does not permit a thorough overview of all criminological research that is going on in the Netherlands. Instead I have described illustrative projects that are characteristic of prevalent trends and interests.

A. Research Financed by the Universities

The largest single category of university-funded research concerns delinquency and deviant juvenile behavior. Some of it is pure theory testing. There is, for instance, a study of Nijmegen's Criminological Institute, where the theoretical model developed by the German theoretician K. O. Opp, on the basis of Sutherland's differential association theory, will be tested. This will be done by submitting a questionnaire to twelve hundred girls and boys aged 12–16 (Bruinsma 1983).

Leiden University researchers are conducting a cohort study on aggressive behavior development in children. A group of children born in the same year will be followed for a number of years. Aggressive and nonaggressive children will be compared. The study includes different subareas of inquiry: a medical and physical aspect investigating neurological defects, birth complications, and the like; a psychological aspect concerning the development of emotional, cognitive, and personality development; and a social and behavioral aspect studying behavior at school, in peer groups, and in parent-child relationships. This study is particularly concerned to test sociobiological theories.

Groningen Criminological Institute is heavily influenced by a number of radical criminologists. They place a heavy emphasis on the social class variable, and this is expressed in the type of studies they undertake. Groningen researchers are conducting a series of studies on the relation between lower-class position and screening decisions by the prosecutor. Other studies on dark number delinquency also relate social class position to the prosecution of offenses. They are also engaged in a number of studies about the relation between unemployment and criminality.

A number of delinquency studies at the Universities of Amsterdam and Rotterdam are concerned with diversion projects, some of them related to specific behavior such as vandalism. Other diversion studies at Amsterdam and Groningen, headed by Andriessen and Jongman, are evaluating programs designed to keep juveniles with repeated police contacts from further involvement with the criminal justice system. Then there are a great many smaller studies on subjects such as schools and delinquency, running away from home and absconding (Angenent 1982), deviant behavior of children in homes, and aftercare of institutionalized children.

With respect to adult crime, the university-funded research also includes studies of a more theoretical or general nature. One example is a history of criminal law in the Netherlands since 1800 in which court, criminal, and prison statistics are used (van Ruller 1980, 1981). Another concerns policy decisions of prosecution, sentencing, and execution over time. Fiselier is developing a model to explain the changes that have taken place in this century in the way criminals are treated. Other examples of such studies include the testing of Eysencks's criminal personality theory by multivariate analysis, and a study conducted by Leuw in which facts about the offense of rape are compared with theories and conceptions of rape.

There is a great deal more current research, varying with the particular researchers' interests or the theoretical orientations of specific criminological institutes. Nijmegen University has developed a number of studies on women and crime (Bruinsma and Dessauer 1979); at Groningen there have been studies on drugs, such as use of drugs among inmates and living conditions of hard-drug users (Erkelens et al. 1979). Wesemann, at Rotterdam, is trying to develop models to introduce cost-benefit analysis into criminal decision making. No doubt these topics look familiar to the American reader. Dutch criminological research is mostly social science research, heavily influenced by American sociology, particularly interaction and labeling perspectives, and radical criminology.

About half of the studies mentioned use quantitative methods. These include the use of files, statistics, reports, and structured interviews. In half of the studies, qualitative methods such as depth interviews and observation are used. The latter approach is preferred when the researcher can get only small samples or has difficulty in getting access to research sources.

B. Research Funded by the Foundation for Pure and Fundamental Research

The *Research Bulletin of the Ministry of Justice*, presenting an overview of all research undertaken in the Netherlands in 1980, mentions two projects sponsored by the foundation. The first, under the direction of Brants-Langeraar of the University of Amsterdam, is a judicial and theoretical study of corporate crime. Its main objective is to devise a theoretical framework for understanding corporate crime, its prosecution, and penalization. Emphasis is given to the relation between the criminally liable corporation as a legal phenomenon and in terms of macroorganizational and sociological factors.

The second project is a historical study of the development of crime reporting in Dutch newspapers since 1800. The research objective is to clarify the relation between changes in crime reporting and other long-term processes, particularly public executions.

C. Research Funded by the Ministry of Justice

A number of extramural studies are fully or partially funded by the Ministry of Justice. Some are of particular interest to individual government departments, which sometimes provide additional funding. This was, for instance, the case for a large qualitative study of long-standing partnership relations other than marriage. In view of the growth of this phenomenon, the question of what legal dispositions should be taken to do justice to other living arrangements than traditional marriage led to an in-depth study of 75 such partnerships including homosexual, lesbian, and heterosexual relations (Straver et al. 1979, 1981).

Other studies include more general aspects of the functioning of the criminal justice system such as the public prosecutor (van de Bunt 1979), the application of penal sanctions, and the comparison of appeal decisions taken by administrative authorities or by an independent court (van Buuren 1981).

Most of the studies funded by the Ministry of Justice have a broad social character with, of course, a judicial angle. Other examples include several studies focusing on women: women and the fear of rape, for example, or the position of women in the legal professions (e.g., Ensink 1981).

Some of these studies could have been conducted equally well by the government's own research center, and in some cases similar, parallel, or preliminary studies were in fact conducted by the center. But there is logic in funding special institutes to do research that is of broader, more general scientific and policy interest, research that takes time, or research that requires a clear and unambiguous independence. Moreover, access to some experimental population groups may be easier when the research is conducted by an outside research institution. Finally, acceptance of results may be greater when the study does not emanate from the Ministry of Justice.

D. Research Conducted by the Research Center of the Ministry of Justice

The center's concerns have changed markedly during the research program's first decade. During the first phase, the center conducted a large number of inventory studies of a descriptive, fact-finding nature; then came an evaluation phase in which important components of the criminal justice system were evaluated on particular aspects of their functioning.

Increasingly, the center is involved in the development and introduction of innovations in penal law and criminal justice practice. This takes the form of action research: the new measure is introduced in experimental form and evaluated. On the basis of the evaluation study, recommendations are made and modifications suggested before definitive introduction of the new measure or the new law. Let me give some examples of the different types of research.

1. *Descriptive, Exploratory Studies.* In order to correct official crime statistics and to get a better understanding of crime trends in our country, the center developed a survey of victims that has been repeated annually, and that has now been taken over by the Dutch Central Bureau of Statistics (van Dijk and Steinmetz 1981). These systematic

surveys have constituted a significant contribution to a better under-standing of crime in the Netherlands. They showed that serious crime has not increased substantially in recent years but that so-called petty crime, such as crime against property, increased considerably. The studies led to a revision of police policy in crime fighting. The police now show a renewed interest in "small" criminality and in crime prevention.

Several studies on the performance of patrol officers and probation workers have caused some surprise and even shock (Junger-Tas et al. 1979*a*, 1979*b*). They showed that crime fighting was only a minor part of the patrol officers' work, compared to tasks of maintaining order and delivering services. The study also demonstrated a certain selectivity in police stop-and-control practice toward nonwhites. The studies on probation showed that probation officers prefer to conduct "therapeu-tic" talks with clients in their offices and to meet with colleagues rather than to render concrete, material services (Spickenheuer and Brand-Koolen 1979). The studies raised some questions about the usefulness of probation work.

2. *Evaluation Studies.*   A large-scale study of police basic training led to a number of recommendations to modify the training program (Jun-ger-Tas et al. 1979*a*, 1979*b*). Several studies were conducted to compare different prison regimes (van der Linden 1978), and to assess the ef-fectiveness of a prison clinic for psychopathic offenders (van Emmerik 1982). A number of studies evaluated the different activities of the probation service and the effects they had on their clients.

Most of these studies were the first of their kind to be conducted in the Netherlands. As they were all accompanied by recommendations for change, they were often threatening to functionaries. It is no wonder therefore that some of them caused considerable concern. Surprisingly enough, this was not so much the case for the police, where there existed a desire for change, as for the probation service, where social workers especially resented criticism of their work, and resistance to change was widespread.

3. *Action Research.*   The center is conducting a number of action research projects. For instance, several experiments concern crime pre-vention: one concerning police target surveillance, one testing out dif-ferent information campaigns, and one based on cooperation with the public and the youth population. The objective is to test out different policy measures, some of which will then, probably after some mod-ifications, be introduced on a broader scale.

Another interesting development concerns the use of experiments and research before new legislation is enacted. Two important legislative proposals are now being investigated. One concerns the introduction in the Netherlands of the Community Service Order practice. There has been no change in the law, but experiments are being conducted in eight of the nineteen court districts. An explicit objective of the new measure is that it should replace short prison sentences (up to six months). An important question concerns the preferable use of the orders: if the prosecutor applies the CSO, we have a diversion measure; if it is the judge, we have a real sentence. Both of these possibilities have been left open. The evaluation will be completed in the beginning of 1984, and on the basis of the results the Minister of Justice will be advised on the form in which the new measures should be included in Dutch penal law.

A similar procedure is followed with respect to a complete revision of juvenile penal law. A special task force appointed by the Minister of Justice in 1978 is reviewing juvenile penal law and has advised experiments with alternative sanctions for juveniles (Rapport van de Commissie 1982). In January 1983, six court districts will start experimenting with two types of sanctions: a Community Service Order for juveniles, and imposed courses or training sessions to improve a youngster's social skills and his functioning in the community. Here again much is left open to the parties concerned: what delinquents and what offenses will be selected for the new measures, what kind of penal measure will they replace, and who will make the decision? The evaluation study will start at the same time as the experiments, following each closely.

It is expected that in two years the final research report and the recommendations on the eventual incorporation of the new measures in juvenile penal law will be delivered to the Minister of Justice. If one considers that so many new laws have unexpected consequences or cannot be applied adequately, I think this extension of the center's activities is especially encouraging, in terms of both better policymaking and accumulation of knowledge about social processes.

III. Some Concluding Remarks

This limited overview of Dutch criminological research may have caused some skeptical reactions among American readers—for example, What about academic freedom? Is not government influence too pervasive? Is there still room for sound academic research?

Of course, there is now and always will be room for sound academic research. Ideally there should be an established division of function between the two kinds of research. The university should be equipped, eventually with the support of nongovernmental funding, to conduct studies of a more fundamental and theoretical character, historical studies, or studies of a specific and delicate nature which are not feasible for government researchers. However, the government will always need a prompt in-house research capacity providing answers to urgent but relatively simple questions. Moreover, the closeness of researchers to policymakers also works the other way around—policymakers become used to the inherent critical quality of research, come to see its usefulness for better decision making, and thus may be inclined to make greater use of research facilities, inside or outside the ministry.

In the past the universities were free to conduct whatever research they were interested in. There was no planning, no specialization, and little quality control. When the government wanted research to be done, the universities were seldom interested; when they were, they were not at all prepared to work under more "commercialized" conditions, implying tight budgeting and deadlines. This is certainly one of the main reasons for the relative weakness of Dutch criminological institutes and the preponderance of government-sponsored research in the Netherlands.

Some important changes in the organization of research are needed to alter this situation. Eight criminological institutes may be too many for so small a country. Some of them could be abolished. Among the others a specialization could be promoted along disciplinary lines (social science and law or history, for example), or along lines of main research interests and qualities. Above all, the university institutes should try to develop integral planning and short- and long-term research programs.

With these changes, the institutes could much better delineate their position, as well as their original contribution to criminology. I think they will end up doing so, if only under the pressure of financial necessity. I hope they will do so, for criminology will flourish only if there is a good balance between free academic research and policy research.

REFERENCES

Angenent, H. L. W. 1982. "Running Away from Home." First report. Groningen: State University, Criminological Institute.
Bruinsma, G. J. N. 1983. *Deviant Socialization*. Nijmegen: Catholic University, Criminological Institute.
Bruinsma, G. J. N., and Dessauer. 1979. *Female Criminality in the Netherlands*. Nijmegen: Catholic University, Criminological Institute.
Buikhuisen, W. 1965. *Achtergronden van nozemgedrag*. Assen: van Gorcum.
Buikhuisen, W., et al. 1968. *Alcohol en verkeer*. Boom: Meppel.
Buikhuisen, W., and J. van Weringh. 1969. *Politie, auto en veilig verkeer—een experiment*. Groningen: Wolters-Noordhof.
Buikhuisen, W., et al. 1969. "Ongeregistreerde criminaliteit onder studenten." *Nederlands Tijdschrift voor Criminologie*.
Buikhuisen, W., and R. W. Jongman. 1972. *Kijken onder invloed. Een experimenteel onderzoek naar de invloed van alcohol op het waarnemen van verkeerssituaties*. Groningen: Wolters-Noordhof.
Coleman, J. S. 1972. *Policy Research in the Social Sciences*. Morristown, N.J.: General Learning Press.
Ensink, B. J. 1981. *Women and Law: The Position of Women Employed in the Legal Profession*. Nijmegen: Catholic University, Law Faculty.
Erkelens, E. H., et al. 1979. *Drugs en detentie: Een beschrijvend onderzoek naar hard-drug gebruikers in een zestal huizen van bewaring*. Groningen: Criminological Institute.
Jongman, R. W. 1971. "Verborgen criminaliteit en sociale klasse." *Nederlands Tijdschrift voor Criminologie*.
Jongman, R. W., and G. J. A. Smale. 1972a. "Ongeregistreerde criminaliteit onder vrouwelijke studenten." *Nederlands Tijdschrift voor Criminologie*.
———. 1972b. "De invloed van leeftijd recidive en sociale klasse op het seponeringsbeleid." *Nederlands Tijdschrift voor Criminologie*.
Junger-Tas, J., et al. 1979a. *The Relationship between Basic Police Training and Policing in Practice*. The Hague: Ministry of Justice.
———. 1979b. *Basic Police Training and Police Performance*. The Hague: Ministry of Justice.
———. 1983. *Backgrounds of Delinquent Behavior and Judicial Intervention*. The Hague: Ministry of Justice.
Nederlands Tijdschrift voor Criminologie. 1968. Vol. 10, no. 3. "Enkele preliminaire beschouwingen over zgn. afwijkend gedrag," by D. Zuithoff. "Afwijkend gedrag sociologisch beschouwd," by D. C. J. van Peype. "De sociologie van het afwijkend gedrag en de criminologie," by G. Snel. "Typen jeugddelinquentie: een empirisch onderzoek," by W. Buikhuisen and R. W. Jongman.
———. 1968. Vol. 10, no. 4. "Erfelijkheid en criminaliteit," by W. Buikhuisen. "Delinquent gedrag en conditioneerbaarheid," by J. J. Hemmel. "Gevangenis en resocialisatie," by J. van Weringh.
———. 1972. Vol. 12. Special issue on "Drugs en schooljeugd."
Rapport van de Commissie herziening strafrecht voor jeugdigen. 1982. *Sanctierecht voor jeugdigen*. The Hague: Ministry of Justice.

Spickenheuer, J. L. P., and M. J. M. Brand-Koolen. 1979. *Het Reclasseringswerk: Houdingen en meningen van medewerkers.* The Hague: Ministry of Justice.

Straver, C. J., et al. 1979 (pt. 1), 1981 (pt. 2). "Tweerelaties, anders dan het huwelijk." "Social and Legal Problems in Connection with Two-Person Relationships Outside Marriage." Unpublished manuscripts. Netherlands Institute for Socio-Sexological Research. Sociological Institute, State University of Utrecht, Fiscal, and Notarial Institute, State University of Leiden.

van Buuren, P. J. J. 1981. *Case Law: Full Appeal/Arob Appeal.* Groningen: State University of Groningen, Administrative Law and Administrative Science Specialist Group.

van de Bunt, J. G. 1979. *The Functioning of the Public Prosecutor.* Utrecht: State University of Utrecht, William Pompe Institute for Penal Law.

van der Linder, B. 1978. *Regiem en recidive.* The Hague: Ministry of Justice.

van Dijk, J. J. M. 1981. "Différence et analogie entre la criminologie pratique et académique." *Déviance et societé.*

van Dijk, J. J. M., and C. H. D. Steinmetz. 1981. *The R.D.C. Victim Surveys 1974–1979.* The Hague: Ministry of Justice.

van Emmerik, J. L. 1982. *Detained at the Government's Pleasure.* The Hague: Ministry of Justice.

van Ruller, S. 1980, 1981. "History of Criminal Law: Long Term Development, 19th and 20th Centuries." Amsterdam: "Bonger" Criminological Institute, University of Amsterdam.

Günther Kaiser

Criminological Research in the Federal Republic of Germany

Criminology in West Germany has come of age since the late 1960s. Until recently, few academics would admit to being criminologists, the volume of research was small, and criminology received little institutional support from the universities and government. Now, however, the volume and quality of work and the institutional recognition of criminology have increased to a point where criminology can fairly be described as a maturing academic specialty in West Germany.

The slow-paced development of criminology in West Germany was in part the consequence of a tension between its methodological affinities to the social sciences and its historical origins and institutional location in criminal law faculties. Dahrendorf (1961, pp. 27–28), in explaining similar tensions in sociology, demonstrated that the debate about whether sociology is value free emanated in part from conflict over sociologists' roles and sociology's functions. This conflict existed between the goals of social research and the goals of social policy. The tension affecting criminology's development resulted from interaction between criminology and criminal law. This tension could be seen in issues of criminal law reform and in academic policy controversies.

Criminologists traditionally occupied a peripheral position within "criminal law theory," a field dominated by academic lawyers. Until the 1970s, this position was reflected in the small number of academic positions for criminologists, the infrequency of university lectures on criminology, and the limited importance of criminology for the bar examinations. This lack of standing and credibility was also manifested

Günther Kaiser is director, Max Planck Institute for International and Comparative Penal Law, Freiburg, West Germany.

in the scant influence of criminologists on the formulation of government policy and legislative proposals.

The stature and institutional recognition of criminology have increased substantially since 1970. Academics interested in criminology in the twenty years following World War II "usually engaged in it secondarily" (Bader 1952, p. 17). Criminologists were considered to be the "court-jesters of jurisprudence." In the early 1960s the first three academic chairs for criminologists were established in the universities at Heidelberg, Tübingen, and Cologne. One of these university positions remained unoccupied for almost a decade. This slight acknowledgment of criminology delayed the development of a competent research community and the establishment of efficient research facilities. Because of this lack of university support and the absence of promising career opportunities, individuals interested in criminology were seldom able to specialize in it. They could not work continuously in the subject and lacked the experience and technical knowledge to evaluate international information and developments critically. Even individuals who specialized in criminology as graduate students had few incentives to continue the research on which they had written dissertations.

This doleful past has given way to a promising future (see Kerner 1972, pp. 35 ff.), reflected both in the greater emphasis given to criminology in the universities' curricula and in the establishment of permanent positions and research facilities. Leading the way for this development has been the recent inclusion of criminology, juvenile court law, and the law of corrections as optional courses in the curricula in law schools (see Kreuzer 1979) and the resulting increase in academic positions at most of the German law schools. Academic positions for those with criminological interests also have increased in forensic medicine, forensic psychiatry, criminal sociology, and social pedagogy. Forensic psychology, however, has remained somewhat understaffed.

Criminology in West Germany today encompasses a variety of disciplines, including forensic medicine, psychiatry, psychology, psychoanalysis, sociology, and criminal law. Even the disciplines of ethnology, humanitarian ethnology, genetics, social pedagogy, and economics include research concerned with traditional criminological subjects. University criminologists, therefore, often occupy interfaculty positions, and criminology is often described as an interdisciplinary subject (Göppinger 1966, p. 5; critically, Sack 1978, pp. 205 ff.; contrarily, Kaiser 1979, pp. 50 ff.).

The momentum that organized criminological research had gathered by the 1970s can be seen in the founding of many research facilities and projects, including the development of various journals—notably *Kriminologisches Journal*, published in Munich, and *Zeitschrift für Soziologie*, published in Stuttgart—publishing criminological research, the collaborative efforts of researchers from different professions, and the adoption by criminologists of research strategies and methodologies from the traditional social sciences.

Since the middle of the 1970s, professors at more than thirty universities in West Germany have been engaged full-time in criminology. In the 1960s lectures on criminology were held at twenty universities for a total of eighty-five hours a week (Kerner 1972, p. 40). By the 1970s, lectures were offered at thirty-three universities for more than 340 hours a week (see Berckhauer 1975).

While these developments are promising, they should not be misinterpreted as evidence of a gigantic increase in the volume of research. In light of the strong intellectual interweaving of criminology with optional courses in juvenile court law and the law of corrections, as well as with criminal law, and the expanded curricula and examination responsibilities of criminological specialists, professors of criminology must devote substantial time and energies to problems of criminal law theory and administration, leaving limited time available for empirical research.

The modern West German criminological research program can be divided into the government and independent research institutes, and the universities. Among the former, the Criminalistics and Criminology Research Unit of the Federal Bureau of Crime (Kube 1978) was first established. Its staff consists of professional and supporting staff, and its primary functions are initiating and coordinating applied research in criminology and criminalistics. The Criminological Research Unit Lower Saxony has nine full-time research workers and is conducting empirical criminological research on the effectiveness of corrections, development of alternatives, and reintegration of released prisoners (Kury 1981). The Max Planck Institute for Foreign and International Penal Law (Criminological Research Unit) includes eight full-time research workers and a substantial number of auxiliary staff, conducting empirical research covering the entire system of crime control (e.g., private crime control in factories; unreported crime; aspects of police activities and of the activities of the Public Prosecutor's Office; fines as sanctions; white-collar crime; prediction and the treatment of juvenile offenders; rehabilitation of released prisoners; victimization and crime) (Kaiser 1975; Johnson 1979; Criminological Research Unit 1982). Criminological research facilities are located at the universities of Bielefeld, Bochum, Bonn, Bremen, Cologne, Frankfurt, Freiburg, Giessen, Göttingen, Hamburg, Heidelberg, Kiel, Konstanz, Mainz, Mannheim, Nurnber-Erlangen, Munich, Münster, Regensburg, Saarbrücken, Tübingen, and Wuppertal. The largest research programs, those employing five or more full-time staff members, are the Max Planck Institute in Freiburg; the research unit of Göttingen University; the Criminological Research Institute Lower Saxony in Hannover; the Institute for Criminology at Tübingen; and the Criminalistics and Criminology Research Unit in the Federal Bureau of Crime in Wiesbaden. A Criminological Central Agency for Federation and State, which has long been planned to coordinate and document empirical research, has not as yet been established.

According to the Justice Department's documentation of research on criminology and criminal justice (Bundesministerium der Justiz 1974, pp. 114 ff.; Hartwieg et al. 1978, pp. 54 ff.; 143 ff.), 135 research positions were devoted to 396 research programs in the 1970s—forty-five in law and criminology, nineteen in psychology, nineteen in medicine, seventeen in sociology, and sixteen in social pedagogy at research institutes. Of the 608 registered criminologists, 26 percent were lawyers, 20 percent psychologists, 19 percent sociologists, 12 percent doctors, and 4 percent pedagogues. Approximately one-third of the research work was devoted to doctoral dissertations. These data are somewhat less impressive when one subtracts the funds, personnel, and effort devoted primarily to teaching and administration. Based on actual research capacity in 1982, only sixty postdoctoral researchers were engaged exclusively in criminological research and approximately two hundred graduate students were doing graduate research work on criminological subjects. By comparison, Szabo (1978, p. 151) estimates that approximately 1,500 individuals in the entire world work more than half-time on research in criminology.

Although twenty years ago it was difficult within the Federal Republic even to obtain Anglo-American literature, today various libraries exist specializing in criminological texts, particularly the library at the Max Planck Institute and the library (*Bibliotheksschwerpunkt*) at Tübingen University, which specializes in criminological texts and research reports published in foreign countries.

The total funds devoted to criminological research in Germany are approximately DM 6 million per year, with personnel costs accounting for the largest expenditure. Less than half of these funds come from the German Research Society, while most of the remaining funds are made available by the individual federal and state departments. Minor contributions also are made by the Max Planck Society, the Volkswagen Foundation, and the various universities.

This short essay reviews the current state of criminological research in West Germany. Section I briefly reviews the subject matter of West German research. Section II considers the nature and extent of government influence and involvement in criminological research, including various radical critiques of governmental influence and the rationales for expansion of in-house governmental research programs.

I. Criminological Research and Theory

The subject-matter trends in criminological research in West Germany are similar to those in other Western countries. Traditionally, research included dissertations on clinical, forensic, and prison psychiatry; individual case studies; and statistical analyses.

Criminology underwent two distinct phases of development between World War II and the 1960s. The first phase, which occurred in the 1950s, involved examinations of juvenile criminology. Studies by Middendorff (1956, 1959) and Heintz and König (1957) introduced and applied information and concepts concerning crime and deviance from Anglo-American sociology. Efforts to institutionalize criminological research failed. Despite this early concentration of interests and research funds on the problems of juveniles, a focus shared with other academic disciplines, insufficient momentum was created to sustain criminology over the long run.

The second phase saw a diversification of efforts beyond juvenile criminology. In the late 1950s, considerable effort was expended on prediction research (e.g., Meyer 1956; Schaffstein 1968). Another central research subject in this period, resulting from the increased use of motor vehicles, was the criminology of traffic offenses (see Kaiser 1970, pp. 13 ff.). Mainly through the efforts of the Bonn criminologist von Weber (1967), research in this period also focused on economic offenses (white-collar crime), the empirical analysis of criminal procedure, and crime control and sanctioning in the workplace (so-called *Betriebsjustiz*). This research, however, received little attention until much later.

In recent years criminological research has broadened as a result of the growing diversity of disciplines represented among serious researchers. Although earlier, as Sack (1971, p. 272) critically commented, criminology was "tight in the grasp of doctors and lawyers," today the number of social scientists involved in criminological research is far greater than the number of doctors or lawyers. On the other hand, an overview of sociological publications in Germany since 1945 reveals that deviant behavior and criminality rank thirty-fifth among the fifty most important fields of sociological research (Lüschen 1979, pp. 169 ff.). Thus, while many sociologists are engaged in criminological research, deviance and social control are relatively minor subjects. Only five sociological chairs at universities are concerned mainly with social deviance and social control.

Sociological concepts and the "sociological dimension" have influenced West German criminology considerably in recent years. A decade ago, the German Research Society's allocation of research funds, as well as the decisions regarding the founding of criminological research institutes, prolonged the "predominance of the legal and medical traditional approaches and thereby extended the apologetic nature of the science of criminology" (Sack 1971, p. 281). Today other scholars having a psychiatric background criticize the sociological orientation of criminology as a "sociological alienation of criminology" and express regret over the lost emphasis of research on the individual offender (Leferenz 1981, pp. 212, 218).

Today criminological research in the Federal Republic is well balanced, as shown by the research requests made over the past few years to the German Research Society. These range from unreported crime, traffic, and economic violations to criminal offender analysis, from private justice and the police to sentencing practice and corrections. For summaries of these efforts, see Kaiser (1975) and Müller-Dietz (1976), each with an inventory. Concerning the German Research Society's new program, "Empirical Research on Penal Sanctions," see Kaiser et al. (1977, pp. 41–50). Concerning research on criminal justice and criminology, see the documentation in Hartwieg et al. (1978).

According to the Federal Justice Department, in the 1970s there were approximately four hundred research projects concerned with empirical criminology (Bundesministerium der Justiz 1979, p. 114; Hartwieg et al. 1978, pp. 54 ff., pp. 143 ff.). Of these, 372 were devoted to research involving primary data. Investigations of crime control, including criminal procedure and the imposition and execution of punishment, dom-

inate these research efforts. Inquiries into the criminology of individual
offenses (business, property, traffic, killings, drugs) follow in second
place, with offender-oriented investigations in a distant third place.
Research on recidivism and female criminality is not extensive.

Many of the registered research projects undertaken either are not
completed or do not result in published reports. Of those projects
sponsored by the German Research Society, for example, fewer than
one-fourth were actually completed. Even fewer attained particular
importance or widespread academic recognition. Some research reports
are so narrowly specialized that they could not contribute to the general
body of knowledge or concepts of criminology.

Seen in their entirety, recent research results and "discoveries," with
a few notable exceptions, appear slight. Among these exceptions are
advances in methodology and theory, including multimethod approaches to the study of unreported crime that combine self-reported
crime, self-reported victimization, and observed criminal behavior, thus
allowing access to in-depth analysis of the relations between crime and
victimization. Furthermore, the study of victimization within a theoretical framework, including both sociological and psychological variables, gives insight into the relevance of different theoretical views of
victimization. In recent years criminological research efforts have concentrated on the development of methodological roots and theoretical
frameworks in the analysis of legal norms, as well as in their implementation in a broader social context. For this reason, "epochal break-
throughs" probably cannot be expected in criminology. The social and
political implications involved in an analysis of the criminal offender
and the quickly changing academic questions concerning humanitarian
and social sciences prohibit the type of definitive evaluations possible
in the medical and natural sciences.

Empirical research in criminology is partly influenced by the focal
programs of te German Research Society. Criminological problems
are also dealt with in several institutions that have developed special
emphases: for example, the influence of mass media on delinquency
and crime control in Münster; research on criminal procedures, mainly
in Göttingen and Mannheim; economic (white-collar) crime research,
chiefly in Freiburg; victimological questions in Mönchen-Gladbach and
Münster; problems relating to drug abuse in Giessen; self-report and
victimization surveys in Bochum, Giessen, and Freiburg; geographical
crime studies in Bochum and Kiel; problems of immigrant workers and
juvenile delinquency in Freiburg and Munich; aspects of crime pro-

phylaxis and defensible space in Hannover, Regensburg, and Wuppertal; and, finally, research relating to the personalities of criminal offenders in Tübingen. Also warranting mention is the interdisciplinary team, including criminologists, in the Federal Republic engaged in the study of terrorism. At this writing, questions concerning organized crime, the economic aspects of crime, the origin of penal norms, the "crimes of the powerful"—outside of economic offenses and environmental crimes—have received scant attention. Biocriminological research (except concerning XXY chromosomes) is completely lacking.

In light of the underdeveloped state of West German criminology as recently as 1970, the developments of the past fifteen years are a major step forward (see Reuband 1982). This evaluation is even more justified when the present literature is compared with that existing in the early 1960s. At that time, there was general concern that German criminological research was in danger of losing any connection to international developments.

II. Government Influence on Criminological Research
An inevitable tension exists in Western nations between the priorities and interests of researchers and the information needs of public officials. Because ultimately government is the source of much of the funding that supports social science research, this disjunction between researchers' and officials' interests sometimes becomes controversial. In this section I discuss three such matters in West Germany: first, the assertion by some criminologists that state officials try to shape research to state ends; second, the allegation that the findings of criminological research do not justify the funds invested; and third, the tension between researchers' theoretical interests and officials' practical needs.

A group of mainly radical criminologists has expressed concern about the potentially insidious influence of state agencies on criminological research through control of funding (Brusten 1981*a*, p. 135). My view is that this concern is exaggerated. The relation between research workers and state agencies is more complex and delicate than critics sometimes acknowledge. The perceived antagonism between "free science" or "free academic criminology" and practice-oriented or state-funded criminological research is overdrawn and artificial. There is no empirical evidence that state agencies and the "power structure of society" are inclined to corrupt or eliminate "free academic criminological research" (Brusten 1981*b*, pp. 61, 71).

Today, researchers' autonomy and ability to pursue their research interests are endangered by other factors. There are sometimes ideological or political pressures from students that make certain research topics taboo. The right of privacy and the efforts to protect records of individuals impose much more formidable impediments to research than do state officials. Officials are not primarily concerned (cf. Schumann 1981, pp. 80, 85) with producing "the scientific rationalization of penal law" or with the "functions of penal law in capitalist societies," nor with providing state agencies with the best possible reservoir of insights favoring the legitimation of particular activities of the system. The main interest of state agencies is in the accumulation of legal and empirical knowledge in order to permit achievement of more rational and humane methods of crime control. Lawyers and officials must search for the empirical groundings of penal philosophy and the justification for penal law, independently of whether they live in capitalist or socialist societies. Only utopians can ignore this intricate question.

Partially, this controversy about state involvement in criminological research results from conflicts between mainstream and radical criminology or, put otherwise, between law-educated and sociology-trained scholars. But it might also be a struggle for resources, influence, and power in criminology, academic policy, and penal policy.

Partly because of these internecine, intracriminological disputes, questions concerning the organization and productivity of criminological research in West Germany have gained increasing attention.

At present, and for the foreseeable future, German criminologists must be prepared to defend their discipline against charges that it is not adequately productive. In light of the approximately DM 6 million expended annually for research and the establishment of a variety of research facilities, one might fear—on the basis of the evidence in Section I—that the investment has been insufficiently productive. Also, one could infer that the research subjects that interest criminologists are not always the same as those that interest state agencies (Hobe 1981; Schwind 1981), the public at large, and international experts.

An evaluation of research productivity, however, must consider that West German criminology is in the final phases of a long and difficult development. Research expenditures are modest when compared with the research backlog and needed investments and with the level of expenditures for other empirical sciences, such as medicine; and the research investments in criminology in other countries, such as Great Britain, the Netherlands, Scandinavia, and the United States, are proportionately much higher. It is unrealistic to expect that this relatively late and absolutely slight investment in criminological research can yield conclusive and definite research findings within a few years.

Criminological research is undertaken for the increase and depth of knowledge in criminological theory. Some research projects are particularly pertinent to practical questions of administration, such as research on sentencing, punishment, corrections, and treatment, but also concerning the police, the judiciary, and the legislature. Research findings, even when incomplete, prepare for the solution of practical problems.

Young lawyers have been particularly stimulated by criminological research, for it makes criminal law more empirical and offers empirical researchers the opportunity to become familiar with the problems of criminal law. The importance of these intermediate social functions for the future development, sophistication, and productivity of research cannot be overestimated. Finally, one should not forget that a generation of young criminologists, who have since become active in the departments of various universities and colleges, were involved in empirical research and were thereby significantly influenced in their professional development.

Still, the weakness and the defects in the development and structure of criminological research cannot be overlooked. There is cause for concern both with deficits in theory development and in theory-guided research and with the hostility displayed by many researchers toward application-oriented analysis. Among the leading concepts and theories in Western criminology, variants of social learning theory, particularly the theory of socialization, are particularly influential in West Germany.

By contrast, the anomie theory is losing influence and varieties of the social control theory are gaining ground. Finally, the struggle with the multiple-factor approach persists, particularly between lawyers and sociologists. These disputes must be seen in the context of a period in which the relation between theory and practice is particularly stressed, but the gap between practice and science has been enlarged.

The reasons for this development lie particularly with the younger academics' reservations toward technocratic models, power, and dominance. Additional causes are the increased emphasis on the political and social implications of crime, a fashion for cynicism, and the stereotyped critical attitudes displayed by many academics toward crime control agencies and personnel. Although tensions between practice and theory are structurally determined and necessary, the potential for conflict is so great that productive, cooperative relations between science and practice are difficult to impossible, unless both sides work to recognize and understand their respective interests and needs.

Partly because of the difficulties involved in reconciling the interests of academic researchers and public officials, officials have increasingly taken certain projects into their own hands (Steinhilper and Berckhauer 1981). These projects concern policy-relevant research on topics such as internal administration, judicial authority, and penal policy (see Schwind 1981). The reorganization of the Criminalistics and Criminology Research Unit in the Federal Bureau of Crime (Kube 1978), the Police Command Academy (Matthes 1974), the Criminology Service for Corrections (§ 166 Law of Corrections [*Strafvollzugsgesetz*]), and the Project for a Criminology Central Agency for Federation and State (Oberthür 1976) are the fruits of these efforts. The independent Criminology Research Institute Lower Saxony was founded in the fall of 1979, and is loosely associated with the Planning and Research Unit in the Lower Saxony Justice Department (Kury 1981, pp. 33–79, 662 ff.). In this institute, policy-relevant research on problems of corrections and community treatment is being undertaken. The concentration of research capacity and personnel in administrative agencies is a natural consequence of the unwillingness of critical or radical researchers to cooperate with public officials. Policy-relevant research however is necessarily dependent on basic research. Research on executive and judicial administration can be productive only to the extent that it is supported and accompanied by independent research efforts. At present there is an emerging mixed research community in which the efforts of agency researchers augment and interact with those of the university and independent researchers.

III. Summary, Conclusions, and Outlook

In the two decades following Radzinowicz's research inventory (1961), the institutionalization of criminology has made considerable progress internationally. In West Germany, criminology has gained a place of "permanent residence" at the university and in the context of research, although it is oriented more toward teaching than toward empirical research. Seen in its entirety, the organizational foundation of criminological research has been broadened to include university, government, and independent research programs, with increasing emphasis on research that is relevant to policy formulation. The German Research Society's research programs and an effort by the Justice Department to coordinate criminological research are attempts to organize and rationalize research efforts. These projects are oriented both thematically and methodologically toward answering the questions presented by social scientists and criminal law specialists.

The following problems and responsibilities confronting criminological research warrant special emphasis in coming years.

1. Research on sentencing, sanctions, corrections, treatment, and crime prevention should continue to be given high priority, including documentation of the selection processes and the effects of sanctioning and also the theoretical understanding of concepts such as control theory, rehabilitation, and general prevention. In addition, auxiliary research on pretrial detention, the judiciary, punishment execution, parole assistance, supervised release, and victim's damages should be undertaken.

2. Emphasis should also be given to crime prevention research. Some empirical studies do exist concerning police and judicial crime prevention tactics. Single studies of "defensible space" were conducted (Rolinski 1980; Hellmer 1982). Systematic studies and theoretical research, however, are lacking, and much more needs to be done.

3. A third research field warranting emphasis is the prediction of recidivism, intensive and career criminality, and the conditions necessary for interrupting criminal careers.

4. A fourth subject for emphasis is victimization. In addition to the prevention of possible victimizations, one should consider victim assistance and damages. Victim surveys need greater sophistication in order to reach beyond present levels of knowledge.

5. A final subject for emphasis concerns the continuous observance of criminality and the development of its indicators and correlates. Here one should consider individual problems such as drug abuse, economic crimes, and crimes committed by foreigners as well as formulating theories concerning the problems researched.

REFERENCES

Bader, K. S. 1952. "Stand und Aufgaben der Kriminologie." *Juristenzeitung* 7:16–19.

Berckhauer, F. H. 1975. "La situation de la criminologie dans l'enseignement universitaire de la République Fédérale d'Allemagne." *Revue internationale de criminologie et de police technique* 28:281–87.

Brusten, M. 1981*a*. "Staatliche Institutionalisierung kriminologischer Forschung." In *Perspecktiven und Probleme kriminologischer Forschung*, edited by H. Kury. Cologne: Heymanns.

———. 1981*b*. "Social control of criminology and criminologists." In *State Control on Information in the Field of Deviance and Social Control*, edited by European Group for the Study of Deviance and Social Control. Leuven.

Bundesministerium der Justiz. 1974. *Rechtstatsachenforschung. Kriminologie*. Dokumentation der laufenden und der in jüngster Zeit abgeschlossenen empirischen Forschungsarbeiten. Bonn: Bundesverlag.

———. 1979. *Rechtstatsachenforschung. Kriminologie*. Bonn: Bundesverlag.

Criminological Research Unit, ed. 1982. *Stock-Taking of Criminological Research at the Max-Planck-Institute for Foreign and International Penal Law after a Decade*. Freiburg: Max Planck Institute.

Dahrendorf, R. 1961. "Sozialwissenschaft und Werturteil." In *Gesellschaft und Freiheit*. Zur soziologischen Analyse der Gegenwart. Munich: Piper.

Göppinger, H. 1966. "Kriminologie als interdisziplinäre Wissenschaft." *Kriminologische Gegenwartsfragen* 7:5.

Hartwieg, O., et al. 1978. *Rechtstatsachenforschung und Kriminologie*. Vol. 2. Bonn: Bundesverlag.

Heintz, P., and R. König, eds. 1957. "Soziologie der Jugendkriminalität." *Kölner Zeitschrift für Soziologie*. 2d special issue. Cologne.

Hellmer, J. 1982. "Stadtbild und Kriminalität." In *Städtebau, Architektur und Kriminalität*, edited by Architektur- und Ingenieurkammer. Schleswig-Holstein: Kiel.

Hobe, K. 1981. "Kriminologische Forschung und Strafgesetzgebung." In *Der Einfluß kriminologisch-empirischer Forschung auf Strafrecht und Strafverfahren*. Heidelberg: Kriminalistik.

Johnson, E. H. 1979. "Comparative and Applied Criminological Research at the Max Planck Institute in Freiburg." *International Journal of Comparative and Applied Criminal Justice* 3 (2): 131–41.

Kaiser, G. 1970. *Verkehrsdelinquenz und Generalprävention: Untersuchungen zur Kriminologie der Verkehrsdelikte und zum Verkehrsstrafrecht*. Tübingen: Mohr.

———. 1975. *Stand und Entwicklung der kriminologischen Forschung in Deutschland*. Berlin: De Gruyter.

———. 1979. "Strafrechtssoziologie—Dimension oder Partitur der Kriminologie? Kriminologie vor dem Tribunal kritisch-radikaler Devianzsoziologie." *Monatsschrift für Kriminologie und Strafrechtsreform* 62:50 ff.

Kaiser, G., et al. 1977. "Antrag auf Einrichtung eines DFG-Schwerpunkts 'Empirische Sanktionsforschung'—Verfahren, Vollzug, Wirkungen und Alternativen." *Monatsschrift für Kriminologie und Strafrechtsreform* 60:41–50.

Kerner, H. J. 1972. "Relationship between Scientific Research and Teaching in Criminology." In *Criminological Research Trends in Western Germany*, edited by G. Kaiser and Th. Würtenberger. Berlin: Springer.

Kreuzer, A. 1979. "Zur Lage des Wahlfachs 'Kriminologie, Jugendstrafrecht, Strafvollzug' im juristischen Studium und Referendarexamen." *Juristische Schulung* 19:526–32.

Kube, E. 1978. "Kriminalistisch-kriminologische Forschung in der Bundesrepublik Deutschland und den USA." *Kriminalistik* 32:439–44.

Kury, H. 1981. "Das kriminologische Forschungsinstitut Niedersachsen e.V. und sein Forschungsprogramm." In *Perspektiven und Probleme kriminologischer Forschung*, edited by H. Kury. Cologne: Heymanns.

Leferenz, H. 1981. "Rückkehr zur gesamten Strafrechtswissenschaft?" *Zeitschrift für die gesamte Strafrechtswissenschaft* 93:199–221.

Lüschen, G., ed. 1979. "Deutsche Soziologie seit 1945." *Kölner Zeitschrift für Soziologie*. Special issue 21. Opladen.

Matthes, J. 1974. "Der Beginn des Forschungsprogramms in der Polizei-Führungsakademie." *Schriftenreihe der Polizei-Führungsakademie* 1:35–38.

Meyer, F. 1956. *Rückfallprognose bei unbestimmt verurteilten Jugendlichen*. Bonn: Röhrscheid.

Middendorff, W. 1956. *Jugendkriminologie*. Ratingen: Henn.

———. 1959. *Soziologie des Verbrechens*. Düsseldorf: Deiderichs.

Müller-Dietz, H. 1976. *Empirische Forschung und Strafvollzug*. Frankfurt am Main: Klostermann.

Oberthür, G. R. 1976. *Kriminologie in der Strafrechtspraxis*. Stuttgart: Enke.

Radzinowicz, L. 1961. *In Search of Criminology*. London: Heinemann.

Reuband, K. H. 1982. "Soziale Probleme und soziale Kontrolle als Gegenstand empirischer Sozialforschung." In *Soziale Probleme und soziale Kontrolle*, edited by G. Albrecht et al. Opladen: Westdeutscher Verlag.

Rolinski, K. 1980. *Wohnarchitektur und Kriminalität*. Wiesbaden: Bundesverlag.

Sack, F. 1971. "Die Idee der Subkultur. Eine Berührung zwischen Anthropologie und Soziologie." *Kölner Zeitschrift für Soziologie* 23:272, 281.

———. 1978. "Probleme der Kriminalsoziologie." In *Handbuch der empirischen Sozialforschung*, edited by R. König. Stuttgart: Enke.

Schaffstein, F. 1968. "Rückfall und Rückfallprognose bei jungen Straffälligen." *Kriminologische Gegenwartsfragen* 8:66–85.

Schumann, K. 1981. "On Proper and Deviant Criminology—Varieties in Production of Legitimation for Penal Law." In *State Control on Information in the Fields of Deviance and Social Control*, edited by European Group for the Study of Deviance and Social Control. Leuven.

Schwind, H. D. 1981. "Kriminologische Forschung und Kriminalpolitik." In *Perspektiven und Probleme kriminologischer Forschung*, edited by H. Kury. Cologne: Heymanns.

Steinhilper, G., and F. H. Berckhauer. 1981. "Kriminologische Forschung als Beitrag zur Kriminalitätsvorbeugung." In *Präventive Kriminalpolitik*, edited by H. D. Schwind et al. Heidelberg: Kriminalistik.

Szabo, D. 1978. *Criminologie et politique criminelle*. Paris: Vrin.

von Weber, H. 1967. "Kriminalsoziologie." In *Handwörterbuch der Kriminologie*. (1977). Vol. 2, 2d ed., edited by R. Sieverts. Berlin: de Gruyter.